The History and Growth of Career and Technical Education in America

Third Edition

The History and Growth of Career and Technical Education in America

Third Edition

Howard R. D. Gordon
Marshall University

WAVELAND

PRESS, INC.

Long Grove, Illinois

For information about this book, contact:
    Waveland Press, Inc.
    4180 IL Route 83, Suite 101
    Long Grove, IL 60047-9580
    (847) 634-0081
    info@waveland.com
    www.waveland.com

*To all CTE students and colleagues in pursuit of excellence
in the field of career and technical education*

*To my former professors at the
College of Agriculture, Science and Education
(formerly the Jamaica School of Agriculture),
Tuskegee Institute, and
Virginia Polytechnic Institute and State University*

*To my parents, wife, children, and relatives
for their love, encouragement, and optimism*

*In memory of the
families and victims of the Virginia Tech tragedy
April 16, 2007*

Contents

Appendices

- Chapter 10 examines the effectiveness of school-to-work.
- Chapter 11 explores the implications of an aging workforce.
- Chapter 12 examines the implications of globalization for career and technical education.
- Chapter 13 reviews selected issues and trends impacting the growth and future of career and technical education.

This book is designed especially for use in teacher education programs of career and technical education. It is uniquely designed for undergraduate and graduate courses in history, philosophy, and foundations of CTE. It will be useful as a source of information to career and technical directors, as well as teachers of career and technical education. This edition has been updated to reflect current preferred usage of the term *career and technical education*, although *vocational education* is still selectively used when it accurately describes CTE in an historical context.

This book is committed to the idea that career and technical education does make a contribution to our educational progress. CTE was added to the school curriculum to achieve a particular set of purposes. Those purposes are still valid for most career and technical educators, in spite of the fact that we now have a society that differs greatly from the society of the early 1900s.

Finally, I wanted to write a book that would not be a crashing bore to read. Colleagues and students who have read the material tell me that for the most part I have succeeded. This work sets forth the historical foundations of career and technical education as they have developed. Knowledge of CTE principles and the story of how they evolved is most important to the future of career and technical education. Career and technical educators need to understand this wealth of historical information if they are involved in planning programs for, advising students in relation to, and making judgments about career and technical education.

Acknowledgments

An ancient saying reminds us, "When you drink the water, remember who dug the well." Many generations of academicians and practitioners provided the scholarship that gave intellectual life to this book.

I am deeply indebted to all the teacher educators, teachers, and their students who have offered comments and constructive criticism, most of which I have tried to address in this edition. Thanks to the following individuals for providing selected photographs for the third edition of this book: Nila Cobb, West Virginia University Cooperative Extension Service; Lou Etta Bowen and Robert McClain, Cabell County Career and Technology Center; Drs. Cecilia Maldonado, Sterling J. Saddler, and Mary Lou Lebo, University of Nevada Las Vegas (UNLV); Nancy Person, Marshall University; and selected personnel at Ebenezer Medical Outreach, Inc. (Huntington, WV).

Special thanks to the staff of Waveland Press, beginning with Gayle Zawilla and Jeni Ogilvie, for their excellent editorial production work.

Preface

History is the cumulative record of our journeys—of people, civilizations, and nations. Whether a novice or a scholar, we are all participants and are able to share its lessons. For five decades or more it has been difficult for people in the field to study the background of career and technical education. The story of career and technical education since 1917 has not been readily available to anyone who desires to develop some background information on its more recent aspects.

This book has been written because there are no other books that focus specifically on the history and growth of career and technical education in America. Students will gain a better understanding of the grassroots information that formed the cornerstone for career and technical education. Today's CTE professionals need to keep current in the materials they use to help tomorrow's workers. However, the history has remained buried in thousands of pages of reports, magazine articles, and other unorganized literature.

Every topic in this book was selected to provide an intimate knowledge of the history and growth of career and technical education in America. The third edition is structured accordingly:

- Chapter 1 presents an overview of the origins of career and technical education in America.
- Chapter 2 introduces the early leaders who influenced CTE curriculum development.
- Chapter 3 describes the impact of land-grant institutions on career and technical education.
- Chapter 4 outlines selected factors that influenced CTE development.
- Chapter 5 traces the evolution of federal legislation that has shaped career and technical education.
- Chapter 6 concerns the participation of women in career and technical education.
- Chapter 7 addresses CTE instructional programs for special-needs populations.
- Chapter 8 discusses CTE programs and teachers.
- Chapter 9 covers career and technical student organizations.

can serve as a powerful tool to facilitate critical conversations, passionate debate, and informed agency and practices.

Although these accomplishments are impressive, what I admire most about Dr. Gordon's text is that he is able to raise tough issues related to career and technical education in a very thoughtful and accessible way. Specifically, aspiring and practicing CTE educators need to grapple with the purpose(s) of career and technical education. All of us must be sensitive to the needs and interest of all learners regardless of race/ethnicity, gender, social class, and special needs. The vision of what has been articulated either as "the new vocationalism" or as career and technical education is reflective of the transformative and democratic potential espoused by John Dewey well over a century ago. However, ultimately it is up to the next generation of career and technical educators to adapt and implement such a vision. I hope you find Dr. Gordon's text to be as powerful a tool as I have for facilitating this transformation.

James A. Gregson, Professor
Adult, Career, and Technology Education
University of Idaho

Foreword

What is the purpose of career and technical education? Is it a curriculum that is intended to prepare students for the world of work? Is it a pedagogical approach that contextualizes academics in way that promotes academic achievement and student engagement? Is it a tool used to transition students from high school to postsecondary education? Is it a "tracking" mechanism used to prepare students for jobs based on social class, race/ethnicity, and/or gender? Is it all of the above? None of the above?

While Dr. Gordon respectfully and skillfully avoids any simplified answers to these questions, he does capture the tensions, contradictions, problems and possibilities of career and technical education. It pleases me that in his third edition he has built upon the philosophical and sociological dimensions as well as the historical ones of his previous texts. Though Dr. Gordon has adopted the new language of career and technical education in the third edition, he understands how critical it is for us not to lose the heritage of what some refer to as the "V word"—vocational education. For how else can we learn lessons from the past so that we can better serve the interests and meet the needs of students, parents, communities, and employers?

My students (who are probably much better reviewers than me) report that it is apparent from Dr. Gordon's book that he has been or is a vocational educator, a vocational teacher educator, a researcher, and a service provider of career and technical education. Because these students are preparing to teach, or are currently teaching, at either the secondary or postsecondary levels—and are from such diverse program areas as agriculture and natural resources education, business and marketing education, family and consumer sciences education, technology and engineering education, and occupational education—they value Dr. Gordon's deep understanding that career and technical education has many shapes and varying purposes, and that context matters.

It is also important to understand that students do not necessarily always value philosophical, sociological, and historical study—something those of us who are passionate about foundational studies find troubling! While *The History and Growth of Career and Technical Education in America* is empirically and theoretically informed, students also find it quite practical, helpful, and relevant. Further, if used artfully, I have found that Dr. Gordon's text

Finally, I gratefully acknowledge Ms. Nhan Hong Pham, former graduate student in the department of Adult and Technical Education, for word processing the third edition of this book.

Howard R. D. Gordon

About the Author

Howard R. D. Gordon is a professor in the department of Adult and Technical Education at Marshall University in Huntington, West Virginia, where he has been a member of the Human Development and Allied Technology faculty since 1991. A native of Jamaica, West Indies, Dr. Gordon has made numerous contributions to the discipline through research, presentations, and publications.

Before joining the faculty at Marshall University, Dr. Gordon worked as a science/horticulture teacher at Prospect Heights High School in Brooklyn, New York, and also as a community college instructor in floral design and management at Florida Community College in Jacksonville, Florida. He is a former Historian of the Association for Career and Technical Education Research (ACTER), an affiliate of the Association for Career and Technical Education (ACTE).

His academic background includes course work at the College of Agriculture, Science and Education (formerly the Jamaica School of Agriculture), a B.Sc. in Animal and Poultry Sciences, and an M.Sc. in Vocational Education/Agricultural Education from Tuskegee Institute. His doctorate is in Agricultural Education with minors in Rural Sociology and Educational Research from Virginia Polytechnic Institute and State University. Dr. Gordon also completed selected postdoctorate courses in medical education at Spartan School of Medicine, Vieux Fort, St. Lucia (West Indies). His present interests are in research design and methodology, history of career and technical education, and preventive/occupational medicine. He has been certified in Agricultural Science Education by the New York State Department of Education. Among his professional affiliations are the American College of Preventive Medicine, the American Educational Research Association, the Association for Career and Technical Education Research, and the Hawaii Educational Research Association.

chapter 1

Early Career and Technical Education in America

The program of career and technical education, as we know it today, had its origin in the early part of the twentieth century. However, the causal factors of the vocational movement in education occurred during the nineteenth century, and the historical roots can be traced to ancient times, with significant European connections.

During the latter part of the nineteenth century, the need for vocational training produced a number of private trade schools. Although there were many different kinds of trade schools, organized for many different purposes, the schools can be described as belonging to one of three types: (1) schools that offered only trade training, (2) schools that offered a combination of trade training and general education, and (3) schools that apprenticed their students to the boards of trustees in addition to offering trade and general education.

In addition to trade schools, a large number of private business schools were organized throughout the nation and supplied vocational preparation for the business world. It was also possible to find a few schools offering instruction in agriculture.

A second major development prior to the beginning of the twentieth century was the establishment of programs—in the public schools—known as manual training, commercial training, domestic science, and agriculture.

At the turn of the twentieth century, some of the farsighted people in the manual training area observed that many of their graduates were using the skills and knowledge gained in manual training classes for vocational purposes. This was not the major intent of manual training programs: the proponents claimed educational rather than vocational purposes. However, the manual training leaders were encouraged to develop a separate system of what was then referred to as vocational education that would achieve vocational goals on purpose rather than by accident. Business leaders represented by the National Association of Manufacturers complained that the factory system had largely destroyed apprenticeship as a source of skilled labor. Finally, the start of World War I cut off a traditional source of the best talent—highly skilled artisan immigrants from Europe.

1

The current structure and growth of career and technical education in the United States are the product of an extensive evolutionary process. Any attempt to address current issues without an understanding of the past will prove arduous at best. With the continually changing federal role in CTE, it has become increasingly important to understand and appreciate the historical evolution of career and technical education in the United States.

This chapter details the origins of CTE in America. Emphasis is placed on the following topics: European influence, apprenticeship in America, the Industrial Revolution, the manual training movement, evolutionary phases of technology development, and redefining career and technical education.

European Influence on Career and Technical Education

Traditionally, CTE has consisted of practical and applied instruction aimed at matching students with work positions in industry and commerce (Benavot, 1983). Because of this purpose, CTE has been known throughout its history by various names, including industrial education, manual education, career education (Grubb and Lazerson, 1975), and more recently, vocational education. Career and technical education's allegiance with the workplace becomes evident when one examines its historical roots, particularly in nineteenth-century Europe.

During the 1800s schools were divided by social class, and the purposes of educational institutions were much different for those who came from wealthy classes than for those from working-class or indigent backgrounds. One of the most obvious differences was that manual training became a central part of the curriculum for the lower classes. In all grades of these schools, handwork was carried on in connection with the other branches of instruction (Bennett, 1937).

Germany was the center of this manual training movement for the middle and lower classes. Unlike France and England, Germany's trade guilds retained their power throughout the nineteenth century and continued to encourage apprenticeship programs. Also, Germany's elementary schooling was both free and compulsory, so there was a ready educational foundation on which to build industrial training (Bennett, 1937). Among the noted exponents of these ideas were Jean Jacques Rousseau and Johann Heinrich Pestalozzi.

Jean Jacques Rousseau (1712–1778)

Rousseau was born in Geneva, Switzerland. In 1762 he published a highly controversial novel, *Émile*. According to Culver (1986), Rousseau's novel was the story of an orphan boy who was removed from society and had access only to his tutor as a companion. The boy discovers cognitive information through objects or things (no books), and in this natural manner he develops physically, intellectually, and morally until he is ready to take his place in society.

Rousseau viewed education as a means to free humankind from social status and permit enjoyment of the senses. In essence, Rousseau advocated that manual arts could serve as a means of mental training and thus paved the way to a new era in vocational education.

Johann Heinrich Pestalozzi (1746–1827)

Pestalozzi was born in Zurich, Switzerland. Davidson (1900) cites that Pestalozzi, who admittedly borrowed from Rousseau's work, believed that formal education must be open to all children, teaching methods should cultivate learning and the desire to learn, and education should be based on facts and the practical circumstances of society as opposed to theoretical constructs.

Pestalozzi's ideas about vocational education can be considered under three headings: the principles of vocational training in agreement with those of other branches of education; his views on industry, its dangers, and means of overcoming them; and finally, his ideas on the education of the poor and his attempts to carry them out in the first decade of the nineteenth century (Silber, 1965). Pestalozzi insisted that children should learn not only to think, but also to do, and hence that education should consist largely of manual labor. Pestalozzi's ideas about the importance of a vocational component in the school curriculum for all students spread across Europe and into the United States. One of his teachers at Burgdorf, Joseph Neef, opened a school in Philadelphia in 1809 based on the Pestalozzian method (Barlow, 1967). Early instruction in manual training in normal schools is directly tied to Pestalozzi's influence. The Oswego State Normal School, organized in 1861 by Edward A. Sheldon (1823–1897), superintendent of schools in Oswego, owed its curriculum and educational philosophy to Pestalozzi (Bennett, 1937). Other schools based on the Oswego model sprang up in neighboring areas. By 1891, similar schools had developed in Massachusetts, New Jersey, Connecticut, Pennsylvania, Maryland, Texas, and California (Report of the Commission, 1893).

Many other nineteenth-century educational reformers contributed to the evolution of career and technical education. Among them were Friedrich Wilhelm Augustus Froebel, Uno Cygnaeus, Otto Salomon, Johann Friedrich Herbart, and Tuiskan Ziller. Their contributions and views of activity, handwork, and industry all emphasized the necessity of vocational education. See Appendix A for a time line summarizing the European–American evolution of vocational education.

Apprenticeship in America

Apprenticeship is the oldest known type of vocational education in the United States. Programs pertaining to apprenticeship have long been a basic method of obtaining occupational competence. Education for the worker took the form of apprenticeship. This type of vocational education was not regarded as part of the school curriculum. The apprenticeship process involves a formal agreement, covering a definite period of time, that binds the employer to provide training in return for the work of the apprentice.

Apprenticeship came to the New World in the early colonial period. This type of training in the colonies resembled that of the mother countries. There were no guilds or similar craft organizations, as such, in colonial America. The English apprenticeship system was modified to suit conditions in the New World, and apprenticeship in colonial America became the most important educational agency of the period of colonization and settlement (Roberts, 1957).

An apprentice carrying a wooden vessel, as tall as himself, on his way to fetch water. Engraving from Braun, *Civitates orbis Terrarum*, 1572.

The custom of apprenticeship that the colonists brought with them from European countries constituted the main form of training for industrial employment until well into the period of machine production. The inadequate labor supply in the colonies and the surplus population in England were the factors promoting the indentured servitude that has been so identified with apprenticeship in this period.

With the development of slavery, this form of white servitude declined. In the New England colonies, where the conditions of apprenticeship were based largely on the English Statute of Artificers of 1562, the educational aspects of apprenticeship were sufficiently stressed to keep it distinct from servitude. The provision for indenture of children of paupers, vagrants, and large families was made to secure for the child (1) training in the trade of the masters, (2) education in the common branches, and (3) instruction in sound ethics. For the poor, at least, the institution of apprenticeship offered the almost sole opportunity to secure an education in colonial times. It was not until well into the nineteenth century that the free public elementary school became an established American institution and gradually relieved apprenticeship of its general education functions (Hawkins, Prosser, and Wright, 1951).

The Statute of Artificers and English Poor Law of 1601

The Statute of Artificers, passed in 1562, transformed apprenticeship from a local to a national system in England. It codified the various local laws and regulations relative to employment of servants and apprentices. This action was necessitated by the countless number of local statutes, many of which were out of date or contradictory. The need to reform had been evi-

dent for some time, and a general law seemed to offer the best possibility for meeting this need (Roberts, 1971).

Late in the sixteenth century, rising prices and growing unemployment created distress among the poor of England. A series of "poor laws" was passed to help impoverished families survive the shift from agriculture to manufacturing that was occurring throughout the country. The English Poor Law of 1601 allowed church wardens and overseers to place children of poor families with an acceptable master until the girls were twenty-one and the boys were twenty-four. The law's basic intent was to equip the children of poor families with a salable skill. This approach was considered very successful and greatly influenced the future direction of career and technical education in America (Thompson, 1973).

Kinds of Apprenticeship

There were two kinds of apprenticeship in America. One was the voluntary form, which followed European customs and traditions but in general was not subject to particular provisions of law, although such agreements were entered in the town records. The second was involuntary apprenticeship, which provided a means of taking care of poor children and orphans. A master, instead of the town, became responsible for their personal and occupational needs (Barlow, 1967).

In general, the traditional elements of apprenticeship agreements were food, clothing, and shelter; religious training; general education as needed in the trade; knowledge, understanding, and experience in the trade skills; and finally, the "mysteries" of the trade, or the techniques that had some elementary scientific basis. Both boys and girls were apprenticed for periods of time varying from five to ten years. Girls usually served until they were eighteen or were married. Apprenticeship started in many instances at the age of eight or nine. Apprenticeship was not a scheme of exploitation but was essentially an educational institution (Seybolt, 1917).

The Apprenticeship Indenture

When a master took an apprentice, he or she entered into a contract (usually written) with the apprentice or the overseer. This contract or indenture, when properly witnessed and recorded, became a public document. As a public record it provided protection to both the apprentice and his or her master. The following apprenticeship indenture made in 1676 illustrates the type of contract used in the New England colonies:

> This Indenture witnesseth that I, Nathan Knight ... have put myself apprentice to Samuel Whidden, of Portsmouth, in the county of Portsmouth, mason, and bound after the manner of an apprentice with him, to serve and abide the full space and term of twelve years and five months ... during which time the said apprentice his said master faithfully shall serve ... He shall not ... contract matrimony within the said time. The goods of his said master, he shall not spend or lend.

He shall not play cards, or dice or any other unlawful game, whereby his said master may have damage in his own goods, or others, taverns he shall not haunt, nor from his master's business absent himself by day or by night, but in all things shall behave himself as a faithful apprentice ought to do.

And the said master his said apprentice shall teach and instruct, or cause to be taught and instructed in the art and mystery as mason; funding unto his said apprentice during the said time, meat, drink, washing, lodging, and apparel, fitting an apprentice, teaching him to read, and allowing him three months toward the latter end of his time to go to school to write, and also double apparel at end of said time. . . . (Erden, 1991, p. 30)

When the apprenticeship was completed, this fact was acknowledged by the master at a town meeting and duly entered into the minutes of the meeting. If the apprentice had given satisfaction, he was permitted to follow his trade. However, if the master was not satisfied with the progress made, the apprentice was forbidden to practice the trade and could, if all parties agreed, continue his apprenticeship program.

Reasons for the Decline of Apprenticeship in America

Following 1807, an industrial revolution similar to that which England had experienced took place in America. As a result of the Industrial Revolution, the apprenticeship program lost its most important characteristics—the personal guidance and instruction by the master. This change in apprenticeship was due to the heavy increases in the demand for manufactured goods that were met by the use of experienced machine operators who did not need a long period of apprenticeship.

Apprenticeship, having already declined in importance in the colonial period, was dealt its heaviest blow by the factory system in the nineteenth century. The reasons for its decline included the following: (1) large groups succeeded small forces of labor; each group was trained to work in a specific task or operation, (2) scattered industries became centralized, (3) industry developed so many subdivisions that training was both expensive and useless, (4) indenture laws gradually became ineffective, (5) many trades became overcrowded because of the large numbers of apprentices who were allowed to learn them, (6) wages were kept very low, (7) young helpers were taught not simply by the technique of some single process but by the "arts and mysteries of a craft," and (8) free public elementary schools developed.

Apprenticeship served as the major source of education and training for the masses. New systems of education and training were beginning to surface in a progressive America that would regulate apprenticeship to serve only a small number of people. While a small number of workers continued to be thoroughly trained through apprenticeship, most workers learned job skills from parents or through on-the-job training—learning job skills through observation, trial and error, and imitation.

Apprenticeship Today

In 1934, a federal committee on apprentice training was created by executive order of the president of the United States (Roberts, 1957). However, it was not until the passage of the Fitzgerald Act in 1937 that statutory provision was made for the establishment and continuing development of a program of apprenticeship. This act authorized the secretary of labor to establish standards to guide industry in employing and training apprentices. The act also provided plans to bring management and labor together to formulate programs for training apprentices, appointing national committees, and promoting acceptance of apprenticeship standards.

By 1940, eleven states had enacted apprenticeship laws and in thirteen others apprenticeship councils had been formed. Recommendations adopted by the International Labor Organization during the summer of 1939 were given wide publicity in the United States, both by labor and by the U.S. Office of Education. These recommendations included provisions for (1) written agreements showing the terms of the agreements and the terms of the apprentice's relationship, (2) learning schedules in various aspects of the trade, (3) a scale of wages with periodic increases, (4) attendance in classes for related instruction, (5) continuous employment, and (6) approval by joint committees of employers and employees (Byer, 1940).

During the thirteen-year period 1941 to 1953, a cumulative total of 687,605 persons registered with authorized apprenticeship agencies to receive training as apprentices. During this period a total of 192,473 registered apprentices completed training, 328,332 left before completion, and 166,800 were still in training at the close of the period. The number of registered apprenticeship systems increased from 760 in 1941 to 50,220 in 1953. This increase was due to newly established systems of apprenticeship and to the registration of previously established nonregistered systems (Roberts, 1957).

Although today's apprentices still work under the terms of formal apprenticeship agreements, they work regular work weeks, reside in their own homes, and earn real wages instead of the "meat, drink, washing, lodging, and apparel" promised to young Nathan Knight.

Apprenticeship in America today is a government credentialing system for developing and recognizing specific skills, competencies, and accomplishments. Credentialing is handled in a manner similar to that of schools and colleges. An individual's registration in a specific program is documented. The apprentice's day-to-day progress toward learning all facets of the target occupation is recorded and matched against the approved, written training outline that describes what functions must be learned, for how long, and where. Apprentices who complete all phases of the prescribed training earn a certificate of completion.

Apprentices are usually high school graduates with manual dexterity or other characteristics directly related to the occupation they want to enter. The average beginning apprentice is twenty-five years old. About two-thirds of the apprenticeable occupations are in the construction and manufacturing

trades, but apprentices also work in such diverse fields as electronics, service industries, public administration, medicine, and health care. The length of an apprenticeship varies depending on the occupation and the standards adopted by the industry. The minimum term of apprenticeship is one year.

On-the-job apprentice training takes place under close supervision of a skilled and experienced craft worker. It is on the job that apprentices learn the practical skills they will need to become skilled craft workers themselves. Apprentices learn the theoretical side of their jobs in technical classes that they usually attend after work. Related training may cover such subjects as mathematics, blueprint reading, and applied English, as well as more technical courses required for specific occupations.

Wages paid to apprentices begin at approximately half those paid to fully trained craft workers. The wages advance rapidly at six-month intervals until the training is completed and apprentices qualify for the full craft-worker wage.

Because apprenticeship combines learning and earning, many different groups must work together to coordinate successful programs. Apprenticeship programs depend on the cooperation of private-sector organizations that control jobs and employers (individually and through trade associations) and sponsor the nation's apprenticeship programs, often in partnership with organized labor unions.

The Industrial Revolution

In the late 1700s, colonial leaders could no longer maintain their Renaissance-based philosophy, especially with the advent of the Industrial Revolution in Great Britain. According to Walter (1993), the arrival of the Industrial Revolution in the United States was delayed until after 1800, largely by restrictive trade laws. Roberts (1957) points out that in 1803 there were only four cotton mills operating in the entire country. Industrial artisans and their apprentices continued to dominate manufacturing in the United States until 1807, when the situation dramatically changed (Walter, 1993). Hawkins, Prosser, and Wright (1951) cite the Embargo Act, the Non-Intercourse Act, and the War of 1812 as the three events that generated the American version of the Industrial Revolution. The combined effects of the three effectively sealed the marketplace to foreign manufactured goods and guaranteed a return on any money invested in U.S. production facilities. Spurred by the no-risk situation, businesspeople quickly sought to apply new technology to their manufacturing operations and to switch to large-scale production. Since the apprenticeship system was unable to supply the subsequent demand for trained workers, the stage was set for new forms of education to emerge.

Among the disadvantages that technology brought were (1) increased accidents, (2) poor working conditions, (3) layoffs when production was not

in line with demand, (4) blacklisting workers who protested the system, and (5) economic chaos for those families who lost their breadwinner. These situations were largely due to the inability of the industrial and political leaders to recognize and meet the changing conditions of the worker.

Charitable groups and societies of mechanics initiated efforts to establish schools to provide factory workers with educational opportunities formerly supplied by the apprenticeship system (Walter, 1993). Bennett (1926) cites the Farm and Trade School, founded in Boston in 1814, as one of the first of this type of institution. Its purpose was to provide orphans the benefits of both academic and vocational preparation.

Generally, 1826 is recognized as the beginning of the *American lyceum movement*, a device for popular adult education through lectures; "scientific farming" was a frequently heard topic (Venn, 1964). In 1823, the first school devoted entirely to practical studies, the Gardiner Lyceum in Maine, was opened. According to Roberts (1957), by 1833 there were about one thousand lyceums in the United States. However, lacking an adequate financial base and facing the distrust of farmers and mechanics, most of them did not last long.

In 1824, a second school of this type addressed the problem of providing the populace with information on the application of technology in the workplace from another angle. The purpose of the Rennselear School in Troy, New York, was to provide teachers of science with the opportunity to apply the scientific principles while studying at actual farms and in production-oriented workshops. The school's mission continued to expand with the addition of Mathematical Arts in 1835, which led to its evolution into the first school of engineering in the United States (Bennett, 1926).

The Manual Training Movement

General Samuel Chapman Armstrong, the son of American missionaries to Hawaii, had headed an African-American regiment during the Civil War. He had been selected for the position due to his extensive experience in educating the illiterate people of Hawaii. Both experiences proved valuable when, in 1866, he was appointed the superintendent of education for African Americans of Virginia. Immediately, he began the development of what became Hampton Institute (Barlow, 1967). Hampton Institute opened in 1868 based on the philosophy that there was dignity in all forms of work and that human beings, regardless of race, could only truly appreciate that which they had earned. Therefore, students at Hampton were expected to work for the school to earn their tuition. This marked the beginning of the manual labor school movement in America. The idea did not originate with Armstrong, who personally had been educated in such a way. While in Hawaii, he had attended the Royal School for Hawaiian Chiefs, where some manual labor was required of everyone (Hall, 1973).

The first U.S. school designed to provide this type of education was the Worcester Polytechnic Institute at Worcester, Massachusetts, which opened in 1868 (Bennett, 1926). The curriculum combined theoretical classes with production work in laboratories, so that students completing the program would be ready for jobs without an apprenticeship period (Walter, 1993).

In 1870, Calvin Woodward introduced shopwork at Washington University as a means of providing his applied-mechanics students with a visual representation of the problems they were attempting to solve (Bennett, 1937). The success of this technique led to the development of specific projects to provide students with practice in the use of tools and machinery (Walter, 1993).

The greatest stimulus to the manual training movement, however, was the Russian exhibit at the Centennial Exposition in Philadelphia in 1876. Victor Della Vos, director of the Imperial Technical School of Moscow, exhibited a system of tool instruction based on the construction of models from plans designed and drawn by students (Wirth, 1972).

John Runkle, president of the Massachusetts Institute of Technology, saw the Russian system of tool instruction as the answer to a problem he had been attempting to solve. Graduates of his engineering program were well schooled in theory and principles, but industries often required them to complete an apprenticeship period because they needed employees who also possessed tool and machinery skills. Runkle was successful in persuading his institution to develop both laboratories to provide engineering students with mechanical skills in 1877, and a secondary-level program, called the School of Mechanic Arts, in 1878. The success of both convinced Runkle that such opportunities should be provided for boys in public schools (Bennett, 1937).

As the manual training movement grew, pressure also grew to increase its availability to all students as part of the public schools. The 1884 convention of the National Education Association in Madison, Wisconsin, became a forum for both advocates and opponents of manual training (Bennett, 1937). Educators in favor of including manual training in the public high schools stressed the general nature of the skills developed and the relationship to academic study of the basic sciences. Those opposed stressed that it was a vocationally oriented substitute for apprenticeship and thus should be limited to separate schools (Walter, 1993).

Despite continued opposition, by the end of the decade manual training as envisioned by Woodward and Runkle had won its prominence in the schools. The shop system, which at once claimed to be a democratic recognition of the importance of the industrial classes and of the learning-by-doing theories of Rousseau and Pestalozzi, was adopted by Woodward as the pedagogical heart of his manual arts program (Venn, 1964). Today, the shop system remains an important part of the legacy of manual arts to career and technical education.

In what could be regarded as a compromise institution, the Baltimore Manual Training High School was opened in 1884 as the first separate manual training school. The mission of this school was to provide both manual and academic training for students. The curriculum offered by this school was replicated in many other cities in America.

The Sloyd (Swedish) System and the Russian System

The sloyd system advocated that manual labor in a prevocational sense should be taught as part of a general education. Selected principles of this system were that the work should be given by a trained teacher, not an artisan; students should make useful articles and not articles of luxury or parts of articles; and the articles were to be made starting with the simple and progressing to the more complex, using models as a guide (Salomon, 1906). In 1888, Gustaf Larson, a teacher of sloyd in Sweden, came to America and established sloyd instruction in Boston. Before long, Larson had to make changes in traditional sloyd methodology to make it work in America. Several of these changes were:

- Swedish models that were first used had no appeal to American youth and had to be replaced with models of interest to students.

- Traditional sloyd emphasized working from models, but American industry developed products from drawings and drawing was already a school subject of importance in general education. The practice of students working from models was replaced with students working from teacher-prepared drawings and later from student-developed drawings.

- The mostly individualized method of instruction was broadened to include more group instruction, which had become successful in American schools.

These adaptations of Swedish sloyd led to the term "American sloyd" (Smith, 1981).

The Russian System, introduced by Victor Della Vos, was essentially a laboratory method of teaching. The method was quite similar to other laboratory work involving a given set of exercises. These exercises were arranged in what was considered to be a logical order for teaching purposes (Struck, 1930).

The major difference between manual training and American sloyd was based on the focus sloyd had on the development of the learner rather than the development of skill in the use of hand tools, and the use of trained teachers rather than the use of skilled craftworkers to teach tool skills. Manual training focused on teaching the use of specific tools by completing exercises or making incomplete objects without sufficient attention directed to individual needs and capacities. Sloyd, on the other hand, placed careful attention on developing capacities of the individual in the selection of graded models and projects that were interesting to youth and on the sequence of instructional tasks based on the capacity of each youth, leading to the completion of useful objects. Other advantages of sloyd over the Russian system of manual training were:

- greater emphasis on the study of form by the use of some models that involved student judgment of shape and proportion rather than the testing of tools,
- greater variety of tasks,
- importance of using completed models, and
- importance of the teacher being a trained educator.

The sloyd movement lasted only a few years, but it did change the way practical art subjects were taught and encouraged the use of trained teachers (Smith, 1981).

Perhaps the greatest contribution of the manual training movement, from the career and technical education viewpoint, was its effect on the perception of what could or should be taught in public schools. This spread of manual training signaled the beginning of a shift, from the belief that the ideal high school curriculum was devoted solely to college preparation, to also reflect the need to prepare students for a variety of career options requiring less than college-level preparation. Coupled with the growing specialization of jobs, this broadening of the high school curriculum also created a need in young people for assistance in choosing which of the many career paths to follow (Walter, 1993).

More than anything else, manual training changed the conception of what might be legitimately taught in the schools; once this was accomplished, the shift to vocational purposes seemed a logical development.

Phases of Technology Development

Many career and technical educators equate the development of technology with the Industrial Revolution. However, technology not only affected industrialization but also had an impact on social, economic, and educational institutions. According to Thompson (1973), most early historians of vocational education were concerned about how the Industrial Revolution affected vocational education programs for production.

Five major phases in the development of technology occurred during the growth of CTE in America.

Phase One: Application of Power to Machines

This first phase of development was characterized by the dominance of the application of power to machines. Thompson (1973) cites inventions such as the loom, the steam engine, and the spinning frame as basic to this era. These inventions were responsible for the establishment of a factory system in America. During this phase, artisans developed a cooperative institute to maintain quality. However, the artisans were not economically viable to purchase the power supply and the power-driven machines.

Phase Two: Introduction of Mass Production

The mid-1800s marked the beginning of the second phase. Factors such as population growth and the Civil War placed increasing demands on production. During this phase, production was characterized as too slow and too costly. An artisan's role in the factory was limited to producing only a single item.

Manufactured goods increased trade, which in turn created additional demands for improvements and new inventions (Thompson, 1973). The profit motive was the major concern of those who controlled business and industry. Therefore, this phase had an influence on the development of mass production through some form of assembly-line techniques. This era of technology development in CTE elevated the artisan to the status of a technician. Industrial growth resulted in more and better-quality goods.

There was no social consciousness on the part of the employer during this phase. Since education was not needed to perform simple work tasks, no "vocational education" was provided to those who performed such tasks (Thompson, 1973).

Phase Three: Influence of Automation

This phase of technological development was often referred to simply as automation (Buckingham, 1961). This era probably began during the time frame when Henry Ford introduced automation. The basic pattern of commonality during this era was multiconnected machines. This phase produced more demands for vocational education and, therefore, an increase in the level of preparation needed by workers in America.

Phase Four: Miniaturization

The fourth phase in the development of technology can be traced to the early 1970s. This phase was characterized by the development of the miniaturization of electronic techniques. Plastics and synthetics became prominent, replacing a majority of materials.

Phase Five: Global Network/Technological Explosion

This phase of technology evolved during the 1980s and 1990s. During the 1980s the videocassette recorder gained prominence as a teaching device in many vocational classrooms. Rapid manufacturing of personal computers was also on the increase. Business and industry saw the introduction of automated teller machines and answering machines as linkage to the "new industrial revolution" in the workplace.

Technology invaded our vocational schools in the 1990s. Career and technical educators purchased new equipment, acquired competence with computer network systems, and developed curricula focusing on new technologies. In many school districts, CTE teachers were leading the technological invasion in the hope of preparing students for the computerized, information-based world in which they would work.

Implications for the Workplace

- Technology must provide the flexibility necessary to meet the escalating client requests for specialized, custom-designed products and services. As a result, workers need both wider varieties of skills and higher levels of technical competence.

- Market mandates for fast turnaround and quick response are forcing further decentralization in management and decision-making skills—fueling an increased demand for production teams that can work together to solve problems, inspect for quality, maximize production and quality, and minimize costs.

- Workers need to handle extreme pressure: they are required to know more about the company and its products or services, to interface frequently with the end users, to take initiative and make decisions based on many more unknowns, and to be dedicated team players.

- Mechanics, technicians, and other "fixers" need to understand complicated manuals and follow complex systems of repair and maintenance. Advances in microprocessors and electronics make existing equipment obsolete in shorter periods of time. As a result, workers need to continually upgrade their technical expertise and broaden the scope of their interpersonal skills to function effectively.

Information technology prepares CTE students to be competent in the information-based, globally connected world of the twenty-first century.

Redefining Career and Technical Education

The growing economic importance of college raises questions about what the role of career and technical education should be. The 1990 federal law defined vocational education, for purposes of federal funding, as preparation for "occupations requiring other than a baccalaureate or advanced degree."

This harks back to the 1917 Smith-Hughes Act, which provided the first federal money for vocational education. At that time only one out of 30 adults had a bachelor's degree or higher educational level (Stern, 1998). However, that proportion has dramatically increased during the twenty-first century among adults who are employed (NCES, 2001). Yet, the restricted definition of "vocational" education has remained.

In spite of the statutory definition, career and technical education itself has been changing. Thousands of high school schools and community colleges have developed new courses of study that prepare students for work as well as for further education, including four-year college or university. Tech Prep, career academies, industry majors, youth apprenticeships, and other innovations have demonstrated the possibility of combining preparation for both college and careers (Bailey and Merritt, 1997).

These innovations have been encouraged by other state and federal legislation, including a provision in the 1990 federal law that required integration of academic and CTE programs, and another provision that authorized money for Tech Prep. The 1994 School-to-Work Opportunities Act, the 1998 Carl D. Perkins Vocational and Applied Technology Amendments, and most recently the Carl D. Perkins Career and Technical Education Improvement Act of 2006 (a reauthorization of the 1998 amendment) also helped stimulate new approaches (Stone and Alliaga, 2005; Stone et al., 2004). According to Stern (1998), "these innovative provisions of federal law may disappear as Congress enacts new legislation. If so, the basic definition of vocational education in federal law will become more important as a guide to state and local practice" (pp. 1, 3).

Career and technical education in high schools and community colleges no longer should be restricted to occupations that do not require a bachelor's or advanced degree. Instead, the statutory definition should encourage collaboration between vocational and nonvocational educators to prepare students both for work and for further education.

Summary

- The foundations of the American educational system were built on the types of education that evolved in Europe. The eighteenth century, or Age of Reason, was an age of democratic liberalism, benevolence, and tolerance. Among the noted exponents of these ideas were Jean Jacques Rousseau and Johann Heinrich Pestalozzi. In the nineteenth century, positive gains of lasting significance were made in the utilization of the elements of industry in education. Pestalozzi's ideas about the importance of the vocational component in the school curriculum spread across Europe and into the United States.

- The apprenticeship laws of the Massachusetts colonies demonstrated a commitment to the concept of public support for both academic and vocational instruction. For more than 150 years colonial America used an American version of apprenticeship as the chief source of education for training the masses. However, as the factory system of production developed, the interest in apprenticeship declined.

- The Industrial Revolution created not only a working class demanding new educational opportunities but also jobs requiring an entirely new type of education. Engineers, designers, and managers needed education that provided both scientific theory and practical applications of the theory.

- The greatest stimulus to the manual training movement was the Russian exhibit at the Centennial Exposition in Philadelphia in 1876. Manual training was not without its critics. Technical education was called a "deceptive farce" by zealous guardians of liberal education who considered it a threat to the intellect and unacceptable in the public schools. In some ways these fundamental arguments are indicative of the problems faced by vocational education in today's society.

- During the 1980s and 1990s world competition increased rapidly, leading to a surge in consumer-driven styles and services; in the twenty-first century these phenomena will continue to escalate the pace of change and the unpredictability in technology and markets. Hence, mass production, standardization, and assembly-line routinization will no longer assume profits through economics of scale. Customers—weary of sameness of clothes, cars, and even home styles—are demanding distinctiveness, quality, and diversity that mass-production techniques cannot meet.

- Defining career and technical education as preparation for both college and careers would eliminate the necessity for students to choose one or the other. It would also give schools no reason to separate students into college-bound and noncollege-bound categories.

Discussion Questions and Activities

1. Justify the reasons for the five major phases of technology development during the growth of career and technical education in America.
2. Distinguish between the characteristics of apprenticeship in colonial America and present-day apprenticeship programs.

3. Differentiate between the principles of the sloyd and the Russian systems.

4. Discuss the effects of technology and changing lifestyles on career and technical education in today's society.

5. Interpret the meaning of the term *indentured apprenticeship*. What functions did it serve?

6. Discuss the factors that caused the decline of apprenticeship in colonial America. What were the effects of the decline?

7. Explain what influenced the American Lyceum.

8. Debate the advantages and disadvantages of technology in career and technical education.

9. Extrapolate the key concepts and ideas of work education proposed by the early educational reformers of Europe.

For Exploration

10. What were some of the arguments for and against including career and technical education subjects into the elementary and secondary schools of America?

11. Compare and contrast the educational principles and methods of instruction of Johann Pestalozzi with present-day career and technical education programs in America.

12. Extrapolate how the lineage of Rousseau, Pestalozzi, and General Armstrong influenced the manual training movement.

13. Read several definitions of career and technical education and select or adapt one with which you mostly agree.

Recommended Educational Media Resources

- *Johann Pestalozzi: The first of the new educators*
  Insight Media
  2162 Broadway
  New York, NY 10024-0621
  1-800-233-9910 or (212)-721-6316
  Web site: http://www.insight.media.com
- *Before the Industrial Revolution*
- *The Industrial Revolution: Part 1*
- *The Industrial Revolution: Part 2*
  Educational Video Network, Inc.
  1336 19th Street
  Huntsville, TX 77340
  1-800-762-0060 or (936)-295-5767
  Web site: https://www.evndirect.com/information.php/page=5

References and Additional Reading

Bailey, T. and Merritt, D. (1997). *School-to-work for the college bound*, MDS-779. National Center for Research in Vocational Education. University of California, Berkeley.

Barlow, M. L. (1967). *History of industrial education in the United States*. Peoria, IL: Chas. A. Bennett.

———. (1976). Independent action. *American Vocational Journal, 51*(5), 31–40.

Benavot, A. (1983). The rise and decline of vocational education. *Sociology of Education, 56*, 63–76.

Bennett, C. A. (1926). *History of manual and industrial education up to 1870*. Peoria, IL: Manual Arts.

———. (1937). *History of manual and industrial arts 1870–1917*. Peoria, IL: Manual Arts.

Buckingham, W. (1961). *Automation: Its impact on business and people*. New York: Harper & Row.

Byer, C. M. (1940). Labor's interest in apprenticeship and vocational education. *AVA Journal and News Bulletin, 15*(1), 30–31.

Culver, S. M. (1986). Pestalozzi's influence on manual training in nineteenth century Germany. *Journal of Vocational and Technical Education, 2*(2), 37–43.

Davidson, T. (1900). *A history of education*. New York: AMS.

Erden, J. V. (1991). Linking past and present, students and jobs. *Vocational Education Journal, 66*(7), 30–32, 69.

Grubb, N. and Lazerson, M. (1975). Rally round the workplace: Continuities and fallacies in career education. *Harvard Education Review, 45*, 451–474.

Hall, C. W. (1973). *Black vocational technical and industrial arts education: Development and history*. Chicago: American Technical Society.

Hawkins, L. S., Prosser, C. A., and Wright, J. C. (1951). *Development of vocational education*. Chicago, IL: American Technical Society.

National Center for Education Statistics (NCES) (2001). *Digest of education statistics*. U.S. Department of Education, Office of Educational Research and Improvement.

Report of the commission appointed to investigate the existing systems of manual training and industrial education (1893). Boston, MA: State of Massachusetts.

Roberts, R. W. (1957). *Vocational and practical arts education*, 1st ed. New York: Harper & Row.

———. (1971). *Vocational and practical arts education*, 3rd ed. New York: Harper & Row.

Salomon, O. (1906). *The theory of educational Sloyd*. Boston: Silver, Burdette.

Seybolt, R. E. (1917). *Apprenticeship and apprenticeship education in colonial New England and New York*. New York: Teachers College Press, Columbia University.

Silber, K. (1965). *Pestalozzi: The man and his work*. London: Butler and Tanner Limited.

Smith, D. F. (1981). Industrial arts founded. In T. Wright and R. Barella (Eds.), *An interpretive history of industrial arts: The relationship of society, education and industrial arts*. 30th Yearbook. American Council on Industrial Arts Teacher Education. Bloomington, IL: McKnight Publishing.

Stern, D. (1998). Removing the ceiling: College and career. *Centerwork, 9*(2), 1, 3.

Stone, J., and Alliaga, O. (2005). Career and technical education and school-to-work at the end of the 20th century: Participation and outcomes. *Career and Technical Education Research, 30*(2), 125–144.

Stone, J., Kowske, B., and Alfeld, C. (2004). Career and technical education in the late 1990s: A descriptive Study. *Career and Technical Education Research, 29*(3), 195–224.

Struck, F. T. (1930). *Foundations of industrial education*. New York: John Wiley and Sons.

Thompson, J. E. (1973). *Foundations of vocational education: Social and philosophical concepts*. Englewood Cliffs, NJ: Prentice-Hall.

Venn, G. (1964). *Man, education and work*. Washington, DC: American Council on Education.

Walter, R. A. (1993). Development of vocational education. In C. A. Anderson and L. C. Ramp (Eds.), *Vocational education in the 1990's, II: A sourcebook for strategies, methods, and materials* (pp. 1–20). Ann Arbor, MI: Prakken Publications.

Wirth, A. G. (1972). *Education in the technological society: The vocational liberal controversies in early twentieth century*. Scranton, PA: Intext Educational.

Leaders Who Influenced Career and Technical Education Curriculum Development

From early apprenticeship programs to the present day, various forms of curriculum and instructional systems have been planned, developed, and implemented. The struggle to introduce career and technical education into all educational curricula has been attributed to Booker T. Washington, an educator and leader; David Snedden, an educational administrator; Charles Prosser, a lawyer; and John Dewey, a philosopher.

Washington emphasized both cognitive and problem-solving skills as essential educational goals. Snedden argued for social efficiency and the need for all students to prepare for useful employment. Prosser was an advocate for integrating CTE into the general curriculum. Dewey saw CTE as a means of liberalizing education. He contended that traditional liberal education did not provide the skills and attitudes necessary for living in an age of science.

This chapter presents an overview of selected leaders who have made significant contributions to the foundation and structure of CTE curriculum development in America.

Historical Role of Booker T. Washington

Perhaps less generally recognized than his leadership skills are the important contributions that Booker T. Washington made to the theory and practice of education—contributions that transcend their time and remain relevant today (Schraff, 2006; Schroeder and Beier, 2005; Brundage, 2003; Wolfe, 1981). Washington, Hampton Institute's most famous graduate, was recommended in 1881 by General Samuel Chapman Armstrong to become principal of a new school in Tuskegee, Alabama (Thornbrough, 1969). With only $2,000, Washington founded Tuskegee Institute based on the same principles that his mentor had established for Hampton Institute. In the years that followed, both Washington and Tuskegee grew in fame and national acclaim. Vocational programs were developed for foundry, electricity, machine shop and stationary engineering, painting, plumbing, carpentry,

Booker T. Washington

blacksmithing, basket making, harness making, brick laying, brick making, wheelwrighting, and tinsmithing. By the time of Washington's death in 1915, Tuskegee owned 2,300 acres of land, 123 buildings, and more than $1,000,000 worth of equipment (Hall, 1973).

Washington defined an educated person as one possessing (1) both cognitive and problem-solving skills, (2) self-discipline, (3) moral standards, and (4) a sense of service. His recognition that true learning is more than memorization was unusual in his day. Only since the twentieth century have we begun to define cognitive learning as the acquisition of knowledge and those thinking skills that enable us to use knowledge to solve problems (Wolfe, 1981). Washington's writings are replete with evidence of his concern for real understanding, not merely book learning:

> Happily the world has at last reached the point where it no longer feels that in order for a person to be a great scholar he has got to read a number of textbooks and that he has got to master a certain number of foreign languages; but the world has come to the conclusion that the person who has learned to use his mind . . . that the person who has mastered something, who understands what he is doing, who is master of himself in the classroom, out in the world, master of himself everywhere, that person is a scholar. (Washington, 1938, p. 18)

The requirement that every Tuskegee student do some manual labor was intended not only to develop self-discipline but also to develop healthy respect for honest labor. In his emphasis on learning by doing, Washington foreshadowed John Dewey and the Progressive Education Movement by nearly two decades. Dewey used this principle as a curricular focus when he established his laboratory school at the University of Chicago in 1896 (Wolfe, 1981). Of his own emphasis on learning by doing, first at Hampton Institute in Virginia (1879–1881) and then at Tuskegee, Washington (1901) wrote:

> Students were admitted to the night school only when they had no money with which to pay any part of their board in the regular day school. It was further required that they must work for ten hours during

the day at some trade or industry and study academic branches for two hours during the evening . . . There could hardly be a more severe test of a student's worth than this branch of the Institute's work. It is largely because it furnishes such good opportunity to test the backbone of a student that I place such high value upon our night school . . . No student, no matter how much money he may be able to command, is permitted to go through school without doing manual labor. (p. 125)

Washington also believed that he could not develop a truly educated person without stressing moral developments:

That education . . . That gives one physical courage to stand in front of a cannon and fails to give him moral courage to stand up in defense of right and justice is a failure. (Washington, 1938, p. 17)

Washington's personal devotion to Tuskegee Institute and to its program exemplified his belief that people must lose themselves in significant, selfless causes in order to find themselves. He lived this ideal by precept as well as by example:

Education is meant to make us give satisfaction and to get satisfaction out of giving it. It is meant to make us get happiness out of service to our fellows. And until we get to the point where we can get happiness and supreme satisfaction out of helping our fellows, we are not truly educated. (Washington, 1938, p. 25)

Views of Booker T. Washington and W. E. B. Du Bois

In 1895 Booker T. Washington delivered his famous "Atlanta Compromise" speech. Washington's philosophy paved the way for the widely acclaimed Washington and Du Bois debates. Washington, a true scholar and leader, was considered to be the major voice in the movement for Black advancement. His beliefs are criticized for having encouraged Black people to cultivate a spirit of "peaceful coexistence" with White southerners. An excerpt from the "Atlanta Compromise" speech reveals some of Washington's beliefs:

Our greatest danger is that in the leap from slavery to freedom we may overlook the fact that the masses of us are to live by the production of our hands, and fail to keep in mind that we shall prosper in proportion as we learn to dignify and glorify common labor, and put brains and skill into common occupations of life; shall prosper in proportion as we learn to draw the line between the superficial and the substantial, the ornamental gewgaws of life and the useful. No race can prosper till [sic] it learns that there is as much dignity in tilling a field as in writing a poem. It is at the bottom of life that we must begin and not at the top. (Moody, 1980, p. 32)

Washington's speech was widely acclaimed by many, including the president of the United States, as a blueprint for Black advancement. However,

W. E. B. DuBois

Washington's speech and philosophy on Black progress was not totally supported by Dr. W. E. B. Du Bois of the same era. Du Bois, born in Great Barrington, Massachusetts, in 1868, was a scholar, author, and historian with a Ph.D. from Harvard. Du Bois believed that it was more important for Blacks to press for the immediate implementation of their civil rights. He believed that Blacks should cultivate personal, aesthetic, and cultural values in the struggle for social emancipation (Lewis, 2003; Moody, 1980). Du Bois is credited for having been a central figure in the founding of the NAACP. As a leader of the Niagara Movement (the first Black protest organization of the twentieth century), Du Bois said, "We want full manhood suffrage and we want it now . . . We want the constitution of the country enforced . . . We are men! We will be treated as men and shall win" (Moody, 1980, p. 33).

It is difficult to assess the impact of the Washington and Du Bois debates on shaping Black involvement in career and technical education. However, there is a shared belief among Blacks that those debates did influence, to some unquantifiable degree, the attitudes of Blacks toward CTE.

Du Bois favored a more traditional academic education but respected Washington as the greatest Black leader of the period. Washington believed that industrial education would build economic self-reliance and help Blacks become better integrated into industrial America. However, Du Bois believed that Washington's program practically accepted an alleged substandard living for the Black race (Hinman, 2005; Moore, 2003; Moody, 1980).

The following excerpt taken from *American Education and Vocationalism, A Documentary History*, reflects Booker T. Washington's belief that the future of his race lay in pursuing manual occupations in the South:

> I believe that we are going to reach our highest development largely along the lines of scientific and industrial education. For the last fifty years, education has tended in one direction, the cementing of mind to matter. Most people have the idea that industrial education is opposed to literary training, opposed to the highest development. I want to correct this error. I would choose the college graduate to receive industrial education. The more mind the subject has, the more satisfactory would be the results in industrial education. It requires a strong mind to build a Corliss engine as it does to write a Greek grammar. (Lazerson and Grubb, 1974, p. 67)

Lazerson and Grubb (1974) further emphasized how important it was for the Black race to learn the following:

As a race there are two things we must learn to do—one is to put brains and skill into the common occupations of life, and the other is to dignify common labor. If we do not, we cannot hold our own as a race. Ninety percent of any race on the globe earns its living at the common occupation of life, and African Americans can be no exception to this rule. (p. 68)

Washington and Du Bois were trailblazers for the pattern of philosophical distinction between vocational and academic education. Washington felt that for the masses of African Americans, the route to success in the financial and social spheres was through the acquisition of the vocational skills that are in demand by today's society. Du Bois felt success would come through the development of those mental faculties that would result in African Americans being competitive at the managerial or executive levels. Unfortunately, both of these arguments still exist today with the resultant dichotomy (Moore, 2003). Members of minority groups tend to view CTE training as inferior to academic education. For those from the minority middle class, CTE continues to be something for someone else's children. Selected quotations of Washington are listed in Appendix B.

Although career and technical education continuously has targeted special populations for access since 1963, both practitioners and researchers increasingly have cited the lack of attention to the vocational education needs of the African-American community (Nall, 1997). This lack of attention was the subject of a national conference in 1977 that sparked the formation of the National Association for the Advancement of Black Americans in Vocational Education with the goal, in part, of promoting research on problems in vocational education idiosyncratic to this community (Porteous, 1980).

The principles that Washington enunciated over a century ago still have validity for vocational educators today. Washington believed that the total environment should be conducive to learning. Based on Washington's views of education, Wolfe (1981) cites the following guidelines for classroom practice in today's society:

- Motivation is essential to genuine learning. There can be no successful learning without persistent, selective, purposeful effort. Therefore, the goals of schooling must be clearly defined, and both faculty and students must be committed to attaining them.
- Because learning is a goal-directed activity, students learn best when education meets their felt needs or purposes.
- Learning is enhanced when the material has meaning to the learner.
- Learning is facilitated when the learner participates in planning the learning experience.
- The holistic nature of learning suggests that learning is always influenced—positively or negatively—by emotions.

From these guidelines, certain principles of skill development emerge:

- Students should never be required to memorize by rote any material that they fail to understand; drill is best when it grows out of practical, real-life situations.

- Skill acquisition involves two stages: integration and refinement. During the first stage, we should give students many contacts with a given skill in a variety of practical situations. During the refinement stage, the student develops precision through repetitive practice.

- Skills should be taught when they can be mastered efficiently by students; that is, students must first have the experiential background that gives meaning to the material to be learned. The level of mastery varies between learners and their different learning styles.

In the twenty-first century, we continue to confront challenges in preparing students for the world of work. Each generation has debated the question of what should be taught in schools. However, the words of Booker T. Washington, written over a century ago, continue to define the mission of education today:

> There never was a time in the history of the country when those interested in education should more earnestly consider to what extent the mere acquiring of the ability to create and write, the mere acquisition of a knowledge of literature and science, makes men producers, lovers of labor, independent, honest, unselfish, and above all good. Call education by what name you please, if it fails to bring about these results among masses it falls short of its highest end. (Fant, 1940, p. 69)

Views of Snedden, Prosser, and Dewey

Education for all was foremost in the early arguments for establishing vocational education. The public secondary schools were serving fewer than 15 percent of the school-age population at the turn of the century, and vocational education was intended to provide programs for those not being served by the public education system. The liberal education of the early 1900s, especially at the secondary level, was neither liberal nor liberating for the masses who did not attend school beyond the sixth grade (Miller, 1985).

David Snedden, Charles Prosser, and John Dewey were advocates of vocational education in the public schools who believed that vocational education had the potential to make public education more democratic.

David Snedden and Charles Prosser

Despite his impoverished childhood, David Snedden moved rapidly up the social and economic ladder. His doctoral work at Columbia University convinced him of the important mission of school in society and of the integral part played by vocational education in schooling. As a faculty member of educational administration at Teacher's College, Columbia University, Snedden greatly influenced his student, Charles Prosser. Therefore, Prosser's philosophy evolved from the teachings of his mentor (Camp and Hillison, 1984).

Snedden was a powerful advocate of the social efficiency doctrine. He believed that schools should prepare individuals for the occupations at which they excelled. After graduate study in 1910, Snedden was appointed commissioner of education for Massachusetts. His appointment came about largely through the influence of powerful industrialists who liked his criticism of literacy education and his advocacy of social efficiency. Frederick P. Fish, founder and president of American Telephone and Telegraph, vocal foe of trade unions and chairman of Massachusetts Board of Education, was most influential in getting Snedden appointed as commissioner (Wirth, 1972). (More detailed information on David Snedden is available at http://www.pembinatrails.ca/charleswood/snedden.htm.)

David Snedden

When Snedden had the opportunity to appoint an associate commissioner of education for Massachusetts, he turned to his former student and disciple, Charles Prosser. After serving in that role for two years, Dr. Prosser went to the National Society for the Promotion of Industrial Education (NSPIE) as executive director. The purpose of the Society was to facilitate the passage of federal legislation for vocational education (Camp and Hillison, 1984).

The importance and need for occupational experience in vocational education were stressed early in the century. Snedden (1910) was clear about his position regarding the role that occupational experience should play in the education of the worker. As one of the early writers on vocational education, Snedden gave prominence to the desirability of occupational experience. Prosser (1913) had much the same point of view as Snedden.

Prosser felt that successful vocational education required combining two elements: (1) practice and thinking about the practice, and (2) doing and thinking about the doing. Prosser's view was that in vocational education practice and theory must go hand in hand; the more intimately they are related to each other, the more the school will contribute to the learner's immediate success in the shop and equip the person for mastery of one's calling.

Practical experience and financial incentives were two areas of emphasis in the writings of Snedden and Prosser. Whether the occupational experience occurred in the workplace or in the shop was not critical to either writer. It was, however, important that the productive experience be as much like the actual workplace as possible. In addition, Snedden believed that the student should benefit from some form of remuneration (Miller, 1985).

Charles Prosser's early work and vision for vocational education were crucial to its development. His pragmatic philosophy made sense to other

Charles Prosser

educators, industrialists, and politicians. Largely because of this work, vocational education gained its first legislation as well as its early operating philosophy. Based on his philosophy, Prosser established sixteen theorems (see Appendix C) that were instrumental in the formation of vocational education. Snedden and Prosser worked closely in promoting vocational education. Together, their influence was important in providing direction for the development of vocational education.

The conditions needed to improve society have changed rapidly since the inception of Prosser's sixteen theorems. In today's society the emphasis is on schooling today for skills tomorrow. These skills are classified as workplace competencies and foundational skills.

Workplace Competencies

- *Resources*—Knowing how to allocate time, money, materials, space and staff.

- *Interpersonal skills*—Knowing how to work on teams, teach others, serve customers, lead, negotiate, and work well with people from diverse cultural backgrounds.

- *Information*—Knowing how to acquire and evaluate data, organize and maintain files, interpret and communicate, and use computers to process information.

- *Systems*—Understanding social, organizational, and technological systems; knowing how to monitor and correct performance; and knowing how to design or improve systems.

- *Technology*—Knowing how to select equipment and tools, apply technology to specific tasks, and maintain and troubleshoot equipment.

Foundational Skills

- *Basic skills*—Reading, writing, arithmetic, mathematics, speaking and listening.

- *Thinking skills*—The ability to learn, to reason, to think creatively, to make decisions, and to solve problems.

- *Personal qualities*—Individual responsibilities, self-esteem and self-management, sociability, and integrity.

John Dewey

John Dewey (1916) saw occupations as central to educational activity. He did, however, express concern about any form of vocational education that would continue the present forms of higher education for those who could afford it while giving the masses a narrow education for specialized occupations under the control of industry.

Lakes (1985) points out that Dewey described youth as adequately prepared if they began to study occupations. By occupation Dewey (1900) meant, " . . . a mode of activity on the part of the child which reproduces, or runs parallel to some form of work carried on in social life" (p. 82). At his experimental elementary school at the

John Dewey

University of Chicago, the occupations were represented in part by shop work, cooking, sewing, textiles, and gardening. Dewey felt that these studies would best prepare students to understand the science of tools and processes used in work, develop an appreciation for the historic evolution of industry, instill favorable group dynamics of shared discovery and communal problem solving, and plan and reflect on the entire process (Lakes, 1985).

Dewey believed that education needed change. Vocational education could, according to him, be the means to induce changes that would improve education. According to Dewey, a right educational use of vocational education:

> . . . would react upon intelligence and interest so as to modify, in connection with legislation and administration, the socially obnoxious features of the present industrial and commercial order. It would turn the increasing fund of social sympathy to constructive account, instead of leaving it a somewhat blind philanthropic sentiment. It would give those who engage in industrial callings desire and ability to share in social control, and ability to become masters of their industrial fate. It would enable them to saturate with meaning the technical and mechanical features which are so marked a feature of our machine system of production and distribution. (1916, p. 320)

According to Miller (1985), considerable argument—frequently public—existed among Dewey, Snedden, and Prosser. Wirth (1972) treats this controversy in detail and labels Prosser's and Snedden's economic philosophy as Social Darwinism.

Origin and Justifications of the Dual System

Early leaders of the vocational education movement viewed vocational education as part of the public system of education in America. However, who should administer such programs, and under what organizational arrangement, was of concern to educational leaders and others in the early part of the twentieth century.

One of the main tenets of Charles Prosser's vision of vocational education was that of a dual system with two clearly separated components, one part being academic and the other vocational. David Snedden also had a similar perspective. Hillison and Camp (1985) argued that Snedden's advocacy of social efficiency was twofold. This doctrine held that it was the responsibility of members of society to contribute to the good of that society by working efficiently and by conforming to social norms. Both perspectives led Snedden, and eventually Prosser, to be strong proponents of the industrialist view of education and the separate or dual system of education.

As early as 1916, Snedden was giving serious consideration to separate vocational facilities (Dutton and Snedden, 1916):

> But the ends of vocational education cannot be achieved merely through courses of general instruction. More and more, in view of the social industrial needs of the time, the demand is that some special fitness be given to those who are to follow a special calling. (p. 143)

Typewriting, stenography, bookkeeping, bricklaying, electrical wiring, plumbing, tailoring, millinery, and some aspects of machine operations were used as examples of separate vocational instruction provided in commercial and trade schools. Snedden further argued that teachers from "regular" schools would be totally unacceptable teaching in the vocational school. He contended that the vocational teacher should be selected from the industry or trade concerned (Barlow, 1967).

The early advocacy of the dual system of education had its critics. For example, the National Education Association believed the concept a serious enough threat to demand alteration of the Smith-Hughes Act (see chapter 5) (Hillison and Camp, 1985). "The Association favors amending the Smith-Hughes Act to prevent the possibility of establishing a dual system of schools in any state" ("A War Platform," 1918, p. 11, cited in Hillison and Camp, 1985).

A second major critic of the dual school system was John Dewey. In *The New Republic*, Dewey (1915a) succinctly stated one of his criticisms:

> I argued that a separation of trade education and general education of youth has the inevitable tendency to make both kinds of training narrower, less significant and less effective than the schooling in which the material of traditional education is recognized to utilize the industrial subject matter—active, scientific and social—of the present day environment. (p. 42)

Dewey (1915b) noted further criticism in a second article published in *The New Republic* in 1915 when he wrote about a vast and costly duplication of buildings, environment, teachers, and administrators. He also noted that the dual educational system would segregate the children of well-to-do and cultured families from those children who would have to work for wages in manual and commercial employment. He continued:

> It is self-evident that under the divided plan either the public must meet the expense of a vast and costly duplication of buildings, equipment, teachers and administrative directors; or else the old schools will have to strip themselves of everything but the rudiments of a traditional bookish education; and the new schools confine themselves to [such] a narrow trade preparation that the latter will be ineffective for every industrial end except setting up a congested labor market in the skilled trades and a better grade of labor at public expense—for employers to exploit. (p. 284)

Hillison and Camp (1985) reported that Prosser and Snedden did not want vocational education to be contaminated by the mistakes or the philosophy of general education. The position advocated by Prosser and Snedden was not universally implemented. Vocational high schools, area vocational centers, and vocational magnet schools resulted directly from that advocacy.

A Redefinition of Manual Training

John Dewey viewed the potential misuse of occupations as purely sensory experiences in skill development. He suggested that nineteenth-century pedagogical theory advocated a complete isolation of the child's learning potential. Dewey believed that faculty psychology programmed the development of the child's abilities into independent training or exercise of separate components. In *Manual Training Magazine*, Dewey (1901) wrote:

> The idea of formal discipline, of the value of isolated and independent training of the so-called faculties of observation, memory, and reasoning, has invaded both physical culture and manual training. Here also we have been led to believe that there is a positive inherent value in the formal training of hand and eye quite apart from the actual content of such training—apart from its social relations and suggestions. (p. 195)

Dewey was aware that one could easily misconstrue educational means (technical proficiency) for educational ends (intelligence). Without an intellectual base, the study of occupations could become primarily utilitarian, as did the ill-fated birdhouse project fad of the 1930s, for example (Barlow, 1967):

> In such cases the work is reduced to a mere routine or custom, and its educational value is lost. This is the inevitable tendency wherever, in manual training for instance, the mastery of certain tools, or the production of certain objects, is made the primary end, and the child is not given, wherever possible, intellectual responsibility for selecting the materials and instruments that are most fit, and given an opportunity to think out his own model and plan to work, led to perceive his own errors,

and find out how to correct them—that is, of course, within the range of his capacities. (Dewey, 1900, pp. 82–83)

The project would not necessarily emphasize the development of a cultural perspective. For example, the creation of a simple breadboard requires more than just the task of planning a board (Diamond, 1936). It might involve an analytical assessment of the role of work in society. According to Lakes (1985), tangential areas of study could include energy conservation, quality of work life, ecological waste, human resource management, and the consumer ethic.

Career and technical education's stigma has developed because of the separation that has been evident in the operation of many programs throughout the decades. Leighbody (1972) cites that many persons reject CTE for their children, not because of a snobbish prejudice but because they fear that when their children enroll in a vocational curriculum they will be cut off from further education and deprived of future educational and career opportunities.

If parental concerns about CTE are not erased, it cannot serve all of the persons it can benefit. A major thrust of the workforce education reform movement is to eliminate the meaningless high school "general" curriculum that moves students to graduation with no clear purpose or promise. In its place would be an academically rigorous career and technical education curriculum that will produce graduates with a grounding in academic basics, job skills, and a focus on a sound career or further education.

Differences in Educational Philosophies: John Dewey and Charles Prosser

John Dewey (1916) argued that education should use a critical democratic approach to raise student consciousness about values, attitudes, and worker responsibilities. He stated that the primary purpose of education in the United States was to foster the growth of democratically minded citizens, and Dewey made no distinction in the education of those who would manage the companies and those who worked on the shop floors. Dewey strongly advocated vocational exploration as a means to acquire practical knowledge, apply academic content, and examine occupational and societal values. However, he adamantly opposed the use of vocational education as merely trade education because it would overemphasize technical efficiency. If this occurred, and some would argue it has, Dewey warned that "education would then become an instrument of perpetuating unchanged the existing industrial order of society, instead of operating as a means of its transformation" (p. 316). Dewey believed that it was education's role to combat social predestination, not contribute to it (Gregson and Gregson, 1991).

In contrast, Charles Prosser advocated an indoctrinational approach for teaching work values and attitudes; students should learn, without question, the

ethical standards of dominant society and the professional ethics of the desired occupational area (Prosser, 1939). Supporters of this approach believed the primary purpose of public education was the development of human capital for the success of the industrial economy. To accomplish this they argued that scientific management principles, drawn from the industrial sector, were employed in the public school setting, creating a hierarchically structured and production-oriented educational system (Spring, 1990). Prosser's sixteen theorems on vocational education support this vision of schooling. Table 2.1 on p. 34 provides a summary of the educational philosophies of John Dewey and Charles Prosser as they relate to vocational education.

Major Dennis Mobley's Philosophy of Career and Technical Education

> To ignore a heritage is to discard a valuable asset.
> —Melvin L. Barlow and Lowell A. Burkett

Many of the present-day members of the Association for Career and Technical Education (ACTE) know little about the great gains made in vocational education during the Mobley era—and some, perhaps, have never heard of M. D. Mobley. Today's career and technical educators must be aware of the struggles and triumphs of the past if they are to understand the present and prepare intelligently for the future.

Mobley served as the executive secretary of ACTE (formerly AVA) for fifteen years (1951–1965). He accepted and promoted an idea advanced by the 1962 Report of the Panel of Consultants on Vocational Education—*Education for a Changing World of Work*. This concept held that vocational education should be "for all people."

Mobley's philosophy of vocational education encompassed enduring ideas and concepts that have transcended the ravages of time. His motivation and beliefs were based on the principles forged from these ideas and concepts that began to emerge with the advent of the vocational movement in education. These principles focused on society's obligation to youth and adults to provide for their occupational well-being as a part of their total education; a recognition of the changing nature of the nation's workforce; a commitment to continued professionalization of vocational education; and a belief that the greatest asset of America was not its tremendous wealth but its ability to use effectively the enormous resources of its people (Barlow and Burkett, 1988).

The following statements, which form the heart of Mobley's philosophy of vocational education, served as his guides (Barlow and Burkett, 1988):

1. *Vocational education must be a part of the total education program.* Mobley was convinced that vocational education was not something separate from education in general. He perceived that a portion of

Table 2.1   Comparison of the Educational Philosophies of John Dewey and Charles Prosser

Philosophical Criteria	Prosser	Dewey
Teaching styles and methodologies	Sequential, begins with basic facts; instructors have strong industrial experience.	Begins with problem-solving results in knowledge base; instructors have strong educational experience.
Administrative structure	Seeks advice from industrial leaders, planners, implementers; cost-effective.	Facilitator of personal choices, advisor.
Personal/school philosophies	Accents the needs of industry.	Accents the needs of individuals.
Benefits of the program	Students gain marketable skills to become productive members of society.	Students gain life skills and adaptability skills.
Prosser-Dewey Dichotomy		
Transferability of skills	Transfer occurs naturally between similar tasks; transfer is not a focus.	Transfer is the focus of a broad education.
Training-to-work transition	Facilitated through current equipment and instructors with industrial background.	Facilitated through focus on transfer.
Development of problem-solving skills	Acquiring a base of knowledge precedes problem-solving skills.	Instruction begins with problem-solving skills.
Continuation of Prosser Philosophy		
Major goal of the school	To meet the needs of industry and prepare people for work.	To meet the needs of individuals and prepare people for life.
Influencing factors on school success	Follow Prosser's sixteen theorems.	Follow guidelines in Dewey's *Democracy and Education*.
Social and Economic Factors		
School climate	Individualized differences are recognized, and all people and types of work are seen as having value.	Individual differences are equalized.
Adequate supplies, space, and equipment	Schools must have adequate supplies, space, and equipment.	Schools need to have adequate supplies, space, and equipment, but students may use transfer skills to cover deficiencies.
Personal motivations	CTE should be reserved for those who are motivated and can benefit.	CTE is for everyone, and everyone can benefit.

Source: Griffin, D., and Herren, R. V. (1994). *North Carolina's first postsecondary technical institution: Past, present, and future*. Unpublished doctoral dissertation, University of Georgia, Athens.

our educational experience should be related to the preparation for entering the workforce.

2. *Vocational education must be available to all people*. Mobley's philosophy regarding the availability of vocational education is illustrated in the stated purpose of the Vocational Education Act of 1963, which he assisted in writing. He was a strong proponent of federal aid; he perceived it as a source for promoting additional programs to include people not embraced by some form of vocational education.

3. *Vocational education must be everybody's concern*. Mobley believed that vocational education should be the concern of all segments of the society and economy. He viewed vocational education as a coalescent vehicle for all aspects of education, parents, students, and policy makers.

4. *Professionalization of vocational education must continue*. Mobley was convinced that the major vehicle for vocational education professionalization was a professional organization. He was an advocate for the support and encouragement of strong organized groups consisting of national, state, and local units.

5. *Youth groups must be considered part of the total vocational education program*. Mobley believed that specialized programs conducted by youth groups benefited students and helped in their preparation for leadership roles.

Summary

- The struggle to introduce vocational education into all educational curricula was attributed to Booker T. Washington, an educator and leader; David Snedden, an educational administrator; Charles Prosser, a lawyer; and John Dewey, a philosopher.

- Washington defined an educated person as one possessing (1) both cognitive and problem-solving skills, (2) self-discipline, (3) moral standards, and (4) a sense of service. His recognition that true learning is more than memorization was unusual in his day.

- Washington's philosophy paved the way for the widely acclaimed Washington and Du Bois debates. Concerned with the practical education of the masses recently freed from slavery, Washington advocated taking what was immediately available: industrial education in a segregated setting.

- Du Bois was convinced that equality required developing a highly educated African-American leadership, a "talented tenth" on an intellectual, social, and political par with Whites.

- Snedden was a powerful advocate of the social efficiency doctrine. He gave prominence to the desirability of occupational experience.

- Prosser's view was that in vocational education, practice and theory must go hand in hand; the more intimately they are related to each other, the more the school will contribute to the learner's immediate success in the shop and equip the person with mastery of one's calling.

- Dewey was a strong advocate for vocational education. He was critical of the existing traditional liberal education of the time and felt that it did not provide the skills and attitudes that individuals needed to live in an age of science. He believed that the curriculum should include a series of situations in which students are involved in solving problems of interest to them, such as the "project method" employed in some manual training schools that engaged students in activities that required thinking as well as doing.

- M. D. Mobley's greatest asset was his ability to work with and get along with all types of people. Mobley was regarded as a humanitarian, public-relations specialist, legislative strategist, and organization leader.

Discussion Questions and Activities

1. Select one career and technical education course you have taught or plan to teach, and develop a statement of philosophy for that particular course.

2. Explain and generalize why it is important for a teacher, an educational department, and a school to have a philosophy of education.

3. Conduct an interview of career and technical and non-career and technical educators regarding their philosophy of career and technical education. What are the similarities? Explain how they are different.

4. Critique the film *Washington–Du Bois debate*. (Information on obtaining this video appears in the next section.)

5. Debate the pros and cons of the following: "The Integration of Academic and Vocational Education."

6. Compare and contrast the educational philosophies of John Dewey and Charles Prosser.

7. Critique the film *Dewey–Snedden debate*. (See p. 37 for further information.)

8. Examine critically and justify the relevancy of Prosser's theorems in today's society (see Appendix C).

For Exploration

9. Discuss how our diverse school population influenced the philosophy of career and technical education.

10. Formulate a statement of philosophy for each of the following educators based on their perception of career and technical education:

    a. Booker T. Washington

    b. David Snedden

    c. Charles Prosser

    d. John Dewey

    e. W. E. B. Du Bois

11. Explain the meaning of the term *Social Darwinism*.

12. Justify the importance of Social Darwinism for workforce education (in the form of career and technical education) to the curriculum of the American high school.

13. Extrapolate the relevancy of Mobley's philosophy of career and technical education in today's society.

Recommended Educational Media Resources

- *Booker T. Washington*
  Educational Video Network, Inc.
  1336 19th Street
  Huntsville, TX 77340
  1-800-762-0060 or (936) 295-5767
  Web site: http://www.evn.com
- *Developing your teaching philosophy and relating it to your students*
- *John Dewey: An introduction to his life and work* (DVD)
  Insight Media
  2162 Broadway
  New York, NY 10024-0621
  1-800-233-9910 or (212) 721-6316
  Web site: http://www.insight-media.com
- *Washington–Du Bois debate*
- *Dewey–Snedden debate*
  Ways to order:
  By phone: (919) 515-1756 or (304) 696-3079
  By fax: (919) 515-9060
  By e-mail: gary_moore@ncsu.edu or Gordon@marshall.edu
  By mail:
  Dept. AEE
  Box 7607
  North Carolina State University
  Raleigh, NC 27695-7607

References and Additional Reading

Barlow, M. L. (1967). *History of industrial education in the United States*. Peoria, IL: Chas. A. Bennett.

Barlow, M. L., and Burkett, L. A. (1988). *The legacy of M.D. Mobley and vocational education*. Alexandria, VA: American Vocational Association.

Brundage, W. Fitzhugh (Ed.) (2003). *Booker T. Washington and black progress: Up from slavery 100 Years later.* Jacksonville: University Press of Florida.

Camp, W. G., and Hillison, J. H. (1984). Prosser's sixteen theorems: Time for reconsideration. *Journal of Vocational and Technical Education, 1*(1), 13–15.

Dewey, J. C. (1900). Psychology of occupation [Monograph]. *Elementary School Record,* No. 3 (April), 82–85.

———. (1901). The place of manual training in the elementary course of study. *Manual Training Magazine, 4,* 193–199.

———. (1915a). Education vs. trade-training. *The New Republic, 28,* 42.

———. (1915b). Splitting up the school system. *The New Republic, 24,* 283–284.

———. (1916). *Democracy and education* (p. 316). New York: Macmillan.

Diamond, T. (1936, March). Responsibility of industrial arts teacher in social problems. *AVA Journal, 25,* 104–106.

Dutton, S. T., and Snedden, D. (1916). *The administration of public education in the United States.* New York: Macmillan.

Fant, C. (1940). *Tuskegee Institute yesterday and today* (p. 69). Tuskegee, AL: Tuskegee Institute Press.

Gregson, J. A., and Gregson, P. (1991, December). *Secondary trade and industrial education work values instruction: Emancipatory or indoctrinational?* Paper presented at the annual meeting of the American Vocational Educational Research Association, Los Angeles, CA.

Griffin, D. A., and Herren, R. V. (1994). *North Carolina's first postsecondary technical institution: Past, present, and future.* Unpublished doctoral dissertation. Athens: University of Georgia.

Hall, C. W. (1973). *Black vocational technical and industrial arts education: Development and history.* Chicago: American Technical Society.

Hillison, J. H., and Camp, W. G. (1985). History and future of the dual school system of vocational education. *Journal of Vocational and Technical Education, 2*(1), 48–50.

Hinman, Bonnie (2005). *A stranger in my own house: The story of W.E.B. Du Bois.* Greensboro, NC: Morgan Reynolds Publishing.

Lakes, R. D. (1985). John Dewey's theory of occupations: Vocational education envisioned. *Journal of Vocational and Technical Education, 2*(1), 41–45.

Lazerson, M., and Grubb, W. N. (1974). *American education and vocationalism* (pp. 67– 68). New York: Teachers College Press, Columbia University.

Leighbody, G. B. (1972). *Vocational education in America's schools.* Chicago: American Technical Society.

Lewis, D. L. (2003). *W. E. B. Du Bois: Biography of a race.* Minneapolis, MN: Tandem Library.

Miller, M. D. (1985). *Principles and a philosophy for vocational education.* Columbus, OH: The National Center for Research in Vocational Education.

Moody, F. B. (1980). The history of blacks in vocational education. *Vocational Education, 55*(1), 30–34.

Moore, Jacqueline M. (2003). *Booker T. Washington, W.E.B. Du Bois, and the struggle for racial uplift.* Lanham, MD: SR Books (imprint of Rowman & Littlefield).

Nall, Hiram (1997). Vocational education and the African American experience: An historical and philosophical perspective. *Journal of Intergroup Relations, 24*(3), 26–48.

Porteous, P. L. (1980). NAABAVE: New rallying point for black concerns. *Journal of Vocational Education, 55*(1), 44–48.

Prosser, C. A. (1913, May). The meaning of industrial education. *Vocational Education*, *2*, 401–410.

———. (1939). *Secondary education and life*. Cambridge, MA: Harvard University Press.

Schraff, Anne E. (2006). *Booker T. Washington: "Character Is power."* Berkeley Heights, NJ: Enslow Publishers.

Schroeder, Alan, and Beier, Anne (2005). *Booker T. Washington: Educator and racial spokesman*. New York: Chelsea House Publications.

Snedden, D. (1910). *The problem of vocational education*. Boston: Houghton Mifflin.

Spring, J. (1990). *The American school 1642–1990*. White Plains, NY: Longman.

Thornbrough, E. L. (Ed.) (1969). *Booker T. Washington*. Englewood Cliffs, NJ: Prentice-Hall.

Washington, B. T. (1901). *Up from slavery* (p. 125). Garden City, NY: Doubleday.

Washington, E. D. (1938). *Quotations of Booker T. Washington* (p. 18). Tuskegee, AL: Tuskegee Institute Press.

Wirth, A. G. (1972). *Education in the technological society*. Scranton, PA: Intext Educational Publishers.

Wolfe, D. C. (1981, November). Booker T. Washington: An educator for all ages. *Phi Delta Kappan*, *63*(3), 205, 222.

chapter 3

Impact of Land-Grant Institutions on Career and Technical Education

In mid-nineteenth-century America, President Barnard of the University of Alabama indicated that vocationalism and the craft society would never have a place in institutions of formal learning:

> While time lasts, the farmer will be made in the field, the manufacturer in the shop, the merchant in the counting room, the civil engineer in the midst of the actual operation of science. (Leslie, 1976, p. 237)

Such views, however, were not present in the earliest days of the university. The first universities specialized in preparing young men for professional callings (Leslie, 1976).

This chapter focuses on career and technical education in the four-year college. It provides information on the following acts: the First Morrill Act, the Second Morrill Act, the Smith-Lever Agricultural Extension Act, and 4-H youth development.

When the university came to America with the founding of Harvard in 1636, it was not for the purpose of preparing professionals. Harvard sought primarily to educate "the men who would spell the difference between civilization and barbarism" (Leslie, 1976, p. 12). Harvard would endeavor to prepare a "learned clergy," schoolmasters, and other servants of society but only through the traditional means; there would be no special job training. This type of education was not viewed as particularly practical either by or for the general populace. Americans placed little faith in those things that were not practical. Commanger (1950) comments:

> The American's attitude toward culture was at once suspicious and indulgent; where it interfered with the more important activities he distrusted it; where it was the recreation of his leisure hours, or his women folk, he tolerated it. For the most part, he required that culture serve some useful purpose. He wanted poetry that he could recite, music that he could sing, and paintings that told a story . . . Education was his religion, and to it he paid the tribute both of his money and his affection; yet, as he expected his religion to be practical and pay dividends, he

41

expected education to prepare for life—by which he meant increasingly, jobs and professions. (p. 10)

The twenty-odd state universities that had been established by 1860 did not turn out graduates who were able to address the practical problems of the day (Thompson, 1973). Agriculture and industry were the principal resources of the American economy, and trained workers were needed to develop their potentials.

The demands for the development of vocational education occurred between 1820 and 1860. In general, the agricultural sector of the economy demanded vocational and practical education. The working individual did not want totally skill-oriented training but, rather, an education more practical than was commonly offered by secondary schools and colleges of the day. If the farmers' problems were to be met, there had to be a "practical" impetus from education. Developing the nation's great agricultural resources required leadership from technically trained persons in public education at the secondary and college level.

Industrial development faced a void caused by a lack of engineers able to deal with the more practical problems of plant layout, machine design, and machine parts. Traditional colleges prepared students for law, medicine, teaching, and the ministry. These four professions would provide gainful employment for only a portion of the population. Among America's expanding masses were thousands of young men who could benefit from advanced training, but who were not interested in the traditional professional training available. Congress responded to some of these practical problems by passing the Morrill Act of 1862 (Thompson, 1973). With the beginning of the land-grant movement, the spirit of vocationalism could no longer be resisted by elitist universities. Leslie (1976) noted that the public universities only feigned resistance; most soon became willing partners in vocational education.

The land-grant mission that evolved was service to the people. It was, in the words of Lincoln Steffens of the University of Wisconsin, "Sending a state to college"; it was "teaching anybody—anything—anywhere" (Leslie, 1976, p. 240). The land-grant university was county agents and agricultural experiment stations; it provided the expertise for anything the people needed or wanted to know. However, it was more than just direct service to the people. The land-grant university meant preparing all kinds of expert professionals that the people might need. The land-grant mission also meant reacting to the immediate needs of the people and anticipating their needs in advance.

Land-grant institutions were called "colleges of agriculture," "colleges of mechanic arts," or "colleges of agriculture and mechanic arts." Their purposes were primarily to educate the farmers and agricultural technicians in increased crop production; to educate the housewife-home economist and her supporting cast in better nutrition, child rearing, and homemaking; and to prepare engineers and technicians for a soon-to-expand industrial society.

Other universities, both public and private, involved themselves in professional education. However, they limited their efforts to those professions that could be characterized as learned—medicine, law, theology. The somewhat tainted professions—the mechanic arts (engineering) and especially agriculture and home economics—were almost the exclusive domain of the land-grant institution.

First Morrill Act (Adopted July 2, 1862)

Senator Justin S. Morrill of Vermont introduced the first land-grant bill in 1857. The bill failed in the Senate, so he reintroduced it in 1859 (Walter, 1993). The bill passed both houses of Congress but was vetoed by President Buchanan. In 1862, Senator Morrill, along with the support of Ohio Senator Benjamin Wade, again passed the Morrill Act for Land-Grant Institutions through both houses. The rationale was to support the legislation for the agrarian community farmer, but Wade took advantage of wartime concerns and illustrated that colleges would be ideal for training officers and engineers for the war effort (Miller, 1993). President Lincoln signed the legislation on July 2, 1862.

The primary purpose of this act was to promote the liberal and practical education of the industrial classes in pursuits and professions of living. Andrews (1918) reported that this act granted 30,000 acres of land to each state for each senator and representative in Congress to which the state was entitled by apportionment under the census of 1860:

> All money derived from the sale of these lands was to be invested by the state in securities bearing interest at not less than 5 percent except that the legislature of the state might authorize the use of not more than 10 percent of capital for the purchase of sites for the college or experimental farm. The interest was to be used for the endowment, support, and maintenance of at least one college where the leading object should be to teach such branches of learning as are related to agriculture and the mechanic arts in order to promote the liberal and practical education of the industrial classes in the several pursuits and professions in life. (p. 10)

It has been held that the Morrill Act authorized the purchase of apparatus, machinery, textbooks, reference books, and materials used for the purpose of instruction and for the payment of salaries of instructors in the branches of learning specified by the Land-Grant Act. In each case of machinery, such as boilers, engines, and pumps that were used to serve both instructional and other purposes, the fund could only be charged with an equitable portion of the cost of such machinery (Miller and Gay, 1914):

> The act prohibited the expenditure of any portion of these funds for the purchase, construction, preservation, or repair of any building or buildings under any pretense whatever, and the salaries of purely administrative officers, such as treasurers, presidents, and secretaries. (p. 238)

The Morrill Act of 1862 was the first legislation passed by the national government to support vocational education. According to Calhoun and Finch (1982), institutions of higher education receiving support under the Morrill Act of 1862 were known as land-grant institutions because their financial support for vocational programs came primarily from the sale of land provided in the act. Table 3.1 lists the 1862 land-grant institutions.

Table 3.1　List of Land-Grant Institutions in 1862

Institution	Date State Accepted Morrill Act	Date Institution Opened to Students	Location
Auburn University	1867	1872	Auburn, AL
University of Alaska	1929	1922	Fairbanks, AK
University of Arizona	1910	1891	Tucson, AZ
University of Arkansas	1864	1872	Fayetteville, AR
University of California	1866	1869	Davis, CA
Colorado State University	1879	1879	Fort Collins, CO
University of Connecticut	1862	1881	Storrs, CT
University of Delaware	1867	1869	Newark, DE
University of Florida	1870	1884	Gainesville, FL
University of Georgia	1886	1801	Athens, GA
University of Idaho	1890	1892	Moscow, ID
University of Illinois	1867	1868	Urbana, IL
Purdue University	1865	1874	West Lafayette, IN
Iowa State University	1862	1859	Ames, IA
Kansas State University	1863	1863	Manhattan, KS
University of Kentucky	1863	1880	Lexington, KY
Louisiana State University	1869	1874	Baton Rouge, LA
University of Maine	1863	1868	Orono, ME
University of Maryland	1864	1859	College Park, MD
University of Massachusetts	1863	1867	Amherst, MA
Michigan State University	1863	1857	East Lansing, MI
University of Minnesota	1863	1851	St. Paul, MN
Mississippi State University	1866	1880	Mississippi State, MS
University of Missouri	1863	1841	Columbia, MO
Montana State University	1889	1893	Bozeman, MT
University of Nebraska	1867	1871	Lincoln, NE
University of Nevada	1866	1874	Reno, NV
University of New Hampshire	1863	1868	Durham, NH
Rutgers State University	1863	1771	New Brunswick, NJ
New Mexico State University	1898	1890	Las Cruces, NM
Cornell University	1863	1868	Ithaca, NY
North Carolina State University	1866	1889	Raleigh, NC
North Dakota State University	1889	1891	Fargo, ND
Ohio State University	1864	1873	Columbus, OH

Institution	Date State Accepted Morrill Act	Date Institution Opened to Students	Location
Oklahoma State University	1890	1891	Stillwater, OK
Oregon State University	1868	1865	Corvallis, OR
Pennsylvania State University	1863	1859	University Park, PA
University of Rhode Island	1863	1890	Kingston, RI
Clemson University	1868	1893	Clemson, SC
South Dakota State University	1889	1884	Brookings, SD
University of Tennessee	1868	1794	Knoxville, TN
Texas A&M University	1866	1876	College Station, TX
Utah State University	1888	1890	Logan, UT
University of Vermont	1862	1801	Burlington, VT
Virginia Polytechnic Institute and State University	1870	1872	Blacksburg, VA
Washington State University	1889	1892	Pullman, WA
West Virginia University	1863	1868	Morgantown, WV
University of Wisconsin	1863	1849	Platteville, WI
University of Wyoming	1889	1887	Laramie, WY

Source: Anderson, G. L. (1976). *Land-grant universities and their continuing challenge*. East Lansing: Michigan State University Press.

Historians agree that neither Senator Justin Morrill, who sponsored the bill, nor the influential Senator Benjamin Wade, who guided it through Congress, had any clear idea of its educational implications. Venn (1964) argued that the implications of the Morrill Act were more extensive than Morrill and Wade had anticipated. Not only did the founding of these colleges enable higher education to be open to a broader public and improve agricultural techniques, but also the concept of integrated academics was first identified. Classical studies ranging from languages and mathematics were integrated for the first time into agricultural and science courses—that is, curricula that were identified as vocational. The vocational and academic curricula were to be integrated without any superior rating, ranking, or qualitative judgment. Accompanying this integration of academics and the development of the experimental farms and extension programs, mechanical arts and agriculture were also given important status and, like science, were taught "as an instrument for molding the societal environment" (Venn, 1964).

The primary difficulty the newly opened institutions encountered was the lack of adequately prepared students for higher education. The result of this perceived failure of public education permanently altered the secondary school curriculum. Leaders in the land-grant institutions realized the problems facing higher education and took it upon themselves to create university high schools. These high schools, run by the land-grant institutions, placed vocational preparation training at the forefront of their curriculum (Miller, 1993).

Second Morrill Act (Adopted August 30, 1890)

The intent of the 1890 Morrill Act was to provide educational opportunity for African-American students. The act mandated that in the southern states, where separate schools were maintained for Blacks, land-grant institutions be opened to both White and Black students or "separate but equal" facilities be established (Bell, 1987). It is interesting to observe, however, that in 1872 the state of Mississippi gave three-fifths of its land-grant funds from the 1862 Morrill Act to Alcorn State University (Moody, 1980). Braxton (1994) noted that Alcorn A&M University became the first Black land-grant institution established under the Morrill Act of 1862. Three other southern states (Virginia, South Carolina, and Kentucky) established land-grant colleges for African Americans as well as colleges for Whites. It was not until the Second Morrill Act of 1890 that all of the southern states established or designated land-grant institutions for African Americans (Baker, 1991).

In 1890, Congress passed the Second Morrill Act, which was an amendment to the Morrill Act of 1862. This act (also known as the Maintenance Act) authorized the application of a portion of the proceeds from sale of public lands under the First Morrill Act for the more complete endowment and support of the land-grant institutions, and for the benefit of agriculture and the mechanic arts. Each state and territory received an amount of $1,500 annually. This amount was to be supplemented by an automatic annual increase of $1,000 until the year 1900 (Hawkins, Prosser, and Wright, 1951).

Miller and Gay (1914) reported that the Second Morrill Act was similar to the original act, but it had the following provisions:

> That in any state in which there has been one college established in pursuance of the act of July second, eighteen hundred and sixty-two, and also in which an educational institution of like character has been established, and is now aided by such state from its own revenue, for the education of colored students in agriculture and mechanic arts, however named or styled or whether or not it has received money heretofore under the act to which this act is an amendment, the legislature of such state may propose and report to the Secretary of the Interior a just and adequate division of the fund to be received under this act between one college for white students and one institution for colored students established as if one said which shall be divided into two parts and paid accordingly, and thereupon such institutions for colored students shall be entitled to the benefits of this act and subject to its provisions, as much as it would have been if it had been included under the act of eighteen hundred and sixty-two and fulfillment of the foregoing provision shall be taken as a compliance with the provision in reference to separate colleges for white and colored students. (pp. 237–238)

The last institution to be organized as a Black land-grant college was Tennessee A&I State College in Nashville in 1912. The state of Tennessee accepted the provisions of the Second Morrill Act in 1891 and established an industrial department at Knoxville College, which it supervised and funded until 1912 (Hall, 1973).

Land-grant institutions for Blacks did not develop as rapidly as those for Whites in the 17 northern states where they were located. The slow growth of these institutions can be greatly attributed to the misappropriation of federal funds entrusted to the states for distribution to these institutions. The Black schools received a fairly equitable share of funds made available under the Morrill Act of 1890 but were denied their equitable share of other federal funds based on population (Guzman, 1952).

A study by Wilkerson (1939) revealed that Blacks constituted from 25 to 27 percent of the population of the southern region in the 1920s and 1930s, but their land-grant colleges received only 3 to 8 percent of all federal funds coming into the region for this type of education. A breakdown of these disparities between 1923 and 1936 is given in Table 3.2.

For many years Black land-grant institutions were largely secondary institutions. This was mainly due to inadequate public schools for Blacks and the lack of Black students prepared to do college work. Their industrial offerings prior to 1930 were confined mostly to manual training and subcollegiate trade courses in occupations that were in harmony with the then prevailing social and economic status of Black men in the South. A study of these schools in 1934 and 1935 revealed that auto mechanics and woodworking, including carpentry, were the most frequently offered trade courses and no course in professional engineering existed (Caliver, 1937).

Table 3.2   Percentage Distribution of Federal Funds to Black Land-Grant Institutions (1923–1936)

Year Ending June 30	All Funds (%)	1862 Land-Grant Funds (%)	Smith-Hughes Funds (%)	Second Morrill, Nelson, Bankhead Jones Funds (%)
1923	6	10	16	29
1924	6	10	15	29
1925	7	7	23	29
1926	6	7	21	29
1927	6	7	31	29
1928	6	15	28	29
1929	5	—	36	29
1930	3	7	23	29
1932	5	10	27	29
1933	5	8	32	29
1934	8	8	16	29
1935	4	12	15	29
1936	5	12	17	29

Note: Information is not available for 1931.
Source: Wilkerson, D. A. (1939). *Special problems of negro education*, pp. 81–82. Washington, DC: U.S. Government Printing Office.

Teacher education became the main function of the Black land-grant institutions when most of their curricula were elevated to the collegiate level in the 1930s. By 1934, eleven of the seventeen institutions offered industrial teacher-education programs (Caliver, 1937). According to Hall (1973), these early programs were extensions of the colleges' vocational trade courses combined with clusters of general and professional education courses, and they attempted to prepare persons to be vocational industrial-education teachers in a four-year sequence. This arrangement was prompted by the need for Black vocational teachers at the secondary level. With the apprenticeship programs closed to Blacks and no specialized vocational schools available to them, it became necessary for these institutions to develop programs to supply the public schools' human-resources needs. It is obvious that the structure of these programs prevented satisfactory attainment of all their objectives, but they did produce a cadre of vocational industrial-education teachers who later pursued successfully advanced degrees at outstanding graduate schools in the North.

Table 3.3 shows the total state appropriations in 1993–94 for land-grant research and extension programs at 33 universities that are designated as land-grant institutions by the U.S. Department of Agriculture. The list includes only those states that have both a predominantly White and a historically Black land-grant institution or system. Healy (1995) reported that such scant support has hamstrung the Black institutions from hiring more professors and developing state-of-the art facilities. Table 3.4 (on p. 50) lists the historically and predominantly Black land-grant institutions in 1890.

West Virginia State University is one of few predominantly Black institutions of higher education that has experienced reverse integration as a result of the U.S. Supreme Court's decision declaring racial segregation illegal. Until 1957, West Virginia State University was similar to the other insti-

West Virginia University (WVU) cooperative extension service is designed to help people use research-based knowledge to improve their lives.

Table 3.3 State Support for Land-Grant Activities at Black and White Institutions

Alabama		Mississippi	
Auburn University	$39,402,500	Mississippi State	
Alabama A&M University*	404,700	University	$29,239,900
Tuskegee University**	0	Alcorn State University*	897,100
Arkansas		**Missouri**	
University of Arkansas		University of Missouri	
at Fayetteville	$34,812,600	System	$31,930,500
University of Arkansas		Lincoln University*	0
at Pine Bluff*	0		
Delaware		**North Carolina**	
University of Delaware	$7,658,900	North Carolina	
Delaware State University*	103,700	State University	$65,951,000
		North Carolina	
		A&T State University*	500,000
Florida		**Oklahoma**	
University of Florida	$83,682,100	Oklahoma State University	$33,049,800
Florida A&M University*	250,000	Langston University*	258,700
Georgia		**South Carolina**	
University of Georgia	$62,000,900	Clemson University	$36,049,800
Fort Valley State College*	382,000	South Carolina	
		State University*	0
Kentucky		**Tennessee**	
University of Kentucky	$37,201,500	University of Tennessee	
Kentucky State University*	1,094,600	at Knoxville	$35,103,900
Louisiana		**Texas**	
Louisiana State		Texas A&M University	$91,909,600
University System	$44,862,400	Prairie View A&M	
Southern University and		University	312,400
A&M College at			
Baton Rouge*	3,000,000		
Maryland		**Virginia**	
University of Maryland		Virginia Polytechnic	
at College Park	$23,518,500	Institute and	
University of Maryland–		State University	$43,308,100
Eastern Shore*	1,263,500	Virginia State University*	613,700

* Historically Black institutions
**A private Black campus, Tuskegee University, is also considered a land-grant institution but receives mostly federal funds.
Note: Figures were obtained from the U.S. Department of Agriculture and Education, through the *Chronicle of Higher Education*, copyright 1995. Reprinted with permission.

Table 3.4   List of Land-Grant Institutions in 1890

Institution	Date State Accepted Morrill Act	Date Institution Opened to Students	Location
Alabama A&M University	1891	1875	Huntsville, AL
University of Arkansas at Pine Bluff	1891	1882	Pine Bluff, AR
Delaware State College	1891	1892	Dover, DE
Florida A&M University	1891	1887	Tallahassee, FL
Fort Valley State College	1890	1891	Fort Valley, GA
Kentucky State University	1893	1887	Frankfort, KY
Southern University	1892	1881	Baton Rouge, LA
University of Maryland– Eastern Shore	1890	1886	Princess Ann, MD
Alcorn State University	1892	1872	Lorman, MS
Lincoln University	1891	1866	Jefferson City, MO
North Carolina A&T State University	1891	1891	Greensboro, NC
Langston University	1890	1898	Langston, OK
South Carolina State College	1868	1896	Orangeburg, SC
Tennessee State University	1868	1912	Nashville, TN
Virginia State University	1870	1868	Petersburg, VA
West Virginia State University*	1890	1891	Institute, WV

*West Virginia State University had been a land-grant institution until the 1950s, when the designation was withdrawn. In 1991, the West Virginia Legislature returned land-grant status to the institution. *Source*: Anderson, G. L. (1976). *Land-grant universities and their continuing challenge*. East Lansing: Michigan State University Press.

tutions in 1890—receiving small appropriations from state and federal governments and training Black students in agriculture-related fields. But that year, responding to the U.S. Supreme Court's decision in *Brown v. Board of Education*, the West Virginia Legislature voted to move all land-grant activities to West Virginia University (WVU) (Jaschik, 1994). However, all of the other states kept their land-grant institutions as such.

Over the years, West Virginia State's White enrollment grew, but most of the students were commuter students. Hall (1973) reported that by 1957 more then 1,000 White students were attending integrated classes at the school. In 1994 its student body was 87 percent White and the resident population was about 80 percent Black (Jaschik, 1994).

West Virginia State University was redesignated as a land-grant institution, meaning the school gets $50,000 a year from the U.S. Department of Agriculture (Jaschik, 1994). In 1991, the West Virginia Legislature returned land-grant status to the institution. Although West Virginia State University has been redesignated as a land-grant institution, the college cannot participate in programs created after 1890 to support Black land-grant institutions. As of 1997, the university was focusing on creating new programs in agribusiness and economics that would help low-income students and state residents.

Territory Land-Grant Institutions

- University of District of Columbia (formerly Federal City College)
- University of Guam
- University of Hawaii (founded in 1907)
- University of Puerto Rico (founded in 1903)
- University of the Virgin Islands

Congress created Federal City College in 1966 as a land-grant college. Finally, by the educational amendments of 1972, the University of Guam (founded in 1952) and the University of the Virgin Islands (founded in 1962) were made land-grant universities. In lieu of land or scrip, these three institutions received a federal endowment—Guam and the Virgin Islands received $3,000,000 each and Federal City received $7,800,000. The University of Hawaii also received cash appropriations instead of land and scrip. Only three of the 1890 institutions—Alcorn A&M, South Carolina State, and Virginia State—shared in the grants of 1862 institutions (Anderson, 1976).

Land-grant universities that are state partners of the Cooperative State Research, Education, and Extension Service can be accessed at: http://csrees.usda.gov/qlinks/partners/state_partners.html.

The Tribal Colleges

Culminating a nearly two-year campaign by the 29 tribal colleges that comprise the American Indian Higher Education Consortium (AIHEC) in October 1994, Congress passed legislation granting them land-grant status. In November 1994, the board of the National Association of State Universities and Land-Grant Colleges (NASULGC), which had strongly endorsed the campaign, voted to admit AIHEC as a system member of the association with one representative as a member of NASULGC's Council of Presidents. In January 1995, AIHEC became the newest member of NASULGC, the nation's oldest higher education association (West Virginia University Extension Service, n.d.).

Land-grant status was conferred on the 29 American Indian colleges in 1994 as a provision of the Elementary and Secondary Education Reauthorization Act. The bill also authorized a $23 million endowment for them, to be built up over five years. The colleges were to receive interest payments from the endowment each year. In addition, the legislation authorized a $1.7 million challenge grant program for higher education programs in agriculture and natural resources, much like the successful program at the 1890 colleges, and $50,000 per school for higher education in agriculture and natural resources (similar to the original Morrill-Nelson funds). The legislation also provided $5 million to the Cooperative Extension Service of the 1862 land-grant institutions in states that also have tribal colleges. Title 1862 institutions were to cooperate with the tribal colleges in setting up joint agricultural extension programs focused on the needs of the American Indian institutions, as identified by the tribal colleges (West Virginia University Extension Service, n.d.).

The 29 colleges named in the 1994 bill comprise all of the American Indian tribal colleges in the nation. Of these, 24 are tribally controlled colleges, two are tribally controlled vocational/technical colleges, two are owned and operated by the Bureau of Indian Affairs, and one is federally chartered. The 29 American tribal colleges are located on or near reservations. Most are two-year colleges and technical schools, but three are four-year institutions, and one offers a master's degree. Located in twelve states, the schools are the most important provider of higher education opportunities for American Indians, serving 14,000 students (almost 10,000 FTE). They have been

Table 3.5   List of American Indian Tribal Colleges*

Alaska	Inupiat University
	Sheldon Jackson College
Arizona	Dine College
California	Hehaka Sapa College at D-Q University
Kansas	Haskell Indian Nations University
Montana	Blackfeet Community College
	Dull Knife Memorial College
	Fort Peck Community College
	Little Big Horn College
	Salish-Kootenai College
Nebraska	Nebraska Indian Community College
New Mexico	Institute of American Indian Arts
	Dine College (formerly Navajo Community College)-Shiprock Campus
	Southwestern Indian Polytechnic Institute
North Dakota	Fort Berthold College Center
	Little Hoop Community College
	Sitting Bull College (formerly Standing Rock Community College)
	Turtle Mountain Community College
Oklahoma	Bacone College
South Dakota	Cheyenne River Community College
	Oglala Lakota College
	Sinte Gleska College
	Sisseton-Wahpeton Community College

* This is not a complete list of all American Indian tribal colleges, but rather a list of those who are recognized as land-grant institutions.
Source: Land Grant Institutions (http:/www.higher-ed.org/resources/LG_tribal_colleges.htm).

notably successful in retaining students and sending them on to four-year colleges and universities. They also provide a variety of community services, such as family counseling, alcohol and drug abuse programs, job training and economic development (West Virginia University Extension Service, n.d.).

A report entitled "The path of many journeys: The benefits of higher education for native people and communities," summarizes the data on the historically low college-going rates of American Indians as well as some signs of increases in recent decades. The report also details the impact on tribal groups and tribal colleges of having more members with college degrees. The report was released in February, 2007, by the Institute for Higher Education Policy and American Indian Higher Education Consortium.

The 1994 Land-Grant Institutions Grants Programs

The primary purpose of the 1994 land-grant institutions is to prepare American Indians to further their education in an environment that is culturally applicable to the students' background. Following are selected programs that are intended to strengthen *research, extension,* and *teaching* capacities in the food and agricultural sciences:

- *Tribal Colleges Education Grants Program*
  Enhances educational opportunities for American Indians through the process of strengthening instructional programs in agricultural sciences.

- *Equity in Educational Land-Grant Status Act of 1994 Program (Tribal Colleges Extension Services)*
  Provides funding for the 1994 land-grant institutions to conduct nonformal educational programs to meet the needs of American Indians.

- *Tribal Colleges Research Grants Program*
  Supports the 1994 land-grant institutions in conducting agricultural research that targets high-priority concerns and interests of tribal, national, or multi-state significance.

- *Tribal Colleges Endowment Fund*
  Encourages and promotes capacity development in teaching programs in the food and agricultural sciences.

Source: Tribal Colleges Land-Grant Institutions Grants Program, 2006.

The Smith-Lever Agricultural Extension Act

In 1914 the Smith-Lever Act was passed. This act completed the land-grant triumvirate—teaching, research, and extension. The Smith-Lever Act provided for a program of cooperative extension work in agriculture and home economics. Merriam and Cunningham (1989) cite several events that made the Smith-Lever Act possible: aggressive promotion by special-interest groups, development of the agricultural sciences, and the creation of a method for knowledge dissemination.

The Smith-Lever Act also formally established the principle that while elementary and secondary education might remain the responsibility of the states, the national government would aid the expansion of higher learning to the "common individual." What this has meant for the land-grant colleges, over and beyond being trendsetters, is that they are routinely funded at set levels from Washington, compared to other colleges and universities (Nichols, 1976).

Provisions of the Smith-Lever Agricultural Extension Act (38 Stat. 372)

Following is a brief summary of the principal provisions of the act.

1. *Cooperative Character of the Work*

   a. It must be carried on in connection with the land-grant college in cooperation with the U.S. Department of Agriculture.

   b. It enables the use of plans that are mutually agreed upon by the Secretary of Agriculture and the land-grant college.

   Procedure: The director of extension draws up, through the state extension staff, plans of work that include the estimated funds necessary for personnel, expenses, and materials to carry them out, subject to the approval of the dean and trustees, regents, or curators of the land-grant institutions. The plans are then forwarded to the administrator of extension, U.S. Department of Agriculture, who, with federal extension staff, checks them for final approval.

2. *Wide Scope of Work*

   a. It provides that work is to be with persons not attending or residents in land-grant colleges. There is no limitation as to age, sex, race, or business.

   b. The subject-matter scope is practically unlimited—"the giving of instruction . . . in agriculture, home economics, and subjects relating thereto."

3. *Educational Character of Work*

   a. The Morrill Acts provide that land-grant colleges are to teach cooperative extension programs.

   b. The act specifies that the "work shall consist of the giving of instruction."

4. *Emphasis on the Demonstration*

   a. The work "shall consist of the giving of . . . practical demonstrations."

   b. It shall impart "information . . . through demonstrations."

5. *Finance and Distribution Based on Rural and Farm Population*

   Congress is authorized to appropriate such sums as it deems necessary. Out of these sums each state, Puerto Rico, and the Federal

Extension Service shall receive funds as indicated by the terms of the current authorizing amended act. These federal funds require some degree of offset from nonfederal funds by the states and Puerto Rico. Certain sums are available to states without offset; in general, the balance of the appropriated sums has to be duplicated by a like amount raised within the state. A small percentage is available to the Secretary of Agriculture to be allotted on the basis of special needs due to population characteristics, area in relation to farm population, or other special problems.

The Federal Extension Service shall receive such amounts as Congress shall determine for administration, technical, and other services and for coordinating the extension work of the department and the several states, territories, and possessions.

6. *Limitations*. Funds may not be used for:

   a. Purchase, erection, preservation, or repair of buildings

   b. Purchase or rental of land

   c. College course teaching

   d. Lectures in college

   e. Other purposes not specified in the act

States determine which college or colleges shall administer the funds. Each college shall make, annually, a detailed report of operations, receipts, and expenditures to the governor of the state and the Secretary of Agriculture. The law gave the Secretary of Agriculture and the state agricultural colleges joint approval authority. It established a national system of cooperative extension education.

Implications for Career and Technical Education

The Morrill Act was the cornerstone for the development of land-grant institutions in America. These institutions have paved the way for leadership, training, and research in specialized fields. Land-grant institutions induced a major redirection in the pattern of higher education in America. Some of the implications for vocational education were as follows:

1. A liberal and practical education was prescribed.

2. The doors of higher education were opened to a wider public audience.

3. Prominent status was given to the mechanical arts, agriculture, and other disciplines.

4. The acceptance of vocationalism was extended to farmers, business professionals, public schools, and various community agencies.

5. The social efficiency of vocational education was widely recognized.

6. Land-grant institutions were perceived as models for solving urban and rural problems.

Today the historic land-grant institutions and their sister state universities address the large and demanding problems of the nation and all humankind—energy and the environment, inflation and recession, and the need for an adequate and nutritious food supply—and accept responsibility for helping to solve them.

The issues facing American society today call for greatly expanded efforts by all of higher education. Yet, no social institution is so uniquely equipped to meet this challenge as the land-grant college or university, an institution that was created to meet precisely this need, and an institution that has a long and distinguished record of such accomplishments.

4-H Youth Development

4-H in the United States is a youth organization administered by the Department of Agriculture Cooperative Extension Service with the mission of engaging youth to reach their fullest potential while advancing the field of youth development. The ideas that epitomize 4-H began to coalesce around the start of the twentieth century, in the work of several people in different parts of the United States who were concerned about young people. A focal point in 4-H is the idea of practical and "hands-on-learning," which came from the desire to make public school education more connected to rural life.

Through 4-H, young people are encouraged to participate in a variety of activities that emphasize a "learning by doing" philosophy.

4-H Clubs

The 4-H organization took shape at the turn of the twentieth century because of a vital need to improve life in rural areas and filled a need for public school education to be more connected to rural life. With its direct connection to 106 land-grant universities, 4-H is often the first experience rural young people have with higher education. The four Hs stand for Heart, Head, Hands, and Health. By introducing improved methods of farming and homemaking, 4-H focused on teaching young people to "learn by doing."

18 USC 707

The 4-H organization came into being because of the work of several people in different parts of the United States. It was Liberty Hyde Baily at Cornell University who first linked youth to nature and the rural environment. Across the country, at state agricultural experiment stations and in rural schools (e.g., O. H. Benson and Jessie Field in Iowa, O. J. Kerns and W. B. Otwell in Illinois, A. B. Graham in Ohio, J. F. Haines in Indiana, and E. C. Bishop in Nebraska), agriculture was promoted and out-of school "clubs" formed that introduced farm and home topics and comparative classes for rural youth.

Beginning with projects such as raising corn and canning tomatoes, and later on through sewing, cooking and baking contests, early 4-H programs were mostly devoted to raising food. Such contests, with their premiums and equipment prizes, demonstrated the value of incentives to encourage young people to learn.

From the Midwest 4-H clubs spread to the south, with Thomas M. Campbell working with African American farmers there and organizing youth clubs among African American youth. Oscar B. Martin coordinated the establishment of clubs in Mississippi. In 1908 a Country Life Commission was established, urging Congress to authorize Agricultural Extension Service through the land-grant university system. Although Congress ignored the recommendation, the movement started on its own.

In 1909, the USDA outlined a proposal for establishing girls' tomato-canning clubs, and in 1910 Marie S. Cromer organized a club using material supplied by the USDA. At the same time, Ella G. Agnew was establishing girls' canning clubs in Virginia. She was the first woman agent appointed by the USDA for farmers' cooperative demonstration work. By 1912, 23,000 canning clubs had been organized with a goal of teaching safe and efficient methods of preserving food. However, girls' clubs soon looked at the entire role of women in the home and community.

Box 3.1   4-H ORGANIZATIONAL STRUCTURE

National Level

- *U.S. Department of Agriculture (USDA)*
  - Congressionally approved home of the organization in which 4-H resides
  - Administered by U.S. Secretary of Agriculture: political appointment by the president
- *Cooperative State Research, Education and Extension Service (CSREES)*
  - One of many agencies within USDA
  - Has 8 units administered by Administrator of CSREES
- *Families, 4-H and Nutrition*
  - One of 8 units within CSREES
  - Administered by Deputy Administrator for F4-HN
- *Youth Development*
  - One of two units within F4-HN and the National Headquarters for 4-H
  - Administered by Director, Youth Development
- *National Program Leaders*
  - Six program leaders provide program and policy leadership and provide financial assistance through securing and managing grants to land-grant universities.

State Level

- *Land-Grant University*
  - State and tribal partner with CES; has many colleges
  - Administered by University President (sometimes called Chancellor).
- *Cooperative Extension Service (CES)*
  - Responsible for outreach and bringing knowledge and research generated at the university to address the local needs of citizens in communities across the state
  - Has many departments or units
  - Administered by Director of Cooperative Extension

- *1862 State Extension Specialists (usually faculty positions)*
  Responsible for translating research to application and supporting county staff and program through teaching, assisting in grant preparation and development of curricula and support materials. CES faculty may be part of the academic department that supports their field of expertise as well as accountable to the extension system.

- *1890 Extension Specialists*
  Deliver programs in counties of regions of the state where needs exist for specific program priorities. All programs focus on the Extension System's nationwide initiatives and provide educational assistance to limited-resource farmers, families and youth helping them acquire skills that improve the quality of their lives and communities.

- *1994 Extension Specialists*
  Deliver programs to American Indian populations on reservations and in native communities in cities across the state.

- *Area/District Extension Specialists*
  - Some states group counties together to provide additional staff support. These areas or districts have offices in one of the counties within the multiple county area.
  - Administered by Area/District Director & State Associate Director 4-H
- *Extension Youth Development*
  - Department within CES responsible for applying knowledge and research related to the growth and development of youth to community youth development efforts across the state.
  - Administered by the State Extension 4-H Leader (sometimes called the Associate Director of 4-H Youth Development)
- *Tribal Extension Youth Development*
  - Department in Tribal College CES responsible for applying knowledge and research related to the growth and development of youth on reservations and in American Indian communities in metropolitan areas
  - Administered by the Tribal Extension Youth Development Director

County Level

1862 schools serve audiences in every county in the U.S. through the county extension system. Since 1890 and 1994 schools have a targeted audience; they do not use a county based delivery system.

- *County Commissioners* approve the county funding of the Extension budgets (elected positions)

- *County Boards* approve direction and implementation of all county Extension programs. The degree to which county agents are accountable to Extension boards varies according to the way in which stat*e funding is distributed to counties in each state (elected positions).*

- *County Extension Educators* are responsible for coordinating the needs of the county with state and county supported Extension outreach and for implementing appropriate program offerings. Usually county offices consist of a team of county agents; typically made up of an Agriculture agent, a Family & Consumer Sciences Agent and a 4-H agent. Some larger counties may have staff to address additional functions. Smaller counties may have fewer staff who share programmatic responsibilities or may share staff with neighboring counties. One of these agents will serve as the County or Multi-county Director. Agents are accountable to both the Director of Extension or designated administrator and to the county Extension council.

- *4-H Agents* are responsible for the delivery of all aspects of the county 4-H Youth Development program. They work with volunteers, parents, youth, schools and community organizations to provide opportunities for youth to master life skills.

- *Volunteer Leaders* are adults and older youth who serve as club leaders, project leaders, camp counselors, etc. Some volunteer leaders work directly with youth and some with other volunteers as trainers and mentors. All are essential to effective 4-H delivery.

Source: Adapted from the United States Department of Agriculture. (2003). 4-H 101 handbook: The basics of starting 4-H clubs. Washington, DC: Cooperative State Research, Education and Extension Service.

By 1914 4-H clubs existed in nearly all states. By 1919 the general structure of local clubs was firmly established, an expansion of projects was encouraged, and relations between club work and vocational education in the schools were defined. By the 1920s and 1930s, the emphasis of the program had become the development of the individual rather than the product produced.

In 1948 a group of American young people went to Europe and a group of Europeans came to the United States on the first International Farm Youth Exchange. Out-of-state trips and international exchanges have been highly educational for hundreds of young people in 4-H. In 2000, 4-H celebrated its 100th anniversary. Today, Cooperative Extension and its 4-H programs serve people in towns, cities, and rural areas with information on agriculture, family living, and community development. Studies show that 4-H members are more motivated to help others, achieve a sense of self-esteem, and develop lasting friendships.

For more information, visit the 4-H home page at http://www.4husa.org.

Source: National 4-H Headquarters. (2002). *4-H in the U.S.A.* Washington, DC: CSREES/USDA.

Summary

- Colleges such as Harvard and Yale were established to prepare persons for the ministry and other professions. This type of education was not viewed as particularly practical either by or for the general populace. Agriculture and industry were the two great resources of the nation, and technically trained workers were needed to develop their potentials.

- The demands for the development of vocational education occurred between 1820 and 1860. In general, the agricultural sector of the economy demanded vocational and practical education.

- Land-grant institutions were called "colleges of agriculture," "colleges of mechanic arts," or "colleges of agriculture and mechanic arts." Their purposes were primarily to educate farmers and agricultural technicians for increased crop production; to educate the housewife-home economist and her supporting cast for better nutrition, child rearing, and homemaking; and to prepare the engineers for a soon-to-expand industrial society.

- The Morrill Act of 1862 was the first legislation passed by the national government to support vocational education. Proposed by Senator Justin Morrill of Vermont, the act granted 30,000 acres of land to each state for each senator and representative it had in Congress. Income from the sale of such lands by the states would be used to create and maintain agricultural and mechanical arts colleges.

- The Second Morrill Act (also known as the Maintenance Act) authorized the application of a portion of the proceeds from the sale of public lands under the First Morrill Act for the more complete endowment and support of the land-grant colleges, and for the benefit of agriculture and the mechanic arts. Each state and territory received an increase of $1,500 annually. This amount was to be supplemented by an automatic annual increase of $1,000 until the year 1900. The Second Morrill Act of 1890 gave new life to land-grant college education for Blacks and other minorities.

- The Smith-Lever Act, known as the Agricultural Extension Act, provided for a program of cooperative extension work in agriculture and home economics. The practice of 50-50 matching began with this act. The state was required to finance one-half of the cost of the extension programs and the federal government the other half. This act also provided farmers and homemakers with a program of cooperative extension work in agriculture and home economics.

- In 1994, 29 tribal colleges gained land-grant status, bringing the total number of land-grant institutions to 105.

- 4-H is unique in the non-formal youth development field because it is a partner with the land-grant university system and has access to the most current knowledge and research provided by those universities related to youth development. In addition, 4-H staff and cooperative extension offices are located in almost every county in the United States and are connected through an extensive electronic network that assures access to the most current developments from the field.

Discussion Questions and Activities

1. What is a land-grant college?
2. Describe the role of the land-grant system in the development of American Indian tribal colleges, and explain the importance of tribal colleges in the American Indian population.
3. Discuss the role of the land-grant system in the development of career and technical education.
4. Describe some of the career and technical education programs that are conducted by the Cooperative Extension Service in your community.
5. Discuss the provisions of the Smith-Lever Agricultural Extension Act.
6. Contrast the provisions of the First Morrill Act with the provisions of the Second Morrill Act.
7. Debate the following topics:
    a. Will the land-grant institutions need to change their mission and goals in order to remain viable?
    b. Should teacher education programs in agricultural education be limited to land-grant universities?
8. Explain the role of Senator Justin S. Morrill in the development of career and technical education.

Library Research

9. Compare and contrast the mission of land-grant institutions with that of non-land-grant institutions.

10. Outline and discuss the tripartite structure of the land-grant system.

11. Research and discuss the impact of collegiate 4-H clubs, 4-H camping programs, and international 4-H clubs on career and technical education programs.

Recommended Educational Media Resources

- *Land for learning: Justin Smith Morrill, architect of American higher education*
  Insight Media
  2162 Broadway
  New York, NY 10024-0621
  1-800-233-9910 or (212) 721-6316
  Web site: http://www.insight-media.com
  Send e-mail orders to: custserv@insight-media.com

- *Toward a common history* (Order #VT0038)
- *From the grassroots: Extension's first 75 years* (Order #VT0144)
  Cabell County WVU Extension Office
  2726 Howell's Mill Road
  Post Office Box 219
  Ona, WV 25545-0219
  1-800-287-8206 or (304) 743-7131

References and Additional Reading

Anderson, G. L. (1976). *Land-grant universities and their continuing challenge*. East Lansing: Michigan State University Press.

Andrews, B. F. (1918). The land-grant of 1862 and the land-grant colleges. *Bulletin No. 13*, p. 10. Washington, DC: U.S. Government Printing Office.

Baker, S. A. (1991). The impact of the civil war on vocational education. *Journal of Vocational and Technical Education, 7*(2), 56–60.

Bell, A. P. (1987, December). Commitment of 1890 land-grant institutions to teacher education in agriculture. *Agricultural Education Magazine, 60*(6), 13.

Braxton, G. J. (1994). *Historically black colleges and universities in the United States*. Washington, DC: National Association of Foreign Students Affairs Publications.

Calhoun, C. C., and Finch, A. V. (1982). *Vocational education: Concepts and operations*. Belmont, CA: Wadsworth.

Caliver, A. (1937). *Vocational education and guidance of Negroes*. Washington, DC: U.S. Government Printing Office.

Commanger, H. S. (1950). *The American mind* (p. 10). New Haven: Yale University Press.

Guzman, J. P. (1952). *1952 Negro yearbook*. New York: William H. Wise.

Hall, C. W. (1973). *Black vocational technical and industrial arts education: Development and history*. Chicago: American Technical Society.

Hawkins, L. S., Prosser, C. A., and Wright, J. C. (1951). *Development of vocational education*. Chicago: American Technical Society.

Healy, P. (1995). The vestiges of Jim Crow. *Chronicle of Higher Education*, *42*(16), 25–26.

Jaschik, S. (1994, April, 27). West Virginia state college regains black land-grant status. *Chronicle of Higher Education*, *40*(34), A22.

Land Grant Institutions (n.d.). Land grant institutions: Native American tribal colleges. Retrieved September 18, 2006, from http://www.higher-ed.org/resources/LG_tribal_colleges.htm.

Leslie, L. L. (1976). Updating education for the profession: The new mission. In G. L. Anderson (Ed.), *Land-grant universities and their continuing challenge* (pp. 237–265). East Lansing: Michigan State University Press.

Merriam, S. B., and Cunningham, P. M. (1989). *Handbook of adult and continuing education*. San Francisco: Jossey-Bass.

Miller, K., and Gay, J. R. (1914). *Progress and achievements of colored people*. Washington, DC: Austin Jenkins.

Miller, M. T. (1993). *The historical development of vocational education in the United States: Colonial America through the Morrill legislation* (ERIC Document Reproduction Service No. ED 360 481).

Moody, F. (1980). The history of blacks in vocational education. *Voc. Ed.*, *55*(1), 30–34.

National 4-H Headquarters (2002). *4-H in the U.S.A*. Washington, D.C: CSREES/USDA.

Nichols, D. C. (1976). Land-grant university services and urban policy. In G. L. Anderson (Ed.), *Land-grant universities and their continuing challenge* (pp. 223–236). East Lansing: Michigan State University Press.

Thompson, J. E. (1973). *Foundations of vocational education: Social and philosophical concepts*. Englewood Cliffs, NJ: Prentice-Hall.

Tribal Colleges Land-Grant Institutions Grants Program (June 30, 2006). USDA, Cooperative state research, education, and extension service. Retrieved March 1, 2007, from
http://www.csrees.usda.gov/nea/education/in_focus/multicultural_if_1994.html.

United States Department of Agriculture (2003). 4-H 101 handbook: The basics of starting 4-H clubs. Washington, DC: Cooperative State Research, Education and Extension Service.

Venn, G. (1964). *Man, education and work*. Washington, DC: American Council on Education.

Walter, R. A. (1993). Development of vocational education. In C. Anderson and L.C. Rampp (Eds.), *Vocational education in the 1990's, II: A sourcebook for strategies, methods, and materials* (pp. 1–20). Ann Arbor, MI: Prakken Publishing.

West Virginia University Extension Service (n.d.). *About the land-grant system*. Retrieved September 18, 2006, from http://www.wvu.edu/~exten/about/land.htm

Wilkerson, D. A. (1939). *Special problems of negro education*. Washington, DC: U.S. Government Printing Office.

chapter 4

Selected Factors that Influenced Career and Technical Education Development

From 1917 to 1918, efforts in vocational education were largely devoted to the needs of the nation during World War I. America's involvement in the war made the rapid and effective training of masses of inexperienced persons an urgent priority. Thousands of civilian workers in the war effort learned their skills in vocational education classes—skills they put to good use in the postwar economy.

As America approached the twentieth century, support for the use of state and federal funds to establish and operate a comprehensive system of vocational education began to increase. Although there was no universal agreement as to what form vocational education should take, there was agreement that changes in the ways of preparing workers were required. Various agencies and organizations expressed interest in providing additional opportunities for vocational education. These groups engaged in studies, passed resolutions, and petitioned legislative bodies to provide financial assistance in establishing programs of vocational education at public expense.

This chapter is concerned with a discussion of selected factors that influenced the development of career and technical education. For convenience these factors are grouped under the following headings: Impact of War Activities, Study Panels, and the Association for Career and Technical Education.

Impact of War Activities

Since 1917, the public vocational schools have trained large numbers of workers for occupations essential to the national economy in both peacetime and wartime. It is not accurate to say that the Smith-Hughes Act was passed because of the possibility of war, but it is apparent that congressional leaders saw a close relationship between the vocational education bill and national preparedness.

The war found America vocationally unprepared. The critical military and industrial shortage of trained workers became an emergency for the newly created Federal Board for Vocational Education. The Federal Board had the responsibility of building a permanent system of vocational education, and its task was to train people in skilled occupations that were useful in combat conditions. Both the War Department and the U.S. Shipping Board requested assistance from the Federal Board in organizing and conducting war classes for various occupations after actual military training (Bauder, 1918). "Thus for the first time in the history of the United States, the schools of America were called upon by the Federal Government to undertake vocational training" (Federal Board for Vocational Education, 1917, p. 10).

Shortly after the approval of the Smith-Hughes Act in 1917, America became involved in World War I. Other major wars that have influenced career and technical education include World War II, the Korean War, and the Vietnam War.

World War I

This was a war that utilized various mechanical forces. To fight a mechanical war, highly trained mechanics, technicians, and experienced supervisory forces were needed, in addition to troops. These needs were the catalyst for newly created and expanded industries. For the production of the necessary equipment and supplies, industry required increasing numbers of trained crafts personnel. The War Industries Board and the Federal Board for Vocational Education met this challenge and took the lead in providing this training. The Federal Board for Vocational Education stated in 1918 that at the request of the United States Army it had "undertaken to aid the Army to secure proper training of conscripted men before they are drafted . . . This bulletin is issued for the purpose of supplying information to school authorities who will undertake this work as a patriotic duty" (p. 3).

The Federal Board for Vocational Education determined that the army needed 200,000 mechanics. In addition, there was a need for radio operators, radio technicians, automobile drivers, gasoline engine technicians, and others. The board then formulated a plan to train personnel, establishing classes in specialized subjects for training men prior to their induction into the service. Training was eventually provided at 125 local induction centers (Federal Board for Vocational Education, 1919).

Beginning July 1, 1917, and continuing until the conclusion of World War I, 62,161 persons were trained for war production jobs. This was in the early stages of the federally aided program of vocational education of less than college grade. After World War I, an upsweep in economy carried America through a period of high-level prosperity that ended with the 1929 economic crash. The industrial activity that followed the 1937 depression proved to be the initial industrial effort for World War II (Seidel, 1951).

World War II

American participation in World War II necessitated the rapid and effective training of large numbers of inexperienced persons. According to

Dennis (1950), the unprecedented feat of training on such a vast scale and in such short time was made possible through close cooperation between the federal government and those vocational schools equipped to handle the problem. Thompson (1973) reported that Vocational Training for War Production Workers (VTWPW) and Vocational Education for National Defense (VEND) were initiated to expand the vocational training programs.

The objective of VTWPW was the immediate employability of the trainee for a specific job. In a large number of instances, new workers received instruction but in other cases, workers employed in civilian production were given "conversion training" for jobs in war industry (Seidel, 1951). VEND was initiated and administered through the same process as the Smith-Hughes Act. A commonality of VEND and VTWPW is that both were largely urban centered and operated to train industrial workers. Several pieces of federal legislation were enacted for vocational training during World War II. It was estimated that the total monetary appropriation was more than $370 million.

The Role of Women in War Industries

The idea of women as peacemakers has a long history. In ancient Athens, the (male) playwright Aristophanes speculated about how women might end the unpopular Peloponnesian War with Sparta (Goldstein, 2002). Women have formed their own organizations to work for peace on many occasions. In 1852, *Sisterly Voices* was published as a newsletter for women's peace societies (Degen, 1974).

As more and more men were inducted into military service in World War II, an increasing number of women were needed in war industries at home. By the end of 1942, women were working in shipyards, aircraft assembly plants, factories, and foundries. In addition to operating trains, aircraft, streetcars, and buses, women were welding, operating cranes, assembling detonators, and operating lathes. "Rosie the Riveter" became an American icon. She was a symbol of the training women received during the war in vocational education programs across the country (Association for Career and Technical Education, 2002).

The number of women trained for the war effort as of

Rosie the Riveter was a symbol of the vocational training women received during World War II.

December 1, 1941 was 11,552, but by April 1943, 741,332 women were enrolled in training programs. Employment opportunities were opening up for older women, married women, and women of color. In some industries, women doing the same work as men were paid the same wages as the men (Association for Career and Technical Education, 2002).

Effects of the Korean and Vietnam Wars

The effects of the Korean and Vietnam wars on vocational education involvement included:

1. A greater need for food and industrial production.
2. A large number of draftees.
3. A decline in unemployment.
4. A subsequent rise in unemployment due to returning veterans entering the labor market.
5. An increased labor supply.
6. An expansion of existing programs and creation of new programs to assist veterans entering the labor market.

Effects of War Training on Career and Technical Education

Foreman training was perhaps the largest direct result of vocational education involvement during the wars (Thompson, 1973). Hawkins, Prosser, and Wright (1951) list ten effects of war training on vocational education. Among the ten are:

- America became conscious of the need for vocational education.
- Adults needed training even after they were employed.
- Women could be trained to do men's work.
- A need arose for short, intensive, teacher-training courses.
- The philosophy was advanced that vocational education was part of the preparation for living needed by all individuals.

Servicemen's Readjustment Act of 1944 (Public Law 78-346)

In June 1944, President Franklin D. Roosevelt signed into law the Servicemen's Readjustment Act of 1944, known as the GI Bill of Rights. The purpose of this act was to assist World War II veterans in readjustment to civilian life. Few requirements were placed on the veterans; they simply were to select the kind of training and/or education they wanted, apply for admission to a recognized training program, and maintain the academic standards necessary to continue in the program. In addition to the direct participants in vocational education, a large number of veterans in college majored in vocational teacher education and taught in vocational programs. Veterans were allowed time for participation in accordance with the time they had been in service. Subsequent legislation guaranteed these benefits to veterans of the Korean and Vietnam Wars.

By taking advantage of the benefits of the Servicemen's Readjustment Act, this veteran completed a course of study in Clinical Laboratory Technology.

Implications

The future will be determined to a great extent by how career and technical education, defense, and industry accept the challenge to work together toward the short- and long-range goals for reducing the shortage of skilled and technical workers for the defense industrial base. Defense industry leaders need to take positive action to improve their industry's image if they want more young people to choose careers with them. The opportunity is there for leaders in defense industries to become more visible in community and school activities where bridges can be built and communications opened.

Defense industries might find it advantageous to participate actively in career days, promote occupational opportunities in industry, speak at school events, arrange plant tours, and in general expose students, counselors, teachers, and administrators to their world in the same way that other business and industry leaders do. Their representatives need to serve on advisory committees and on school boards, taking actions that make them important to students and administrators. Only in this way will they be assured that their points of view will be incorporated into local decision making.

One valuable lesson that must not be forgotten is that our strength as a country—in war or in peace—lies in the effective cooperation, effort, and adaptability of our citizens. It is imperative that as a nation we continue to maintain our ability to produce and the faculty to adjust ourselves to sudden, unexpected demands on our human resources if we are to retain our position as a people confident of our destiny. However, we can no longer afford to waste *any* of our resources, *especially* our human resources.

Study Panels

Before discussing the history and objectives of these national panels, it is crucial to understand the importance of the National Association of Manufacturers, the Douglas Commission, and the National Society for the Promotion of Industrial Education.

The National Association of Manufacturers

The National Association of Manufacturers (NAM) was organized January 22, 1895, at a convention held in Cincinnati, Ohio (Roberts, 1971). NAM was organized in response to a period of economic depression and was keenly interested in securing an adequate supply of trained workers and reducing the power of the growing labor movement. Its Committee on Industrial Education issued a report in 1905 citing high dropout rates and the failure of the apprenticeship system as justification for the creation of a separate system of trade schools. The first report advocated that the schools be funded through corporate or private endowments rather than through public funds. Seven years later, however, the committee modified its position. Recommendations made in their 1912 report included:

- The creation of German-style continuation schools;
- The development of courses centered on the needs of local industry;
- The administration of the schools by coalition of business and labor to ensure that industrial education not be corrupted by educators the way manual training had been; and
- The use of federal funds to improve industrial education as the Morrill and Hatch Acts had improved agricultural education (Wirth, 1972).

The National Association of Manufacturers' 2005 skills gap report (as cited in Stone, 2005) revealed that about four-fifths of U.S. manufacturers indicated they are facing a moderate to severe shortage of qualified workers. Stone (2005) noted that many jobs requiring postsecondary technical degrees and short-term skill certificates remain unfilled. This scenario probably suggests that there are areas of deficiency in the preparation of students for the global workforce. The NAM and the Manufacturing Institute (as cited in Reese, 2007, p. 16) list the following facts about manufacturing that make it essential to the U.S. economy and security:

- *It nurtures the economy.* Every $1.00 in manufacturing goods generates an additional $1.37 worth of additional economic activity—more than any other economic sector.
- *It invents the future.* Manufacturers are responsible for more than 70 percent of all private-sector research and development, which ultimately benefits other manufacturing and non-manufacturing activities.

- *It competes internationally.* The United States is the world's largest exporter; 61 percent of all U.S. exports are manufactured goods, double the level of 10 years ago.

- *It generates productivity increases.* Over the past decades, manufacturing productivity gains have been more than double that of other sectors. These gains enable Americans to do more with less, increase our ability to compete, and facilitate higher wages for most employees.

- *It provides more rewarding employment.* Manufacturing compensation averages more than $66,000, the highest in the private sector, and manufacturers are leaders in employee training.

- *It pays the taxes.* Manufacturing has been an important contributor to economic growth and tax receipts at all levels of government, contributing one-third of all corporate taxes collected by state and local governments.

The success of the manufacturing industry is vital to our nation's economy, and career and technical education is vital to ensuring U.S. success in the current global workforce. To learn about some of the equipment and software used in CTE manufacturing programs, visit these Web sites:

www.autodesk.com
www.labvolt.com
www.solidworks.com
www.TECedu.com

The Douglas Commission of Massachusetts

Various vocational historians have suggested that present CTE programs originated in Massachusetts with the report of the Douglas Commission. This commission was also called the Commission on Industrial and Technical Education (the term then used for CTE). This commission was directed to investigate the present facilities and needs for vocational education. As McCarthy (1950) points out:

> It must be remembered that the Douglas Commission was created not only because of the inadequacy of manual training programs in the public schools, but because the land-grant colleges failed to serve the needs of agriculture or industry on the workers' level. (p. 5)

As provided for by the legislature, in 1905 Governor William Douglas of Massachusetts appointed a commission composed of representatives of manufacturing, agriculture, labor, and education (Walter, 1993). The Douglas Commission criticized existing manual training programs and called for a more industrially oriented educational system. The commission's most controversial proposal, however, was for the establishment of public trade schools independent of the existing educational system.

The Douglas Commission Report concluded that lack of industrial training for workers increased the cost of production. The report stated that workers with general intelligence, technical knowledge, and skill would command the world market. The Douglas Commission emphasized that the foundation for technical success required a wider diffusion of industrial intelligence and that this foundation could only be acquired in connection with the general system of education in which it would be an integral part of the curriculum from the beginning (Barlow, 1976). The Douglas Commission Report was an instrumental landmark in the development of vocationalism in the public schools.

Venn (1964) notes that the recommendations of the Douglas Commission Report were enacted into law in 1906, giving impetus to the initial formation of national groups such as the National Society for the Promotion of Industrial Education. The national study panels had the benefit of this report as a model to guide them. The report was also influential in the passage of the Smith-Hughes Act of 1917.

National Society for the Promotion of Industrial Education

Labor and management could not agree on urban programs and had little interest in rural programs. Rural-dominated state legislatures were not going to vote money for vocational programs because most of the eligible schools would be located in the cities (Venn, 1964).

In 1906 the National Society for the Promotion of Industrial Education (NSPIE) brought its study of vocational education needs to the public's attention. According to Barlow (1976), two leaders of manual training, Dr. James P. Hanly and Professor Charles R. Richards, assembled a group of thirteen representative leaders at the New York City Engineers Club on June 9. This gathering was followed by another meeting of about 250 persons on November 16 (Thompson, 1973). As a result of this meeting, the National Society for the Promotion of Industrial Education was organized on November 16, 1906.

The major objectives of NSPIE were:

1. To bring to public attention the importance of industrial education as a factor in the industrial development of America and to provide opportunities for the study and discussion of the various phases of the problem.

2. To make available the results of experiments in the field of industrial education.

3. To promote the establishment of institutions of industrial training.

The members of the society consisted of educators, manufacturers, mechanics, businessmen, and representatives of other occupations.

Dr. Charles Prosser served as executive secretary of NSPIE in 1912 (Roberts, 1957). Subsequently this organization and its successor, the National Society for Vocational Education, served as a means of discussing issues of vocational education. The society was instrumental in advocating the appointment in 1914 of the National Commission on National Aid to Vocational Education.

Various national panels were appointed to study vocational education intensively. These panels were responsible for recommending changes that would permit the growth of vocational education. During the period from 1914 to 1968 there were six national panels responsible for reporting on vocational education. Five of the six panels were appointed by the president of the United States. The six panels were:

- Commission on National Aid for Vocational Education, 1914
- Committee on Vocational Education, 1928–1929
- National Advisory Committee on Education, 1929–1931
- Advisory Committee on Education, 1936–1938
- Panel of Consultants on Vocational Education, 1961–1962
- National Advisory Council on Education, 1967

Commission on National Aid to Vocational Education, 1914

President Woodrow Wilson responded to a joint resolution of Congress in 1914 and appointed a special nine-member commission to study the issue of federal aid to vocational education. The Commission on National Aid to Vocational Education (a video is available; see end-of-chapter information) included Senator Hoke Smith of Georgia, who served as chair; Representative Dudley Hughes of Georgia; and Charles Prosser, secretary of NSPIE. Dr. Prosser was regarded as the guiding figure of the national commission. The commission had various meetings that involved the gathering of information to answer six basic questions:

1. What is the need for vocational education?
2. Is there a need for a federal grant (assuming a need for vocational education)?
3. What vocational programs require federal grants?
4. To what extent should the federal government extend federal grants for vocational education to the states?
5. What amount of money is needed (the proposed legislation)?
6. What standards are required for the federal government to grant monies to the states for vocational education?

Individuals as well as representatives of national organizations and the various departments of the federal government submitted replies to the commission's questionnaire, both in person and by mail. Barlow (1976) cites Captain Douglas MacArthur (destined for later fame in World War II and Korea) as one of the respondents. In less than sixty days the commission had created a two-volume report of nearly 500 pages on the six basic questions (Commission on National Aid, 1914). The report included the following recommendations:

- Funding support for precollege level programs in public schools.
- Federal aid designed to prepare students over the age of fourteen for employment.

- Support for three types of schools: full-time schools, with 50 percent of the time in vocational instruction; part-time schools for employed youth; and evening schools for adult workers.
- Federal grants for training vocational teachers.
- Grants for paying part of the salaries of vocational teachers.
- Funds for vocational teachers to conduct research activities.
- Public supervision of schools receiving federal funds.
- Assurance that schools receiving federal grants are less than college grade.
- Development of some form of administrative structure to supervise grants on a statewide basis.
- A federal board to oversee distribution of federal grants.

Committee on Vocational Education, 1928–1929

This was the only national committee during that time period not appointed by the president of the United States. The committee did not function as its sponsors intended it should, and soon after its appointment it was phased out.

National Advisory Committee on Education, 1929–1931

This committee was appointed by President Hoover and the Department of the Interior. The first meeting resulted in the creation of a conference, where recommendations were made to:

- Amend the Smith-Hughes Act of 1917 and all subsequent acts dealing with vocational education by repealing those provisions that require state matching of federal funds.
- Abolish the Federal Board for Vocational Education, transferring its remaining functions and staff to the proposed Department of Education.

Advisory Committee on Education, 1936–1938

President Roosevelt appointed a group of twenty-four members to work on this committee. Dr. Floyd W. Reeves served as the committee chairperson. The president requested that the committee conduct a study focusing on the following three areas: (1) the existing programs for federal aid to vocational education; (2) the existing relationship of training to academic education and to prevailing economic and social conditions; and (3) the extent to which there was a need for expanded programs in vocational education. This advisory committee made six recommendations:

- to review the basic statutes with the specific intent of removing restraining provisions,
- to consolidate all federal funds for vocational education of less than senior college grade into a single fund,

- to transfer to the states the determination of educational activities deemed vocational,
- to continue and expand plant training programs,
- to provide for those states that have separate schools for Blacks to receive a just and equitable share of federal funds, and
- to establish a minimum age of seventeen for instruction designed to prepare for a specific trade, and the age of fourteen for participation in all special fields of education (but this could be waived for club work for rural boys and girls) (National Advisory Committee on Education, 1938, pp. 206–207).

Panel of Consultants on Vocational Education, 1961–1962

Each year a committee of the Congress of the United States conducts hearings on appropriations for all government agencies. These hearings are held to decide if adjustments of appropriations for any activity of the federal government are necessary, and the committee's conclusions are embodied in a recommended budget. During the hearings on the federal budget for the fiscal year 1961, there was a recommendation to reduce the amount of funds allocated to vocational education by $2 million (Roberts, 1971).

Vocational education had major issues to resolve, and a reduction in expenditure of federal funds was scarcely an appropriate aid toward meeting the required vocational adjustments. Roberts (1971) suggested that federal aid for vocational education was ill-timed because of social, economic, and technological changes. The reduction in the appropriation was inconsistent with the needs of the nation, and the committee restored the $2 million to the budget (Barlow, 1976). This led to the appointment of a task force to make a comprehensive study of vocational education.

During the presidential election year of 1960 the American Vocation Association sought the opinions of the candidates about vocational education. Barlow (1976) reported that both John F. Kennedy and Richard M. Nixon voiced their support for vocational education. President Kennedy, in a special message to Congress on February 20, 1961, empowered the creation of a panel of consultants to study vocational education:

> The National Vocational Education Acts first enacted by Congress in 1917 and subsequently amended have provided a program of training for industry, agriculture, and other occupational areas. The basic purpose of our vocational education effort is sound and sufficiently broad to provide a basis for meeting future needs. However, the technological changes which have occurred in all occupations call for a review and reevaluation of these acts, with a view toward their modernization.
>
> To that end, I am requesting the Secretary of Health, Education and Welfare to convene an advisory body drawn from the educational profession, labor, industry, and agriculture as well as the lay public together with representatives from the Departments of Agriculture and Labor to

be charged with the responsibility of reviewing and evaluating the current National Vocational Education Acts, and making recommendations for improving and redirecting the program. (U.S. Congress, 1961, 107, Part 2, 2391)

This panel consisted of twenty-five members representing vocational education, business, labor, education, government, and the press. The panel was chaired by Dr. Benjamin C. Willis, superintendent of schools for the city of Chicago. The panel was responsible for reviewing and evaluating vocational education with the objective of improving and redirecting the programs offered. The panel released its report in the spring of 1963 in "Education for a Changing World of Work." This report served as a basis for modernizing and improving job training, and it set the stage for the passage of the Vocational Education Act of 1963.

The panel's general recommendations were that in a changing world of work, vocational education must:

1. Offer training opportunities to the 210 million noncollege graduates who would enter the labor market in the 1960s.

2. Provide training or retraining for the millions of workers whose skills and technical knowledge must be updated as well as those whose jobs will disappear due to increasing efficiency, automation, or economic change.

3. Meet the critical need for highly skilled craftworkers and technicians through education during and after the high school years.

4. Expand the vocational and technical programs consistent with employment possibilities and national economic needs.

5. Make educational opportunities equally available to all regardless of race, sex, scholastic aptitude, or place of residence (Panel of Consultants on Vocational Education, 1963).

The panel suggested that federal aid to specific occupational categories be discontinued and support increased for five clientele groups and services: (1) high school youth (expansion of present occupational programs); (2) high-school-age youth with academic, socioeconomic, or other handicaps; (3) post–high-school opportunities; (4) unemployed or underemployed youth; and (5) services to assure quality (instructional materials, occupational counseling, and various forms of research).

National Advisory Council on Vocational Education, 1967

This council grew out of the 1963 Vocational Education Act and was required by that act to make a report on vocational education every five years. The National Advisory Council on Vocational Education (NACVE) was appointed in 1967 by President Lyndon B. Johnson. The focus of this committee was the enlargement of the concept of vocational training and the necessity to more effectively integrate the poor, unemployed, and underemployed into the economic system. Dr. Martin Essex of Ohio chaired the twelve-member advisory council, and its report was released in 1968.

The first report of NACVE stated that the majority of Americans felt vocational education was designed for somebody else's children. It further accused the nation of intellectual snobbery where vocational education was concerned (Calhoun and Finch, 1982). "Clearly, in the minds of some," Leighbody (1972) states, "the goal of vocational education is to meet the needs of those who are less fortunate economically, socially, and intellectually" (p. 9).

The report of the 1967 Advisory Council concluded that vocational education is not a separate discipline within education; rather, it is a basic objective of all education and must be a basic element of each person's education (Leighbody, 1972).

Association for Career and Technical Education

The National Society for Vocational Education met in Cleveland, Ohio, December 3–5, 1925, for its nineteenth annual convention. The name of the society was changed to the American Vocational Association (AVA), the new constitution was adopted, and the proposed amalgamation with the Vocational Education Association of the Middle West was endorsed. As president of the newly formed American Vocational Association, the Cleveland convention elected Edwin A. Lee, director of the Division of Vocational Education, University of California, whose plan had stimulated the new union. The American Vocational Association (1926) stated that:

> Lee's vigorous acceptance of the responsibility inspired confidence among those who did not know him before. They know now that they have a vital force at the head of the new organization; and those who have known him longer can vouch for the fact that he is an efficient administrative officer. (p. 208)

The spirit and morale of the convention delegates seemed suddenly to be lifted by their act of amalgamation. Dennis (1926), who was to become executive secretary, wrote:

> We find ourselves in a situation where leaders in vocational education have a fine faith in each other and a greater belief in the great work in which we are all endeavoring to do our part. (p. 4)

The final step in the amalgamation awaited only the action of the Vocational Association of the Middle West. This action was taken unanimously at the Des Moines Convention, March 17–20, 1926. No regret was expressed concerning the demise of the old organization; only the hope and promise of the future occupied the attention and thoughts of the delegates. Charles A. Prosser addressed the convention on the topic "The Magic Chance of Vocational Education."

> If you want the magic chance get in on the new movement. That's the chance in manual training; that's the chance in vocational education. Manual training, vocational education and art education have made more progress than any other departments of education. (Bennett, 1926, p. 353)

The first convention of the new organization—the American Vocational Association—was held December 2–4, 1926, in Louisville, Kentucky.

From AVA to ACTE

What's in a name? Shakespeare states, "That which we call a rose by any other name would smell as sweet." In an effort to mold its image around the portrait of modern workforce education, on December 13, 1998, the American Vocational Association changed its name to the Association for Career and Technical Education (ACTE).

The assembly of delegates at the association's annual convention in New Orleans approved the name change by a vote of 333–67, an 86 percent favorable margin (Association for Career and Technical Education, 1999a). This name change was in response to the concern about the image of vocational education and the use of the term "vocational" in the name of the association. The entire process began in early 1995 when the board of directors began to assess the views of members, prospective members, and other stakeholders. This process included focus groups, surveys, communications, and open forums. Some reasons for the name change are listed as follows:

- Trying to change people's views of the term "vocational" was ineffective. No matter what was said, "vocational" was viewed as noncollege-bound training meant for someone else's children.

- Nonmembers cited the use of the word "vocational" in the name of the organization (AVA) as a major reason they did not become members.

- Policy makers, businesspeople, parents, students, educators, and the media generally have a negative opinion about the word "vocational," associating the word with outdated or lower-level skills and programs of the past.

- Many state departments had changed their names and no longer used the word "vocational" in their titles.

State associations across the country have taken heed to the changing times and the need to have a name that reflects modern career and technical education. The following states have adopted "Association for Career and Technical Education" as of August 25, 1999: Alabama, Colorado, Georgia, Illinois, Indiana, Kentucky, Mississippi, Missouri, Nebraska, Nevada, New Mexico, North Carolina, North Dakota, Pennsylvania, South Carolina, South Dakota, Utah, Washington, West Virginia, and Wyoming (Association for Career and Technical Education, 1999b). On January 1, 2000, the Ohio state association became the Ohio Association for Career and Technical Education. New York changed its association name to New York Occupational Association.

Career fairs play an essential role in the promotion of CTE programs and selected benefits provided by ACTE.

Objectives and Purposes of ACTE

The Association for Career and Technical Education is a national organization for CTE professionals with state affiliates representing some 40,000 members composed primarily of CTE teachers, supervisors, teacher educators, counselors, administrators, special support personnel, and graduate students. The mission of the ACTE is to provide educational leadership in developing a competitive workforce.

The multi-faceted purpose of ACTE is to:

- Assume and maintain active national leadership in the promotion of career and technical education.
- Render service to state or local communities in stabilizing and promoting CTE.
- Provide a national open forum for the discussion of all questions involved in CTE.
- Unite all the CTE interests of the country through membership representative of the entire country (American Vocational Association, 1986).

The major objectives of ACTE include:

- *Professional development*—Encourage career development, professional involvement, and leadership among members.
- *Program improvement*—Foster excellence in career and technical education.
- *Policy development*—Advocate national policy to benefit CTE.
- *Marketing*—Marketing of career and technical education (American Vocational Association, 1992; American Vocational Association, 1995).

The Association for Career and Technical Education is composed of the following divisions:

- Administration
- Agricultural Education
- Business Education
- Employment and Training
- Guidance
- Health Occupations Education
- Family and Consumer Sciences
- Marketing Education
- New and Related Services (including an international division)
- Special Needs
- Technical Education
- Technology Education
- Trade and Industrial Education

ACTE holds an annual convention, usually in December. The convention city is selected on a rotating basis so that the meeting is held in various parts of the nation. ACTE publishes *Techniques* (formerly the *Vocational Education Journal*) monthly, September through June with a combined November/December issue. The name change to *Techniques* went into effect in September 1996. Other publications of ACTE include: *Career Tech Update* (the newsletter that replaced *Vocational Education Weekly*), *School-to-Work Reporter*, and *Legislative Update*.

ACTE maintains its national headquarters at 1410 King St., Alexandria, VA 22314 (http://www.acteonline.org). The leadership of ACTE includes an executive director, a president, vice presidents representing the divisions of ACTE, and five regional vice presidents. Each state is entitled to send a number of delegates to the annual convention based on the state's percentage of national membership. Official business of delegates is consummated in the meeting of the house delegates at the annual convention.

Summary

- Shortly after the approval of the Smith-Hughes Act in 1917, America became involved in World War I. Other major wars that have influenced vocational education include World War II, the Korean conflict, and the Vietnam War. Two major benefits from the effects of war training were: (1) the country became conscious of the need for vocational education, and (2) the philosophy was advanced that vocational education was a part of preparation for living needed by all normal individuals rather than a device for keeping youth in school or for taking care of delinquents.

- The National Association of Manufacturers was organized in response to a period of economic depression. The NAM was keenly interested in securing an adequate supply of trained workers and reducing the power of the growing labor movement.

- Public discussion and interest in the educational needs of the labor force were stimulated by the report of the Douglas Commission. Governor Douglas of Massachusetts, responding to a legislative mandate, appointed a Commission on Vocational Education composed of nine representatives from manufacturing, agriculture, education, and labor to investigate the need for vocational education, to determine the extent of existing programs meeting this need, and to make recommendations regarding how to modify existing programs to serve a vocational purpose.

- A number of separate national panels, committees, and commissions were appointed to study vocational education intensively. Most of these groups were created to find ways of improving the status of vocational education. The panels were to study the existing condition of vocational education and recommend what changes were needed.

- Founded in 1926, Association for Career and Technical Education (formerly AVA) is committed to helping members grow personally and professionally, and to improving CTE programs nationwide. ACTE's mission is to provide educational leadership in developing a competitive workforce. ACTE seeks to provide the kind of foresight and direction America needs to develop a productive, competitive workforce and to position our nation as a leader in the global marketplace.

- Throughout World War II, vocational education served the country well by maintaining a well-trained war industry workforce and by assisting in preinduction training. The nation's farmers and homemakers also aided the war effort at home through their dedication to producing goods and services. However, when the war was won, there were new challenges for vocational education.

- In an effort to mold its image around the portrait of modern workforce education, the American Vocational Association changed its name to Association for Career and Technical Education on December 13, 1998.

Discussion Questions and Activities

1. Extrapolate the activities of the Federal Board for Vocational Education in training people for World War I.

2. Explain how the War Production Training Program of World War II was organized.

3. Justify the need for the types of training that were provided in the World War II War Production Training Program.

4. Compare and contrast the activities of the following organizations:

    a. the Douglas Commission

    b. the National Society for the Promotion of Industrial Education (NSPIE)

    c. the Commission on National Aid to Vocational Education

5. Extrapolate the recommendations of the Advisory Committee on Education.

6. Explain the role of the Association for Career and Technical Education in the development and growth of CTE.

7. View the following video: *The Commission on National Aid to Vocational Education: A reenactment of the 1914 hearing* (see the Recommended Educational Media Resources section below).

8. Discuss the impact of study panels in the development of career and technical education.

For Exploration

9. Determine the influence that war training had on vocational education.

10. Assess the impact of the Servicemen's Readjustment Act on the development and growth of vocational education.

11. Describe the influence of career and technical education on the training of women in today's military industry.

12. All but a few state departments have changed their names and no longer use the word "vocational" in their titles. Document the history of the use of the word "vocational" by your state department organization.

Instructor-Coordinated Activity

13. The events of September 11, 2001, changed our nation and our world. Career and technical educators had to deal with their own shock, fear, and sadness while also helping students in schools to cope with the horror. Conduct a panel discussion from a variety of perspectives on the impact of September 11 (acts of terrorism) and what it means to career and technical education.

Recommended Educational Media Resources

- "The GI Bill," *The News Hour with Jim Lehrer* [Date: 07/04/00, MLN 6802]

    View online at http://pbs-newshour/video (click on "Streaming Video" link).

- *Patriot voices* (Show #2503)
- *Patriot soldier, two wars* (Show # 2505)
  Tony Brown Productions
  2214 Frederick Douglass Blvd., Suite 124
  New York, New York 10036
  Web site: http://www.tonybrown.com/booksandtapes.html
  E-mail: mail @tbol.net
  (718) 264-2226

- *September 11*
  American Federation of Teachers
  555 New Jersey Ave., N.W.
  Washington, DC 20001-2079
  1-202-879-4400
  http://www.aft.org/pubs-reports/american_teacher/sept02/911.html.

References and Additional Reading

American Vocational Association (1926). The A.V.A. *Industrial Education Magazine*, *27*(7), 208.

———. (1986). AVA at 60: The past is prologue. *Vocational Education Journal, 61*(8), 23.

———. (1992). American Vocational Association annual report 1991. *Vocational Education Journal, 67*(1), 31.

———. (1995). Inside AVA. *Vocational Education Journal, 70*(2), 13.

Association for Career and Technical Education (1999a). Inside ACTE. *Techniques, 74*(2), 51.

———. (1999b). Inside ACTE. *Techniques, 74*(8), 62.

———. (2002). Answering the call to duty. *Techniques, 77*(2), 26-31.

Barlow, M. L. (1976). 200 years of vocational education 1776–1976. *American Vocational Journal, 51*(5), 21–108.

Bauder, W. T. (1918, September). Training the fighting mechanics. *Manual Training Magazine, 20*(1), 1–10.

Bennett, C. A. (1926). The merger wins unanimously at Des Moines. *Industrial Education Magazine, 28*(11), 353.

Calhoun, C. C., and Finch, A. V. (1982). *Vocational education: Concepts and operations.* Belmont, CA: Wadsworth.

Commission on National Aid to Vocational Education (1914). *Annual report.* Washington, DC: U.S. Government Printing Office.

Degen, M. L. (1974). *The history of the women's peace party.* Baltimore, MD: John Hopkins University Press.

Dennis, L. H. (1926, February). The Cleveland convention. *American Vocational Journal, 1*(1), 4.

———. (1950, February). Vocational education for American youth. *American Vocational Journal, 25*(2), 5.

Federal Board for Vocational Education (1917). *First annual report*, p. 20. Washington, DC: U.S. Government Printing Office.

———. (1918). *Bulletin number 2*, p. 3. Washington, DC: U.S. Government Printing Office.

———. (1919). *Third annual report*, p. 66. Washington, DC: U.S. Government Printing Office.

Goldstein, J. S. (2002). *International relations: Brief edition*. Boston: Addison Wesley Longman.

Hawkins, L. S., Prosser, C. A., and Wright, J. C. (1951). *Development of vocational education*. Chicago: Harper and Row.

Leighbody, G. B. (1972). *Vocational education in America's schools: Major issues of the 1970s* (p. 9). Chicago: American Technical Society.

McCarthy, J. A. (1950). *Vocational education: America's greatest resource* (p. 15). Chicago: American Technical Society.

National Advisory Committee on Education (1938). *Annual report* (pp. 206–207). Washington, DC: U.S. Government Printing Office.

Panel of Consultants on Vocational Education (1963). *Education for a changing world of work*. Washington, DC: Office of Education, U.S. Department of Health, Education, and Welfare.

Reese, S. (2007). Manufacturing success. *Techniques, 82*(3), 14–16.

Roberts, R. W. (1957). *Vocational and practical arts education*. 1st ed. New York: Harper and Row.

———. (1971). *Vocational and practical arts education*. 3rd ed. New York: Harper and Row.

Seidel, J. J. (1951, May). Vocational education in the national mobilization. *American Vocational Journal, 26*(5), 5, 7.

Stone, J. R., III (2005). The neglected majority—revisited. *Journal of Career and Technical Education, 21*(2). Retrieved October 17, 2006, from http://scholar.lib.vt.edu/ejournals/JCTE/v21n2/stone.html.

Thompson, J. E. (1973). *Foundations of vocational education: Social and philosophical concepts*. Englewood Cliffs, NJ: Prentice-Hall.

U.S. Congress (1961). *Journal of Proceedings, 107*, Part 2, 2391. Washington, DC: U.S. Government Printing Office.

Venn, G. (1964). *Man, education and work*. Washington, DC: American Council on Education.

Walter, R. A. (1993). Development of vocational education. In C. Anderson and L. C. Rampp (Eds.), *Vocational education in the 1990s, II: A sourcebook for strategies, methods, and materials* (pp. 1–20). Ann Arbor, MI: Prakken Publishing.

Wirth, A. G. (1972). *Education in the technological society*. Scranton, PA: Intext Educational.

Legislative History and the Changing Workforce

In the last quarter of the nineteenth century as America moved to establish public secondary schools, there were battles over the role of classical and practical education programs. With more students going to school, the narrow classical curriculum did not satisfy the proponents of an expanded practical education curriculum.

In 1905, proponents of vocational education argued that a broader curriculum was needed to prepare people for the new industrial age. They wanted youth and adults to have a chance for better careers. They were unhappy that only 8 percent of youth graduated from high school, and almost all male graduates went to college while female graduates went into white-collar work (Plawin, 1992). These advocates also were concerned about America's ability to compete in world agricultural and industrial markets. Eventually they developed a coalition to press for federal legislation.

Chapter five is organized according to the legislative history of career and technical education and today's changing workforce.

Pre-1917 Laws and Bills

Career and technical education has a long history in America. Since the Land Ordinance of 1785 and Northwest Ordinance of 1787, the federal government has demonstrated continued interest in the education of its citizenry. Although 1917 marked the first significant legislation relating to vocational education, several pieces of supportive legislation were passed earlier. The most significant of these pre-1917 laws include the following:

- *Ordinance of 1785.* Congress required that certain western lands be divided into thirty-six sections, with the sixteenth section set aside for the support of education (Fitzpatrick, 1933).
- *Northwest Ordinance of 1787.* Congress specified (Thorpe, 1909): "Religion morality, and knowledge being necessary to good government and the happiness of mankind, schools and the means of education shall be forever encouraged" (p. 961). By the time that Ohio, the

first state in these new western territories, was admitted to the Union, the practice of setting aside the sixteenth section of each township to support education was firmly established. Without entering directly into education of various states, through these two acts the federal government expressed an interest in the education of the nation's citizens (Calhoun and Finch, 1982).

- *1887 Hatch Act*. Provided $15,000 to each state for the development of agricultural experiment stations.

- *The Davis and Dolliver-Davis Bills*. In 1907 Representative Charles R. Davis of Minnesota introduced his first bill providing federal aid for industrial education. This bill proposed to allocate federal funds to agricultural high schools for teaching agriculture and home economics, and to secondary schools in urban communities for teaching mechanical arts and home economics. Senator Dolliver introduced a revised version of the Davis Bill into the U.S. Senate in 1910. However, the National Society for the Promotion of Industrial Education voiced objections to the Dolliver-Davis Bill. Senator Dolliver died in 1910, and friends did not seek the bill's passage but instead concentrated on the Page Bill of 1911 (Roberts, 1957).

- *The Page Bill*. Carroll S. Page, a U.S. Senator from Vermont, was prominent among the early federal supporters of vocational education. According to True (1929), in March 1911 Senator Page introduced a bill proposing federal appropriations to the states. Roberts (1971) points out that the Page Bill provided for a division of funds in states that maintained separate schools for Blacks in proportion to the population of the two races. The bill also provided for evening schools. The Page Bill was amended in the Senate in 1912.

Page felt keenly that the actual preparation for the majority of farm, shop, and home tasks should begin in the high school. Page was unsuccessful in getting congressional action on his proposed legislation. When it became evident that the Page Bill would not pass, the National Society for the Promotion of Industrial Education and other interested individuals suggested that Congress establish a commission on national aid for vocational education (Miller, 1985).

Authors of Federal Legislation for Career and Technical Education

Smith, Hughes, George, Perkins . . . the names read like a roster of CTE's hall of fame. Their leadership has led to some of the most important pieces of legislation in career and technical education in this country.

Hoke Smith and Dudley Hughes

In January 1914, Congress authorized the president to appoint a commission to study national aid for vocational education. On December 7, 1915, Senator Hoke Smith of Georgia, committee chairman, introduced Senate Bill 703 to promote vocational education; to cooperate with the states in promotion of such education in agriculture, trades, and industries and in the preparation of teachers of vocational subjects; and to appropriate money and regulate its expenditure (Plawin, 1992).

On February 10, 1916, Representative Dudley M. Hughes of Georgia, also a member of the commission, introduced similar legislation in House Bill 11250. The House Committee on Education, which quickly approved it, filed a report that stated:

> It is especially designed to prepare workers for the most common occupations in which a great mass of our people find useful employment . . . to give training of a secondary grade to persons more than 14 years of age for . . . employment in the trades and industries, in agriculture, in commerce and commercial pursuits, and in callings based upon . . . home economics. (Plawin, 1992, p. 31)

President Woodrow Wilson signed the Smith-Hughes Vocational Education Act into law on February 23, 1917. Thus, these two Georgians became partners, sponsored the Smith-Hughes Act, and gave the nation what has proved to be one of its greatest assets, vocational education.

Walter F. George

It is significant in the legislative history of vocational education that in six Senate terms, Walter F. George sponsored every federal act for vocational education since the Smith-Hughes law of 1917. These are the George-Reed, George-Ellzey, George-Deen, and George-Barden Acts. Senator George's efforts culminated in vocational education funds totaling more than $40,000,000 for fiscal 1958 alone. According to Mobley (1957), "When George of Georgia spoke, his fellow senators—and the world—listened with respectful attention."

Senator George suggested that he never thought vocational training should interfere with a well-rounded academic course of study, but that the two could well be brought together, beginning at the secondary level—for, after all, he added, "most of our people do not go to college anyhow." He then continued:

> I don't mind saying that I got very great inspiration from reading about the work of Booker T. Washington, a famous African American educator. Booker T. Washington had advanced knowledge of the practical, purely utilitarian side of schooling. His method and his pretty [sic] well-grounded belief was that practical education was the way up for his race. (Williams, 1950, p. 3)

Carl D. Perkins

In the decade of the 1950s, the baby boomers entered school and the so-called "space race" began. The turbulent 1960s were punctuated by civil rights marches, drug addiction, assassinations, and the Vietnam War. During this time Representative Carl D. Perkins of Kentucky emerged as a strong advocate for vocational education. He served as the primary force in writing, introducing, and supporting legislation that became the Vocational Education Acts of 1963 and 1984. The latter was named the Carl D. Perkins Vocational Education Act (Baker, 1991).

Major Vocational Legislation 1917–1984

The Constitution of the United States makes no provision for federal support or control of education. However, the federal government has long considered career and technical education to be in the national interest and has provided federal legislation in support of CTE. Beginning with the Morrill Act in 1862, which established land-grant colleges aimed at preparing people for the "agricultural and mechanical arts," the federal government has had an enduring interest in vocational education (Wrench, Wrench, and Galloway, 1988). The following descriptions highlight the major provisions of these important pieces of legislation.

Smith-Hughes Act (Public Law 64-347)

Situation—World War I (The Germans had demonstrated superior vocational preparation.)

Study Group—Commission on National Aid to Vocational Education, 1914

The Smith-Hughes Act of 1917 was the first vocational education act, and it contained several specific elements that contributed to the isolation of vocational education from other parts of the comprehensive high school curriculum. For example, in order to receive federal funds under Smith-Hughes, each state was required to establish a state board for vocational education. This requirement led, in some states, to the establishment of a board separate from the State Board of Education. Thus, two separate governmental structures could exist at the state level. This in turn fostered the notion of vocational education as separate from academic education. Lynch (2000) reported that the Smith-Hughes Act was influenced by a variety of social, economic, and political forces; its primary objective was to offer youth an alternative to the general curriculum that existed at that particular period of time.

The Smith-Hughes Act tended to promote a segregated curriculum, with agriculture, homemaking, and trade and industrial education segments separated not only from academic programs, but from all other vocational programs as well. The impact of this separation has been felt through subsequent decades in the development of separate training programs, separate teacher organizations, and separate student organizations.

The Federal Board for Vocational Education created by the Smith-Hughes Act consisted of the following members:

- secretaries of commerce, agriculture, and labor
- the commission of education
- three appointed citizens (Plawin, 1992)

The Smith-Hughes Act was to have been a grant in perpetuity. However, during July of 1997, the Smith-Hughes Act was repealed.

George-Reed Act of 1929 (Public Law 70-702)

The George-Reed Act, introduced by Senator Walter F. George and Representative Daniel A. Reed of New York, authorized an increase of $1 million annually for four years (1930–1934) to expand vocational education in agriculture and home economics. The administration of agricultural education and home economics were similar to the provisions of the Smith-Hughes Act with the following exceptions: (a) agricultural education funds were allotted on the basis of farm population rather than rural population, (b) home economics education funds were allotted on the basis of rural population rather than urban, and (c) the George-Reed Act was an authorization for funds whereas Smith-Hughes Act was an appropriation. The George-Reed Act was approved by President Calvin Coolidge on February 5, 1929.

George-Ellzey Act of 1934 (Public Law 73-245)

The George-Ellzey Act was sponsored by Senator George and Representative Lawrence F. Ellzey of Mississippi. The act authorized $3 million annually for three years, to be apportioned equally in agriculture, home economics, trade, and industrial education. In a sense, it replaced the temporary George-Reed Act. The George-Ellzey Act was signed by President Franklin D. Roosevelt on May 21, 1934.

George-Deen Act of 1936 (Public Law 74-673)

Situation—Recovering from the impact of the Great Depression
Study Group—Advisory Committee on Education 1936–1938

The George-Deen Act, authored by Senator George and Representative Braswell Dean of Georgia, authorized approximately $14 million a year for vocational education in agriculture, home economics, trade, and industrial education. The George-Deen Act was significant because marketing occupations were recognized for the first time. Money was also authorized for teacher education programs. Unlike the Smith-Hughes Act, it was an authorization, not a permanent act. Mobley (1956) cites the late Dr. Lindley H. Dennis, then American Vocational Association Executive Secretary, for planning the strategy and organizing the support for this legislative victory. The George-Deen Act was signed by President Franklin D. Roosevelt on June 8, 1936.

George-Barden Act of 1946 (Public Law 79-586)

The George-Barden Act was authored by Senator George and Representative Graham A. Barden of North Carolina as an amendment to the George-Deen Act. It authorized a larger appropriation from $14 million to $29 million annually. One of the major factors contributing to this legislation was the need to provide a means for thousands of returning World War II veterans to acquire employable skills in a rapidly expanding economy (Calhoun and Finch, 1982). This was a time of post-war industrial boom, when American needed cars instead of tanks. Mason, Furtado, and Husted (1989) cite the following major provisions of the George-Barden Act:

1. This act authorized $10 million for agricultural education, to be allocated among the states on the basis of farm population.
2. Authority was given in the act for the expenditure of funds in support of two youth organizations in agriculture: the Future Farmers of America and the New Farmers of America.
3. The act authorized $8 million for home economics, the basis of allotment being the rural population of the state.
4. It also authorized $8 million for trade and industrial education, to be allocated among the states on the basis of nonfarm population.
5. Funds for marketing occupations were limited to support for part-time (cooperative) and evening courses for employed workers—no preparatory courses in other fields were authorized.

The act provided that after June 30, 1951, not more than 10 percent of these funds could be used for the purchase or acquisition of equipment. The George-Barden Act was signed by President Harry S. Truman on August 1, 1946.

George-Barden Amendments of 1956 (Public Law 84-911)

In 1956, in response to the shortage of qualified nurses, the George-Barden Act was amended to add practical nursing ($5 million) and fishery occupation ($375,000) to a list of approved areas of instruction (Venn, 1964). Area vocational programs were provided with an annual authorization until 1962.

National Defense Education Act of 1958 (Public Law 85-864)

The National Defense Education Act of 1958 was passed during the Cold War period following the Soviet Union's successful launch of *Sputnik I*, the first human-made earth satellite, into space in 1957. *Sputnik* installed a sense of fear among Americans that U.S. technology could not compete with that of the U.S.S.R. This fear, coupled with the added tension caused by a recession, resulted in a fiercely competitive desire to reform the U.S. educational system, particularly in the sciences.

This was the first act to stress the importance of science, mathematics, foreign language, and technical competencies. The focus of this act was on providing vocational training for youths, adults, and older persons, including related instruction for apprentices, designed to fit them for employment as technicians or skilled workers in scientific or technical fields.

Following is a summary of the major provisions of the National Defense Education Act.

- Assistance to state and local school systems for strengthening instruction in science, mathematics, foreign languages, and other critical subjects.

- Improvement of state statistical services.

- Improvement of guidance counseling, testing services, and training institutes.

- Funds for higher education, student loans, and fellowships.

- Funds for experimentation and dissemination of information on more effective use of television, motion picture, and related media for educational purposes.

- Funds to maintain vocational education for technical occupations, such as data processing, necessary to the national defense.

Manpower Development Training Act of 1962 (Public Law 87-415)

In 1962 there was fear that automation and technological change would cause unemployment among heads of families. According to Evans and Herr (1978), the Manpower Development Training Act was created to ease this dislocation by authorizing funds for training and retraining of unemployed and underemployed adults. A large sum of money ($370 million) was authorized to be spent over a three-year period.

This act was a milestone in providing training for those who were economically disadvantaged and were not being served in regular vocational programs. Eligible trainees and potential job openings were identified by the state employment service. State vocational education departments contracted for the courses and experiences that matched the identified needs. Preference for retraining was given to unemployed and underemployed workers who had at least three years experience in gainful employment. A unique feature was the provision for payment of subsistence benefits during training.

Vocational Education Act of 1963 (Public Law 88-210)

Situation—A reaction to too much emphasis on service and unemployment
Study Group—Panel of consultants on vocational education

The year 1963 was the most significant in the legislative history of vocational education since passage of the 1917 Smith-Hughes Act. As a result of a 1963 study ("Education for a Changing World of Work"), the Perkins-Morse Bill, better known as the Vocational Education Act of 1963, was signed into law by President Lyndon B. Johnson, marking a new era for vocational education.

The purposes of the act were varied. However, its major goals were to maintain, extend, and improve existing programs of vocational education and to provide part-time employment for youth who needed the earnings to continue their schooling on a full-time basis. The intent of the act was to ensure that persons of all ages in all communities would have ready access to vocational training or retraining of high quality, suited to their personal needs, interests, and abilities. The law also stipulated that funds be used for persons who have academic, socioeconomic, or other handicaps that prevent them from succeeding in a regular vocational education program. Mason, Furtado, and Husted (1989) reported that for the first time, vocational education was mandated to meet the needs of individual students and not just the employment needs of industry.

This legislation did not stipulate funds for the various vocational education services; instead it stipulated them for particular types and ages of persons. Ninety percent of the authorized funds were to be allotted to the states on the basis of formulas. According to Calhoun and Finch (1982), the formula that was used required that 50 percent of the allotted funds be used for the 15 to 19 age group, 20 percent for the 20 to 25 age group, 15 percent for the 25 to 65 age group, and 5 percent for all groups regardless of age.

Vocational Education Amendments of 1968 (Public Law 90-576)

As a result of an NACVE study, the Vocational Education Act of 1963 was amended in October of 1968; these changes are referred to as the Vocational Education Amendments of 1968. These amendments replaced all previous federal legislation for vocational education except the Smith-Hughes Act, which was retained for sentimental reasons as the first legislation passed by the federal government for secondary vocational education.

The purpose of the 1968 amendments was to provide access for all citizens to appropriate training and retraining, which was similar to the purpose of the Vocational Education Act of 1963. The major differences were that the 1968 amendments emphasized vocational education in postsecondary schools and broadened the definition of vocational education to bring it closer to general education. The Vocational Education Act of 1963 authorized the appropriation of millions of dollars for vocational education in an attempt to find solutions to the nation's social and economic problems in a time of social and political violence and unrest.

Under the amendments, federal funds could be used for:

- High school and postsecondary students.
- Those who have completed or left high school.
- Those in the labor market in need of retraining.
- Those who have academic, socioeconomic, or other obstacles.
- Those who are mentally retarded, deaf, or otherwise disabled.
- Construction of area vocational school facilities.
- Vocational guidance for all persons mentioned.

- Ancillary services (preparation of state plans, administration, evaluation of programs, teacher education, etc.)
- Training in private schools under contract with public schools.

Comprehensive Employment Training Act of 1973 (Public Law 93-203)

After a decade, the Manpower Development Training Act was replaced by the Comprehensive Employment Training Act (CETA). The principal effect of this new act was to transfer decision making from Washington to local and state governments (Evans and Herr, 1978).

One of the unique features of CETA was its funding pattern. The act established the delivery concept of a prime sponsor. The occupational education, training, and other employment services programs were conducted in conjunction with local units of government known as CETA prime sponsors. Prime sponsors provided a variety of employment and training services by contracting with approved public and private agencies.

In general, the special provisions of the Comprehensive Employment Training Act included:

1. Consolidation of previous labor and public service programs;
2. Authorization of funds for employment counseling, supportive services, classroom training, training on the job, work experience, and public service employment; and
3. Incorporation of essential principles of revenue sharing, giving state and local governments more control over use of funds and determination of programs.

Vocational Education Amendments of 1976 (Public Law 94-482)

Congress added several new clauses to its declaration of purpose in the 1976 vocational amendments. One new purpose for the authorization of funds was to ensure that states improved their planning by involving a wide range of interested agencies and making use of all available resources for vocational education. With the advent of the women's liberation movement, another purpose was to assist states in overcoming sex discrimination and sex stereotyping in vocational education programs.

The Vocational Education Amendments of 1976 extended and increased funding of the Vocational Education Act of 1963 and the Vocational Education Amendments of 1968. The major thrusts of the Vocational Education Amendments of 1976 were to:

1. Extend, improve, and, where necessary, maintain existing programs of vocational education;
2. Develop new vocational education programs; and
3. Provide part-time employment for youths who need the earnings to continue their training on a full-time basis.

With these purposes identified for a major portion of the legislation, the Vocational Education Amendments of 1976 revised the preceding acts to provide for continued support in the form of state grants, supplemented by additional categories that reflect priorities identified by Congress. These added categories included vocational guidance and counseling, pre-service and in-service training for personnel, renovation and remodeling of facilities, and grants to overcome sex bias.

Job Training Partnership Act of 1982 (Public Law 97-300)

The Job Training Partnership Act (JTPA) replaced CETA, which expired on September 30, 1982. JTPA was intended to establish programs to prepare youth and unskilled adults for entry into the labor force and to afford job training to economically disadvantaged individuals facing critical barriers to employment.

The statute enlarged the role of state governments and private industry in federal job training programs, imposed performance standards, limited support services, and created a new program of retraining displaced workers (Mason, Furtado, and Husted, 1989).

Carl D. Perkins Vocational Education Act of 1984 (Public Law 98-524)

The Carl D. Perkins Vocational Education Act of 1984 amended the Vocational Education Act of 1963 and replaced the amendments of 1968 and 1976. The act consisted of two major goals, one economic and one social. The economic goal of the act was to improve the skills of the labor force and prepare adults for job opportunities. The social goal was to provide equal opportunities for adults in the vocational education. The act changed the emphasis of federal funding in vocational education from primarily expansion to program improvement and at-risk populations.

Reform and Vocational Education

Education reforms began in the early 1980s and have focused on secondary education, prompted by concern about the nation's declining competitiveness in the international market, the relatively poor performance of American students on tests of educational achievement (both nationally and internationally), and complaints from the business community about the low level of skills and abilities found in high school graduates entering the workforce.

A review of the literature on education reforms finds a consensus that there have been two waves of reform since 1980—both focused on secondary education (Asche, 1993). The first wave, sometimes characterized as academic reform, called for increased effort from the current education system: more academic course requirements for high school graduation, more stringent college entrance requirements, longer school days and years, and an emphasis on standards and testing for both students and teachers.

Beginning in the mid-1980s, a second wave of school reform arose, based in part on the belief that the first reform effort was not thorough enough to improve education for all students. Sometimes referred to as "restructuring," the second wave called for changes in the way schools and the educational process were organized.

The reform movement—and particularly its first phase—received major impetus from the publication in 1983 of *A Nation at Risk*, the report of the National Commission on Excellence in Education (1983). This report observed that the United States was losing ground in international economic competition and attributed the decline in large part to the relatively low standards and poor performance of the American educational system.

The publication of other reports such as *America's Choice: High Skills or Low Wages, Workforce 2000*, and reports from the Secretary's Commission on Achieving Necessary Skills (SCANS) have shifted the debate away from a narrowly defined set of academic or general competencies, technical and specific job skills, interpersonal abilities, and behavioral traits, including motivation. These reports and the attention given to them have lifted career and technical education from relative obscurity to a place of prominence in the ongoing debate surrounding school reform. Each of the reports stressed issues such as:

1. Lengthening the school day and the school year.
2. Increasing the number of units (credits) required for high school graduation by specifying additional units in English, mathematics, science, and social studies.
3. Raising the entrance requirements for state colleges and universities.
4. Restructuring the high school curriculum by prescribing five "new basics"—four years of English, three years of mathematics, three years of social studies, and one-half year of computer science, and requiring college-bound students to have two years of a foreign language.

Career and Technical Education: 1990s–21st Century

This section discusses various pieces of legislation that had an influence on the growth of career and technical education during the 1990s and on into the twenty-first century.

Carl D. Perkins Vocational and Applied Technology Education Act of 1990 (Public Law 101-392)

On September 25, 1990, President George Bush signed into law the Carl D. Perkins Vocational and Applied Technology Act. The new name—Vocational and Applied Technology Education—signaled congressional interest in emphasizing the application of the academic and vocational skills necessary to work in a technologically advanced global society. The Carl D. Perkins Vocational and Applied Technology Education Act of 1990 amended and extended the Carl D. Perkins Vocational Education Act of 1984.

For the first time, the act was directed toward "all segments of the population." Congress, in enacting Perkins II, set the stage for a three-pronged approach to better workforce preparation: (1) integration of academic and vocational education, (2) articulation between segments of education engaged in workforce preparation—epitomized by congressional support for Tech Prep, and (3) closer linkages between school and work.

All these changes represented a major shift in the ways vocational education historically has been provided in America. Earlier provisions, initiated and promulgated by Congress and accepted by vocational educators since the days of the Smith-Hughes Act, tended to separate and isolate vocational teachers, students, and curriculum from the rest of the school community.

In addition, there were two more components of the Perkins Act marking serious departures from past practice. They dealt with funds distribution and accountability. As a result of problems perceived to exist under prior legislation, Congress, in Perkins II, bypassed the state agency decision makers by allocating the vast bulk of the funds directly to local education agencies, thus removing virtually all distributional discretion from state officials. In addition, the act explicitly required states to develop systems of performance measures and standards for secondary and postsecondary career and technical education.

Congress thus provided a template for the CTE portion of the merging strategy for preparing the workforce of the future. Its three core approaches marked a significant departure from past vocational education acts, not by emphasizing the separation and segregation of vocational education but rather by emphasizing its integration with academic instruction, between secondary and postsecondary institutions, and with business and labor. The historical separation of vocational and academic education was a powerful barrier to integration, and the ultimate success of this initiative depended on the willingness of policy makers and practitioners at the federal, state, and local levels to stay the course.

Major Flaws of the Carl D. Perkins Vocational Applied Technology Act of 1990

Swanson (1991) cited five major flaws in the Carl D. Perkins Vocational Applied Technology Education Act of 1990:

1. *Purpose/funding did not match*. The act's formulas for implementation and funding were addressed to a totally different purpose. The act did more to erect barriers than to remove them.

2. *Micromanagement*. Members of Congress had not been prepared, either professionally or by experience, to manage these tasks they have mandated. Conducting hearings is not an adequate way to acquire this training or experience.

3. *Legislated learning.* Learning is as difficult to legislate as morality. Congress should leave both to more competent hands. Legislated learning appears to be an attempt to guarantee tracking.

4. *Legislated methodology.* With its legislated instructional methodology, Congress makes curricula easy to "McDonaldize"—a precondition for curricula to become marginal, even trivial. If teaching quality is declining, Congress should begin to take the blame as it continues to legislate methodology.

5. *Mistrust of democracy.* State legislative functions were ignored in the act. The act appeared to assign most of its implementation to congressionally prescribed entities and to reduce the ability of state and local government to administer whatever remains.

School-to-Work Opportunities Act (STWOA) of 1994 (Public Law 103-239)

The School-to-Work Opportunities Act was passed to address the national skills shortage by providing a model to create a highly skilled workforce for our nation's economy through partnerships between educators and employers. The STWOA emphasized preparing students with the knowledge, skills, abilities and information about occupations and the labor market that will help them make the transition from school to post-school employment through school-based and work-based instructional components supported by a connecting activity's component. Key elements of STWOA included (a) collaborative partnerships, (b) integrated curriculum, (c) technological advances, (d) adaptable workers, (e) comprehensive career guidance, (f) work-based learning, and (g) a step-by-step approach.

A summary of vocational funding for 2001 and 2002 is provided in Table 5.1. For the purpose of observing trends in funding CTE programs, see Appendix E for a summary of major events concerning the growth of CTE preparation and retraining.

Personal Responsibility and Work Opportunity Act of 1996 (Public Law 104-193)

President Clinton signed the new welfare reform bill, the Personal Responsibility and Work Opportunity Act of 1996, into law on August 22, 1996. While career and technical education is by no means a welfare program, some policy makers argued that there were opportunities for linkages with other agencies. Therefore, it was important that C&T educators participate in the state's decision-making process to ensure an appropriate role for CTE.

As part of the enacted Personal Responsibility and Work Opportunities Act of 1996, recipients of welfare were required to work within two years of receiving federal assistance. This work requirement was expected to be phased in over a six-year period. Welfare recipients were allowed to count

Table 5.1   Funding for Vocational Education (FY '01, FY '02, in Millions)

PERKINS	FY '01 Enacted Funding	President's FY '02 Request	Congress's Final FY '02 Budget	Change from FY '01
Basic state grants	$1,100,000,000	$1,100,000,000	$1,180,000,000	+$80,000,000
Tribally controlled postsecondary institutions	$5,600,000	$5,600,000	$6,500,000	+$900,000
Nat'l programs	$17,500,000	$12,000,000	$12,000,000	−$5,500,000
Occ. and empl. information (Sec. 118)	$9,000,000	$0	$9,500,000	+$500,000
Tech Prep	$106,000,000	$106,000,000	$108,000,000	$2,000,000
Tech Prep demonstration	$5,000,000	$5,000,000	$5,000,000	$0
Perkins Total	$1,234,100,000	$1,223,600,000	$1,321,000,000	+$77,900,000
Pell Grant Maximum	$3,750	$3,850	$4,000	+$250

Source: Personal communication with Nancy O'Brien and Alisha Dixon of ACTE's Office of Government Relations, March 4, 2002.

up to twelve months of CTE training as "work," and teenage parents were allowed to use high school attendance as part of their work requirements.

Under the original law, a state could allow 20 percent of its welfare population to count CTE as work; subtracting the 6 percent of teen parents under the cap, 14 percent of those receiving CTE would be adults. Under the new agreement, the 1997 percentage of adults served by career and technical education dropped to 7.5 percent, or 30 percent of the 25 percent of recipients required to work (see Table 5.2). The percentage of adults who could count CTE as work increased through FY 1999 as the percentage of people required to work went up, but dipped when teen parents came back under the cap in FY 2000. This action taken by Congress reduced career and technical education's role to serve adult welfare recipients.

Suggestions for Teaching Welfare Clients

Welfare clients have several needs. Many are severely deficient in basic skills and unfamiliar with the world of work. Years of dependency have contributed to a loss of self-esteem and confidence. Following are some suggestions for meeting these needs in your classroom or programs:

- Make learning relevant.
- Adjust to different learning styles.
- Make your expectations clear.
- Maintain frequent contact.

Table 5.2   Percentage of Adults Served by Vocational Technical Education: Welfare Original Law versus New Provisions

Fiscal Year	Original Law			New Provisions
	% Adults Served by			
	% Required to Work	% Served by Education	% Adults Served*	Career and Technical Education
1997	25	20	14	7.5 (30% of 25%)
1998	30	20	14	9.0 (30% of 30%)
1999	35	20	14	10.5 (30% of 35%)
2000	40	20	14	6.0* (30% of 40%)
2001	45	20	14	7.5* (30% of 45%)
2002	50	20	14	9.0* (30% of 50%)

* 6%, for teen parents subtracted from % served by education.
Source: Personal communication with Bridget Brown of AVA's Office of Government Relations, August 8, 1997.

- Establish a peer support network.
- Emphasize co-op and apprenticeship programs. Help strengthen the connection between learning and employment.

The Personal Responsibility and Work Opportunity Act was last authorized on February 8, 2006, as Title VII, Subtitle A of Public Law 109-171.

Workforce Investment Act of 1998 (Public Law 105-220)

On August 7, President Clinton signed into law the Workforce Investment Act (WIA). The Job Training Partnership Act (JTPA) was officially repealed and replaced by the provisions of the Workforce Investment Act in July 2000.

Highlights of the Workforce in Investment Act

1. The Workforce Investment Act consists of a *state workforce investment board* that assists each governor in developing the state's five-year strategic plan for providing job-training services in the state. This plan must be submitted to the U.S. Secretary of Labor.

2. The law also consists of *local workforce investment boards* that are responsible for setting training policy at the local level in conjunction with the state plan.

3. *Local service delivery areas* must be established throughout each state. In designating the local areas, the governor must consider geographic areas served by local education agencies and postsecondary educational institutions, the extent to which such local areas are consistent with labor market area, the distance individuals will have to travel to receive services, and the resources available in the local area to administer job-training activities effectively.

4. The law requires that a *one-stop delivery system* be established in each local area. The law encourages states to retain existing one-stop delivery systems where they have been established, if they are working effectively. The local board is authorized to designate or certify the one-stop operators through a competitive process. Entities eligible to be designated one-stop centers include postsecondary educational institutions, employment service agencies, private nonprofit organizations (including community-based organizations), private for-profit agencies, or a government agency. The one-stop delivery system provides core services and access to intensive services and authorized training services. The one-stop delivery system must make services available through at least one center in each local area in the state.

5. The law authorizes the use of *individual training accounts* (ITAs) (vouchers) through which participants choose training from among qualified providers. The individual training accounts are used to deliver training services with only a few exceptions, including on-the-job training, customized training, and training provided by community-based or private organizations to populations that face multiple barriers to employment. The states have flexibility in determining how the vouchers will be distributed in the local areas and how much the vouchers will be worth.

6. Local areas use job-training funds to initially provide *core services* to adult and dislocated workers through the one-stop center system. Core services include outreach and intake, initial assessments of skill levels, job-search and placement assistance, career counseling, identifying job vacancy listings, assessment of skills necessary for jobs in demand, and the provision of information about available training services. All adults are eligible to receive core services. Funds can also be used to provide *intensive services* to unemployed and incumbent workers who are unable to obtain employment through core services. Intensive services include comprehensive and specialized assessments of skill levels, diagnostic testing, in-depth interviewing to identify employment barriers, the development of individual employment plans, group or individual counseling and career planning, case management services, and short-term prevocational services.

7. *Authorized training services* are available to individuals who meet the eligibility requirements for intensive services but are still unable to find employment. These individuals must also be deemed able to benefit from a particular job-training activity that is linked to employment opportunities in the local area. In addition, individuals must be unable to obtain other grant assistance (including Federal Pell Grants) before qualifying for authorized training. Authorized train-

ing includes occupational skills training, on-the-job training, programs that combine workplace training with related instruction, skill upgrading and retraining, job-readiness training, and adult education and literacy activities provided in combination with other authorized training services. Individuals receiving these types of training services are served primarily through individual training accounts.

8. The law stipulates that to be eligible to provide job-training services, the local board must certify a provider with guidance by the governor. *All institutions eligible to participate in Title IV student aid programs of the Higher Education Act are automatically initially eligible to be providers of job training services*; however, they must provide performance information to the state in subsequent years to maintain eligibility.

9. *Accountability* is an important part of the system. At the state level, the law established performance indicators for adult and dislocated-worker programs. The accountability measures are broadly defined in the statute and include entry into unsubsidized employment, retention in unsubsidized employment six months after entry into the workforce, earnings received six months after entry into employment, and attainment of a recognized credential where appropriate. In addition, the law stipulates customer-satisfaction indicators, which consist of evaluations of employers and participants of services received.

10. The law established a *Twenty-First Century Workforce Commission* to study matters related to the information technology workforce. The commission was composed of 15 members, five each appointed by the President, the Majority Leader of the U.S. Senate, and the Speaker of the U.S. House of Representatives. Three members were representatives of state and local government; three were educators from elementary, secondary, vocational, or postsecondary institutions; and eight were representatives of business.

11. Eligibility for *Work-Flex* expanded to all states. Under this provision, governors could be granted authority to approve requests for waivers of the law submitted by their local workforce areas. These workforce flexibility plans must detail the expected outcomes to be achieved by the waivers. *Governors may also request a waiver* for a state or area of the state by submitting a plan to the U.S. Secretary of Labor. The plan must include an identification of the provisions to be waived, the actions the state or local area has taken to remove state or local regulatory or statutory barriers, the goals of the wavier and expected programmatic outcomes, a description of the individuals affected by the waiver, and the process to be used to monitor the implementation of the waiver.

12. States may submit a *unified plan* to ensure the coordination of, and avoid duplication among, workforce development activities for adults and youth, adult education, and secondary and postsecondary

vocational education. Fourteen different programs are eligible for the state unified plan including, to name a few, the Vocational Rehabilitation Act, the Food Stamp Act, and programs authorized under the Community Services Block Grant Act. Secondary vocational education can be included in a unified plan only if it is agreed to by the state legislature.

13. The law provides that states shall not be prohibited from *testing job-training participants for the use of controlled substances*, but, if they do, funds to carry out testing must come from administrative expenses, not from money allocated to carry out job-training services. Also, states may sanction individuals who test positive for drugs with a six-month ban from programs for the first positive test, and a two-year ban for subsequent positive tests.

WIA Incentive Awards

In May of 2001 the U.S. Department of Labor, in collaboration with the Department of Education, announced that six states were eligible to apply for Workforce Investment Act (WIA) incentive awards. The six states had until June 18, 2001 to submit their applications for the incentive funding to the Department of Labor.

The states qualified for a share of $10.08 million available because they had taken the lead on implementing provisions of the WIA one year ahead of the full implementation date. In order to qualify, a state must have exceeded performance levels agreed to by the secretaries, governor, and state education officer for outcomes in state-operated employment and adult education programs. Goals included placement after training, retention in employment, and improvement in literacy levels. The six eligible states were Florida ($2,645,125), Indiana ($1,308,726), Kentucky ($1,400,631), Texas ($3,000,000), Utah ($882,167), and Vermont ($843,351) (Association for Career and Technical Education, 2001).

The differences in theme and detail between JTPA and WIA have important implications for career and technical education at both the secondary and postsecondary levels.

Youth Services

JTPA had two separate youth-funding streams, disadvantaged youth and summer youth, with the summer-youth stream receiving by far the larger funding (Employment and Training Administration [ETA], 1998b). WIA replaces these with a single youth-funding stream.

WIA requires individual assessment of skill levels and service needs and development of an individual service strategy for each youth participant. WIA requires all youth programs to make 10 program elements available to each participant (ETA 1998a):

• Tutoring, study skills, and instruction leading to completion of secondary school

- Alternative secondary school services
- Summer employment opportunities directly linked to academic and occupational learning
- Paid and unpaid work experiences, including internships and job shadowing
- Occupational skill training
- Leadership development opportunities
- Supportive services
- Adult mentoring
- Follow-up services for not less than 12 months after participation
- Comprehensive guidance and counseling, which may include drug and alcohol abuse counseling and referral

In line with development theory and practices (National Youth Employment Coalition, 1999), WIA prescribes more basic outcomes for youth (attainment of work readiness, occupational skills, and employment) than for adults (both employment and attainment of educational and occupational credentials) (Kaufman and Wills, 1999). The clear intent of WIA (Wonacott, 2000) is to move away from short-term interventions and toward the long-term development of young people.

Secondary CTE programs that wish to provide WIA youth services must accommodate the changes introduced by WIA—focus on long-term development rather than short-term intervention; summer employment as only one part of an integrated, year-round program to increase youth's work readiness, occupational skills, and employment; provision (or contract with another provider for provision) of all 10 required program elements; assessment of each youth's skills levels and service needs; development of an individual service strategy for each youth; and limits on funding devoted to non-low-income and in-school youth (Wonacott, 2000).

Adult and Dislocated Worker Services

Unlike JTPA, WIA eliminated economic disadvantage as an eligibility criterion (ETA, 1998a). Instead, three levels of services for adults and dislocated workers (and youth aged 19–21 receiving services under adult funding) are to be accessed sequentially. More extensive levels of service are for individuals unable to obtain employment through the more basic services.

Community and technical colleges that provide CTE programs (Feldman, 1998) should note that training services are the last resort; WIA has a clear emphasis on placing adults and dislocated workers in employment as quickly as possible, with the least intensive intervention needed for placement. However, intensive services such as assessment, counseling, and prevocational education—provided by many community and technical colleges under JTPA—remain an integral part of the WIA system.

Governance and Structure

WIA's provisions for governance and structure allow plenty of opportunity for involvement of CTE providers, especially at the postsecondary level, as eligible members of state or local boards and local youth councils, as eligible one-stop operators, and as eligible providers of youth, core and/or intensive services. At the very least, CTE providers should develop and maintain contact with local boards, youth councils, and one-stop operators to make their interest in WIA activities known and promote their services.

Providers and Performance Accountability

Consistent with the performance-based approach in the Government Performance and Results Act (ETA, 1998a), WIA emphasizes outcomes rather than management control. To implement those goals, WIA sets up a system of performance indicators including core indicators and customer satisfaction indicators, which are identified in the legislation. Each state negotiates an acceptable level of statewide performance on each core and customer satisfaction indicator with the Secretary of Labor; each state then negotiates local performance levels with each local area.

Core indicators measure participant outcomes (Wonacott, 2000). One set is applied to younger youth (ages 14–18): diploma or equivalent attainment rate, skill attainment rate, and retention rate (e.g., in advanced training or apprenticeships). Another set is applied separately to adults and dislocated workers: entered employment rate, employment retention after 6 months, earnings change after 6 months, and educational/occupational credential rate upon employment. The same set of adult/dislocated worker indicators also applies to older youth (ages 19–21) served under the adult funding stream, except that the educational/occupational credential rate applies upon entry into postsecondary education, advanced training, or employment. Participants served under more than one funding stream are counted in each applicable indicator.

Implications of WIA for Career and Technical Education

CTE providers who make youth services available under WIA must provide information on the three core indicators for younger youth; those who make training services available for adults must provide information on the four core indicators for adults. CTE providers may need to develop the capacity to collect and report performance information in order maintain eligibility after the initial period. In particular, postsecondary educational institutions may find it difficult to use unemployment insurance information to identify employment, earnings, and retention outcomes of adults, dislocated workers, and older youth (Feldman, 1998); they may wish to take advantage of provisions in WIA for help in meeting extraordinary costs.

Postsecondary institutions should also take full advantage of the requirement that governors solicit recommendations on statewide performance levels from service providers in the state and take them into account in setting state performance levels. Finally, the possibility of local boards adjusting statewide performance levels upward means that CTE providers will want to play an active role in local decision making (Wonacott, 2000).

Individual Training Accounts

Eligible training providers are required to furnish one-stop operators with information on their training programs and outcomes for program participants; one-stop operators then make that information available to participants, who use it to make informed choices about which qualified training program best meets their individual needs. As training providers, CTE providers will need to ensure not only that they furnish one-stop operators with required information but also that one-stops in turn provide accurate and current information to participants.

The Workforce Investment Act Amendments of 2005 (S. 1021)

On January 4, 2005, the Job Training Act (H.R. 27) was introduced to reauthorize the Workforce Investment Act. The purpose of S. 1021, the WIA Amendments of 2005, was to improve the workforce investment system created under the Workforce Investment Act of 1998.

The major themes of the WIA reauthorization provisions are (Lordeman, 2005):

- Increasing flexibility to meet state and local needs;
- Providing workers with the training they need to obtain new or better jobs;
- Providing employers with a trained workforce to compete in the global marketplace;
- Improving upon the existing one-stop career center delivery system to ensure that it can respond quickly and effectively to the changing needs of employers and workers in the new economy and can address the needs of special populations, including individuals with disabilities;
- Removing barriers that have discouraged business involvement in workforce training, while finding new mechanisms to increase and improve business and industry and influence job-training decisions in communities;
- Encouraging job training and employment services to be demand driven and responsive to the needs of employers, both large and small; and
- Improving access to services in all areas, including rural areas.

Special changes to WIA include:

- Reducing the number of required members on local workplace boards to reduce bureaucracy, and encourage business involvement in local job training decisions;
- Maintaining the ability of local workforce areas to agree upon equitable contributions from partners for infrastructure funding. If the local area cannot reach an agreement, the governor would determine appropriate contributions (subject to certain caps);

- Involving the state workforce investments boards to provide a comprehensive statewide workforce development system to serve all individuals;
- Increasing the emphasis on ensuring that individuals with disabilities have physical and programmatic access to workforce activities at one-stop centers and approved training providers;
- Maximizing services to the business sector to make the system more demand driven and responsive to employers' needs, including small employers;
- Creating more realistic and relevant performance measures to assess the effectiveness of local workforce areas in helping people obtain and remain in jobs with good wages and stable careers;
- Ensuring that individuals are placed in jobs, education, or training that lead to comparable pay;
- Revising reporting requirements for entities that wish to be job-training providers, in response to complaints that current requirements discourage entities from participating as providers;
- Taking steps to improve coordination of all workforce programs, including requiring the co-location of employment service programs with WIA one-stops, and making the Temporary Assistance for Needy Families (TANF) program a mandatory partner at one-stop centers (unless the governor of the state chooses not to make TANF a mandatory partner);
- Adding community-based job training programs for training in high-growth, high-wage, and high-demand occupations;
- Improving youth job-training activities by directing more resources to those out-of-school youth who are most in need of assistance; and
- Enhancing assistance to youth ages 16 to 21 who face barriers to employment (Lordeman, 2005).

Carl D. Perkins Vocational and Technical Education Act of 1998 (Public Law 105-332)

On October 31, 1998, President Clinton signed the Carl D. Perkins Vocational and Technical Education Act (PL 105-332). The 1998 act replaced the 1990 federal vocational education law and authorized vocational programs for five years. The act went into effect on July 1, 1999. A summary of major provisions of the law follows.

Authorization of Appropriations

The law authorized Congress to appropriate "such sums as necessary" to fund the basic state grant. Of the total amount appropriate, 1.25 percent was reserved for American Indian programs, 0.25 percent for Native Hawaiian programs, and 0.2 percent for outlying areas. Another $4 million was authorized to carry out activities for tribally controlled postsecondary vocational and technical institutions.

State Allotment

The structure was the same as previously maintained for the federal-to-state allotment of funds. The U.S. Secretary of Education allocated funds to each state by a formula based on the following:

- 50 percent of the population aged 15–19
- 20 percent of the population aged 20–24
- 15 percent of the population aged 25–65
- 15 percent of the sum of the three categories above.

Small states were guaranteed to receive at least 0.5 percent of the total grant amount.

Within-State Allotment

The law required that 85 percent of funds allocated to the state be distributed to local programs; 15 percent of funds were reserved at the state level. The 10.5 percent set-aside historically included within Perkins for single parents, displaced homemakers, single pregnant women, and programs that promote sex equity in vocational education was eliminated. Also eliminated was the mandatory requirement that states employ a gender equity coordinator.

Of the 85 percent of funds directed at the local level, states had the option of reserving up to 10 percent of those funds distributed to programs in geographic areas that met at least two of the four following criteria:

- The area is rural,
- It has a high population of vocational and technical students,
- It has a high percentage of vocational and technical students, or
- It is a community that has been negatively impacted by the changes made to the formula that distributes monies to secondary schools.

Accountability

The eligible agency was required to establish state performance measures consisting of core indicators of performance that, at a minimum, included measures of:

- Student attainment of challenging state-established academic, and vocational and technical, skill proficiencies;
- Student attainment of a secondary school diploma or its recognized equivalent, a proficiency credential in conjunction with a secondary school diploma, or a postsecondary degree or credential;
- Placement in, retention in, and completion of postsecondary education or advanced training, placement in military service, or placement or retention in employment; and
- Student participation in and completion of vocational and technical education programs that lead to nontraditional training and employment.

State Plan and Distribution of Funds

The law reported 22 specific elements in the state plan, including:

- The vocational-technical activities to be carried out;
- How comprehensive professional development would be carried out;
- How interested parties would be involved in the development of the plan;
- How funds would be distributed between secondary and postsecondary programs;
- How programs would be annually evaluated;
- Program strategies for special populations;
- How individual entities receiving funds would be involved in the development of state-adjusted levels of performance;
- How technical assistance would be provided at the local level;
- How funds would be used to serve individuals in state corrections agencies; and
- How funds would be used to link secondary and postsecondary education.

Regarding the distribution of funds to postsecondary education, the minimum postsecondary grant award remained unchanged at $50,000.

State Leadership Activities

There were eight required state uses of leadership funds:

- An assessment of programs, including how the needs of special populations were being met;
- Developing, improving, or expanding the use of technology in vocational and technical education;
- Professional development programs, including in-service and pre-service training;
- Support for vocational and technical programs that improve the academic, vocational, and technical skills of students through the integration of academics with vocational and technical education;
- Providing preparation for nontraditional training and employment;
- Supporting partnerships among local education agencies, institutions of higher education, adult education providers, and other entities;
- Serving individuals in correctional institutions; and
- Support for programs for special populations that lead to high-wage, high-skill careers.

In addition, the law listed 12 permissible state uses of funds, including technical assistance, improvement in career guidance, Tech Prep, cooperative education, support for family and consumer science programs, support for business and education partnerships, and support to improve or develop new vocational and technical education courses.

Local Uses of Funds

The law also identified required and permissive local uses of funds. There were eight required uses of funds:

- To strengthen the academic, and vocational and technical skills of students;
- To provide students with strong experience in and understanding all aspects of an industry;
- To develop, expand, or improve the use of technology;
- To provide professional development programs to teachers, counselors, and administrators;
- To develop and implement evaluations of programs, including an assessment of how the needs of special populations are being met;
- To initiate, improve, expand, and modernize programs;
- To provide services that are of sufficient size, scope, and quality to be effective; and
- To link secondary and postsecondary programs, including Tech Prep.

In addition, the law listed 15 permissive local uses of funds, including local education and business partnerships; mentoring and support services; leasing, purchasing, upgrading, or adapting equipment; improving and developing new courses; teacher preparation; support for nontraditional training and employment; and providing for career guidance and academic counseling, work-related experience, and programs for special populations.

Tech Prep

The law authorized Tech Prep as a discrete program with its own authorization ceiling. The law also authorized the appropriation of "such sums as necessary" to support Tech Prep. Tech Prep is defined as a program that:

- Combines, at a minimum, two years of secondary education (as determined under state law) with a minimum of two years of postsecondary education in a nonduplicative, sequential course of study;
- Integrates academic and vocational/technical instruction, and utilizes work-based and worksite learning where appropriate and available;
- Provides technical preparation in a career field such as engineering technology, applied science, a mechanical, industrial, or practical art or trade, agriculture, health occupations, business, or applied economics;
- Builds student competence in mathematics, science, reading, writing, communications, economics, and workplace skills through applied, contextual academics, and integrated instruction, in a coherent sequence of courses;
- Leads to an associate or a baccalaureate degree or a postsecondary certificate in a specific career field; and
- Leads to placement in appropriate employment or to further education.

National Activities

A national assessment of vocational education activities was authorized to provide for an independent assessment and evaluation of programs funded with Perkins dollars. The law authorized the U.S. Secretary of Education to conduct activities in the areas of national research and demonstrations, as well as development, capacity building, and technical assistance.

Special Populations/Gender Equity Provisions

Special populations were defined in the law to include individuals with disabilities; individuals from economically disadvantaged families, including foster children; individuals preparing for nontraditional training and employment; single parents, including single pregnant women; displaced homemakers; and individuals with other barriers to educational achievement, including individuals with limited English proficiency.

The No Child Left Behind Act of 2001 (Public Law 107-110)

These reforms express my deep belief in our public schools and their mission to build the mind and character of every child, from every background, in every part of America.

—President George W. Bush

On January 8, 2002, President George W. Bush signed into law the landmark No Child Left Behind Act of 2001 (NCLB), the reauthorization of the Elementary and Secondary Education Act (ESEA). The law reflects a remarkable consensus on how to improve the performance of America's elementary and secondary schools while at the same time ensuring that no child is trapped in a failing school.

Provisions of the Act

NCLB, as a reauthorization of the ESEA, incorporates the principles and strategies that include increased accountability for states, school districts, and schools; greater choice for parents and students, particularly those attending low-performing schools; more flexibility for the states and local educational agencies (LEAs) in the use of federal education dollars; and a stronger emphasis on reading, especially for our youngest children.

Increased accountability. NCLB was intended to strengthen Title I accountability by requiring states to implement statewide accountability systems covering all public schools and students. These systems must be based on challenging state standards in reading and mathematics, annual testing for all students in grades 3–8, and annual statewide progress objectives ensuring that all groups of students reach proficiency within 12 years. Assessment results and state progress objectives must be broken out by poverty, race, ethnicity, disability, and limited English proficiency to ensure that no group is left behind. School districts and schools that fail to make adequate yearly progress (AYP) toward statewide proficiency goals will, over time, be subject to improvement, corrective action, and restructuring measures aimed at getting them back on course to meet state standards. Schools that meet or exceed AYP objectives or close achievement gaps will be eligible for State Academic Achievement Awards.

More choices for parents and students.   NCLB significantly increases the choices available to the parents of students attending Title I schools that fail to meet standards, including immediate relief-beginning with the 2002–03 school year—for students in schools that were previously identified for improvement or corrective action under the 1994 ESEA reauthorization.

LEAs must give students attending schools identified for improvement, corrective action, or restructuring the opportunity to attend a better public school, which may include a public charter school, within the school district. The district must provide transportation to the new schools and must use at least 5 percent of its Title I funds for this purpose, if needed.

For students attending persistently failing schools (those that have failed to meet state standards for at least three of four preceding years), LEAs must permit low-income students to use Title I funds to obtain supplemental educational services from the public- or private-sector provider selected by the students and their parents. Providers must meet state standards and offer services tailored to help participating students meet challenging state academic standards.

To help ensure that LEAs offer meaningful choices, the law requires school districts to spend up to 20 percent of their Title I allocations to provide school choice and supplemental educational services to eligible students.

In addition to helping ensure that no child loses the opportunity for a quality education because he or she is trapped in a failing school, the choice and supplemental service requirements provide a substantial incentive for low-performing schools to improve. Schools that want to avoid losing students—along with the portion of their annual budgets typically associated with those students—will have to improve or, if they fail to make AYP for five years, run the risk of reconstitution under a restructuring plan.

Greater flexibility for states, school districts, and schools.   One important goal of No Child Left Behind was to breathe new life in the "flexibility for accountability" bargain with states first struck by President George H. W. Bush during his historic 1989 education summit with the nation's governors at Charlottesville, Virginia. Prior flexibility efforts have focused on the waiver of program requirements; NCLB moves beyond this limited approach to give states and school districts unprecedented flexibility in the use of federal education funds in exchange for strong accountability for results.

New flexibility provisions in NCLB include authority for states and LEAs to transfer up to 50 percent of the funding they receive under four major state grant programs to any one of the programs, or to Title I. The covered programs include Teacher Quality State Grants, Educational Technology, Innovative Programs, and Safe and Drug-Free Schools.

The law also includes a competitive State Flexibility Demonstration Program that permits up to seven states consolidate the state share of nearly all federal state grant programs—including Title I, Part A Grants to Local Educational Agencies—while providing additional flexibility in their use of Title V innovation funds. Participating states must enter into five-year performance agreements with the Secretary covering the use of consolidated funds, which may be used for any educational purpose authorized under the ESEA. As part of their plans, states also must enter into up to 10 local performance agreements with LEAs, which will enjoy the same level of flexibility granted under the separate Local Flexibility Demonstration Program.

The competitive Local Flexibility Demonstration Program would allow up to 80 LEAs, in addition to the 70 LEAs under the State Flexibility Demonstration Program, to consolidate funds received under Teacher Quality State Grants, Educational Technology State Grants, Innovative Programs, and Safe and Drug-Free Schools programs. Participating LEAs would enter into performance agreements with the Secretary of Education and would be able to use the consolidated funds for any ESEA-authorized purpose.

Putting reading first.   No Child Left Behind stated President Bush's unequivocal commitment to ensure that every child can read by the end of third grade. To accomplish this goal, the new Reading First initiative significantly increases the federal investment in scientifically based reading instruction of children for special education services due to a lack of appropriate reading instruction in their early years.

NCLB fully implements the President's Reading First initiative. The Reading First State Grant program will make six-year grants to states, which will make competitive subgrants to local communities. Local recipients administer screening and diagnostic assessments to determine which students in grades K–3 are at risk of reading failure and provide professional development for K–3 teachers in the essential components of reading instruction.

The Early Reading First Program makes competitive six-year awards to LEAs to support early language, literacy, and pre-reading development of preschool-age children, particularly those from low-income families. Recipients use instructional strategies and professional development drawn from scientifically based reading research to help young children to attain the fundamental knowledge and skills they will need for optimal reading development in kindergarten and beyond.

Other major program changes.   The No Child Left Behind Act of 2001 also put the principles of accountability, choice, and flexibility to work in its reauthorization of other major ESEA programs. For example, the law combines the Eisenhower Professional Development and Class Size Reduction programs into a new Improving Teacher Quality State Grants program that focuses on using practices grounded in scientifically based research to prepare, train, and recruit high-quality teachers. The new program gives states and LEAs flexibility to select the strategies that best meet their particular needs for improved teaching that will help them raise student achievement in the core academic subjects. In return for this flexibility, LEAs are required to demonstrate annual progress in ensuring that all teachers teaching in core academic subjects within the state are highly qualified.

NCLB also simplified federal support for English-language instruction by combining categorical bilingual and immigrant education grants that benefited a small percentage of limited-English-proficient students in relatively few schools into a state formula program. The formula program will facilitate the comprehensive planning by states and school districts needed to insure implementation of programs that benefit all limited-English-proficient students by helping them learn English and meet the same high academic standards as other students.

Other changes support state and local efforts to keep schools safe and drug-free, while at the same time ensuring that students—particularly those who have been victims of violent crimes on school grounds—are not trapped in persistently dangerous schools. As proposed in No Child Left Behind, states must allow students who attend a persistently dangerous school, or who are victims of violent crime at school, to transfer to a safe school. States also must report school safety statistics to the public on a school-by-school basis, and LEAs must use Federal Safe and Drug-Free Schools and Communities funding to implement drug and violence prevention programs of demonstrated effectiveness. Box 5.1 shows an overview of previous federal CTE legislation.

Carl D. Perkins Career and Technical Education Improvement Act of 2006 (PubLic Law 109-270)

On August 12, 2006, President George W. Bush signed the Carl D. Perkins Career and Technical Education Improvement Act of 2006. The provisions of the act are outlined below.

Background

- The reauthorization process began in 2004.
- The House and Senate approved legislation overwhelmingly in July 2006.
- The president signed into law August 12, 2006, reauthorizing it through 2012.

Themes

- Accountability and program improvement.
- Secondary–postsecondary connections.
- Links to rigorous academics.
- Stronger focus on business and industry.

Structure of Law

- Basic State Grant (Title I).
  – National Programs (Section 114).

Box 5.1   Overview of Previous Federal CTE Legislation

Periods of Vocational Legislation	Policy Objectives and Tools
1917–1963	Provide trained workers for growing semi-skilled occupations and retain more students in secondary education through: • Expansion of separate CTE schools and programs • Funds for basic maintenance of programs • Focusing on agriculture, industry, and home economics for high school students
1963–1968	Improve and expand career and technical education through: • Separate funds for innovative programs, research, and curriculum development • Support for construction of regional area vocational schools • Support for adult training and retraining (postsecondary CTE) • Encouragement to states to promote CTE equity and better service to disadvantaged students
1968–1990	Improve career and technical education and facilitate access through: • Periodic encouragement to states to distribute some funds by a community's economic need and levels of student disadvantage • Establishment and expansion of set-aside funds to serve special population groups • Prohibiting the use of most federal funds for maintenance of programs • Continuation of set-aside funds for program improvement
1990–1998	Expansion of equal access and emphasis on academic quality through: • Introducing intrastate and intradistrict funding rules: distribution to agencies and schools weighted by special populations • Promoting "integration" of academic and CT education and "all aspects of the industry" • Set-aside funds for new programs linking secondary and postsecondary CTE: Tech-Prep. • Requirement that states develop performance standards.

Source: U.S. Department of Education (2004). National assessment of vocational education: Final report to Congress, p. 3. Washington, DC: Office of the Under Secretary, Policy and Program Studies Service.

The distribution of Perkins funds within their state is of great interest to these teacher educators.

- Tribally Controlled Postsecondary Institutions (Section 117).
- Occupational and Employment Information (Section 118).
- Tech Prep (Title II).

Funding Distribution

- Incentive grants were eliminated.
- Increased money for small states, if overall funding increases.
- Within-state allocation stays the same—state administration maintained at 5%.
- Local funding stays the same.
- Funds still must be spent on CTE.

Accountability

- Separate secondary and postsecondary indicators.
- New local requirements.
- More specific improvement plan and sanction language.
- Must have valid and reliable measures.

Accountability—Secondary Indicators

- Academic achievement—on NCLB assessments.
- Technical attainment—industry standards when possible.

- Attainment of (I) a diploma, (II) a GED, (III) a proficiency credential in conjunction with a diploma.
- NCLB graduation rates.
- Placement in postsecondary, military, or employment.
- Participation and completion of non-traditional programs.

Accountability—Postsecondary Indicators

- Technical attainment—industry standards when possible.
- Attainment of industry recognized credential, certificate, or degree.
- Retention in postsecondary (including transfer to 4-year).
- Placement in military or apprenticeship, or placement or retention in employment—including high skill, high wage, or high demand.
- Participation and completion of non-traditional programs.

Accountability—Negotiations

- Every two years.
- Federal-state very similar to current law.
- Locals will either accept state performance levels or negotiate with states on new local levels.
- Must show continuous improvement.

Accountability—Improvement Plans

- If a state or local fails to meet at least 90% of a performance level on any indicator, they must develop and implement an improvement plan.
- Secretary of Education or State will provide technical assistance.

Accountability—Subsequent Action

- If a state or local:
  - Fails to implement an improvement plan,
  - Fails to make any improvement within a year after implementing plan,
  - Fails to meet 90% of an indicator 3 years in a row,
- Then funds can be withheld (fully or partially).

Uses of Funds

Definition of Career and Technical Education (CTE):

- Eliminates the restriction on preparation for careers requiring a baccalaureate degree.
- Does not affect funding.

Uses of Funds—State Requirements

- Assess CTE programs funded, including focus on special populations.
- Develop, improve, or expand the use of technology in CTE.
- Provide professional development.
- Support the integration of academics and CTE.

- Provide preparation for nontraditional fields and high-skill, high-wage occupations.
- Support partnerships.
- Serve individuals in state institutions.
- Support for programs for special populations.
- Technical assistance for local recipients.

Uses of Funds—State Permissive

- Notable additions:
    - Activities that facilitate transition from 2-yr. to 4-yr.
    - Incentive grants for locals.
    - Entrepreneurship education and training.
    - Career academies, career clusters.
    - Technical assessments and data systems.
    - Recruitment and retention of educators.
    - Section 118 activities.

Uses of Funds—Local Requirements

- Strengthen academic and technical skills of students through integration.
- Link secondary and postsecondary education, including through Programs of Study.
- Provide experiences in all aspects of an industry.
- Develop, improve, or expand technology.
- Provide professional development.
- Develop and implement evaluations of CTE programs.
- Initiate, improve, expand, and modernize CTE programs.
- Provide activities of sufficient size and scope to be effective.
- Provide activities to prepare special populations for high-skill, high-wage, or high-demand occupations that lead to self-sufficiency.

Uses of Funds—Local Permissive

- Notable additions:
    - Activities that facilitate transition from 2-yr. to 4-yr.
    - Entrepreneurship education and training.
    - Development of Programs of Study.
    - Development and support of small, personalized career-themed learning communities.
    - Pooling a portion of funds with other recipients for innovation.
    - Expanding postsecondary programs offerings at more accessible times/formats.

Programs of Study

- Incorporate and align secondary and postsecondary education.
- Include academic and CTE content in a coordinated, non-duplicative progression of courses.
- May include the opportunity for secondary students to acquire post-secondary credits.
- Lead to an industry-recognized credential or certificate at the postsec-ondary level, or an associate or baccalaureate degree.
- Identify and address current or emerging occupational opportunities.
- Build on Tech Prep, career clusters, career pathways, career acade-mies.
- State develops in consultation with locals.
- Locals must offer the required courses of at least one Program of Study (and can offer more).
- Foundational elements already in place.

Tech Prep

- States must show greater coordination with Basic State Grant—sin-gle plan.
- States may combine Tech Prep and Basic State Grant funding streams.
- If combined, funds treated as Basic State Grant dunds.
- If kept separate, new definitions and accountability for consortia.

Implications for Today's Global Workforce

Federal support for career and technical education is a critical element in meeting students' and employers' needs. Since the passage of the Smith-Hughes Act in 1917, the federal government has provided funding to states and localities to bolster the improvement and expansion of occupationally oriented education. Congress also has recognized the need for leadership and cost-effective information sharing by providing support for those activi-ties at the national level to assist educators and students.

Federal legislation directing this funding has evolved through the years to reflect the needs of students, the changing economy, and the diversifica-tion of the workforce. At times, more national activities have been needed to determine how needs are changing. At other times, greater emphasis has been placed on the needs of states and localities to address growing student populations, the need to infuse new technologies into the classroom, or other demands of local business and industry to meet workforce needs.

The demand for new technologies, the changing demographics of the workforce reflecting increasing numbers of minorities and women, and the increase in academic and technical skill levels needed in almost every employment sector require that Congress carefully consider the need for greater federal support for career and technical education. This authorization will have an influence on the growth of American society throughout the twenty-first century.

To keep America's place in the global economy secure, the federal investment in CTE must support the improvement of academic and occupational skills and the expansion of access for all students in these programs. To meet these needs of students and the workplace, it is imperative that integration of core of academic and C&T education continue. To ensure emphasis on this priority, governance of CTE must remain within the purview of education and not be segregated from other education reform efforts.

Career and technical education provides the initial opportunity for students to explore career options in a setting that takes into account the broad range of every student's needs—from career guidance and counseling to course work that stresses the academic and occupational applications of the subject matter. Strong CTE as part of effective education reform efforts will significantly reduce the need for "second-chance" job-training efforts, increase the earning power and educational achievements of its students, and improve our nation's ability to compete in the global marketplace.

Summary

- Although 1917 marked the first significant legislation relating to career and technical education, several pieces of supportive legislation were passed earlier. Some of the most important pieces of U.S. legislation occurred under the leadership of Hoke Smith, Dudley Hughes, Walter F. George, and Carl D. Perkins.

- The primary unifying force for CTE in America has been federal legislation. Since federal vocational dollars were the only education funds that flowed from federal government to the states until the 1958 National Defense Education Act, federal policy played a primary role in shaping current programs.

- A broad education reform movement began in the early to mid-1980s, prompted by concerns about America's competitiveness in the international economy and the poor performance of American students on international tests. The movement called for greatly improved academics, to be achieved primarily through increased education standards and accountability (both teacher and student).

- In the mid-to-late 1980s, a second wave of reform sought to go beyond academics and accountability. Unlike the first wave, it tended to focus on nonacademics and college-bound students and to emphasize the restructuring of secondary curricula and organizations. The movement also included many educators and researchers intent on reforming career and technical education.

- The Carl D. Perkins Vocational and Applied Technology Education Act Amendments of 1990 spurred significant changes in CTE. The emphasis of this act was on increasing the links between academic and occupational skill development, secondary and postsecondary education, and business and education.

- The School-to-Work Opportunities Act was passed to address the national skills shortage by providing a model to create a highly skilled workforce for our nation's economy through partnerships between educators and employers.

- The Personal Responsibility and Work Opportunity Act, a welfare reform bill, was signed into law on August 22, 1996, requiring recipients of welfare to work within two years of receiving federal assistance.

- Quality programs depend on qualified educators with access to continuous professional development activities, state-of-the-art technology, and student support services; equity in access to programs; integrated academic and occupational curricula based on industry approved standards; and opportunities for work-site learning experiences for all students. As the evolution toward higher technology in the workplace continues, the focus of federal support for career and technical education must be on redoubling efforts to strengthen these links.

- The Workforce Investment Act of 1998 provided the framework for a unique national workforce preparation and employment system designed to meet both the needs of the nation's business and the needs of job seekers and those who wanted to further their careers. The goals of the Workforce Investment system were as follows:
  – to increase the employment, retention, and earnings of participants;
  – to increase occupational skill attainment by participants;
  – to improve the quality of the workforce;
  – to reduce welfare dependency; and
  – to enhance the productivity and competitiveness of the nation.

- The major changes in the Carl D. Perkins Vocational and Technical Education Act of 1998 involved new accountability measures and the treatment of funding for special populations. Regarding accountability, each state was responsible to negotiate expected levels of performance with the Secretary of Education within four broad categories: attainment of academic and vocational-technical proficiencies; attainment of a secondary school degree, GED, or postsecondary degree or credential; placement, retention, and completion of postsecondary education; placement in military service or employment; and participation in and completion of programs that lead to nontraditional training and employment. The 10.5 percent funding included within Perkins that was set aside historically for special populations was eliminated, as was the requirement that each state employ a gender equity coordinator. However, the law required that state and local plans show how these populations would be served, and make assessments and evaluations to show if the needs of these populations were being met.

- The No Child Left Behind Act is based on the principles of increased flexibility and local control, stronger accountability for results, expanded options for parents, and an emphasis on effective teaching methods.

- The most notable provisions of the Carl D. Perkins Career and Technical Education Improvement Act of 2006 are that it uses the term *career and technical education* instead of *vocational education* throughout, maintains the Tech Prep Program as a separate federal funding stream within the legislation, and maintains state administrative funding at 5 percent of a state's allocation.

Discussion Questions and Activities

1. Name the legislative ordinances prior to 1900 that had an impact on career and technical education.

2. What was the first major legislation appropriating funds for vocational education programs at secondary schools?

3. Name the members of the Federal Board of Vocational Education as designated by the Smith-Hughes Act.

4. What were the principal provisions of the Smith-Hughes Act?

5. In what way did the George-Reed, George-Ellzey, and George-Deep Acts differ from the Smith-Hughes Act?

6. What were the major differences between the George-Barden Act and the Smith-Hughes Act?

7. Under which act was marketing education (formerly distributive education) first appropriated?

8. Prepare brief biographical sketches of the following authors of federal legislation:

   a. Hoke Smith

   b. Dudley Hughes

   c. Walter George

   d. Carl D. Perkins

9. Read and report on at least three articles on federal legislation pertaining to career and technical education.

10. What was the impact of the National Defense Education Act on vocational education?

11. State the purpose of the Manpower Development Training Act of 1962. What were the conditions that led to this legislation?

12. State the principal provisions of the Vocational Education Act of 1963.

13. What are the differences between the Vocational Education Act of 1963 and the 1968 Vocational Education Amendments? How are they similar?

14. What was the purpose of the Comprehensive Employment and Training Act?

15. What was the difference between the Comprehensive Employment Training Act and the Manpower Development Training Act?

16. In what way did the Job Training Partnership Act affect career and technical education? Why do you believe these programs were established?

17. State the major differences between the 1984 Carl D. Perkins Vocational Education Act, the 1976 Vocational Education Amendments, and the 2006 Perkins reauthorization.

18. Debate the following topics:
    a. The Carl D. Perkins Vocational and Applied Technology Education Act is not the worst piece of federal legislation ever passed.
    b. The Smith-Hughes Act is the most significant federal legislation passed affecting the development and growth of career and technical education.

19. Interview a CTE teacher and a CTE director. Ask both of them which of the following is most needed most by career and technical education: funds, better equipment and facilities, community support, or business and industry support. Then ask the CTE director how federal legislation can help with these needs.

20. What were the principal provisions of the School-to-Work Opportunities Act?

21. What was the impact of the School-to-Work Opportunities Act on CTE in your community? In your state?

For Exploration

22. Conduct an interview with parents and teachers in your community to determine their attitudes toward the NCLB Act.

Library Research

23. Compare and contrast the features of the Workforce Investment Act with the former Job Training Partnership Act (JTPA).

24. Compare and contrast the Perkins Vocational and Applied Technology Education Act with the Perkins Vocational Technical Education Act of 1998.

25. Compare and contrast the Perkins Vocational Technical Education Act of 1998 with Carl D. Perkins Career and Technical Education Improvement Act of 2006.

References and Additional Reading

Asche, M. (1993). *The impact of educational reform on vocational education*. Berkeley, CA: National Center for Research in Vocational Education.

Association for Career and Technical Education (2001). *Six states eligible for WIA incentive awards*. Alexandria, VA: Author.

———. (2007). Perkins Reauthorization. ACTE Online. Retrieved February 7, 2007, from http://www.acteonline.org/policy/legislative_issues/Perkins-new.cfm.

Baker, S. A. (1991). The impact of the civil war on vocational education. *Journal of Vocational and Technical Education, 7*(2), 56–60.

Calhoun, C. C., and Finch, A. V. (1982). *Vocational education: Concepts and operations*. Belmont, CA: Wadsworth.

Employment and Training Administration (1998a). *Implementing the workforce investment act of 1998*. Washington, DC: U.S. Department of Labor (ERIC Document Reproduction Service No. ED 427 177).

———. (1998b). *Workforce investment act of 1998*. Washington, DC: U.S. Department of Labor (ERIC Document Reproduction Service No. ED 425 334).

Evans, R. N., and Herr, E. L. (1978). *Foundations of vocational education*, 2nd ed. Columbus, OH: Charles E. Merrill.

Feldman, L. (1998). *The workforce investment act: Implications for community colleges*. Washington, DC: American Association of Community Colleges.

Fitzpatrick, J. C. (Ed.) (1933). *Journals of the Continental Congress, 1774–1789*, Vol. 2, pp. 373–386. Washington, DC: U.S. Government Printing Office.

Kaufman, B. A., and Willis, J. L. (1999). *User's guide to workforce investment act of 1998*. Alexandria, VA: Association of Career and Technical Education (ERIC Document Reproduction Service No. ED 435 808).

Lordeman, A. (May 17, 2005). The workforce Investment Act of 1998 (WIA): Reauthorization of job training programs. Congressional Research Service (order code RL322778). Washington, DC: Library of Congress.

Lynch, Richard L. (2000). High school career and technical education for the first decade of the 21st century. *Journal of Vocational Education Research, 25*(2). Retrieved February 7, 2007, from http://scholar.lib.vt.edu/ejournals/JVER/v24n2/lynch.html.

Mason, R. E., Furtado, L. T., and Husted, S. W. (1989). *Cooperative occupational education and work experience in the curriculum*. 4th ed. Danville, IL: Interstate Printers and Publishers.

Miller, M. D. (1985). *Principles and a philosophy for vocational education*. Columbus, OH: The National Center for Research in Vocational Education.

Mobley, M. D. (1956). History of federal funds for vocational education. *American Vocational Journal, 31*(9), 99.

———. (1957). Walter F. George. *American Vocational Journal, 32*(7), 3.

National Alliance of Business (1983). *A pocket guide to the Job Training Partnership Act of 1982*. Washington, DC: National Alliance of Business.

National Commission on Excellence in Education (1983). *A nation at risk: The imperative for educational reform*. Washington, DC: U.S. Department of Education.

National Youth Employment Coalition (1999). *Lessons learned from 51 effective youth employment initiatives*. Washington, DC: Author (ERIC Document Reproduction Service No. ED 437 447).

Plawin, P. (1992). 1917–1992: A vocational education era. *Vocational Education Journal, 67*(2), 30–32.

Roberts, R. W. (1957). *Vocational and practical arts education*, 1st ed. New York: Harper and Row.

———. (1971). *Vocational and practical arts education*, 3rd ed. New York: Harper and Row.

Swanson, G. I. (1991). Vocational education and the United States Congress. *Vocational Education Journal, 66*(1), 30–31, 45.

Thorpe, F. N. (Ed.) (1909). *The federal and state constitutions, colonial charters, and other organic laws*, Vol. 2, p. 961. Washington, DC: U.S. Government Printing Office.

True, A. C. (1929). *A history of agricultural education in the United States*. Washington, DC: U.S. Department of Agriculture, Pub. No. 36, U.S. Government Printing Office.

U.S. Department of Education (2002). The Elementary and Secondary Education Act (The No Child Left Behind Act of 2001). Retrieved September 4, 2006, from http://www.ed.gov/policy/elsec/leg/esea02/index.html.

———. (2007). Career and Technical Education: Legislation & Policy Guidance. Office of Vocational and Adult Education. Retrieved February 7, 2007, from http://www.ed.gov/about/offices/list/ovae/pi/cte/index.html.

Venn, G. (1964). *Man, education and work*. Washington, DC: American Council on Education.

Williams, C. (1950). Vocational educators honor U.S. Senator Walter F. George. *American Vocational Journal, 25*(4), 3.

Wonacott, M. E. (2000). The workforce investment act and CTE. *In Brief* (No. 6). National Dissemination Center for Career and Technical Education.

Wrench, R. C., Wrench, J. W., and Galloway, J. D. (1988). *Administration of vocational education*. Homewood, IL: American Technical Publishers.

chapter 6

Participation of Women in Career and Technical Education

One of the most remarkable phenomena of the last three decades has been the entrance of women in the workplace in record numbers. Their increasing presence in the corporate world, government, and politics is the result of many factors including the changing attitudes of society toward working women. Whether for social, economic, or personal reasons, women have changed their roles in society by attaining a higher education level and increasing their participation in the labor market. This chapter addresses the historical work roles of women in career and technical education, legislative breakthroughs affecting women, and selected problems associated with sex equity.

Historically, CTE has consisted of practical and applied instruction aimed at matching students with work positions in industry and commerce (Benavot, 1983). Compared to other educational fields, CTE more immediately satisfies Herzberg's (1966) notion that the primary function of any organization should be employment and the need for man [sic] to enjoy a meaningful existence. It is this purpose of connecting school and work that makes CTE an important focus for equity work.

Career and technical education is also a particularly useful field to examine because its framework has tended to be, and is presently, more responsive to political and economic factors than philosophical positions (Ray, 1968). As many writers have suggested, inequalities exist or are prolonged for economic and workplace reasons. In fact, economic factors have been used as reliable indicators of what areas of equity have been achieved (Harvey and Noble, 1985). The concept of equity corresponds in these terms to "the preferred shape of the distributional curve or the just distribution of economic resources in society" (Hewlett, 1977, p. 31). According to Osipow (1973):

> Perhaps the most significant area of concern for advocates of equal rights for women lies in the topic of careers, especially as these rights concern equality of opportunity, treatment, remuneration and advancement, but also they concern the general social attitude toward women's careers, marriage, and family responsibility. (pp. 255–256)

As Lewis (1985) has pointed out, years of schooling for women, especially minorities, do not automatically translate into improved economic status. Rather, it is the link of "specialized schooling to career development" (p. 382) that makes a difference. In essence, developing sex equity in education through development of occupational skills and employment possibilities for women is a pragmatic, economic approach to equity that can be accomplished through career and technical education (Burge and Culver, 1989).

Historical Work Roles of Women in Career and Technical Education

Throughout the nineteenth and early twentieth centuries in the United States, vocational educators took their cues of what and whom to teach from the needs and desires of the workplace. Originally, this teaching, along with theories of career development and work, focused almost exclusively on men (Roby, 1976). However, as women's presence in the workplace increased, a movement evolved for educating women in their new roles.

In the early part of the nineteenth century, thousands of women became part of the labor force in textile factories (Foner, 1987) or by selling or trading fruits and vegetables (Marshall and Paulin, 1987). Despite their growing numbers in the workforce, the role of a "good woman" was still perceived as staying home, tending the family and house. Consequently, during this time women were trained in a domestic and ornamental capacity. It was seen as the duty of females to "regulate the concerns of every family," so instruction geared toward making women good mothers or good "mistresses of families" was appropriate (Willard, 1987, p. 22). Ornamental instruction for economically disadvantaged women focused on drawing, painting, and "elegant penmanship, music, and grace of motion." Such instruction was perceived as

The increasing presence of women in the corporate world, government, and politics is the result of many factors, including their rising level of education.

important because it was not wise to allow female youth "to seek amusements for themselves" (Willard, p. 24).

Experiential learning was an important part of the curriculum in both the eighteenth and nineteenth centuries after the publication of Rousseau's *Émile* in 1762. Émile, an orphan boy removed from society, discovers knowledge through things or objects (books are banned), and in this natural manner develops physically, intellectually, and morally until he is ready to take his place in society. As a consequence of such thinking, children were required to do manual training, to learn by doing. However, not all children learned to do the same things. Boys, for example, learned to saw and to dig and to cultivate gardens (Green, 1969). They also practiced bookbinding and other skills. Girls, however, were more likely to learn spinning, weaving, cooking, and sewing. Girls were also more likely targets for moral instruction because they were responsible for maintaining "a moral home environment" (Gutek, 1999, p. 34).

It wasn't until the Civil War that women began to play an increasingly important role in industry and the production of goods. During World War I and World War II, the shortage of male workers and the industrial expansion necessitated by war created many new jobs for women in factories, sewing rooms, and munitions plants. Perhaps in recognition of new, limited opportunities for women, as early as 1874 the Kansas State Agricultural College "allotted [women] to take courses in drawing and do shop work in scroll sawing, carving, and engraving." For most young women, however, there was a department of sewing, work in household economy, and "a very progressive course in household chemistry" (Bennett, 1937, p. 314). For young men, ship work was the emphasis, with importance also attached to mathematics, science, and drawing (Bennett, 1937). Ten years later, at Toledo Manual Training School in Toledo, Ohio, there was a clearly defined system of vocational training for girls that differed from that offered to boys. Boys' shop work included carpentry, wood turning, forging, welding, chipping, and the study of machinery and gas engines. In contrast, the "domestic economy" outlined for girls included light carpentry; wood carving; clay modeling; instruction in preparing and cooking food; care of the sick; cutting, making, and fitting of garments; and household decoration (Clark, 1892).

During the Civil War women were employed as government clerks for the first time. As well as being trained differently from men, women would now be paid differently. Congress appropriated funds for the salaries of these women in 1864, but the appropriation set a cap of $600 a year for female government clerks, less than half the salary paid to male clerks (Baker, 1977). Taking the government cue, private industry also employed women for 50 percent of the wages men received for the same work. More than seventy years later, Westinghouse, maintaining this wage differential, stipulated in personnel manuals that the lowest-paid male job was not to be paid a wage below that of the highest-paid female job, regardless of the job content and value to the firm (Westinghouse Industrial Relations Manual: Wage Administration, Nov. 1, 1938, and Feb. 1, 1938, cited in Heen, 1984).

Not only was a wage differential the norm when men and women performed the same job, but women also were typically relegated to only a few jobs. For example, in 1870, 88 percent of women who were gainfully employed were in only ten occupations, among them domestic servant, seamstress, teacher, milliner, and nurse. By 1900, of 252 occupations listed by the U.S. Department of Labor, more than 90 percent of women were in 25 of them (Marshall and Paulin, 1987). This sex segregation was such a part of employers' and employees' perceptions that only after the equal-opportunity legislation of the 1950s did it become illegal for employers to specify sex of applicants for job openings listed in the newspaper (Shaw and Shaw, 1987).

In the short history of our country, women have been limited in their labor-force participation and in their wage earning potential simply because of their gender. This lack of economic independence has done little to destroy inequitable policies and attitudes in all of society, and, in human capital terms, paints a dismal picture for all women, especially those middle-aged and older (Shaw and Shaw, 1987). Young single mothers too are a group increasing in number and in economic disadvantage (Burge, 1987). Although improvements in breaking down barriers have been made, CTE enrollments mirror limited labor-force roles with narrow, sex-typed enrollment patterns.

Legislative Breakthroughs Affecting Women

The Smith-Hughes Act of 1917 provided the first federal funding for public school programs in agriculture, trade, industrial, and home economics education. Reflecting the sex-role norm of the times, the first two programs were specifically designed for males, and home economics was included to provide education for homemaking and occupations relating to the female homemaker role.

Thus, from the beginning, vocational education programs were intentionally sex typed. This separation of training for males and females continued with no legislative direction for change until the Equal Pay Act of 1963 was passed. This act, considered the first significant legislation relating to vocational equity, called for the end of discrimination on the basis of sex in payment of wages for equal work. This law was soon followed by Title VII of the Civil Rights Act of 1964 prohibiting discrimination in employment on the basis of sex, race, color, religion, and national rights (Burge and Culver, 1989). The scope of Title VII was more extensive than that of the Equal Pay Act.

Title IX of the Education Amendments of 1972 was landmark legislation responsible for banning discrimination on the basis of sex in education. Title IX provided that "no person in the United States shall, on the basis of sex, be excluded from participation in, be denied the benefits of, or be subjected to discrimination under any educational program or activity receiving federal financial assistance." The Women's Educational Equity Act of 1974

(Public Law 93-380) provided for funding of projects to advance education between women and men (Burge and Culver, 1989). As Fishel and Potter (1977) noted, this act along with provisions for many aspects of education specifically provided for expansion and improvement of programs for women in vocational education and career education.

Despite the passage of Title IX and the Women's Educational Equity Act, the 1970s and 1980s did not experience much change in vocational enrollment patterns from the previous years. Legally required opportunities, or at least lack of discriminatory policies, were not sufficient to attract many students into programs considered nontraditional for their sex (Burge, 1990).

With an understanding that more dramatic efforts had to be implemented, Congress appropriated the first funds for sex equity in conventional programs through the Educational Amendments of 1976. These funds required the development and implementation of programs to eliminate sex discrimination, sex bias, and sex-role stereotyping. To comply with the 1976 directives, each state was required to employ a full-time sex equity coordinator to (a) provide specific leadership in eliminating those barriers that inhibit equal access to vocational education, (b) offer technical assistance to local educators, and (c) develop a public relations program. With limited funding, some small gains were made as a result, but enrollment patterns remained relatively unchanged because the gender-traditional influences of the cultural arena were pervasive and firmly established (Burge, 1990).

With the passage of the Carl D. Perkins Vocational Education Act in 1984, increased emphasis was placed on gender equity in vocational programs. In addition to the 1976 amendment requirements, states were directed to expend an 8.5 percent set-aside of their vocational federal funds to provide vocational education and training leading to marketable skills and support services for single parents, homemakers, and displaced homemakers. Another set-aside, 3.5 percent, was authorized for programs to eliminate sex bias and stereotyping and to increase sex equity in vocational programs. This money was the largest federal provision ever made for the vocational preparation of females (National Coalition for Women and Girls in Education, 1988) and for the support of males in nontraditional roles.

This legislation has resulted in many equity efforts nationwide. The effects of these sex-equity programs, while considered successful by participants, are still largely unmeasured, and sex-segregated enrollment patterns still continue. The 1990 reauthorization of the vocational education amendments provided a similar significant amount of federal funding related to eliminating the problem of gender inequality. Money for single-parent and homemaker programs and for efforts to increase the numbers of students in programs nontraditional to their gender will continue (U.S. Congress, 1990).

Equity Status in Career and Technical Education

While acknowledging the important role career and technical education plays in our society, numerous studies, reports, and evaluations have repeatedly documented that sex segregation exists in the CTE system (National Coalition for Women and Girls in Education, 1988). Among CTE programs, business, cosmetology, health occupations, and home economics have been the domain of women; agriculture, auto mechanics, building trades, and technology education have been areas considered appropriate for men. In fact, in the seven traditional CTE program areas, six tend to be heavily sex typed (only marketing education is not) and nontraditional for one sex or the other. Yet, in spite of historically traditional workforce patterns and sex-related occupational stereotypes, vocational educators have been somewhat successful in attracting students into programs dominated by the other gender. Nontraditional students are those program enrollees, both male and female, who enroll in areas of study traditionally considered appropriate only for the opposite sex (Culver and Burge, 1985b).

Other groups often categorized as nontraditional vocational students are those females for whom paid employment is not a part of their self-perception. These women have been, or perceive their future roles to be, situated only in the domestic sphere. Any work for pay outside the home is viewed as a nontraditional option by this group. Examples of such women include displaced homemakers (displaced by death of a spouse, divorce, or separation), and many female single parents and teenage mothers. The number of women in these categories represents a significant portion of the total population, and they are a group in extreme economic need (Burge, 1990). Though education programs may provide some help, Cardenas and First (1985) have pointed out that pregnant and parenting teens are the young women most discriminated against in schools. These authors also note that a disproportionate number of these young women are minority students.

Women's Enrollment in Nontraditional CTE Programs

Before the passage of Title IX of the Education Amendments of 1972, which prohibited sex discrimination in federally supported programs, little attention was given to providing women with occupational preparation offered by vocational education. In the 1971–1972 school year, nearly three million girls and women were enrolled in occupationally specific high school and postsecondary programs. Girls and women could be, and were, excluded from some vocational programs simply on the basis of their sex (Vetter and Hickey, 1985).

Relations implementing Title IX were not issued until 1975. During the interim three years, advocacy groups of vocational educators researched where women were being serviced in vocational education. Since women's enrollments were primarily in home economics, health occupations and office occupations, sex-equity provisions were included in the vocational education section (Title II) of the Education Amendments of 1976 (Vetter and Hickey, 1985).

Despite the gains women have made in seeking employment, they continue to be segregated into a few occupations that require skills equal to those required in many male-dominated occupations (National Commission on Working Women of Wider Opportunities for Women, 1990). Yet these female-intensive areas continue to provide substantially lower pay. In the same patterns that occur in the workforce, women are at a disadvantage in selecting and completing gender-nontraditional, CTE programs that would train them for higher-paying jobs. Yuen (1983) has noted that the results of much of the research about women suggest that even if discriminatory institutional barriers to career development are removed (and to some extent, this has occurred through federal legislation), most women need special support services to succeed in completing preparation for male-intensive employment. While the social and political climate presents significant limitations, the willingness of career and technical educators to be innovative in their recruitment and retention activities can make a difference in individual lives. With adequate information about necessary support services, including emotional support, dependent care, self-esteem enhancement, skill assessment, basic skill development, and job-seeking strategies, C&T educators can better counteract tenacious beliefs about stereotypical workplace roles for women. Burge (1990) suggested that one way to make up for women's inequality in higher-paying jobs (or in some cases, any job at all) is to learn more about the techniques for changing workplace inequalities and to develop strategies to improve Affirmative Action programs.

If a more equitable society is to be developed, a conscious effort must be made by parents, teachers, and counselors to liberate young people from many sex-role stereotypes prevalent in our society and help them to become independent human beings who choose their future vocational occupations after consideration of all available possibilities. Following are several strategies that could broaden the range of nontraditional opportunities for girls and women in career and technical education:

- Provide career exploration activities.
- Provide information on nontraditional careers to families.
- Select texts and materials free from sex bias.
- Provide women students with role models.
- Treat students equally.
- Develop mentorship programs.
- Bring nontraditional students and nontraditional workers to the attention of all students through panel presentations and career-day conferences.
- Recognize the achievements of nontraditional students.
- Include assertiveness training as part of an overall curriculum.
- Work with employers to assist them in obtaining highly skilled workers, regardless of gender.

Educators must take precautions to ensure that neither sex discrimination nor bias affects students' attitudes toward, access to, enrollment in, or completion of nontraditional programs that may lead to higher-paying jobs. Moreover, educators should help forge new pathways that overcome barriers that have historically limited opportunities based on gender and encourage students to explore nontraditional training and employment.

For these purposes, four leading CTE and gender equity organizations—the Association of Career and Technical Education (ACTE), the National Alliance for Partnerships in Equity (NAPE), the National Association of State Directors of Career Technical Education Consortium (NASDCTEc), and the National Women's Law Center (NWLC)—founded the "Programs and Practices That Work: Preparing Students for Nontraditional Careers" Project. The purpose of the project is to help schools eliminate the subtle and unintended, as well as the overt, barriers that students face in enrolling in and completing nontraditional CTE courses and programs. "In helping schools address these barriers we aim to improve students' access to these courses and programs toward the goal of enhancing students' economic self-sufficiency and personal fulfillment" (Association of Career and Technical Education, 2005).

Selected Problems Associated with Sex Equity

Three terms need to be defined with regard to sex-equity issues: sex bias, sex stereotyping, and sex discrimination. *Sex bias* is behavior, attitude, or prejudice resulting from the assumption that one sex is superior to another. *Sex stereotyping* is the attribution of behaviors, abilities, interest, values, and roles to an individual or group on the basis of sex. *Sex discrimination* is the denial of opportunity, privilege, role, or reward on the basis of sex (Butler, 1989).

According to Dykman (1997), when trainers are invited to schools or workplaces to do classes on sex equity, they may be working against the following attitudes:

- *Sex stereotyping.* Learned thought processes often associate women with specific, often submissive, feminine roles and men with masculine, dominant roles.

- *Sex-role spillover.* Sometimes male workers will act out against female co-workers because they don't meet their expectation of "affectionate" female behavior.

- *Pack mentality.* The majority group often holds members of a minority to higher standards.

- *Somebody else's problem.* Male co-workers (or students) often fail to see any potential for harassment in their behavior because they believe only the behavior of supervisors can contribute to a sexually hostile environment.

Sex-role stereotyping is harmful to women, both economically and psychologically. Females in career and technical education, as in the workplace, generally expect to have few fields of work to choose from and are segregated into a small number of occupational areas. These female-intensive areas are typically low paying and carry low prestige when compared to the areas of the occupational spectrum that are male-intensive (Biddlecombe et al., 1989). An important goal for C&T educators is to eliminate this clustering of women in a restricted range of occupations. Helping women broaden their occupational participation will encourage the development of a more equitable income distribution between men and women (Reider, 1977). In addition, traditionally female-intensive areas, while usually low paying, are often crucial for the well-being of our society. Efforts to increase the income potential and status of child- and health-care workers, for example, can provide another approach to enhancing the economic status of women (Burge, 1990).

Sex-role stereotyping is also harmful to males. Although workforce preparation and pay inequities controlled by a patriarchal system usually favor men, societal expectations place males in restrictive roles. Young boys learn early that they are expected to "prove" their masculine identity, typically by excluding certain natural human characteristics—nurturing others, being aesthetic, sensual, emotional—that have been labeled as feminine (Gordon, 1981). Stitt (1988) has described the destruction inherent in stereotyping males: "The price of defining masculinity as toughness, aversion to scholarship, devotion to business, and indifference to physical danger, however, is exorbitantly high. Ill-considered myths about what a man is, impair social relationships and compromise career development" (p. 12).

As men break traditional patterns and seek more active home and parenting roles, employers may lack sensitivity to males' potential conflicts between home and work, thus further compounding these problems (Couch, 1989).

Sex Bias and Sex Stereotyping

Sex bias and sex stereotyping in education and occupations in the late 1960s and 1970s were documented by Vetter, Sechler, Lowry, and Canora (1979). They concluded that, at the time, interests in occupations perhaps tended to be sex stereotyped more for "real" choices than for "ideal" choices. Family members (parents, in particular), the mass media, and nearly every element of public education had been criticized in the literature for helping perpetuate rigid sex roles that limit people's vocational options to those traditional to their sex. Experimental studies had shown that sexist language and sexist instructional materials had affected the responses of students (Vetter, 1993).

At the high school level, studies of the High School and Beyond (HSB) database indicated that students in programs nontraditional for their sex (30 percent or fewer), whether male or female, held higher self-concepts than their counterparts in traditional programs (Culver and Burge, 1985b). On the whole, males were found to have more positive self-concepts than females. HSB students in traditional female programs had the highest job aspirations (measured by the Duncan Socioeconomic Index). Women stu-

dents in male-intensive, female-intensive, and nonsex-intensive programs
had higher aspirations than males in each of these groups (Culver and
Burge, 1985a).

Employers of nontraditional vocational graduates indicated that sex stereotypes are a major barrier to such employment (Burge, 1983). Eighteen
percent of the employers surveyed believed some jobs in their business could
not be filled effectively by a man, and 24 percent believed that some could
not be filled effectively by a woman. Thus, while employers indicated the
problem was that the clients or consumers would be uncomfortable with
nontraditional workers, employers themselves were also uncomfortable
(Vetter, 1993).

Harassment

In 1978, the largest problem identified by women students in nontraditional high school vocational education programs (fewer than 25 percent)
was harassment by male classmates (Kane and Frazee, 1978). Fewer problems were reported in relation to teachers. Harassment was much diminished
for women, which has obvious implications for policies of class assignment.
When few women are enrolled in a nontraditional program, it would be helpful to assign them to the same class. Where only one or two women are
enrolling in a program, support groups for women in different programs
could be helpful. Teachers must be made responsible for combating the "turf-
ism" expressed by traditional male students. When women are no longer a
novelty in class, as is now the case in some nontraditional programs, this
problem may fade as male students expect the women to be there, as evi-
denced in the New York City high schools (Schulzinger and Syron, 1984).

Between 1991 and 1996, the percentage of companies that reported at
least one sexual harassment claim grew from 52 percent to 72 percent. Sexual harassment costs the typical Fortune 500 company $6.7 million a year in
increased absenteeism, staff turnover, low morale, and low productivity
(Dykman, 1997).

The same concerns can apply in the education arena. Sometimes a
school's funding is tied to how well it improves gender equality. One example is the School-to-Work Opportunities Act, which requires state and local
administrators to show how their plans will increase opportunities for
women (and other groups) in careers that are not traditional for their gender
(Dykman, 1997). These requirements and liabilities have increased awareness of gender equity between employers and vocational educators.

Following are several suggestions for C&T educators for dealing with
the issue of sexual harassment:

1. Develop a comprehensive sexual harassment policy for dissemination
   to administrators, staff, students, and parents.
2. Parents, students, staff, and lawyers should participate in writing the
   policy.

Inequalities still exist for women in access to formal education, work-based training, lifelong learning, and new technology training.

3. Student support groups should be available for students in nontraditional vocational classes.
4. Develop a process to continuously monitor and evaluate your policy.
5. Provide workshops to train administrators, staff, and students about sexual harassment.

Lack of Support

A statewide study in West Virginia (Sproles, 1987) indicated that for nontraditional completers of vocational programs (less than 20 percent), friends, relatives, and school personnel were perceived as less helpful than for completers of more traditional choices. Vocational teachers were perceived as being more helpful than parents and friends by the traditional respondents, whereas parents were more helpful for the nontraditional respondents.

Houser and Garvey (1985), in studying California women in vocational education programs, found that nontraditional students differed from traditional students primarily in the support received from female friends and family members. Additionally, compared to a group of students who had considered nontraditional programs but then enrolled in traditional programs, nontraditional students reported receiving more encouragement from school personnel.

When students complete a CTE program, they should be ready for placement on the job. A major concern of students in nontraditional programs is whether they will find employment (Hollenback, 1985). Hollenback indicates that faculty members must encourage potential employers to hire nontraditional students at adequate salaries and with adequate opportunities for job advancement.

Recognizing these problems and others related to male sex-role stereo-typing can help vocational educators identify equity as an area that benefits both sexes.

Institute for Women in Trades, Technology, and Science (IWITTS)

The Institute for Women in Trades, Technology, and Science (IWITTS) is dedicated to integrating women into the full range of trades, technology, and science careers in which they are underrepresented. IWITTS is a national nonprofit 501(c)3 organization founded in 1994, under the incorporated name of New Traditions for Women, Inc. IWITTS works with teachers of career and technical education, science, and math; guidance counselors; school-to-work directors and School-to-Work coordinators; gender equity coordinators; and administrators (IWITTS, 1999).

Information on IWITTS is available at the following Web sites: http://www.iwitts.com, or http://www.womentechworld.org.

Revisitation of Title IX: Gender Segregation in CTE at the High School Level

Title IX, which required all educational programs receiving federal financial assistance to provide opportunities to women and girls, reflected the belief that females could enjoy the same educational opportunities as males, if compliance with strict equity requirements were mandated and enforced (Wonacott, 2002). A report by the National Women's Law Center (NWLC) (2002) analyzed career and technical education in 12 states, 30 years after the enactment of Title IX. While substantial progress has been made, the report suggested that gender segregation still exists in career and technical education. Young men matriculate into programs that lead to higher-wage jobs and self-sufficiency, while young girls tend to enroll in programs that lead to much lower earning power. Young women and girls face widespread sex discrimination in high school career and technical education programs across the country. Pervasive sex segregation, sexual harassment in the classroom, discrimination in counseling and recruiting, and other gender-based bias were creating serious barriers to their future earning power, according to the study. As a result of these findings, NWLC filed 12 Petitions for Compliance Review. The petitions requested Title IX investigations of—and demanded remedies for—sex discrimination in career and technical education across the country (NWLC, 2002).

According to the American Association of University Women:

> In 2001, the National Coalition for Women and Girls in Education (NCWGE), which AAUW chairs, published a report entitled Invisible

Again: The Impact of Changes in Federal Funding on Vocational Programs for Women and Girls (Link to cite: http://www.ncwge.org/perkins.pdf). This study was designed to examine the impact the shift from Perkins to WIA funding had on special populations. Overall, the study found that in most states, special populations were dramatically underserved, and that women were having a hard time transitioning from being either stuck in a low-wage job or being dependent on welfare to getting the skills and education they needed to find more family-sustaining employment. . . . Women who do not earn a bachelor's degree—and constitute an important population group for career and technical education programming—earn only 68 percent of male workers' median income. To shrink the wage gap for skilled workers, participation and achievement in career and technical education should not be bound to gender segregation and stereotypes, harassment or barriers that prevent girls and women—including single mothers, displaced homemakers and former welfare recipients— from becoming self-sufficient. (AAUW, 2004)

Thirty years after Title IX, boys were still steered toward courses that led to a traditionally male, and higher paying, career in technology and the trades, while girls were taking programs focusing on lower paying jobs such as cosmetology and child care. National patterns of sex segregation, based on data in 12 states, revealed that 96% of cosmetology students were female, as are 87% of those enrolled in child care courses, and 86% of those enrolled in health aide preparation courses. Meanwhile, 90% of the students enrolled in carpentry, automotive, and plumbing were boys. The pattern of sex segregation is even worse in some states. For example, in Florida, 99% of the students in cosmetology were female, while 100% of the students taking plumbing were male (NWLC, 2002). There is evidence that some change has occurred in access to career and technical education programs. For example, females received 85% of all bachelor's degrees in family and consumer sciences (from the 10 postsecondary institutions with the highest enrollment),

As of 2002, 96 percent of cosmetology students were women.

but some programs attract a more gender balanced mixed of students (Firebaugh and Miller, 2002).

There is persuasive evidence that gender bias, gender segregation, and gender discrimination still exist and still have a baneful effect on access and opportunity. For example, four predominantly female career and technical education high schools in one city offered an average of 1.75 advanced placement courses per school; for 11 predominantly male schools in the same city, the average was 3.89 courses (National Coalition for Women and Girls in Education [NCWGE], 2002). Also, women in nontraditional jobs constituted only 12 percent of working females, in spite of the great disparities between nontraditional and traditional jobs for females (NCWGE, 2002).

Wonacott (2002) argues:

> However, to say bias, segregation, and discrimination exist is one thing; to say whether those are on the increase or decrease is quite different. Some data indicate, for example, that there is movement toward greater gender balance in some career and technical education program enrollments, hence more equitable access to career and technical education programs. However, those data are partial, reflecting program enrollments in certain states and may not reflect the situation in other states. (p. 4)

According to Bae and others (2000), comprehensive nationwide data typically do not specifically address career and technical education programs and effects. For example, in 1970, the median annual earnings of female high school graduates were only 50 percent of males' earnings; those of female bachelor's degree holders, only 57 percent of males' earnings. By 1997, those disparities had been reduced to 64 percent and 78 percent, respectively, at the two levels. "Therefore, although disparities still exist, earnings appear to be less unequal than formerly—but the data presented allow conclusions only on the effects of education in general, not on the effects of career and technical education in particular" (Wonacott, 2002, p. 4).

Discussions concerning how to achieve more equitable access typically appear very logical: on the face of it, it makes sense to call for full implementation of Title IX requirements for issuing federal programs or for the return to the previous Perkins Act requirement and funding for full-time state sex equity coordinators (NCWGE, 2002; NWLC, 2002). Wonacott (2002) reported that previous legislative and regulatory requirements have fallen far short of producing genuinely equitable access across the board to career and technical education programs and to the benefits they can provide.

> It appears that access to career and technical education and to its benefits is not perfectly equitable; however, it is apparently better than it was thirty years ago. Efforts to improve access by eliminating gender bias, segregation, and discrimination have not been completely effective—but they have presumably had some effect. Maybe the reality is that gender bias, segregation, and discrimination will be always be a danger in career and technical education; efforts to combat and eliminate them will always be needed; attention to equal access for all will always be in order. (p. 4)

Workforce Participation of Women in Developing Countries

Men enjoy greater privileges; women bear greater burdens.
—Paul Harrison

Gender continues to be a strong determinant of education, training, and work opportunities, even though public policy in many countries has encouraged—or expected and depended on—women's participation in the workforce. Cultural patterns differ among the kinds of work roles open to women at any point in time. Societies have evolved from the age of hunting and gathering to a time of agrarian pursuits, through the industrial era and into the information/knowledge age with little substantive change in women's work responsibilities and opportunities. However, in most countries women still do not have broad access to the range of work and education or training opportunities that would enable them to rise above the lower-income strata of their culture (Daines, Hartenstein, and Birch, 2000).

Economic accumulation in poor countries is closely tied to the status of women in those societies (Nusebaum and Glover, 1996). Most attention in the past has focused on men as supposedly the main generators of capital. Government and international agencies concentrated on work performed by male wage earners, which appears in financial statistics such as the GDP. Women's work, by contrast, often is not paid for in money and does not show up in financial statistics (Goldstein, 2001).

Access to Training

Given the conditions of uncertainty that confront women in their work lives, access to education and training, information, and technology remain the main strategies for advancing human life and society (International Labour Organization, 1998).

According to the International Labour Organization (ILO) (1998), inequalities persist throughout the following areas:

- *Access to formal education.* Unequal enrollments of males and females are most evident in developing countries.

- *Access to vocational training.* Education and training systems reinforce gender-based occupational segregation in the workforce, thereby limiting access to a wide range of occupations.

- *Access to work-based training.* Discrimination in employer-provided training especially affects women. Employers are less likely to invest in initial or further training for women because of their higher rates of job-learning due to family responsibilities, and because they may be part-time or temporary workers.

- *Access to lifelong learning.* Lifelong learning opportunities tend to be most available to those who already work in high-level jobs.

- *Access to training programs for the unemployed.* These programs may underrepresent women when (a) women are not registered as unemployed, (b) the training programs lack such related support provisions as child care, or (c) male-focused occupations are targeted.
- *Access to new technology training.* Skill development in such areas as information and communications technology is critical if women are to progress.

Women play a major role in agricultural production in most developing countries (Cloud, 1986; Creevy, 1986). In some cases, women manage a substantial share of the small farms because men have migrated to find other work; in Malawi, for example, women are reported to manage one-third of rural farm households (Spring, Smith, and Kayuni, 1985). Elsewhere in Africa, women provide 50 to 80 percent of the labor for such tasks as marketing, sowing, and weeding. Women have not had equal access to extension services, however, nor for that matter to the complementary general education that enhances the effect of extension information on productivity. Extension programs also often miss the poorest farmers and smallest farms, in part because it is easier to work effectively with the better-educated owners of large farms (Middleton, Ziderman, and Adams, 1993).

Participation rates of women in career and technical education (the proportion of females of secondary-school age attending vocational schools) are lower than those for men in developing countries. More important are gender differences in fields of study. Female CTE students are concentrated in white-collar-related fields of study, while men predominate in blue-collar trades. Census data from Israel reveals that, of those individuals who have completed secondary vocational education and for whom a course of study is known, 83 percent of males were concentrated in blue-collar fields of study, while 89 percent of females were concentrated in white-collar fields (Neuman and Ziderman, 1991).

According to Middleton, Ziderman, and Adams (1993), data on career and technical training in six Latin American countries reaffirm the channeling of women into "female" areas of study. More than 80 percent of the students in such fields as secretarial and clerical studies, beauty care, and handicrafts were women; in some cases, 95 to 98 percent of the students were women (beauty care in Argentina and Colombia; handicrafts in Argentina). In contrast, on average women constituted less than 10 percent of students in such fields as motor vehicle mechanics, electricity, electronics, and technician training.

Great literacy deficits remain among adult women, especially in such areas as sub-Saharan Africa and southern and western Asia. Girls' school enrollments in primary and secondary schools now equal boys' in most developed countries, as well as in Latin America and the Caribbean (Daines, Hartenstein, and Birch, 2000).

More women now enroll in colleges and universities, but there are wide disparities among countries, ranging from enrollments nearly equal to that of men (in developed countries, and some in Southern Africa, Latin America, and the Caribbean) to fewer than 30 women per 100 men in sub-Saharan African and Southern Asian countries (United Nations, 1991).

Except for in Africa, women have made rapid gains in advanced training for law and business. By 1984, enrollments of men and women in those fields were nearly equal to that within developed regions, Latin America, and the Caribbean (Daines, Hartenstein, and Birch, 2000). The proportion of women primary school teachers also increased everywhere, but with wide regional differences. Men outnumber women in secondary-school teaching in all regions except Latin America and the Caribbean (United Nations, 1991). Women's work in Muslim countries is not properly accounted for due to cultural factors.

A study by the Academy Project (Maguire, 2001) finds women in developing countries face considerable obstacles in gaining access to information technology (IT). The study concludes that unless gender is considered when telecommunications policy is formulated and IT programs are designed, women risk greater social and economic marginalization. Among the obstacles to women's access to IT, according to the study, are low levels of literacy and education, language, time, cost, geographical location of facilities, social and cultural norms, and insufficient computer and information management skills. The study warns that the gender divide in Internet access is particularly acute in rural areas, where women make up 60 percent of the population. The study cites examples of how IT is already creating increased employment and income-generation opportunities for women in developing countries. In India these range from staffing call centers to operating small businesses offering Internet access, as well as developing software.

Implications for Workforce Education

With the global progression of the industrial age and its concern for efficiency, policy makers and C&T educators need to continue emphasizing the importance of matching the skills of the labor force with the needs of the labor market over individual development and fulfillment through meaningful work. Daines, Hartenstein, and Birch (2000) proposed an agenda for vocational/technical education that revisits the need to provide for individual development as well as the need to serve society. An agenda that focuses on education and training for women might highlight such actions as the following:

1. Support and actively contribute to the future development of basic education and literacy programs.

2. Examine practices that may contribute to gender-related socialization patterns leading to segregated occupations.

3. Develop strategies that effectively engage and sustain individuals in nontraditional occupations.

4. Emphasize programs that meet the needs of the information age.

5. Establish partnerships to build commitment, extend resources, and improve effectiveness.

6. Develop a multifaceted approach. For example, the U.S. Agency for International Development (1997) uses six major interventions to address gender issues, including (a) awareness raising and promotional/ advocacy campaigns, (b) career information and counselors services, (c) professional development, (d) mentors, (e) work-based learning, and (f) parental involvement.

Studies show that development projects often fail because women are left out of the development process, even though they may have primary responsibility. One reason for this is a lack of data on what women do. More research needs to be conducted on women's role in developing countries. Experience has shown that these roles change from country to country and even within countries. The call to integrate women into development is an attempt to rectify previous neglect of women by development planners and to fit women into plans where they previously have been left out.

Summary

- In the early part of the nineteenth century, thousands of women first became part of the labor force in textile factories. Despite their growing numbers in the workforce, women were perceived as "better" if they stayed home, tending family and house. It wasn't until the Civil War that women played an increasingly important role in industry and the production of goods. During World War I and World War II, the shortage of male workers and the wartime industrial expansion created many new jobs for women in factories, sewing rooms, and munitions plants.

- The Smith-Hughes Act of 1917 provided the first federal funding for public school programs in agriculture, trade, industrial, and home economics education. The first three programs were specially designed for males, and home economics was included to provide women with an education for homemaking. From their inception, vocational programs were intentionally sex typed. This separation of training for males and females continued with no legislative direction for change until the Equal Pay Act of 1963 was passed. This act, considered the first significant legislation relating to vocational equity, called for the end of discrimination on the basis of sex in payment of wages for equal work.

- In the 1970s, Congress recognized the expanding role of women in the workforce. Congressional reports accompanying the 1976 Amendments to the Vocational Education Act noted that most women will work during at least some portion of their adult lives; that women constitute a large growing part of the labor force; that most women work out of necessity; and that in spite of all this, working women are concentrated in a few lower-income occupational areas.

- To remedy this situation, Congress included provisions in the 1976 amendments to eliminate sex bias and sex stereotyping in vocational education, and (later) to serve displaced homemakers. Recipients' responses to these provisions were initially very limited, prompting Congress to strengthen and expand the provisions in subsequent legislation.

- Other federal laws, including the Carl D. Perkins Vocational Act of 1984 and the Carl D. Perkins Vocational and Applied Technology Act of 1990, challenged business, industry, labor, and education to develop policy, procedures, and practices promoting racial and sex equity. The 2006 reauthorization of Perkins continues to push for race and gender equity.

- Some of the problems associated with sex equity are: sex bias, sex stereotyping, lack of support, and sexual harassment. Recognizing these problems and others related to male sex-role stereotyping can help C&T educators identify equity as an area that benefits both sexes.

- In many cases females were denied entry into training programs for higher-wage, traditionally male, industry and technical occupations. Gender stereotyping in guidance and counseling practices and materials, bias in teacher practices, and harassment by other students discouraged nontraditional enrollment by females and in practice restricted career and technical education opportunities for females to lower-wage, traditionally female, health and cosmetology occupations. In short, systematic practices and expectations steered females into family and consumer sciences and away from shop or auto mechanics. In the long run, the most damaging consequence of such gender bias was to limit female access to the benefits of career and technical education—the living wage that provides females the same economic self-sufficiency that males have long enjoyed.

- Women in developing countries play an important role in agricultural production and are involved in virtually all aspects of subsistence/food cultivation.

- Women's increased participation in the labor force has occurred during a time when rapid technological advantages, substantive political and social transitions, and dramatic shifts in the world economy have affected the work situations of both men and women.

- Although career and technical education and training are essential to development in the information age, women in developing countries continue to experience unequal access.

- Women's access to technology and training is a basic requirement for their participation in the global information economy. Education is the single most important factor for increasing the ability of girls and women to take advantage of information technology opportunities. Beyond increasing access to basic education, girls and women must be equipped with skills for a range of roles in information technology as users, creators, designers, and managers.

- Women as well as men must be consulted and involved in all aspects of project development and implementation in developing countries. In order to be involved, women need to have the same opportunities available to them that have been available to men.

Discussion Questions and Activities

1. Discuss the differences between requirements of Title IX (Education Amendments of 1972) and the provisions of the Education Amendments of 1976 that pertain to sex discrimination and sex bias.
2. What career and technical education training is currently available to women in your local community?
   a. How flexible are these courses in terms of time and place?
   b. To what extent are they concentrated on the traditional low-paying jobs?
3. In view of the important role of women in meeting the nation's need for trained workers, how can career and technical education training programs for women be strengthened and expanded to provide employment opportunities for women at all levels of educational attainment?
4. Discuss the historical work roles of women in CTE.
5. Differentiate between sex stereotyping and sex discrimination.
6. List and discuss some suggestions for C&T educators to utilize in addressing the issue of sexual harassment.
7. What are the major factors determining the level and nature of female enrollment in career and technical education?
8. Discuss what the world would be like in a developed country such as the United States if women withdrew from the labor market. What would the scenario be like for a developing country?

Library Research

9. What are women's special career and technical education needs?
10. What programming is provided for minority women and poor white women who live in rural areas and have less than a high school education?

Debate

11. Is equal opportunity for females in career and technical education a "myth" or a "reality"?

12. Has there been an increase in equitable access to career and technical education programs and the benefits they can provide in the twenty-first century?

References and Additional Reading

American Association of University Women (2004). Vocational education and the Perkins Act. June 2004 position paper. Washington, DC: AAUW Public Policy and Government Relations Department. Retrieved April 4, 2007, from http://www.aauw.org/issue_advocacy/actionpages/positionpapers/perkins.cfm.

Association of Career and Technical Education (2005). Forging new pathways: Promising practices for recruiting and retaining students in career and technical education programs that are nontraditional for their gender. Programs and Practices That Work: Preparing Students for Nontraditional Careers Project. Retrieved February 15, 2007, from http://www.napequity.org/pdf/Report2005_PPTW_Final.pdf.

Bae, Y., Choy, S., Geddes, C., Sable, J., and Synder, T. (2000). *Trends in educational equity of girls and women*. Washington, DC: National Center for Education Statistics, U.S. Department of Education.

Baker, R. K. (1977, July). Entry of women into federal job world at price. *Smithsonian, 8*, 83–85.

Benavot, A. (1983). The rise and decline of vocational education. *Sociology of Education, 56*, 63–76.

Bennett, C. A. (1937). *History of manual and industrial education. 1870 to 1917*. Peoria, IL: The Manual Arts Press.

Biddlecombe, L., Browne, J., Charlton, B., Dowden, H., Northcott, C., Onslow, J., Priestly, J., and Thompson, J. (1989). *Learning the hard way*. London: Macmillian.

Burge, P. L. (1990). Vocational education gender-equity research priorities for the 1990s. *Journal of Vocational Education Research, 15*(3), 1–19.

———. (1987). *Career development of single parents*. Information Series No. 324. Columbus, OH: ERIC Clearing house on Adult, Career, and Vocational Education. The National Center for Research in Vocational Education.

———. (1983). Employers' perceptions of nontraditional vocational guidance. *Journal of Studies in Technical Careers, 5*, 299–306.

Burge, P. L., and Culver, S. M. (1989). Vocational education: A pragmatic, economic approach to equity. *Journal of Vocational and Technical Education, 6*(1), 3–12.

Burke, J. Bruce and Johnston, Michelle (2006). *Equity in American education*. Charleston, SC: BookSurge Publishing.

Butler, D. (1989). *Title IX for cutting the tape to sex equity in education programs and activities*. Charleston: West Virginia Department of Education.

Cardenas, J., and First, J. M. (1985). Children at risk. *Educational Leadership, 43*(1), 4–8.

Clark, I. E. (1892). *Art and industry*. Washington, DC: U.S. Bureau of Education.

Cloud, K. (1986). *Gender issues in AID's agricultural program: How efficient are we?* Washington, DC: USAID.

Couch, A. S. (1989). Career and family: The modern worker's balancing act. *Vocational Education Journal, 64*(6), 24–27.

Crain, Soudien, Kallaway, Peter, and Breier, Mignonne (Eds.) (2006). *Education, equity and transformation*. Norwell, MA: Kluwer Academic Publishers.

Creevy, L. E. (1986). *Women farmers in Africa*. Syracuse, NY: Syracuse University Press.

Culver, S. M., and Burge, P. L. (1985a). Expected occupational prestige of students in vocational programs nontraditional for their sex. *Journal of Studies in Technical Careers, 7*, 231–240.

———. (1985b). Self-concept of students in vocational programs nontraditional for their sex. *Journal of Vocational Education Research, 10*(2), 1–10.

Daines, J., Hartenstein, H., and Birch, G. (2000). Women, education, and training: Old challenges in a new age. In D. R. Herschbach and C. P. Campbell (Eds.), *Workforce preparation: An international perspective* (pp. 22–42). Ann Arbor, MI: Prakken Publications.

Dykman, A. (1997, April). Taking aim at bias in school and the workplace. *Techniques, 72*(4), 19–21.

Firebaugh, F. M., and Miller, J. R. (2002). Diversity and globalization: Challenges, opportunities, and promises. *Journal of Family and Consumer Sciences, 92*(1), 26–36.

Fishel, A., and Potter, J. (1977). *National politics and sex discrimination in education*. Lexington, MA: Lexington Books.

Foner, P. S. (1987). Women and the American labor movement: A historical perspective. In K. S. Koziara, M. H. Moskow, and L. D. Tanner (Eds.), *Working women: Past, present, future* (pp. 154–186). Washington, DC: The Bureau of National Affairs.

Goldstein, J. S. (2000). *International relations,* 4th ed. New York: Addison Wesley Longman.

Gordon, R. (1981). *Ties that bind: The price of pursuing the male mystique*. Washington, DC: Project on Equal Education Rights.

Green, J. A. (1969). *The educational ideas of Pestalozzi*. Originally published by W. B. Clive (1914). New York: Random House.

Gutek, G. L. (1999). *Pestalozzi and education*. Long Grove, IL: Waveland Press.

Harvey, G., and Noble, E. (1985). Economic consideration for achieving sex equity through education. In S. Klein (Ed.), *Handbook for achieving sex equity through education* (pp. 17–28). Baltimore, MD: The Johns Hopkins University Press.

Heen, M. (1984). A review of federal court decisions under Title VII of the Civil Rights Act of 1964. In H. Remick (Ed.), *Comparable worth and wage discrimination: Technical possibilities and political realities* (pp. 197–219). Philadelphia: Temple University Press.

Herzberg, F. (1966). *Work and the nature of man*. Cleveland, OH: World Publications.

Hewlett, S. (1977). Inequality and its implications for economic growth. In I. Horowits (Ed.), *Equity, income, and policy* (pp. 29–48). New York: Praeger.

Hollenback, K. (1985). *Developing an equity handbook for community college personnel: A resource to increase female enrollment in nontraditional vocational education programs*. Final report. Pueblo, CO: Pueblo Community College (ERIC Document Reproduction Service No. ED 266 253).

Houser, B. B., and Garvey, C. (1985). Factors that affect nontraditional vocational enrollment among women. *Psychology of Women Quarterly, 9*, 105–117.

Institute for Women in Trades, Technology and Science (1999). *About the institute for women in trades, technology and science*. Alameda, CA: Author.

International Labour Organization (1998). Women and training in the global economy. In *World employment report 1998–99: Employment in the global economy—How training matters* (pp. 139–162). Geneva, Switzerland: Author.

Jossey-Bass Publishers (2002). *The Jossey-Bass reader on gender in education* (Jossey Bass Education Series) Hoboken NJ: John Wiley & Sons.

Kane, R. D., and Frazee, P. E. (1978). *Women in nontraditional vocational education in secondary schools.* Arlington, VA: RJ Associates.

Klein, Susan, Dwyer, Carol Anne, Fox, Lynn, Grayson, Dolores, Kramarae, Cheris, Pollard, Diane, and Richardson, Barbara (Eds.) (2007). *Handbook for achieving gender equity through education.* Mahwah, NJ: Lawrence Erlbaum.

Koch, Janice and Irby, Beverly (Eds.) (2005). *Defining and redefining gender equity in education: A volume in research on women and education.* Charlotte, NC: Information Age Publishing.

Lewis, S. (1985). Achieving sex equity for minority women. In S. S. Klein (Ed.), *Handbook for achieving sex equity through education* (pp. 365–390). Baltimore, MD: The Johns Hopkins University Press.

Maguire, M. F. (November/December, 2001). Gender, information technology, and developing countries. *Techknowlogia*, 58–59.

Marshall, R., and Paulin, B. (1987). Employment and earnings of women: Historical perspective. In K. S. Koziara, M. H. Moskow, and L. D. Tanner (Eds.), *Working women: Past, present, future* (pp. 1–36). Washington, DC: Bureau of National Affairs.

Middleton, J. Ziderman, H., and Adams, A.V. (1993). *Skills for productivity: Vocational education and training in developing countries.* New York: Oxford University Press.

National Commission on Working Women of Wider Opportunities for Women (1990). *Women and nontraditional work.* Washington, DC: Author.

National Women's Law Center (2002). *Title IX and equal opportunity in vocational and technical education: A promise still owed to the nation's young women.* Washington, DC: Author.

NCWGE (National Coalition for Women and Girls in Education) (1988). *Working toward equity: A report on implementation of the new equity provisions of the Carl D. Perkins Vocational Education Act.* Washington, DC: Displaced Homemakers' Network.

Nusebaum, M., and Glover, J. (1996). *Women culture and development: A study of human capabilities.* New York: Oxford University Press.

NWLC (National Coalition for Women and Girls in Education) (2002). *Title IX at 30: Report card on gender equity.* Washington, DC: Author.

Neuman, S., and Ziderman, A. (1991). Vocational schooling, occupational matching, and labor market earnings in Israel. *Journal of Human Resources*, 26(2), 256–281.

Osipow, S. H. (1973). *Theories of career development.* Englewood Cliffs, NJ: Prentice-Hall.

Ray, E. M. (1968). Vocational, technical, and practical arts education: Social and philosophical framework. *Review of Educational Research*, 38(4), 309–325.

Reider, C. (1977, April). *Women, work, and vocational education.* Occasional Paper No. 26. Columbus, OH: The National Center for Research in Vocational Education.

Roby, P. A. (1976). Toward full equality: More job education for women. *School Review*, 84(2), 181–212.

Schulzinger, R., and Syron, L. (1984). *Inch by inch: A report on equal opportunity for young women in New York City's vocational high schools.* New York: Center for Public Advocacy Research.

Shaw, L. B., and Shaw, R. (1987). From midlife to retirement: The middle-aged woman worker. In K. S. Koziara, M. H. Moskow, and L. D. Tanner (Eds.), *Work-*

ing women: Past, present, future (pp. 299–331). Washington, DC: The Bureau of National Affairs.

Sleeter, Christine E., and Grant, Carl A. (2006). *Making choices for multicultural education: Five approaches to race, class, and gender,* 5th ed. Hoboken, NJ: John Wiley & Sons.

Spring, A., Smith, G., and Kayuni, F. (1985). *Women farmers in Malawi: Their contribution and participation in development projects.* Washington, DC: USAID Office of Women in Development

Sproles, E. K. (1987). Perceptions by nontraditional and traditional agricultural students toward their high school preparation and work barriers. *Journal of the American Association of Teacher Educators in Agriculture, 28*(2), 18–24.

Stitt, B. A. (1988). Male stereotyping isn't fair. *Vocational Education Journal, 63*(8), 12–14.

———. (1990). *The Carl D. Perkins Vocational and Applied Technology Education Act* (P.L. 101–392). Washington, DC: U.S. Government Printing Office.

Suki, Ali, Mauthner, Melanie L., and Benjamin, Shereen (Eds.) (2005). *The politics of gender and education.* New York: Palgrave Macmillan.

U.S. Congress (1974). Women's Equity Act of 1974 (P.L. 93-380). Washington, DC: U.S. Government Printing Office.

United Nations (1991). *The world's women 1970–1990: Trends and statistics* (Social Statistics and Indicators, Series K, No. 8). New York: Author.

United States Agency for International Development (1997). *Human capacity development in the 21st century.* Washington, DC: Author.

Vetter, L. (1993). Sex equity programs and vocational education. In C. Anderson and L. C. Rampp (Eds.), *Vocational education in the 1990s, II: A sourcebook for strategies, methods, and materials* (pp. 225–242). Ann Arbor, MI: Prakken Publishing.

Vetter, L., and Hickey, D. R. (1985). Where the women are enrolled. *Vocational Education Journal, 60*(7), 26–29.

Vetter, L., Sechler, J., Lowry, C. M., and Canora, V. (1979). *Factors influencing nontraditional vocational education enrollments: A literature review.* Columbus, OH: State University, National Center for Research in Vocational Education.

Wells, J. (1983). *Statement of the National Coalition for Women and Girls in Education.* Washington, DC: National Coalition for Women and Girls in Education.

Willard, E. (1987). *A plan for improving female education.* Originally published by Middleburg College (1918). Marietta, GA: Larlin Corporation.

Wonacott, M. E. (2002). *Equity in career and technical education: Myths and realities,* No. 20. Columbus: ERIC Clearinghouse on Adult, Career, and Vocational Education, The Ohio State University.

Yuen, C. Y. (1983). Internal barriers for women entering nontraditional occupations: A review of the literature. *Occupational Education Forum, 12*(2), 14–39.

chapter 7

Participation of Special-Needs Populations in Career and Technical Education

The term *special-needs populations* is generally used to describe individuals who are (1) members of minority groups, (2) limited-English speaking and physically and/or mentally disabled, (3) economically and/or academically disadvantaged; or (4) gifted and talented.

Uniqueness of needs was recognized in the early development of vocational education. The Commission on National Aid to Vocational Education (1914) expressed particular concern about persons leaving school at an early age: One-half of the children who entered elementary schools in the United States in 1914 remained to the final elementary grade, and only one in ten reached the final year of high school. On the average, 10 percent of the children left school at 13 years of age; 40 percent left by the time they were 14; 70 percent by the time they were 15; and 85 percent by the time they were 16 years of age. On the average, the schools retained pupils as far as the fifth grade, but in some cities large numbers left in earlier grades.

Vocational education was intended to help change schools' inability to retain students. However, the commission's judgment was that special emphasis was needed on education for early dropouts who were already employed. The commission responded to these special needs by recommending part-time schools, the purpose of which was twofold:

1. To increase the general intelligence of young workers and teach them to better understand their social and civic duties.

2. To increase their industrial intelligence and skill and develop capacity for advancement within a given trade if such opportunity exists, or if not, to prepare for some skilled and remunerative work in another line (Commission on National Aid to Vocational Education, 1914).

In the 1960s and 1970s, much of the legislation passed by Congress dealt with providing equal education for all. Never before had there been such an emphasis on providing vocational education for all students, no matter what their race, sex, age, national origin, language, or economic level. Laws enacted during this period include the Civil Rights Act of 1964, the Economic Opportunity Act of 1965, the Elementary and Secondary Education Act of 1973, the Comprehensive Employment Training Act of 1973, the 1974 Education Amendments for the needs of limited-English-proficient (LEP) students, the Education for All Handicapped Children Act of 1975, and the Vocational Educational Amendments of 1976, which mandated changes designed to enable vocational education to better serve all people, including special-needs populations.

This chapter examines the historical relationship between ethnic groups and career and technical education and also the participation of special education students in CTE.

Historical Relationship between Ethnic Groups and CTE

As America continues to be the land of opportunity, the makeup of the workforce continues to change dramatically. Minority groups are growing at an unprecedented rate, especially Asian-Americans and Hispanics. According to the U.S. Census Bureau (2000), for the first time since the early 1930, one of every ten Americans was foreign born, due mainly to explosive growth in the Hispanic population. By the year 2050, the U.S. Census Bureau (2004) projects the following racial/ethnic distribution: 55 percent White, 21 percent Hispanic, 14 percent Black, 9 percent Asian, and 1 percent American Indian.

There is no doubt that minorities are inadequately represented in professional roles in career and technical education. CTE professionals who have worked with minority youth have noted that these youth seem to be less interested in CTE than are non-minority youth. However, there is a paucity of data to substantiate this observation.

Ogbu (1986) argued that minorities who were incorporated into American society against their will are different from the White majority and from

Attracting and retaining minorities should be a top priority for CTE.

other minorities such as immigrants. He called these groups "castelike minorities" and gave as examples Blacks, Hispanics, and American Indians. Boykin (1986) expanded on this theme by proposing the theory that minorities must cope within three areas. Everyone, including Whites, interacts within the "mainstream" or majority culture. Next, there is a separate minority culture that groups like Blacks, Hispanics, and Asian Americans contribute to and experience. Finally, each minority group has its own distinct actions, reactions, and experiences that fit into the majority culture with varying degrees of success.

Longstreet (1978) suggested that ethnic groups are unique according to several aspects of style: verbal and nonverbal communication, orientation modes, social value patterns, and intellectual modes. Longstreet used these aspects to conduct observations of minority and nonminority students in classroom settings. Studies by Marshall (1989), Metzger (1985), and Valverde (1988) that explored the underrepresentation of minorities and women in professional administrative jobs in education suggest that stereotyping, discrimination, constraints imposed by self and family, low career aspirations, lack of confidence and initiative, and lack of sponsors are causes for low participation by these groups.

African Americans

African Americans have a long history and tradition of participation in career and technical education. Between 1619 and 1846 there were numerous apprenticeship programs for slaves. Manual labor schools for African Americans began to open in many parts of the South in the 1830s (Jennings, 1991). Several private industrial institutions, such as Tuskegee and Hampton, were founded. Leaders such as Frederick Douglass and Booker T. Washington spoke strongly in favor of expanding participation of African Americans in vocational education after the post–Civil War period. From 1910 to 1930 public secondary schools began to offer manual training for African Americans.

While the manual training movement had stressed the benefit to education of the integration of manual and intellectual training, a major purpose of industrial and vocational education was to meet the labor needs of industry. However, it also offered an educational response to two social and economic challenges: the huge influx of rural poor and newly free, uneducated, and unemployed African Americans in the South (Du Bois, 1903; Lazerson and Grubb, 1974). Educators and industrialists were concerned about the immigrants' high attrition rate in secondary schools that left them uneducated, unskilled, and unprepared for life as industrial workers. For the urban immigrants and other poor, educators prescribed socialization and training in the values of hard work and proper homemaking, which in schools translated into woodworking or industrial arts for boys and sewing, cooking, or home economics for girls (Lazerson and Grubb, 1974).

During the first decade of the twentieth century, the educational opportunities of African-American women slowly expanded. Local Black industrial training schools became public high schools, and larger industrial training institutes were converted into colleges. Some of the new schools offered more academic work, and some expanded their vocational offerings as traditional trades became obsolete. For their daughters, African-American families were interested in education that would ensure that the young women could avoid domestic work. Of the new vocational areas, African-American women most often chose the fields of nursing, cosmetology, or printing. Nursing and cosmetology were popular and open to African-American women because these services were needed in the African-American community, and the work fit into the accepted women's roles. The printing field was opening up to women because print shops on campuses were expanding and men were choosing other fields of vocational work (Ihle, 1986).

After 1930, as industrial development demanded more skilled workers, a reversal occurred in vocational education as Whites claimed access to the better jobs. White schools began emphasizing industrial training while Black schools offered more academic education (Ogbu, 1978). In addition, the depression caused increased competition between Black and White schools for limited educational funds, so these public school systems, already separate, became even more unequal. By 1935, African Americans in the South were underrepresented in vocational education programs that received federal funds, and Black institutions were less likely to receive funds. While southern White students were equally likely to be enrolled in agriculture (36 percent), home economics (34 percent), and trade and industries (30 percent), African-American students were most likely found in agriculture (55 percent) and home economics (29 percent) with only 16 percent in trade and industry programs. The lower participation by African-American students in the trades most likely reflected the exclusion of African Americans from practicing in these occupations (Anderson, 1982). In addition, although distributive (sales) occupations had been funded in vocational education by the George-Reed Act of 1929, these programs were not offered in most Black schools (Ogbu, 1978).

During the 1930s, African-American educators attempted to reduce educational and economic inequities in the North and the South through a Black vocational guidance movement that sought to improve the vocational counseling for African-American students. They saw that African-American students were either aspiring to very low-level occupations or expecting to pursue an academic or professional education. These educators believed that more information on the wide range of middle-level skilled occupations would lead African-American students to choose more of these occupations (Anderson, 1982). However, this movement had very little effect on the lower participation of Black students in the more lucrative job paths, due to the severity of the depression and the continuing exclusion of Blacks from these occupations. Instead, during the 1940s, the demand for civilian labor during World War II created more opportunities for African-American men and women than any vocational guidance or training had been able to do.

African-American educational strategy finally moved away from vocational education and instead encouraged African-American youth to aim for entrance into colleges and universities (Anderson, 1982). Thus, Du Bois' vision that African-American youth should strive for the highest level of education was finally fulfilled.

Black agricultural educators concerned about increasing the number of Black students in vocational agriculture note that most vocational agriculture teachers are White (Bowen, 1987). The historically and predominantly Black 1890 land-grant agricultural and mechanical colleges provide excellent training for many Black agricultural researchers and teachers (Taylor, Powers, and Johnson, 1990). However, the percentage of Black faculty at historically White 1862 land-grant colleges, which train the majority of vocational agriculture teachers, has remained very low (Bowen, 1987). In addition, while the percentage of Black students majoring in agriculture at the bachelor's level has not changed, the percentage of Black students obtaining master's degrees in agriculture has decreased. Consequently, the percentage of agricultural faculty who are Black is not likely to increase (Larke and Barr, 1987).

These studies offer various historical and structural reasons why African Americans might be found in lower-level vocational programs. According to Arnold and Levesque (1992):

> A history of being limited to lower-level vocational education programs and occupations may explain any lingering overrepresentation in lower-level vocational education programs. However, it is also possible that Blacks may be underrepresented in the higher-level programs due to continuing racism and structural biases. (p. 20)

The 2000 Census reported that the growth of the Black population rose to 34.7 million from 30 million in 1990, an increase of 16 percent.

Booker T. Washington, the prominent African American educator, promoted vocational education (CTE) because he perceived it would provide economic self-reliance and help African Americans integrate into America. On the other hand, W. E. B. Du Bois, another prominent African American educator, had a preference for academic education over vocational education (CTE). Du Bois believed that academic education was the cornerstone to progress and the solution to racial conflicts for African Americans (Nall, 1997). Nall reported that:

> Neither Washington nor Du Bois was totally right or wrong. African Americans need to use all available resources to expand options and opportunities for African American youth. Unfortunately, the argument still exists today with the resultant dichotomy. Many African Americans tend to view vocational education [CTE] as inferior to academic education, and when they acknowledge that some African Americans should acquire training, it is usually for someone else's children. This view partly derives from the fact that African Americans have historically been allowed access to vocational training that prepared them for the low-paying jobs traditionally held by African Americans rather than that

leading to high-paying jobs. This view is likely to persist until African Americans are prepared for and gain access to the high-quality training that provides the skills necessary for successful entry into the technical workforce of the 21st century. (p. 46)

Hispanics

Although limited data availability often leads researchers to treat Hispanics as if they were a homogeneous group, the U.S. Hispanic population is diverse. The three largest Hispanic subgroups are Mexican Americans, Puerto Ricans, and Cubans. Recent immigrants from Central and South America constitute a fourth group (National Center for Educational Statistics, 1995). These subgroups are concentrated in different parts of the United States, their economic circumstances vary, and the timing of their immigration differs.

The issue of participation is central to career and technical education. Consequently, researchers have extensively explored the factors that influence participation. However, little information exists about participation as it specifically relates to Hispanics. This situation has serious implications given the current Hispanic socioeconomic and demographic trends.

According to Peng (2006):

> A teacher, a student, a businessman, a politician—these titles are finding their way into a group that once went unnoticed. The increasing Hispanic population is contributing to the changing face of America and the Pine Belt. A 2005 report from the U.S. Census estimates there are 42.7 million people who are of Hispanic origin—making them the largest ethnic or raise minority at 14 percent of the nation's population. This is double the population of 15 years ago. The Hispanic population was 32.8 million, according to the 2000 Census and in 1990, the Census reported 22.4 million. However, today's count on the Hispanic population still may not paint an accurate picture. These numbers do not include some migrant workers in the U.S. (p.1).

By 2050, the total number of U.S. residents of Hispanic descent is expected to reach 98 million (Hankin, 2005).

The Hispanic population is growing even faster in the Pacific Northwest (Cook, 1986). While Hispanics are increasing in number, they have not benefited substantially from the economic growth of the 1980s and 1990s. Sotomayor (1988) reported that Hispanic workers are more likely to work in unskilled occupations. This situation held true especially for Hispanic women; wages remained low even though Hispanic females' participation in the workforce grew. Valdivieso (1985) noted that Hispanic children were more likely to live in poverty (70.5 percent) than were Whites (47.6 percent) or African Americans (68.5 percent).

Furthermore, the educational outlook for Hispanics remains grim. As a group, many Hispanics 20 to 24 years old have not graduated from high school (Valdivieso, 1985). In addition, dropout rates remain high. Sotomayor (1988) reported that, based on national survey data, 31 percent of 18-year-old Hispanics had not completed high school or obtained a general equivalency degree (GED). Oakes (1990) found that in elementary and secondary schools, students who were Hispanic, African-American, low-income, inner-city residents, or in "low-ability" classes had fewer opportunities than other students to participate in traditional academic mathematics and science programs for the following two reasons. First, Hispanic, African-American, and low-income students were more likely than White and middle-income students to be assessed as low in academic ability and placed in lower-level tracks. Second, students in majority Black or disadvantaged schools were exposed to fewer demanding programs. Students in low tracks and in less advantaged schools were exposed to fewer math and science resources such as highly qualified teachers, equipment, and development of higher-level skills. Consequently, these lesser opportunities perpetuated race and social class differences in math and science achievement.

In 1991, at the associate's degree level, Hispanic men were slightly less likely than White men to major in other technical/professional fields but were more likely to major in arts and sciences. Hispanic women were more likely than White women to earn associate's degrees in arts and sciences and in business but were less likely to earn degrees in health-related fields. Between 1987 and 1991, differences in the fields studied by Hispanics and Whites at the associate's degree level narrowed for men and widened for women (NCES, 1995).

At the bachelor's degree level, in 1991, Hispanics were more likely than Whites to major in social and behavioral sciences and were less likely to major in technical/professional fields. Overall, Hispanic–White differences in the fields studied at the bachelor's-degree level narrowed between 1977 and 1991, although almost all of the decrease occurred between 1977 and 1985 (NCES, 1995). Hispanics are less likely to complete postsecondary credentials in large numbers and do not complete programs considered to lead to high-skill, high-wage work (Maldonado, 2006).

Wirsching and Stenberg (1992) suggested that length of residency, marital status, and educational attainment were predictive of participation of Hispanics in career and technical education. Factors predictive of nonparticipation included age, barriers to participation (situational, institutional, and psychosocial), and degree of acculturation.

American Indians

Career and technical education for American Indians needs to be understood in the context of all American Indian education, which in turn operates within the context of American Indian life. Originally, the federal government assumed full responsibility for the education of American Indians, as their isolation on tax-exempt reservations provided states and localities with a rationale to withhold education (as well as other publicly supported) services. According to Hudson (1994), in the 1800s the federal government focused on two efforts to use education to attract American Indians. First, the government supported missionary education through various religious groups; the goal was to Christianize American Indians, providing them with basic literacy skills. Some of the mission schools that were established on reservations during this period still operate today, although as part of a more diverse education system.

The federal government's second effort focused on schools run by the Bureau of Indian Affairs (BIA). By 1900, the BIA had established twenty industrial training schools, providing instruction in basic literacy. The acknowledged goal of these schools was to "take the Indian out of the Indians." To help meet this goal, the training schools operated as off-reservation boarding schools, separating youth from the "negative" influences of their families and tribes. According to one historian, "the underlying intention of this policy of relocation was to assimilate American Indians into the dominant culture." Children were placed in boarding schools in the early primary grades, and the schools were notorious in their attempts to eradicate any vestiges of traditional Indian cultures (Slater, 1992).

In the twentieth century, acceptance of American Indian cultures was espoused by anthropologists and reformers, and, through their efforts, by policy makers. This new view culminated in the 1928 Meriam report, which was harshly critical of the ethnocentric and indoctrination methods used by the boarding schools. Relatively rapid and major changes followed in the philosophy and practice of American Indian education. Within five years, twelve boarding schools were closed or converted to day schools, and curricula began to include information on American Indian culture. Efforts to reform American Indian education were assisted by a congressional study that revealed the deplorable living conditions on reservations. This study led to the passage of the 1934 Indian Reorganization Act (Hudson, 1994).

It was in the Indian Reorganization Act that the federal government first promulgated the notion of "self-determination" for American Indians. The act increased tribal self-government and input into education, encouraged cultural and religious pluralism, and supported economic development for reservations. American Indian teachers were trained; textbooks were published in American Indian languages; and "community" schools, designed to serve multiple tribal needs, became the new focus of the BIA's education efforts.

In the 1950s and 1960s, known as the Termination Era, the government reverted to the philosophy that American Indians should be encouraged to integrate into the larger society. Financial support for 100 tribes was ended, a number of reservations were eliminated, and a federal relocation program was implemented to move American Indians to urban centers. The effects of this policy were marked:

> The majority of Native Americans who left the reservations became part of the undereducated, working poor—those engaged in part-time or lower-paid manual labor. Many of these people . . . left the reservations

but returned, unable to cope with urban life. The failure of so many Native Americans to adapt outside the reservation hastened the end of the termination policy. (Blood and Burnham, 1994, p. 25)

The civil rights movement of the 1960s also helped end the Termination Era, as the rights of minorities, including American Indians, were enforced with new legislation. In 1970, the Nixon administration returned federal policy to one of self-determination for American Indians. Although the 1972 Indian Education Act provided funds for adding Indian history and culture to educational programs, the larger focus of the new federal effort was to shift administrative responsibilities to tribes rather than to increase funding. Thus, in 1975, the Indian Self-Determination and Education Assistance Act became the first of a series of laws that shifted federal administrative responsibilities to tribal leaders.

During the early 1990s, most American Indians were enrolled in the public school system. About 85 percent of American Indian K–12 students attend public schools, while 10 percent attend federally funded BIA schools and 5 percent attend private schools (Slater, 1992). At the postsecondary level, the federal government has attempted to increase educational opportunities for American Indians on reservations by funding a number of postsecondary institutions on or near these sites. Hudson (1994) reported that in the early 1990s the BIA funded 24 tribally controlled postsecondary institutions, including 2 vocational institutes, 18 community colleges, and 4 four-year colleges. According to Hudson (1994), about 14 percent of all American Indian postsecondary students attend these tribally controlled institutions. An additional five U.S. colleges and two Canadian colleges also serve American Indians.

Values held by individuals with special needs are not always congruent with those of C&T educators. More importantly, they need not be congruent. The cultural values of one group do not need to be bent to fit the values of the dominant culture. Recognition and acceptance of the differences are usually what is needed. Marjorie Bear Don't Walk (1976) presents the position of the American Indians:

> There developed a joke among Indians that if you sent any Indian to the moon, he/she would find a way to return to the reservation. Most of us do return to our reservations; most of us would prefer to be trained on or near our own homes. Most of us would like to find jobs on our own reservations. (p. 132)

Career and technical educators who accept this expression of desire will find an initial basis for providing CTE different from that of the past. However, the educational needs of American Indians do not end merely with reservation-based and reservation-oriented programs. Other important aspects must be addressed, as well. It must be determined whether training for a new social and economic role will cause a communication gap between American Indian students and their parents and families. It is also important to determine how emotional support can be provided to help students and family members adapt to the new situations (Bear Don't Walk, 1976).

The following organizations are involved in the work of providing educational opportunities for American CTE Indians.

- *The American Indian Higher Education Consortium*
  Founded by, and jointly governed by, the tribal colleges, AIHEC supports the work of the colleges and the national movement for tribal self-determination.
  www.aihec.org

- *The American Indian College Fund*
  This nonprofit organization is the nation's largest provider of privately funded scholarships for American Indians.
  www.collegefund.org

- *The Office of Indian Education Programs*
  The OIEP is part of the Bureau of Indian Affairs, an agency within the U.S. Department of the Interior, and was established to carry out the federal government's education commitment to Indian tribes.
  www.oiep.bia.edu

- *Office of Indian Education*
  An office of the U.S. Department of Education, OIE supports the efforts of local education agencies, postsecondary institutions and tribes.
  www.ed.gov/about/offices/list/ous/oese/oie/index.html

- *The Indian Education Professional Development Program*
  Funded by the U.S. Department of Education, Office of Indian Education, the program provides professional development grants to qualified American Indians to become teachers, administrators and teacher aides.
  www.ed.gov/legislation/FedRegister/announcements/2003-3/
  072403d.html

- *Center for Indian Education*
  The Center for Indian Education promotes studies in American Indian/Alaska Native policy and administration that contribute to the quality of scholarship and effective practices in education, professional training and tribal capacity building. It is housed in the College of Education at Arizona State University. The Center also publishes the *Journal of American Indian Education*.
  www.coe.asu.edu/cie

Limited-English-Proficient CTE Students

Diversity in America is hugely affected by immigration. Worldwide, more than 150 million people live in a country different from their birthplace; more than a quarter of these people chose to live in the United States. By 2050, the U.S. population is expected to grow by 129 million, and of this number, 75 million are expected to be immigrants (Doyle, 2002).

Helping students improve their English proficiency will likely lead to higher levels of self-efficacy and academic achievement.

Hankin (2005) reported that:

> Traditionally, immigrants to the United States came from Western and Central Europe. Irish, English, Germans, and Italians flooded Ellis Island in pursuit of the American dream. While they came with their own languages, cultures, and traditions, they had, by and large, one key thing in common: They were more or less "white." (p. 66)

This situation has changed rapidly over the past few decades. Since the 1965 Immigration Act lifted restrictions on immigration from non-Christian countries, America has seen an influx of immigrants representing many more races and creeds, and until recently, the number of White immigrants has steadily declined. In 1970, 62 percent of foreign-born U.S. residents were of European and non-Hispanic descent. By 1997, this figure had dropped to just 17 percent, a percentage that has held steady since (Hankin, 2005). More White immigrants have been coming to the United States recently from Eastern Europe, Africa, the former Soviet Union, and even Canada. About ten times more White immigrants came to America from the Soviet Union during the 1990s than during the 1980s. From 1997 to 2000, the share of the total foreign-born U.S. residents who were White and from Africa increased from 30 percent to 38 percent. During the same period, the share of foreign-born black residents from Africa decreased by 10 percent (Hankin, 2005).

There are more than 40 million people in the United States who speak a native language other than English (Oxford et al., 1989). Although the majority of this population is Spanish speaking, it also includes persons who are Asian, European, Middle Eastern, African, and American Indian. For example, between 1915 and 1985 more than 1 million refugees entered the United States: 730,000 from Southeast Asia, 100,000 from the former Soviet Union, 60,000 from other Eastern European countries, 30,000 from Latin America, 25,000 from the Near East, and 12,000 from Africa (Crandell, 1985). Several countries from the Caribbean are also included in this growing population.

Unlike some other special population groups, the number of nonnative speakers of English is expected to increase significantly. In fact, according to a study by Johnson and Packer (1987), immigrants represent the largest share of the increase in the population and the workforce since the First World War.

Access to Career and Technical Education

> As a subset of the language minority student population, the limited-English proficient student population has been estimated at [as many as] 5 to 7.5 million. . . . As a proportion of the total school-age population, LEP students could comprise . . . as much as 17% of the total. (Anstrom, 1996)

Ensuring access to CTE for special-needs populations was one predominant theme of the Perkins Act. It was included because limited-English-proficient (LEP) students are generally underrepresented in CTE programs at both secondary school and adult education levels. At the secondary level, LEP students' greater vocational coursetaking is mainly confined to occupational courses and reflects to some extent the provision of work preparation courses specifically designed for these students. According to National Assessment of Vocational Education (NAVE) (1994), LEP students have less access to vocational schools than do other students.

Some school systems have had legal action sought against them for failing to provide access. In other words, they were discriminating against student entrance into vocational education programs based on their national origin. Historically, such suits are governed by the 1974 *Lau* decision made by the U.S. Supreme Court (*Lau v. Nichols*). The decision that a San Francisco school district was discriminating against 3,000 Chinese-speaking students was made based on Title VI of the Civil Rights Act of 1964, which prohibits exclusion from programs and denial of benefits to any person on the basis of race, color, or national origin (Bradley and Friedenberg, 1988). To more adequately meet the needs of LEP students, federal funds should be more closely targeted in institutions with a large concentration of immigrant populations.

Since 1976, the Office of Vocational and Adult Education of the U.S. Department of Education has funded a modest number of bilingual vocational training (BVT) programs. Probably the most important contribution made by these federal programs is development of the BVT model, often considered to be the most effective instructional delivery for LEP vocational students (Friedenberg and Fields, 1993).The BVT model consists of the following seven components:

1. Target recruitment specifically to LEP students.

2. Institute assessment procedures.

3. Use bilingual instructions and materials; simplify English.

4. Provide vocational English as a second language.

5. Offer counseling and support service.

6. Promote job development and placement.

7. Coordinate the previous six elements so that each supports the other (Friedenberg and Fields, 1993).

In 2006, the U.S. Department of Education announced a new initiative—the LEP Partnership:

> In order to design instruction better and improve academic performance for the Nation's more than 5 million limited English proficient (LEP) students, educators need to understand what these students know and don't know, and need to build knowledge and develop strategies and tests to maximize the participation of LEP students in the academic life of our schools (U.S. Department of Education, 2006a).

According to the U.S. Department of Education (2006b), The LEP Partnership will:

- help states measure what LEP students know and what they have yet to learn in all subjects so instructional decisions can be based on valid and reliable data.

- Provide technical assistance and support to states to allow them to continue their ongoing development of valid and reliable assessments.

- Identify best practices in providing accommodations to LEP students that do not compromise accuracy or academic achievement.

Participation of Special Education Students in Career and Technical Education

Career and technical education has a long history of serving special education students. Since the Americans with Disabilities Act (ADA) took effect in 1992, employers, professionals in vocational rehabilitation, and educators generally are turning more to C&T educators for answers to questions such as the following:

- How do you determine if an employee with a disability is ready to work?

- How do you decide if the functions of a job can be done by alternative means?

- How do you ensure that a student with a disability will get needed support once he or she is enrolled in a vocational education program? (Morrissey, 1993)

The ADA defines an *individual with a disability* as "one who has a physical or mental impairment that substantially limits one or more major life activities, one who has a record of such a disability, or is regarded as having such a disability" (Morrissey, 1993, p. 23). By law, educators must now provide programming and services to special populations, including individuals with disabilities.

According to Wonacott (2001), CTE is at the forefront in providing a significant source of benefits to students with disabilities. However, secondary CTE teachers need to be knowledgeable of the following factors impacting students with disabilities:

• The rights of students

• The planning process involved in meeting their needs

• The types of disabilities and accommodations required

The National Assessment of Vocational Education (as cited in Harber, 2005, p. 42) reported that although students with disabilities are not being counseled into CTE as a group, they are the recipients of a system that prepares them well for the challenges of the workforce.

Education of the Handicapped Amendments of 1990 (PL 101-476)

This act, which began in 1975 as The Education of All Handicapped Children Act, was revised in 1983 and 1986 as Education Handicapped Act Amendments and was amended again in 1990, when its name was changed to the Individuals with Disabilities Education Act (IDEA). This act, as amended, was passed by Congress for educating disabled children and youth.

Individuals with Disabilities Education Act Amendments of 1997 and 2004 Reauthorization

On June 4, 1997, President Clinton signed into law amendments of the Individuals with Disabilities Education Act (IDEA) (Public Law 105-17). Career and technical education teachers need to be well informed about the specifics of the legislation that address the "transition" from school to a career.

IDEA's definition of transition services are defined (in section 602) as a coordinated set of activities for a student with a disability, designed within an outcome-based process that promotes movement from school to postschool activities. This includes postsecondary education, vocational training, integrated employment (including supported employment), continuing and adult education, adult services, independent living, and community participation. Transition services are based on the individual student's needs, taking into account the student's preferences and interests, and include instruction, related services, community experiences, the development of employment and other postschool adult living objectives and, when appropriate, acquisition of daily living skills and functional vocational evaluation.

The law also requires, beginning at age 14 and updated annually, a statement of students' transition service needs according to their individualized education program (IEP). This includes such components as advanced placement in career and technical education courses. Beginning at age 16, the law requires a statement of the interagency linkages needed for students' planned outcomes. At least one year before the student becomes a legal adult, the law requires a statement that the student is aware of his or her rights under the legislation (section 614).

Before the Education for All Handicapped Children Act (EHA) and the present IDEA as amended in 1997 and reauthorized in 2004, opportunities were limited for many disabled children. Under the present IDEA, however, public schools are required to offer a free appropriate public education to every eligible child with a disability in the least restrictive environment appropriate to their individual needs (Weishaar et al., 2007; Armstrong, 2001).

Purposes of IDEA 1997

The purposes of the 1997 IDEA were as follows:

- To assure that all children with disabilities have available to them . . . a free appropriate public education that emphasizes special education and related services designed to meet their unique needs;
- To assure that the rights of children with disabilities and their parents . . . are protected;
- To assist states and localities to provide for the education of all children with disabilities; and
- To assist and assure the effectiveness of efforts to educate all children with disabilities.

IDEA 2004 Reauthorization

The Individuals with Disabilities Education Act was reauthorized on December 3, 2004, as Public Law 108-446. The Individuals with Disabilities Education Act is a critical federal investment in the future of our nation. By ensuring that all students with disabilities have access to a free appropriate public education in the least restrictive environment, this law provides a framework for school systems across the nation to use in delivering an individualized education program to millions of children.

According to Weishaar and colleagues (2007), when IDEA was reauthorized in 2004, it was renamed the *Individuals with Disabilities Education Improvement Act*, and it contained many references to the No Child Left Behind Act:

> References included the participation of children with disabilities in state and district assessment systems, goals for children with disabilities that reflected goals for all children, the flexible use of funds from the IDEA to carry out school-wide programs under the NCLB, and a man-

date that all personnel were adequately prepared to work with children, subject to the provisions in the NCLB. (p. 38)

West and Taymans (1998) made the following recommendations for working with students with disabilities:

- Ask students about their strengths and disabilities; discuss any accommodations they use;
- Ask students about modifications that would make the classroom or workplace more user friendly;
- Provide the IEP team, students, and parents with labor-market information related to students' occupational area;
- Keep standards high and give students positive feedback based on their achievements and skill acquisition;
- Communicate with special education teachers and school-to-careers transition specialists; ask them for advice;
- Provide the IEP team, students, and parents with transition assessment information, such as a list of postsecondary options;
- Provide the IEP team with a list of skills and competencies taught in your vocational area; and
- Provide the special education teacher with a list of vocabulary used in the vocational classroom.

Implications of IDEA for Career and Technical Education Teachers

CTE teachers can be instrumental in assisting students with disabilities because of the nature of their work. They can provide the opportunity for students to acquire the skills they need to make the transition from school to life. Career and technical education teachers also have a thorough understanding of the employment process and the workplace. Consequently, they can contribute significantly to the transition process of a student with disabilities by contributing to the student's IEP (West and Taymans, 1998).

Because of their focus on the workplace, the majority of career and technical teachers also practice strategies that promote social skills—another benefit to students with disabilities. Some career and technical education teachers pair or group students to utilize cooperative learning and practice teamwork skills. This strategy also promotes decision making and builds self-confidence. Through some simple efforts career and technical education teachers can play an important part in assisting students' transition from school to life (West and Taymans, 1998).

> If America is to continue to grow and prosper, said former President Clinton in an address to members of Congress and the Office of Special Education, . . . We cannot afford to ignore talents, energy, and creativity of . . . Americans with disabilities. (Armstrong, 2001, p. 29)

Rate of Participation

Wagner (1991) observes that students with disabilities often need training in both work-related behaviors and specific job skills, if they are to function effectively in the competitive job market when they leave high school. A study by Wagner et al. (1993) explored the relationship of career and technical education to school performance for students with disabilities. This analysis included a comparison of how students who took CTE classes in high school fared in making the transition to adult roles and responsibilities, compared with other students. The data came from the National Longitudinal Transition Study of Special Education Students (NLTS). The NLTS is a nationally representative sample of more than eight thousand students in all eleven federal special education disability categories.

Wagner and others (1993) used the NLTS data to examine whether disabled students who took career and technical education in their most recent year in secondary school were more likely to have positive outcomes than nonvocational students, both during secondary school and in their early postschool years. The outcomes include (a) school performance as measured by students' school attendance, (b) grade performance as measured by whether students received one or more failing course grades, and (c) persistence in school, as measured by whether the students dropped out. The postschool outcomes included enrollment in postsecondary CTE or trade school and incidence of paid employment.

The Wagner study (1993) found a consistent pattern of relationships between enrollment in occupationally oriented career and technical education and better school performance. Students who had occupational training were absent from school significantly fewer days than students who did not have such training, other factors being equal. Similarly, students taking occupationally oriented CTE were significantly less likely to drop out of school when other confounding factors (such as disability and gender differences) were controlled. The NLTS estimates show that the likelihood of dropping out rather than persisting in school was three percentage points lower for CTE students than others. The analysis also indicates that CTE students were about three percentage points less likely than others to have failed a course.

Those youth who had been out of high school for up to two years and had taken secondary CTE classes were 8 percent more likely to have attended a postsecondary CTE school in previous years than were nonvocational students. In addition, students who took CTE in their last year in secondary school were 9 percent more likely to be competitively employed than youth who had not taken CTE. Wagner (1993) also reports that if the secondary career and technical education included work experience, the likelihood of employment increased an additional 14 percent beyond the increased probability associated with CTE enrollment alone.

The NLTS findings suggest that secondary career and technical education does appear to have potential for improving both school performance and postschool outcomes of disabled students.

Characteristics of CTE Participants at the Secondary Level

Students may be taking career and technical education for different reasons. Historically, students enrolled in career and technical education to prepare for entry-level jobs after high school. Meeting this objective called for developing skills in a particular occupational area and likely encouraged students to "concentrate" their course taking as a way to maximize their appeal to potential employers. Federal law, particularly in Perkins II and III, supported this goal by promoting school implementation of, and student participation in, "sequences" of related career and technical education courses.

Despite these efforts, however, the clear trend in career and technical education course taking has been toward "exploring" across occupational program areas rather than "concentrating." Among students who earn at least 3.0 occupational credits (investors), concentrating was a less common way to organize course work in 2000 (58.3 percent) than it was in 1982 (72.8 percent), when a higher proportion of students were taking three or more credits in multiple program areas. Similarly, students were much less likely to take advanced course work in their area of concentration than in 1982 (U.S. Department of Education, 2004).

These data suggest that fewer students may now view developing skills in a specific program area as their main objective for enrolling in career and technical education. Focus group discussions with students in career and technical education courses (U.S. Department of Education, 2004) suggest a variety of other reasons for their participation: to gain career exposure, to help them select or prepare for a college major, to use as a fall-back if college or other career plans fail to materialize, to pursue a leisure interest, or to take courses that present less of an intellectual challenge than do other courses (Table 7.1).

Who participates in career and technical education has been a continuing policy concern. While federal legislation in the 1960s and 1970s aimed to improve access to career and technical education for certain special populations, the debate is whether vulnerable groups are overrepresented in and well-served by CTE. Some previous reports suggested that by the early 1990s, vocational education had come to be stigmatized as a high school track for students with low levels of academic achievement, special needs or behavioral problems (Boesel et al., 1994b).

It appears that some states and districts have worked to strengthen the appeal of career and technical education courses—for example, moving away from training for what used to be considered blue-collar jobs, such as manufacturing, secretarial work, and child care, toward programs in pre-engineering, information technology and education (U.S. Department of Education, 2004). Policy makers and educators remain committed to providing access to CTE for students from special populations. However, many believe that the quality of CTE programs is unlikely to improve without attracting a broader segment of the student population or that the participa-

Table 7.1   Student Perspectives on Reasons for Participating in Career and Technical Education

Reasons	Illustrative Quotations
Help select or prepare for a college major	I took a variety of courses because I didn't know what I wanted to do in college.
	I think it's a head start. You know that you liked it in high school, so when you get to college you'll have better idea what to take.
	I took mine to prepare for college. You're better off in college if you've taken these courses. I took accounting, business management and a few others.
	I plan on majoring in agricultural for a career. [These courses] will give me a better background for college courses.
Fallback strategy	I want to become a lawyer. I'm taking auto tech to have something to fall back on.
	My mom said that I should take it because you don't know what's going to happen.
	I also want to be a singer and it (cosmetology) makes a good back-up plan.
Enrich everyday life	I want to know how to do a bit of everything.
	Fixing cars is something I like to do, something I can do. Also, I save money fixing cars myself.
	Accounting is something that you can use every day. You can help prepare taxes for yourself and others.
	Computer classes help with school work, to be able to type school papers.
Balance the pressure of academic course work	... something different from regular school work.
	You don't do the same thing every day. It's not all book work.
	It is an alternative to the regular "just go to class" ... Hands-on. I took them because I figured they'd be easy. I need a break.
	I took building maintenance because it was an easy "A."
	I chose voc. ed. because I didn't want to take Spanish and physics.
Immediate job preparation	I can get a license in July. I picked voc. ed. to get experience while I'm young so I can get a job at an early age.
	Yeah, foods. My sister and I are going to start this catering business.
	I took up the trade of welding so that I could find a job right out of high school.

Source: U.S. Department of Education. (2004). National assessment of vocational education: Final report to Congress, p. 29. Washington, DC: Office of the Under Secretary, Policy and Program Studies Service.

tion of a more diverse set of students will signal that quality improvements are being made. For these reasons, it is important to examine the characteristics of students involved in career and technical education.

African American students participate in career and technical education somewhat more, and Asian students somewhat less, than students in other racial or ethnic groups (U.S. Department of Education, 2004). There is little evidence of any statistically significant change in participation in CTE by race or ethnicity during the last decade (Table 7.2). However, in 1998 African American students earned more CTE credits (4.3 credits) and Asian students earned fewer CTE credits (3.2) than did students from other racial and ethnic groups (4.0 credits each for Hispanic, White, and American Indian students). Among all students in 1998, African Americans earned a higher share of their total CTE credits (17.4 percent) than did Asians (12.6 percent), and Asian students earned a lower share than did students from all other racial and ethnic groups (Levesque, 2003).

There were also some differences according to race and ethnicity in term of specific CTE programs in which students participated during the last decade (Table 7.3). African American students, for example, were more likely to concentrate their career and technical studies in health, food service and hospitality, personal services (such as cosmetology) and business services—occupations with projected job growth but below average earnings—and less likely to concentrate in agriculture. Comparatively high proportions of Hispanic students concentrated in agriculture, marketing, personal services, and health. Asian students were most likely to participate in health programs and much less likely to gravitate toward agriculture or trade and industry programs, including construction.

Students with limited English proficiency (LEP) are much less likely than other students to participate in an occupational program. The participation of LEP students in career and technical education has fluctuated since 1990, perhaps because the small sample of these students who can be identified in the data makes trend analysis less reliable. However, the data indicate that LEP students in twelfth grade earned significantly fewer CTE credits (3.2) in 1998 and were less likely to be occupational concentrators (8.7 percent) than were twelfth-grade students with English language proficiency (who earned 4.0 CTE credits, and of whom 25.1 percent were concentrators) (Table 7.3).

Career and technical education continues to serve somewhat disproportionate share of students with disabilities and does so in the more traditional program areas. In 1998, students with disabilities represented 2.8 percent of all high school graduates, but 4.2 percent of all occupational concentrators (Levesque, 2003). As in previous years, these students were much more likely to become concentrators (37.5 percent) and to earn substantially more CTE credits (5.9 credits) than students without disabilities (24.6 percent and 3.9 credits) (Table 7.2). In fact, students with disabilities took a much higher share of their CTE credits (23.5 percent) than did other students (15.7 percent) (Levesque, 2003). This course-taking emphasis may shift as the No Child Left

Table 7.2   Participation Measures, by Student Characteristics: 1990 to 1998

Student Characteristics	Average Number of Vocational Credits Earned			Percentage of Students Who Are Occupational Concentrators		
	1990	1998	Change	1990	1998	Change
All Students	4.2	4.0	−0.2	27.8	25.0	−2.8*
Gender						
Male	4.3	4.3	+0.0	32.3	30.7	−1.6
Female	4.1	3.8	−0.3*	23.6	19.9	−3.6*
Race or Ethnicity						
Native or American Indian	4.6	4.0	−0.6*	38.0	25.5	−12.5
Asian or Pacific Islander	3.1	3.2	+0.1	16.6	16.8	+0.2
African American	4.4	4.3	−0.1	27.3	27.2	−0.1
Hispanic	4.1	4.0	−0.1	27.9	22.9	−5.0
White	4.2	4.0	−0.2	28.5	25.3	−3.2*
Disability Status						
Has disability	6.0	5.9	+0.1	42.2	37.5	−4.7
None indicated	4.1	3.9	+0.2	27.4	24.6	−2.8*
English Proficiency						
Limited (LEP)	2.9	3.2	+0.3	12.4	8.7	−3.7
Proficient	4.2	4.0	−0.2	27.8	25.1	−2.7*
Grade 9 Mathematics						
Geometry or higher	2.7	3.0	+0.3	12.0	17.5	+5.5*
Pre-algebra or algebra	3.9	4.1	+0.2	25.3	26.2	+0.9
No or low math	5.3	4.8	−0.5**	39.3	29.6	−9.7**
School locale[1]						
Urban	3.7	3.6	−0.1	21.4	23.1	−1.7
Suburban	3.6	3.6	0.0	21.9	21.5	−0.4
Rural	4.8	4.8	0.0	31.3	31.0	−0.3
School income level						
Low	n/a	4.7	n/a	n/a	29.2	n/a
Medium	n/a	4.1	n/a	n/a	26.8	n/a
High	n/a	3.2	n/a	n/a	15.7	n/a

[1] A comparable school locale variable was not available in 1990, so 1992 data were used instead.

n/a = not available or missing data.

LEP = Limited English proficient.

* Statistically significant at the 1.96 critical level for comparison between 1990 and 1998.

**Statistically significant at the 2.58 critical level for comparison between 1990 and 1998.

Source: U.S. Department of Education. (2004). National assessment of vocational education: Final report to Congress, p. 38. Washington, DC: Office of the Under Secretary, Policy and Program Studies Service.

Table 7.3   Percentage of High School Graduates Who Concentrated in Selected Occupational Programs, by Student Characteristics: 1988

Student Characteristics	Agri-culture	Busi-ness	Health	Food/ Hosp.	Child Care	Personal Services	Tech.	Trade/ Industry
All Students	2.6	4.8	1.9	0.5	0.6	0.8	2.2	9.8
Gender								
Male	3.5	3.2	0.7	0.4	0.1	0.2	2.4	18.5
Female	1.8	6.3	3.0	0.5	1.0	1.4	2.2	1.7
Race or Ethnicity								
Native or American Indian	2.5	3.6	—	—	—	—	2.3	13.6
Asian or Pacific Islander	0.8	3.7	2.1	0.3	0.1	—	2.1	6.7
African American	0.8	7.0	4.7	1.4	0.6	1.3	1.7	7.2
Hispanic	1.5	4.3	2.1	0.2	0.5	1.3	1.8	9.1
White	3.2	4.6	1.3	0.3	0.6	0.7	2.4	10.6
Disability Status								
Has disability	6.9	4.0	1.4	0.8	0.7	2.4	1.5	18.7
None indicated	2.4	4.9	1.9	0.5	0.6	0.8	2.3	9.5
English Proficiency								
Limited (LEP)	—	2.2	—	—	—	—	—	5.2
Proficient	2.6	4.9	1.9	0.5	0.6	0.8	2.3	9.8
Grade 9 Mathematics								
Geometry or higher	1.2	3.4	3.3	0.2	0.3	0.2	3.1	4.6
Pre-algebra or algebra	2.9	5.4	1.6	0.5	0.7	0.9	2.1	10.2
No or low math	2.8	4.6	1.3	0.8	0.6	1.2	1.9	14.4
School Locale								
Urban	0.4	4.7	3.4	0.7	0.8	1.1	1.5	8.0
Suburban	1.2	3.7	1.1	0.5	0.6	0.8	2.5	8.9
Rural	6.1	6.4	1.4	0.3	0.4	0.6	2.5	12.5
School Income Level								
Low	1.1	3.2	1.3	0.3	0.6	0.7	1.7	
Medium	2.9	4.8	1.9	0.5	0.6	0.7	2.4	
High	4.0	6.5	3.6	0.1	0.3	1.1	1.9	

— = sample too small to computer mean.

LEP = Limited English proficient

Source: U.S. Department of Education. (2004). National assessment of vocational education: Final report to Congress, p. 39. Washington, DC: Office of the Under Secretary, Policy and Program Studies Service.

Behind Act becomes fully implemented and states are required to more consistently include special-needs students in academic assessment reporting.

There is little support, however, for a prediction made in a report by the National Assessment of Vocational Education (NAVE) (Boesel et al. 1994a) that students with disabilities are becoming more concentrated in career and technical education. Although data between 1982 and 1990 show a modest trend in that direction, it was not sustained during the 1990s. In addition, with special-needs students accounting for less than 5 percent of all concentrators nationally, the notion of career and technical education in general as a "dumping ground" for these students is not warranted. Although students with disabilities are represented in some of the traditional CTE program areas—agriculture, construction, mechanics and repair, and materials production (Table 7.3)—some of these areas prepare students for occupations with substantial job growth, earnings, or both. For example, automotive mechanics, electricians, and welders all had earnings in 2000 above the median and are projected to experience above-average employment growth as well (Bureau of Labor Statistics, 2001).

Career and technical education is more prevalent in small, generally rural communities than other locales. Although rural schools serve 32.3 percent of all public school graduates across the nation, these same schools serve 40.1 percent of all occupational concentrators. In contrast, urban and suburban schools account for 26.2 and 33.8 percent of concentrators, respectively (compared to 28.4 percent and 39.3 percent of all graduates) (Levesque, 2003). The numbers of CTE credits earned remained steady across all types of locales since 1990, but students in rural schools still earned more credits (4.8) in 1998 than did students in urban and suburban schools (each group averaged 3.6 credits) (Table 7.2).

Rural students tend to focus their career and technical education studies in different occupational programs than do urban or suburban students (Table 7.3). A much higher share of rural students concentrate their CTE course taking in agriculture, and to a lesser extent in construction and business, than do students who live in other locales. On the other hand, rural students are less likely to concentrate in marketing, food service and hospitability, and personal and other services—all occupations with relatively low annual earnings. Rural students are also much less likely than urban students to concentrate in the growing field of health care, although they do so at rates similar to those of their suburban peers. In other occupational program areas, there are no statistically significant differences among students who live in urban, suburban, or rural areas in terms of the extent to which they concentrate in these fields.

Challenges for Career and Technical Educators

Minorities today face an uncertain future regarding their participation in career and technical education. If planned and administered in ways that reflect quality, CTE is not only an important tool for preparation for minority workers but also a way for America to overcome a growing social and economic crisis—the deterioration of living conditions for many of its citizens. Because of the economic and demographic development in America, there is now a window of opportunity for all minorities in career and technical education. This opportunity will not be realized, however, if basic challenges are not met and resolved by the CTE community.

Before describing these challenges, it is important to emphasize that the American CTE community does have the potential and leadership capabilities to respond to these challenges that could strengthen America's social productivity. Jennings (1991) described at least five major social and economic challenges facing all educators concerned with issues related to race, ethnicity, and the preparation of the workforce for the 1990s and beyond:

1. *Demography*—Today's demographic scenario presents economic opportunities not just for minorities but for the entire nation. However, CTE will become increasingly important as a channel for providing minorities with career skills for the job market.

2. *Changing economy*—The deterioration of living conditions for poor and working-class Americans has led to what social scientists call a "permanent underclass" of young Blacks and Hispanics who have not been integrated into the American economy.

3. *Changes in the labor force*—According to the *Workforce 2000* report, most labor force growth will come from groups in the population that have been traditionally underutilized and suffer from labor market problems. Women, minorities, and immigrants could account for more than 70 percent of the net additions to the labor. Career and technical education is the arena where many of these new workers can be trained and channeled into the higher-paying jobs of the unfolding market in the next several years.

4. *How workers are trained*—This challenge is to find ways to impart CTE, including advanced technologies skills, to groups that generally have not been served effectively by American public schools.

5. *The politics of race*—Racial and ethnic tensions still characterize social relations in American society. The CTE community has a chance to turn potential confrontation into political and social opportunity.

Suggestions for Career and Technical Educators

Following is a list of suggestions to help C&T educators face the challenges concerning special-needs populations:

- Expand school programs, formal and informal, to include opportunities for minority students to authenticate their own intellectual growth and to share in their knowledge and experience.

- Improve the image of CTE between minority youth and professionals.

- Fund a study to determine more accurate numbers of minorities participating in CTE and the program types in which they participate.
- CTE department heads should be sure that special-needs C&T educators and special-needs courses include state-of-the-art information on serving LEP students.
- Devise methods of determining the readiness of minority students to cope with the challenges of college and graduate study. This involves going beyond traditional testing programs that have failed to discover potentially excellent minority students because they reveal more about one's past opportunity than about one's present potential.
- Encourage state directors to provide leadership regarding professional activities devoted to enhancing racially and ethnically diverse learning environments.
- Provide support for more ethnic minority doctorates in CTE to ensure a future pool of talent for research on ethnic (as well as other) issues in CTE, and to ensure future role models.
- Staff CTE programs with people who are knowledgeable about minority cultures and are good role models and mentors for these groups.
- Relate the research and extension activities of the university to the needs of the total population of the state including urban Blacks, Hispanics, American Indians, and poor Whites. Somehow, the notion has to be reinforced that this public benefaction known as a university must serve all of the people.

Summary

- In the 1960s and 1970s, much of the legislation passed by Congress dealt with providing equal education for all. As part of its efforts to help special population students, the Perkins Act requires states to provide assurances that these students have equal access to career and technical education, and that localities ensure their full participation in programs with Perkins money.
- Minorities that were incorporated into American society against their will are different from the White majority and from other minorities such as immigrants. Ethnic groups are unique according to several aspects of style: verbal and nonverbal communication, orientation modes, social value patterns, and intellectual modes. Stereotyping, discrimination, constraints imposed by self and family, low career aspirations, lack of confidence and initiative, and lack of sponsors are causes for low program participation by these groups.
- Education is the real hope for American minorities; experience tends to confirm this. When minorities, including Blacks, Hispanics, and

American Indians, have received adequate and meaningful education, they have tended to be successful in cultures like that of the United States. While several types of education are crucial to this success, CTE has demonstrated that it occupies a central position in minority affairs.

- In the past several decades, career and technical education has become more concerned with the role of serving persons with disabilities and has made progress in adapting and refining programs to prepare these "students at risk" vocationally. The Education of All Handicapped Children Act of 1975 launched an organized effort to provide a free appropriate public education for all children with disabilities from ages 3 to 21. This act provided a number of grants to states and local school systems to improve CTE and related services for individuals with special needs.

- The Individuals with Disabilities Education Act (originally the Education of Handicapped Children Act) was designed to ensure that all children with disabilities have access to free appropriate public education that emphasizes special education and services to meet their unique needs. Career and technical education teachers have a thorough understanding of the employment process of the workforce. Consequently, they can contribute significantly to the transition process of a student with disabilities by contributing to the student's individualized education program (IEP).

- Many students with disabilities enroll in career and technical education in order to develop job skills so that they can be employed and live independently and can benefit from CTE in the same ways as all students.

- Special-needs groups and the individuals who make up special-needs groups are a special challenge for career and technical education. Defining, identifying, accepting, adapting, creating, and giving are terms that indicate separate challenges. In some cases, good solutions to these challenges are yet to be found.

- Clearly, the evolution of racial and ethnic composition of our population will have an impact on the career and technical education workforce of the future. Every human resource function, from recruiting through communication, will need to serve a mixed population. One set of benefits will not fit all, and one language may not even fit all. Business and industry will need to understand the mix—culture, similarities and differences, communication styles, and training needs.

- Career and technical education serves an array of students, with most from the middle range of academic and income advantage. However, those who have disabilities or are male, come from lower-income or rural schools, or enter high school with low academic achievement, participate more substantially than do other students. These patterns were generally stable during the 1990s, although CTE appeared to be attracting relatively more academically talented students. There was less progress on overcoming gender differences in particular career and technical education courses that students choose.

Discussion Questions and Activities

1. Describe some special programs in your state that provide support services for career and technical education students from special populations.
2. What are the patterns of access and participation for minorities in career and technical education at the secondary level in your state?
3. What are the patterns of access and participation for minorities in career and technical education at the postsecondary level in your state?

Library Research

4. Determine the best strategies for increasing the participation of minority students from low socioeconomic backgrounds in career and technical education.
5. According to research, minority students are less likely to participate in the following career and technical courses at the postsecondary level: agriculture, home economics, and trade and industry. What are some of the possible reasons for this?
6. Identify some ways of providing more minority faculty as role models for minority students enrolled in career and technical education.
7. Develop a historical review documenting how much impact vocational education had on helping the early-twentieth-century immigrants adjust to the working world of America.
8. Describe what is being done today through career and technical education to help immigrants.
9. Examine critically the Individuals with Disabilities Education Act Amendments of 1997 and the subsequent IDEA 2004 reauthorization. Explain how they affect career and technical educators.
10. What role does career and technical education play in filling the void that sometimes exists in the education of special-needs students?
11. How does or can career and technical education improve the outcomes of secondary students who choose to enroll in CTE programs?

Recommended Educational Media Resources

- *Sitting Bull and the Great Sioux Nation*
  The History Channel
  http://www.historychannel.com/store
  1-800-708-1776

- *The immigrant experience: The long, long journey*
  Educational Video Network, Inc.
  1336 19th Street
  Huntsville, TX 77340
  1-800-762-0060 or (936) 295-5767
  Web site: https://www.evndirect.com
- *The shackled immigrants* (Show # 2203)
  Tony Brown Productions
  2214 Frederick Douglass Blvd., Suite 124
  New York, NY 10036
  (718) 264-2226
  Web site: http://www.tonybrown.com/booksandtapes/html
  E-mail: mail@tbol.net
- *Working with students from the culture of poverty* (DVD)
- *Dealing with diversity in the classroom* (DVD)
- *A new I.D.E.A. for special education: Understanding the system and the new law* (DVD)
  Insight Media
  2162 Broadway
  New York, NY 10024-0621
  1-800-233-9910 or (212) 721-6316
  Web site: http://www.insight-media.com
  E-mail: custserv@insight-media.com

References and Additional Reading

Anderson, J. D. (1982). The historical development of Black vocational education. In H. Kantor and D. B. Tyack (Eds.), *Work, youth, and schooling* (pp. 180–222). Stanford, CA: Stanford University Press.

Anstrom, K. (1996, summer). Defining the limited-English-proficient student. *Directions in Language Education, 1*(19) (summer). Washington, DC: National Clearinghouse of Bilingual Education.

Arnold, C. L., and Levesque, K. A. (1992). *Black Americans and vocational education: Participation in the 1980s.* Macomb, IL: National Center for Research in Vocational Education.

Armstrong, R. (2000). Is the new IDEA a good idea? *Techniques, 76*(3), 29.

Bear Don't Walk, M. (1976). Options for Native Americans in vocational education. In J. E. Wall (Ed.), *Vocational education for special groups* (pp. 125–135). Sixth yearbook of the American Vocational Association. Washington, DC: American Vocational Association.

Blood, P., and Burnham, L. H. (1994). *Meeting the vocational needs of the Native Americans* (pp. 21–25). Washington, DC: Library of Congress, Federal Research Division.

Boesel, D., Farrar, B., Hollinger, D., Hudson, C., Masten, C., Myers, R., Scheiderman, S., and To, Duc-Le (1994a). *National assessment of vocational education, interim report to Congress.* Washington, DC: U.S. Department of Education, Office of Educational Research and Improvement. NLE 98-2003.

Boesel, D., Hudson, L., Deich, S., and Masten, C. (1994b). *National assessment of vocational education, final report to Congress, volume II: Participation in and quality of vocational education.* Washington, DC: U.S. Department of Education, Office of Educational Research and Improvement.

Bowen, B. E. (1987). A minority perspective on minorities in agriculture. *Agricultural Education Magazine, 60*(6), 3–4.

Boykin, A. W. (1986). The triple quandary and the schooling of Afro-American children. In U. Neisser (Ed.), *The school achievement of minority children* (pp. 57–71). Hillsdale, NJ: Lawrence Erlbaum Associates.

Bradley, C. H., and Friedenberg, J. E. (1988). *Teaching vocational education to limited-English proficient students.* Bloomington, IL: Meridian.

Bureau of Labor Statistics (2001). *2000 national occupational employment and wage estimates.* Washington, DC: U.S. Department of Labor.

Cook, A. R. (1986). Diversity among Northwest Hispanics. *Social Science Journal, 23*(2), 205–216.

Commission on National Aid to Vocational Education (1914). *Vocational education, Vol. 1.* Washington, DC: U.S. Government Printing Office.

Crandell, J. A. (1985). *Directions in vocational education for limited-English proficient students and adults.* Occasional paper No. 109. Columbus: The Ohio State University, National Center for Research in Vocational Education (ERIC Document Reproduction Service No. ED 264 436).

Doyle, R. (February, 2002). Assembling the future. *Scientific American, 286*(2), 30.

Du Bois, W. E. B. (1903). *The souls of Black folk.* Rev. ed. New York: Bantam.

Friedenberg, J. E., and Fields, E. L. (1993). Ethnic minority participation in vocational education. In C. Anderson and L. C. Rampp (Eds.), *Vocational education in the 1990s, II: A sourcebook for strategies, methods, and materials* (pp. 212–224). Ann Arbor, MI: Prakken Publishing.

Hankin, H. (2005). *The new workforce: Five sweeping trends that will shape your company's future.* New York: AMACOM.

Hudson, L. (1994). *National assessment of vocational education, final report to Congress volume IV: Access to programs and services for special populations.* Washington, DC: Office of Educational Research and Improvement, U.S. Department of Education.

Ihle, E. (1986). *Black women's vocational education: History of Black women's vocational education in the South, 1865–present.* Instructional modules for educators, Module II (Module prepared for the Women's Educational Equity Act Program, U.S. Department of Education). Harrisonburg, VA: James Madison University.

Jennings, J. (1991). Minorities and vocational education: The challenges. *Vocational Education Journal, 66*(4), 20–21, 45.

Johnson, W., and Packer, A. (1987). *Workforce 2000: Work and workers for the 21st century.* Indianapolis, IN: D. Hudson Institute.

Larke, A., Jr., and Barr, T. P. (1987). Promoting minority involvement in agriculture. *Agricultural Education Magazine, 60*(6), 6–7.

Lazerson, M., and Grubb, W. N. (1974). *American education and vocationalism: A documentary history, 1870–1970.* New York: Teachers College Press.

Levesque, K. (2003). *Public high school graduates who participated in vocational technical education: 1982–1998.* Washington, DC: U.S. Department of Education, Institute of Education Services, National Center for Education Statistics. NCES 2003-024.

Longstreet, W. S. (1978). *Aspects of ethnicity.* New York: Teachers College Press.

Maldonado, C. (2006). Does generation status matter? An examination of Latino college completers. *Online Journal for Workforce Education and Development,*

1(5), 1–28. Retrieved November 2, 2006, from http://wed.siu.edu/journal/volum5/latino.htm.

Marshall, C. (1989). *More than black face and skirts: New leadership to confront the major dilemmas in education.* Charlottesville, VA: National Policy Board for Educational Administration (ERIC Document Reproduction Service No. ED 318 089).

Metzger, C. (1985). Helping women prepare for principalships. *Phi Delta Kappan, 67,* 292–296.

Morrissey, P. (1993). The ADA and vocational education. *Vocational Education Journal, 68*(8), 22–24.

Nall, H. (1997). Vocational education and the African American experience: An historical and philosophical perspective. *Journal of Intergroup Relations, 24* (3), 26–48.

National Center for Education Statistics (NCES) (1995). *The condition of education 1995: The educational progress of Hispanic students.* Washington, DC: Office of Educational Research and Improvement, U.S. Department of Education.

Oakes, J. (1990). Multiplying inequalities: The effects of race, social class, and tracking on opportunities to learn mathematics and science (National Science Foundation Report R-3928-NSF). Santa Monica, CA: Rand.

Ogbu, J. U. (1978). *Minority education and caste: The American system in cross-cultural perspective.* New York: Academic Press.

———. (1986). The consequences of the American caste system. In U. Neisser (Ed.), *The school achievement of minority children* (pp. 19–56). Hillsdale, NJ: Lawrence Erlbaum Associates.

Oxford, R., Lopez, K., Stupp, P., Peng, S., and Gendell, M. (1989). *Projections of non-English language background and limited-English proficient persons in the United States to the year 2000.* Rosslyn, VA: InterAmerica Research Associates.

Peng, J. (2006). *Celebrating heritage.* Retrieved September 18, 2006, from http://www.hattiesburgamerican.com/apps/pbcs.dill/article?AID=/20060917/LIFESTYLE/6.

Slater, G. (1992). *Principal issues regarding Native Americans.* Papers presented at the Design Conference for the National Assessment of Vocational Education. Washington, DC: Office of Educational Research and Improvement, U.S. Department of Education.

Sotomayor, M. (1988). Educational issues and Hispanic populations in the U.S.A. *Journal of Vocational Special Needs, 10*(3), 7–9.

Taylor, W. N., Powers, L., and Johnson, D. M. (1990). The 1890 institutions at 100. *Agricultural Education Magazine, 63*(2), 8–9.

U.S. Census Bureau (2004). *Dynamic diversity: Projected changes in U.S. race and ethnic composition 1995 to 2050.* Retrieved February 28, 2007, from http://www.census.gov/ipc/www/usinterimproj.

U.S. Department of Education (2004). *National assessment of vocational education: Final report to Congress.* Washington, DC: Office of the Under Secretary, Policy and Program Studies Service.

———. (2006a) Letter to Chief State School Officers regarding the LEP Partnership. Retrieved February 7, 2007, from http://www.ed.gov/about/inits/ed/lep-partnership.

———. (2006b). Building partnerships to help English language learners. Retrieved February 7, 2007, from http://www.ed.gov/nclb/methods/English/lepfactsheet.html.

Valdivieso, R. (1985). *Hispanics and education data.* Washington, DC: National Center for Education Statistics.

Valverde, L. A. (1988). The missing element: Hispanics at the top in higher education. *Change*, *20*, 11.

Wagner, M. (1991). *The benefits of secondary vocational education for young people with disabilities: Findings from the national longitudinal transition study of special education students*. Menlo Park, CA: SRI International (ERIC Document Reproduction Service No. ED 272 570).

Wagner, M., Blackorby, J., Cameto, R., and Newman, L. (1993). *What makes a difference?: Influences on postschool outcomes of youth with disabilities*. Menlo Park, CA: SRI International.

Weishaar, M. K., Borsa, J. C., and Weishaar, P. M. (2007). *Inclusive Educational Administration*, 2nd ed. Long Grove, IL: Waveland Press.

West, L. L., and Taymans, J. (1998). Keeping up with the new IDEA. *Techniques*, *73*(4), 25.

West, R. F., and Shearon, R. W. (1982). Differences between black and white students in curriculum program status. *Community/Junior College Quarterly*, *6*(3), 239–251.

Wirsching, T., and Stenberg, L. (1992). Determinants of Idaho Hispanic female participation in adult vocational education programs. *Journal of Vocational Education Research*, *17*(3), 35–61.

chapter 8

Career and Technical Education Instructional Programs and Teachers

This chapter examines many salient features of career and technical education programs. The major areas of focus are: organization of CTE at the secondary level, CTE program areas of study, CTE teachers, and selected entities influencing growth in career and technical education programs.

Career and Technical Education at the Secondary Level

Career and technical education at the secondary level is a large and complex system. Like academic subjects, CTE courses are available at various grade levels and include both introductory and advanced offerings. But far more so than academic subjects, secondary career and technical education is provided in diverse institutions. Understanding where and how CTE courses are offered provides important context for interpreting who participates in career and technical education, how it is implemented, and what its outcomes are.

Because nearly all public high school graduates earn credits in career technical education, it follows that most secondary schools offer at least some form of career learning. Recent evidence suggests that at least 11,000 high schools, more than two-thirds of such schools nationally (Table 8.1), provide at least one of the common occupational programs. These schools include the following (Hudson and Shafer, 2002):

- *Close to 9,500 comprehensive high schools.* These schools typically have an academic focus, but some have large career and technical education programs. Charter schools, many of which have career or occupational themes, are also included in this category.

- *About 1,000 career and technical education high schools.* These schools emphasize career and technical education instruction but also offer the full set of academic courses required in a high school curriculum; students spend a full day at the school.

181

Table 8.1   Percentage of Public High School Institutions, by Type, Locale, and Percentage Offering Selected Occupational Programs: 1999

	Percentage Distribution of Public High School Institutions			
Locale	Comprehensive High School	CTE High School	Area or Regional CTE Center	Percentage of Schools Offering CTE
Overall	89.2	4.6	6.2	66.5
Urban	84.2	10.3	5.5	72.9
Suburban	89.7	4.4	2.9	63.9
Rural	90.3	3.1	6.6	66.5

Source: U.S. Department of Education. (2004). National assessment of vocational education: Final report to Congress, p. 21. Washington, DC: Office of the Under Secretary, Policy and Program Studies Service.

- *About 800 area or regional career and technical education schools.* These schools usually provide only CTE instruction; students typically attend part-time and receive their academic instruction at their home high school.

Compared to comprehensive high schools, both types of career and technical education schools are considered to offer higher-quality occupational instruction because of their superior equipment and facilities and the greater depth and breadth of training these specialized institutions provide. However, most secondary career and technical education is provided in comprehensive high schools (Boesel et al., 1994, p. 3), with some courses also offered in middle schools.

Regardless of where it is offered, secondary career and technical education comprises three types of courses (Figure 8.1, pp. 184–185):

- *Specific Labor Market Preparation (occupational education).* Teaches skills and knowledge required in a particular occupation or set of related occupations—such as health, business, and food service and hospitality—included in the 10 broad occupational program areas defined by the National Center for Education Statistics (NCES), some with subspecialty areas. This category includes cooperative education, in which students earn school credit for work experience related to a specific occupational program.

- *General Labor Market Preparation.* Provides general employment skills that are not specific to any particular occupational area, such as courses in typing or keyboarding, introductory technology education, career education, and general work experience.

- *Family and Consumer Sciences Education.* Intended to prepare students for family and consumer roles outside the paid labor market, including consumer and home economics.

These courses can be expected to attract different types of students across various grade levels.

Career and technical education is an option for high school students. With input from parents, students choose to enroll in a CTE high school or an area career and technical education center, if one is available; at comprehensive high schools, they choose to take CTE courses in place of study hall or other elective offerings, such as art, music, or more advanced academic courses. The elective nature of career and technical education has important implications for policy because efforts to improve the rigor or structure of career and

Principles of food selection, preparation, preservation, and some knowledge of chemistry are demonstrated by these Family and Consumer Sciences students.

technical education will likely affect how many and which students participate.

Students can also choose to, and do, take career and technical education courses in varying numbers and with different objectives in mind. Many schools offer sequences ("programs") of related, increasingly advanced courses in one or several specific occupational areas (e.g., health, drafting, child care). However, actual course taking does not necessarily follow these organized offerings. Most career and technical education courses and programs have no prerequisites, with students being free to enroll in courses across occupational areas and levels, although some choose to focus on a single occupation (Boesel et al., 1994, pp. 85–87). The exceptions are specialty career preparation programs like career academies and youth apprenticeships, in which students define sequences of CTE and academic courses.

Because involvement in career and technical education varies, it is difficult to identify a group for evaluation purposes whose participation and outcomes can be accurately measured. There are several possibilities (U.S. Department of Education, 2004):

- *Career and technical education course taker*: Graduate earning any credits in any form of career and technical education
- *Occupational investor*: Graduate earning three or more credits in occupational courses, regardless of how these credits are organized; made up of two subgroups (concentrators and explorers).

Figure 8.1   Course Taxonomy

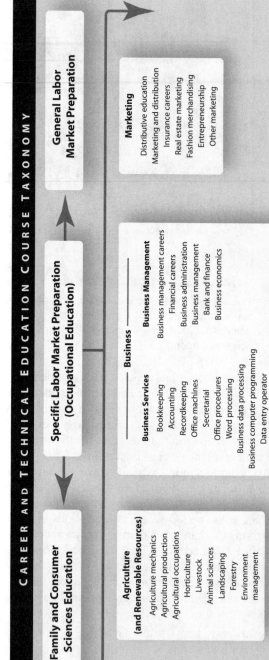

CAREER AND TECHNICAL EDUCATION COURSE TAXONOMY

Family and Consumer Sciences Education

Specific Labor Market Preparation (Occupational Education)

General Labor Market Preparation

Agriculture (and Renewable Resources)
Agriculture mechanics
Agricultural production
Agricultural occupations
Horticulture
Livestock
Animal sciences
Landscaping
Forestry
Environment management

Health Care
Health occupations
Health technology/laboratory
Nursing assisting
Dental assisting
Dental technology

Protective Services (and Public Services)
Criminal justice
Fire fighting
Human services

Business

Business Services
Bookkeeping
Accounting
Recordkeeping
Office machines
Secretarial
Office procedures
Word processing
Business data processing
Business computer programming
Data entry operator

Business Management
Business management careers
Financial careers
Business administration
Business management
Bank and finance
Business economics

Marketing
Distributive education
Marketing and distribution
Insurance careers
Real estate marketing
Fashion merchandising
Entrepreneurship
Other marketing

Technology

Computer Technology
Computer appreciation
Computer mathematics
Computer applications
Computer programming
Data processing
Computer and information sciences

Communications Technology
Yearbook production
Broadcast management
Film making and production
Telecommunications
Radio/television production
Videotape production
Other communications
Other communication technologies

Other Technology
Electronic technology
Electromechanical technology
Industrial production technology
Chemical technology
Engineering technologies

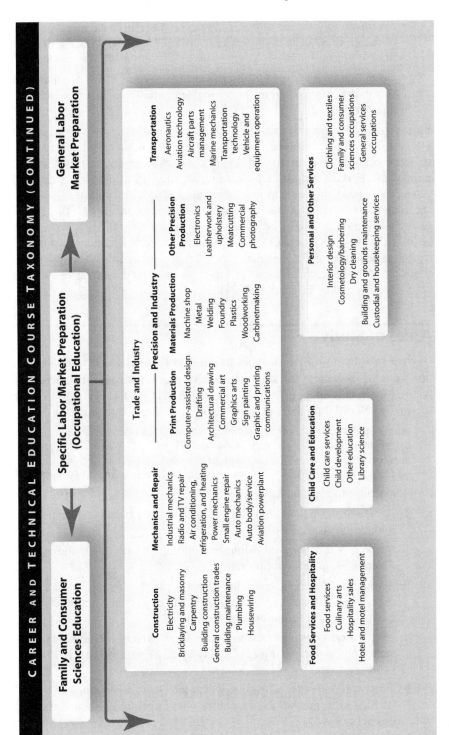

CAREER AND TECHNICAL EDUCATION COURSE TAXONOMY (CONTINUED)

Family and Consumer Sciences Education

Specific Labor Market Preparation (Occupational Education)

General Labor Market Preparation

Trade and Industry

Construction
Electricity
Bricklaying and masonry
Carpentry
Building construction
General construction trades
Building maintenance
Plumbing
Housewiring

Mechanics and Repair
Industrial mechanics
Radio and TV repair
Air conditioning, refrigeration, and heating
Power mechanics
Small engine repair
Auto mechanics
Auto body/service
Aviation powerplant

Print Production
Computer-assisted design
Drafting
Architectural drawing
Commercial art
Graphics arts
Sign painting
Graphic and printing communications

Materials Production
Machine shop
Metal
Welding
Foundry
Plastics
Woodworking
Carbinetmaking

Other Precision Production
Electronics
Leatherwork and upholstery
Meatcutting
Commercial photography

Transportation
Aeronautics
Aviation technology
Aircraft parts management
Marine mechanics
Transportation technology
Vehicle and equipment operation

Food Services and Hospitality
Food services
Culinary arts
Hospitality sales
Hotel and motel management

Child Care and Education
Child care services
Child development
Other education
Library science

Personal and Other Services
Interior design
Cosmetology/barbering
Dry cleaning
Building and grounds maintenance
Custodial and housekeeping services
Clothing and textiles
Family and consumer sciences occupations
General services occupations

- *Occupational concentrator*: Graduate earning three or more occupational credits but in a single program area (e.g., health care or business services).

- *Occupational explorer*: Graduate earning three or more occupational credits but in more than one program area (e.g., business services and agriculture).

From a policy perspective, however, concentrators are not the only group of interest. The larger population of all students (44.5 percent) who earn three or more occupational credits, of which concentrators are a subset, is also important. Perkins grants are distributed to institutions—districts and schools—to fund courses and programs, not individual students. Therefore the federal investment is similar, whether students concentrate their CTE course taking in a single occupational program area (26.0 percent) or "explore" across several areas (18.5 percent). Together, concentrators and explorers account for the vast majority of credits earned in CTE or occupational education. Each of these groups was examined in NAVE analyses (U.S. Department of Education, 2004).

Areas of Study

The Association for Career and Technical Education (ACTE) features hundreds of programs for students. Each program division has a broad-based foundation of people dedicated to educating today's students for tomorrow's world. Members of these divisions include educators in:

middle/junior high schools	community and technical schools/colleges
secondary schools	vocational schools
career centers	comprehensive high schools
adult education facilities	other related institutions and organizations

Programs fall into eight major areas of study:

1. *Agricultural education*, including horticulture, agricultural mechanics, and agribusiness.

2. *Business education*, including accounting, office occupations, and business management programs.

3. *Marketing education*, including general merchandising, apparel and accessories marketing, real estate, financial services and marketing, business and personal services marketing.

4. *Family and consumer sciences education*, which encompasses consumer and homemaking education as well as occupational fields such as food services.

5. *Trade and industrial education*, which includes a wide range of trades, such as auto mechanics, carpentry, metalworking, graphic arts, and cosmetology.

6. *Health occupations education*, such as for practical nursing, registered nursing, medical and dental assistants, and radiologic technicians.

7. *Technology education*, which concerns materials, processes, and technologies that are used in manufacturing, construction, transportation, communication, and other components of industries.

8. *Technical education*, which involves a variety of technical occupation fields such as communications, engineering-related technologies, and computer sciences.

All of these areas of study list the following goals:

- Provide professional development, program recognition, and program-improvement activities and products.

- Provide effective advocacy for the profession in both technical and academic arenas and promote a unified direction for the profession.

- Increase the flow of new members to the profession/division and encourage their continued involvement so that they remain active participants.

Agricultural Education

Career and technical education in agriculture, in some form, has always been an integral part of American life. Hamlin (1956) points out that an agricultural school for orphans was established in Georgia in 1734 or shortly thereafter and a similar school, the Bethesda School in Savannah, Georgia, was founded in 1740.

Teaching agriculture in public schools of less than college grade apparently began in certain elementary schools in Massachusetts in 1858. Teaching agriculture in a public secondary school can be traced back to Elyria, Ohio, in 1902. The first agricultural teacher was employed by a public school in Carroll County, Georgia, in 1903. Groups that later developed into 4-H clubs began in 1900. These groups received their initial impetus from county and local school superintendents in Illinois, Iowa, Mississippi, and Ohio (Hamlin, 1956).

Agricultural education has consistently changed in its instructional programs to meet the needs of a dynamic, rapidly changing industry. Agriculture is becoming highly scientific and technical in such new frontiers as biotechnology, which deals with genetic engineering and tissue culture. Agricultural education is responding with more programs like agriscience, which consists of a series of laboratory courses that emphasize the basic biological and physical science principles and practices with agriculture (Scott and Sarkees-Wircenski, 1996).

Along with the educational institutions listed for all divisions of ACTE, the Agricultural Education Division also includes educators in two-year colleges and land-grant universities. In addition to the previously mentioned goals for all ACTE areas of study, the mission of the Agricultural Education Division is to prepare students for successful careers and a lifetime of choices in the global agriculture and natural resources system.

Greenhouse technology has provided more access to exotic plants, along with more job opportunities for CTE students.

Agricultural programs prepare students for a wide range of career options. Like other areas of vocational education, more attention is being given to integrating academic subjects such as communications, mathematics, and science to the applications of technology. Agricultural education is offered in grades 7 through 14 in more than 7,600 high schools and 570 postsecondary institutions in America. Many students begin career awareness and exploration programs in agriculture in the middle and junior high school years and continue this area of interest in the high school agriculture program. Some students continue their education for two or more years by enrolling in community colleges and four-year colleges or universities, where they earn associates' degrees or baccalaureate degrees in agriculture or related areas (Lee, 1994).

Agricultural occupation clusters are composed of groups of related courses or units of subject matter that are organized for carrying on learning experiences concerned with preparation for, or upgrading in, occupations requiring knowledge of and skills in agricultural subjects. The functions of agricultural production, supplies, mechanization, products, ornamental horticulture, forestry, agricultural resources, and related services are emphasized in the instruction designed to provide opportunities for students to prepare for, or to improve their competencies in, agricultural occupations (Mason and Husted, 2002).

The delivery system for vocational agriculture utilizes three major components: classroom and laboratory instruction, leadership development (FFA), and supervised agricultural experience programs. According to Lee (1994), classroom and laboratory instruction involves teaching students the underlying concepts and principles of agriculture and providing them with opportunities to apply what they have learned in a "hands-on" environment. Supervised agricultural experiences (SAE) involve structured learning activities that build on what has been learned through classroom and laboratory instruction. The FFA provides opportunities for students to become involved in a variety of career development events and professional development activities.

In the mid-1980s the profession began exploring innovative program approaches such as aquaculture, agrimarketing, infusing agricultural sciences into the curriculum, infusing international agricultural education into the instructional program, and so forth. All approaches were designed to maintain or increase student interest and enrollment in a program developed and delivered primarily to prepare people for employment in production agriculture, agribusiness, and natural resources occupations. However, in many instances, programs designed to emphasize vocational education were being threatened and, in many cases, phased out (Cox, McCormick, and Miller, 1989).

U.S. educational reform was launched in large part because of the tremendous impact of the National Commission on Excellence in Education report, *A Nation at Risk* (1983). The intent of this reform was to improve the quality of education, especially at the basic level. In 1985, then Secretary of Education Terral Bell, and Secretary of the U.S. Department of National Academy of Sciences' Board on Agriculture John Block undertook a companion comprehensive study of "Vocational Agriculture in Secondary Schools" (Cox, McCormick, and Miller, 1989).

Data from the National Longitudinal Study of the High School Class of 1972 revealed the following facts about agricultural education graduates:

- Agricultural education graduates participated less frequently in postsecondary programs when compared with nonagricultural education graduates.
- Participation in agricultural education had no substantive effect on postsecondary education attainment.
- Socioeconomic background variables (i.e., community, gender, ethnicity, father's education, mother's education, student's ability, and number of semesters completed of agricultural education) explained 29.77 percent of the variance in educational attainment (Gordon, 1985).

Results of this study suggested that (1) more emphasis should be placed on counseling students to consider continuing their education beyond high school; (2) secondary and postsecondary agricultural educators should clearly articulate their curricula programs; and (3) more effort should be made to advise high school agricultural education students on the postsecondary opportunities available in their chosen career areas.

Vo (1997) cites that less than 2 percent of the jobs in America's agricultural industry relate to production. Most are nonproduction jobs, such as:

college professor	agronomist	geneticist
livestock commission agent	biochemist	winery supervisor
agricultural construction engineer	weed scientist	expert sales manager
rural sociologist	log grader	mammalogist
environmental conservation officer	land surveyor	farm appraiser

As agriculture moves from small family farms to large business conglomerates and technology replaces tradition, education must adapt. Career and technical education must step in to replace the body of knowledge that used to be passed from generation to generation, and it will play an important role in opening the door to the growing new opportunities in the field. It is hard to overstate the significance of an industry that has successfully fed and clothed the people of its own country for so many decades. Agriculture not only ensures our very survival by providing us with our basic needs of food and clothing, it also contributes to our strength and prosperity.

Recent years have seen massive changes in the industry as a whole. At one time, approximately one-quarter of the U.S. population lived on farms; today it is less than two percent. The USDA classifies a noncommercial farm as an establishment that sells between $1,000 and $50,000 worth of produce per year, and a commercial farm as one that sells more than $50,000 (Reese, 2001). Unfortunately, this means that the number of smaller family farms will decrease as many more will have to consolidate into larger, commercial ones in order to survive (Reese, 2001). In the past, the majority of agricultural knowledge and expertise was acquired by growing up on the farm. The fundamentals were learned early, and then newer developments in the industry could be acquired though educational institutions or cooperative extension services.

With fewer family farms, the formal education of our future agricultural workforce will have to begin at a different level. Adding to the need for more agriculture education is the ever-increasing level of technology being utilized in the industry. Career and technical education will become more important than ever in preparing for a successful future in agriculture. Agriculture has long been an *art* practiced by a special group of people. However, *science* has begun to play a greater path in agricultural production. There are now satellites that can transmit precise soil information for maximizing yield with the correct amount of fertilizer and seed. There are collars for dairy cows that open gates, dispense feed, and track milk production and vaccination schedules. While technology today is providing more information than farmers have ever had available to them, they must utilize that information to maximize production. Career and technical education can provide the knowledge to use these tools of technology along with the more traditional tools of the trade.

Business Education

In colonial times, the apprentice usually had to discover the skills needed for business success and master them on his own. The demands of ambitious apprentices who urged employers to teach them bookkeeping after working hours resulted in organized business training. This practice played a major part in the formation of vocational business education. Practical experience supplemented by study of "rules" became the foundation for advancement in business in the colonial period. According to Walker, Huffman, and Beaumont (1956), some rudimentary business courses were offered by individual teachers and by schools during the seventeenth and eighteenth centuries. Penmanship and an advanced arithmetic known as "casting accounts" were taught privately in Latin grammar schools.

Late in the eighteenth century, before the advent of private business schools, bookkeeping was taught by individuals. Early in the nineteenth century, business training became more specialized in "commercial" schools. Lack of leadership and status of business educators enabled traditionalists to retard the business education development in public schools for many years. As late as 1910, only one of seven high schools taught business-related subjects. The first organized course to prepare business teachers was given in Philadelphia in 1898 (Walker, Huffman, and Beaumont, 1956).

Business education has had to change curriculum and instructional practices continuously to keep pace with changes in business equipment, organization, policy, and market demands. Instruction evolved to focus on skill development with word processing and other computer programs, information management systems, high-speed copiers and optical scanners, laser printers, and modern/more complex fax machines. Business principles and concepts have also changed focus from secretarial office procedures to management systems and entrepreneurship, from a focus on the local economic community to an international one, and from computer applications to information systems (Phillips, 1994). Business management was the most popular undergraduate major in 1994, making up 21 percent of all baccalaureate degrees earned that year (National Center for Educational Statistics, 1997).

Along with the educational institutions listed for all divisions of ACTE, the Business Education Division also includes educators in two-year colleges as well as postsecondary, baccalaureate, master's, and doctoral degree programs.

Marketing Education

The first comprehensive investigation of retail occupations was made in 1905 by the Women's Educational and Industrial Union in Boston, a society for the advancement of women in industrial work. Conditions revealed by this investigation motivated Mrs. Lucinda Wyman Prince to establish classes in retail selling as part of the society's activities. Within two years applicants for admission had to be turned away (Brown and Logan, 1956). The principles developed by Mrs. Prince have greatly influenced vocational practices. Mrs. Prince felt that the daily experiences of pupils must be the basis for the curriculum, that instruction should be largely individual, and that training should prove itself in practice on the job.

Scattered and sporadic efforts to develop retail training continued through the first two decades of the century. The Committee of Nine of the National Education Association recommended in 1903 that advertising be included in the high school commerce curriculum. Retail sales training patterned on the original Boston plan began in Providence, Rhode Island, in 1910. Two years later Mrs. Prince organized the first retail training cooperative program in the Boston high schools. By 1915, the National Retail Dry Goods Association created the position of education director and appointed Mrs. Prince to this position (Brown and Logan, 1956).

CTE graduate students access their data through state-of-the-art computer technology.

The objectives of marketing education have changed since they were first introduced to secondary school programs in Boston in 1912. At that time, the objective was to provide cooperative training in retail store work for the purpose of improving the lot and quality of work of sales personnel (Haas, 1972).

Marketing education is the instructional program designed to prepare individuals for the major occupational areas within marketing and management. Marketing, simply defined, is the selling of ideas, products, and services of all kinds to identified and qualified markets. Marketers manage the massive system of distribution that brings goods and services to industrial users and consumers worldwide. Marketing includes information gathering, recruiting, image building, promoting, training, campaigning, financing, lobbying, researching, and communicating. Marketing is a process that can be adapted to virtually every economic, social, or public activity and is an essential ingredient in making our free enterprise system work (Distributive Education Clubs of America [DECA Inc.], 1992).

The changing way of life in America is reflected the development of marketing education. It is recognized that there is a marketing/distribution economy that has had an impact on the social fabric of the twentieth and twenty-first centuries. For several decades, people engaged in marketing education reported that two of every three jobs involved the distribution of goods and services, and they felt that the public schools should prepare students to work in these jobs and careers (Leventhal, 2002).

Many of the elements of distributive education programs have been the catalyst for other concepts. Among the first state directors of marketing education, women were well represented, which was also true at the local level among teacher-coordinators. Thus, this field was truly one of the first in education that was of equal opportunity. Moving from retailing and merchandising, the field moved to wholesaling, industrial marketing, and now to electronic marketing. Students should be prepared for industrial marketing by way of classroom instruction. When students learn about industrial products as part of product information, they are presented with information about the various non-textile material such as plastic, rubber, metals, wood, glass, electronics, and masonry, and about how they are manufactured and marketed. Gaining this understanding facilitates a student's ability to work in an industrial manufacturing setting with related marketing functions (Leventhal, 2002).

Another impact of marketing/distributive education was in competency-based instruction. The "mother" of this concept was Lucy Crawford of Virginia Polytechnic Institute and State University, who did pioneering work in organizing the taxonomy for marketing and then worked on tasks/performances /objectives for each occupation. Her work was cited in modules and other publications developed at Center for Career and Technical Education at the Ohio State University for the broad field of trade and industrial education and comprehensive career and technical education. Another method used in marketing education was the project method based on a central theme of teaching/learning activity that students worked on and completed under the supervision of the teacher coordinator. Educators have also extolled the virtues of portfolio assessment, in which students demonstrate their work and competence. This is another version of the project method, as is cooperative learning.

Instruction for marketing education is a combination of hard skills and soft skills. Students learn occupational skills that include marketing skills, self-development/personality development, getting along with co-workers/ supervisors/customers and leadership skills. In the field of education, all teachers are responsible for student learning in the areas of cognitive skills, psychomotor skills, and affective skills. The affective area is based on emotions/attitudes/values that are essential in working in the field of marketing. Career and technical educators have been concerned about the value systems of students and how they fit into the workplace. Providing related supervised work experience as part of the school's marketing education program is an established component. From the early 1900s, on-the-job training was an important ingredient of the curriculum. The federal guidelines for distributive education specified half a day in school and half a day of related supervised work experience—paid, for at least 15 hours a week (Leventhal, 2002). The pioneering efforts in placing and supervising students in the workplace have led marketing education teacher-coordinators to be recognized as the experts in cooperative education strategies. As retirements result in personnel changes in the schools, there is a greater need to re-educate new CTE administrators to the opportunities that are available to students through marketing education.

Nearly one-third of our nation's public schools offer marketing education programs. Data have shown that 8.7 percent of public high school graduates completing one or more courses in specific labor market programs of CTE have been enrolled in marketing education programs (Scott and Sarkees-

Wircenski, 1996). Employment of advertising, marketing, promotions, public relations, and sales managers is expected to increase faster than the average for all occupations through 2010 (Bureau of Labor Statistics, 2002).

Along with the educational institutions listed for all divisions of ACTE, the Marketing Education Division also includes educators in two-year colleges, four-year baccalaureate degree programs, and marketing teacher-education programs. In addition to the previously mentioned goals for all ACTE areas of study, the mission of the Marketing Education Division is to advance marketing education and to enhance and develop students' education and awareness of marketing theory and practices.

Family and Consumer Sciences Education (formerly Home Economics Education)

The early developments in home economics education were scrutinized by educational leaders who attended the Lake Placid, New York, conferences held annually from 1899 to 1908. These leaders were convinced that too little was being done in education to improve home and family living. Promoted by Mr. and Mrs. Melville Dewey and Ellen H. Richards, a sanitary engineer at Massachusetts Institute of Technology, these conferences attracted the participation of such leaders (as chairpersons of committees) as Caroline Hunt, Abby Marlatt, Marion Talbot, Helen Kinne, Alice Norton, Ann Barrows, and Isabel Bevier. Their deliberations covered school (elementary, secondary, vocational) and evening college and university programs, and the training of teachers. Home economics was defined by the Lake Placid Conference participants and later replaced the terms domestic science, domestic art, domestic economy, household science, and household arts. In their last conference in 1908, this group endorsed the Davis Bill, then in Congress, designed to give national financial assistance to the teaching of home economics (Lawson and Creighton, 1956).

Advanced Clothing Construction offers experimentation in construction techniques, fabric, and design compatibility, preparing students for careers in the fashion industry.

The new conceptual framework for home economics education was developed and accepted by those participating in the

Scottsdale, Arizona, Conference of October 23, 1993. The tripartite mission of family and consumer sciences is empowering individuals, strengthening families, and enabling communities (American Home Economics Association, 1994).

In addition to the educational institutions listed for all divisions of ACTE, the Family and Consumer Sciences Education Division also includes educators in two-year colleges and four-year baccalaureate degree programs.

In 1998 and 1999, the American Association of Family and Consumer Sciences (AAFCS) polled state administrators of family and consumer sciences programs about the forecasted supply and demand for family and consumer sciences educators. The poll was an attempt by AAFCS to respond quickly to increasing expressions of concern from members of the profession. Although not every state responded to the request for information, the results provided a national "snapshot" of the shortage of family and consumer sciences educators (American Association of Career and Technical Education, 2000).

According to Reese (2004), among the rallying cries in the twenty-first century are that we must strengthen family values, prevent violence in our schools, and do our part in serving our communities. Yet, there is a field of education that addresses most of these issues—family and consumer sciences. "Those who think that these courses are simply about cooking are sadly mistaken, and that misconception may mean that their school is missing out on the benefits that a strong family and consumer sciences education program can offer" (Reese, 2004, p.18).

The mission of family and consumer sciences education is to prepare students for family life, work life, and careers in family and consumer sciences by providing opportunities to develop the knowledge, skills, attitudes, and behaviors needed for:

- Strengthening the well-being of individuals and families.
- Becoming responsible citizens and leaders in family, community, and work settings.

Interior Design provides students with principles and elements of design, design theory, and actual "hands on" training through its internship component and community projects.

This welding program, certified by the American Welding Society, provides students with entry-level welding skills.

Fundamentals of automotive technology, including basic engine concepts, brake systems, and suspension and steering systems, are offered at this career and technology school.

Upon successful completion of this course, these students will receive a technical certification of competency and can achieve a national certificate through the National Center for Construction Education Research.

- Promoting optimal nutrition and wellness.
- Managing resources to meet the needs of individuals and families.
- Balancing personal, home, family, and work life.
- Using critical- and creative-thinking skills to address problems in diverse family, community, and work environments.
- Facilitating successful life management, employment, and career development.
- Functioning effectively as providers and consumers of goods and services.
- Appreciating human worth and accepting responsibility for one's actions and success in family and work life (Stewart, 1994).

Most secondary students enroll in one or more CTE courses before they graduate with nearly half of those students enrolled in consumer and home-making courses.

Trade and Industrial Education

The 1876 Centennial Exposition in Philadelphia showed America how far behind it lagged in the current theories. After seeing the Russians exhibit the typical exercises used as a basis for tool instruction, a number of industrial communities established evening classes to upgrade workers, notably in drawing. Because school authorities failed to consult and cooperate with factory employers or workers, these classes accomplished little, and they all but disappeared in twenty-five years (Britton and Fick, 1956). To meet this crisis, the National Society for the Promotion of Industrial Education was formed in 1906.

The major goal of trade and industrial education is for students to develop sufficient knowledge and skills to secure initial employment or advancements through experiences that (a) focus on performance skills required in an occupational field; (b) provide an understanding of and use of functional technology related to a chosen occupational area; (c) prepare individuals to deal effectively with personal and group relationship problems; (d) assist individuals in developing desirable work habits, ideals, and attitudes essential to job performance; and (e) provide relevant instruction to enable individuals to develop critical-thinking and problem-solving skills, manipulative skills, safety judgments, technical knowledge, and related occupational information preparing individuals for meaningful, productive employment in vocational industrial pursuits (National Association of Trade and Industrial Education, 1994).

Along with the educational institutions listed for all divisions of ACTE, the Trade and Industrial Education Division also includes educators in two-year colleges and four-year baccalaureate degree programs. In addition to the previously mentioned goals for all ACTE areas of study, the mission of the Trade and Industrial Education Division is to advance trade and industrial education through the development of sound practices in trade and industrial education programs and services.

Health Occupations Education

A limited number of programs in practical nursing were in operation after the Smith-Hughes Act of 1917, which broadly defined nursing as a trade and thus included under the trade and industrial provisions of the act (Calhoun and Finch, 1982). In 1956, practical nursing was included as part of the federal vocational education program. Venn (1964) points out that the program was usually conducted through a hospital or medical center, often with the cooperation of the local school district or a junior college.

The health occupations program is designed to acquaint individuals with the career options in the health services industry and to provide the knowledge, skills, and attitudes necessary to succeed in the wide field of health care. Employment in the health services industry will continue to grow almost twice as fast as total nonfarm wage-and-salary employment. Demand for health-care professionals is spurred by an aging population, new medical technologies that allow treatment of previously untreatable illnesses, and the growth of outpatient and home care. According to the U.S. Department of Labor (2007):

- As the largest industry in 2004, health care provided 13.5 million jobs—13.1 million jobs for wage and salary workers and about 411,000 jobs for the self-employed.
- Eight out of 20 occupations projected to grow the fastest are in health care.
- More new wage and salary jobs created between 2004 and 2014— about 19 percent, or 3.6 million—will be in health care than in any other industry.

Four main issues have influenced the development of health-care occupations at the secondary level: the unequal value of health care, questionable quality of health care, skyrocketing costs, and responsibility for or control of health services (Sands, 1971). These four issues are still relevant in the development of health care in today's society.

Along with the educational institutions listed for all divisions of ACTE, the Health Occupations Education Division also includes educators in four-year baccalaureate degree programs. In addition to the previously mentioned goals for all ACTE areas of study, the mission of the Health Occupations Education Division is to advance health-occupations education and its capability to equip students with skills for life and career success.

Technology Education

In October 1904, Professor Charles R. Richards, director of manual training at Columbia University, suggested the term "industrial arts" be substituted for manual training. The term was first used to designate work that developed as a reaction against the formalized courses inherited from Froebel (Foles, Coover, and Mason, 1956). It was Froebel's recognition of the central importance of manual/industrial education that led to the major position that manual training later occupied in kindergarten and elementary school.

Technology education (formerly industrial arts education) is an instructional program that acquaints people with their technological environment and provides them with a broad knowledge of the applications of technology in daily life. The Carl D. Perkins Vocational and Applied Technology Education Act of 1990 (PL 101-392) defined technology education as "an applied discipline designed to promote technological literacy which provides knowledge and understanding of the impacts of technology including its organizations, techniques, tools, and skills to solve practical problems and extend human capabilities in areas such as construction, manufacturing, communication, transportation, power, and energy" (American Vocational Association, 1990).

According to the International Technology Education Association (1993), technology education programs propose to help students:

- Develop an appreciation for the importance of technology.
- Make informed occupational and career choices.
- Apply tools, materials, processes, and technical concepts safely and efficiently.
- Make wise consumer choices.
- Make appropriate adjustments to a rapidly changing environment.
- Recognize and deal with forces and trends that influence the future.
- Apply critical-thinking and problem-solving skills.
- Discover and develop individual talents.
- Apply creative abilities.
- Apply academic skills and the content of other school subjects.

As an integral part of the school's curriculum, technology education teaches students to understand, use, and control technology in an experimental laboratory environment. Students are taught the application of mathematics and science and how to use knowledge of technology to solve an array of practical problems in the areas of communications, manufacturing, construction, transportation, power, and energy.

Along with the educational institutions listed for all divisions of ACTE, the Technology Education Division also includes educators in two-year colleges and four-year baccalaureate degree programs. In addition to the previously mentioned goals for all ACTE areas of study, the mission of the Technology Education Division is to advance technology education and its capability to develop technological literacy for life and employment.

Technical Education

The main thrust of technical education can be traced to the 1940s, when the U.S. Office of Education recognized and proclaimed the need to train technicians who would work on jobs that required more limited competencies than those of professional engineers but more than those needed by skilled mechanics. As industry mushroomed after World War II, there were increasing demands for technical workers (Calhoun and Finch, 1982).

McMahon (1970) suggests that preparation for a technical occupation requires:

> An understanding of, and ability to apply, those levels of mathematics and science appropriate to the occupation. And in those occupations that can be properly defined as technical, the mathematics and science required is more advanced than that required for a middle-type craft or skilled-trades occupations. (p. 23)

Measurement, blueprint reading, lather and mill operations, and basic CNC programming are some of the areas explored by students in the machine trades curriculum.

The definition of *technical* is still somewhat unclear, with colleges, universities, vocational-technical schools, and technical institutes formulating their own definitions. However, Scott and Sarkees-Wircenski (1996) defined technical occupations as occupations that required workers to use higher levels of math, science, and technology to make decisions on the job than is normally required in skilled-trades occupations.

The majority of technical education programs are offered at public and private postsecondary institutions including community colleges, technical institutes, technical centers, engineering schools, and four-year colleges offering technical programs of less than baccalaureate degree programs.

Career technical educators should build on the following six initiatives to design their programs during the twenty-first century (Lynch, 2000):

1. Make sure your curriculum represents career fields that are projected to experience employment growth.

2. Bring contextual learning and teaching methods into high school classrooms throughout the curriculum.

3. Include work-based learning experiences in the curriculum.

4. Improve authentic assessment of student achievement.

5. Reconfigure high school vocational programs to become career academies—or schools within schools—that include top-notch teachers (academic and career and technical) who execute courses and related learning experience, collaboratively with business and industry.

6. Refocus our thinking of the proverbial K–12 school system into a pre-K–14-and-beyond system that includes the conceptual components of model Tech Prep programs. Yesterday's version of the high school diploma for most students, most places, most of the time is insufficient in today's workplace.

Implications for Career and Technical Education Programs and Policies

The United States is shifting from a manufacturing- to a service- and information-based economy. This trend has two important implications for CTE programs. It signals an ongoing shift in the education and training fields that are required of the U.S. workforce as well as the levels of that education and training. The occupations with the highest projected growth rates are generally in the computer technology and health fields. Those with the highest projected increase in number of jobs are somewhat more varied, although they also include several health occupations. While the occupations with the highest projected growth rates have relatively high education and training requirements, those with the highest projected increase in number of jobs have relatively low education and training requirements.

Implications are that while some emerging occupations have high education and training requirements, the majority of jobs still demand relatively low education and training levels. There is consensus in the research literature that there are trends toward greater education and training requirements and a greater need for critical thinking, personal responsibility, and social skills among workforce participants. However, these trends are not uniform across industries and occupations, and some disagree about their magnitude. Although researchers have long identified the association between increased educational attainment and better labor market outcomes, the disparity in incomes between those with more and less education has increased in recent years. Some argue that this means that education and training are increasingly crucial for narrowing the income gap and for preventing the creation of a society of haves and have-nots. CTE at the postsecondary level appears to offer the best hope for bringing the educationally, socially, and economically disadvantaged into the mainstream of American life.

Credentials and Work Experience of CTE Teachers at the Secondary Level

Teacher quality has increasingly become a focus of policy makers' interest in regular K–12 education, but less attention has been paid to how well career and technical teachers are being prepared for their jobs. The availability, experience, priorities, and practices of teachers can be expected to affect the quality of instruction and therefore of career and technical education overall. Larger issues concerning the preparation and hiring of career and technical educators have become increasingly important as the economy and federal career and technical policy have changed. The issues of teacher supply and qualifications are important to the ongoing development of the field.

Most states do require from sixteen to 200 hours of pedagogical preparation in the first year of teaching, typically obtained through workshops or college courses. Many states also require licensure in occupations such as cosmetology, health technologies, plumbing, and auto mechanics. In addition, twelve to eighteen states require individuals within the first year of teaching, or preservice teachers lacking work experience, to pass National Occupational Competency Testing Institute (NOCTI) tests (Lynch, 1993).

The educational attainment of vocational teachers as a group remained about the same in 1990–91 and 1993–94 (Table 8.2). Although there was a small decrease in the percentage of teachers with a master's degree, the percentage of vocational education teachers with a doctorate or first-professional degree increased slightly. In both 1990–91 and 1993–94, about 8 percent of vocational education teachers had less than a bachelor's degree; 47 percent had a bachelor's degree; and the rest (about 45–46 percent) had some type of advanced degree.

About the same proportion (47 percent) of vocational and academic teachers held bachelor's degrees as their highest degree in 1993–94 (Table 8.2). Vocational education teachers were more likely to have less than a bachelor's degree (8.3 versus 0.5 percent), while academic teachers were more likely to have a master's or doctorate/first professional degree.

Educational attainment varied markedly by vocational education program area. Trade and industry and technical teachers and those teaching in more than one vocational field were generally least likely to have a bachelor's or advanced degree in 1993–94 (Table 8.2). About 39 percent of trade and industry teachers, 32 percent of "mixed" vocational teachers, and 16 percent of technical teachers held less than a bachelor's degree. This may reflect the practice in some states of counting industry experience in place of education in hiring some vocational education teachers (American Vocational Association, 1993). In contrast, agriculture, business, career education, home economics, and industrial arts teachers were more like academic teachers in terms of their educational attainment, with less than 6 percent of these groups having less than a bachelor's degree.

According to a report by Levesque et al. (2000), CTE teachers were generally older than academic teachers; however, they are similar in years of teaching experience. CTE teachers may have been older than their academic peers because they began teaching at an older age, possibly after obtaining industry experience.

Table 8.2 Percentage Distribution of Public School Teachers of Grades 9–12 according to Highest Educational Degree, by Teaching Assignment and Vocational Program Area: 1990–91 and 1993–94

Teaching Assignment and Vocational Program Area	1990–91					1993–94				
	Less than Bachelor's	Bachelor's	Master's	Educational Specialist	Doctorate or First Professional	Less than Bachelor's	Bachelor's	Master's	Educational Specialist	Doctorate or First Professional
Total	1.7	45.4	46.4	5.3	1.3	1.7	46.3	45.6	5.3	1.1
Teaching assignment										
Vocational education	8.3	45.5	41.4	4.5	0.3	8.3	46.7	38.7	5.6	0.7
Academic education	0.3	45.7	47.4	5.1	1.5	0.5	46.8	46.6	4.9	1.2
Special education	0.2	42.5	47.0	8.4	1.9	0.2	41.3	49.4	8.2	0.9
Vocational program area										
Agriculture	1.5	51.3	42.7	3.9	0.6	1.7	51.9	42.7	2.5	1.2
Business and accounting	0.6	43.1	50.4	5.6	0.3	0.7	48.2	44.5	6.5	0.1
Career education	0.5	42.7	47.5	9.2	0.0	5.5	39.1	42.1	10.6	2.7
Health occupations	17.9	44.4	26.1	11.6	0.0	15.1	49.5	20.4	15.0	0.0
Family and consumer sciences	0.3	58.8	37.9	2.7	0.4	0.1	59.2	36.3	3.4	1.0
Industrial arts	4.0	46.9	44.8	4.3	0.0	2.4	45.7	45.2	5.1	1.6
Technical	24.7	39.0	33.1	3.2	0.0	16.0	46.3	34.3	0.9	2.5
Trade and industry	45.4	29.3	21.8	3.3	0.2	39.1	29.5	24.6	6.6	0.2
Other	18.1	43.4	32.2	4.8	1.6	12.5	40.0	41.0	6.4	0.1
Mixed*	2.9	41.8	57.7	3.6	0.0	32.2	34.8	25.0	7.1	0.9

Note: Percentages may not add to 100 due to rounding. Estimates appearing as 0.0 may be nonzero but less than 0.05.

* "Mixed" indicates that the teacher taught equal proportions in two or more vocational subjects.

Source: National Center for Education Statistics (NCES) (2000). Vocational education in the United States: Toward the year 2000, p. 96. Washington, DC: Office of Educational Research and Improvement, U.S. Department of Education.

Value of Occupational Experience and Formal Education

The tendency for career and technical education teachers to have less education and more work experience than academic teachers is most heavily concentrated in trade and industrial education. According to Lynch (1993), this pattern of less education and more work experience goes back many years.

> Beginning with the . . . 1917 Smith-Hughes Act and continuing to the present time, nearly all states substitute years of work experience [for] college preparation [in] certifying MI teachers. In fact, only Hawaii and Wisconsin require the baccalaureate degree for initial certification. . . . Seven states require a baccalaureate degree and five states require an associate degree for full certification. Beginning teachers in 43 states may teach T&I programs without any college credits. (p. 11)

The fact that career and technical education teachers in general, and trade and industry teachers in particular, have less formal education and more occupational experience than others has been at issue for some time. There is controversy about whether trade and industry teachers, or any teachers, should be able to teach in public schools without a college degree. Career and technical education teachers are more likely to have industry experience than other secondary teachers but continue to be less academically prepared (U.S. Department of Education, 2004).

Unlike the specifications for academic teachers in the No Child Left Behind Act, the Perkins Act does not require grantees to define a highly qualified CTE teacher or to set goals for ensuring that students in career and technical education programs have access to one. Two factors that might be important in those qualifications are industry experience and academic background. Because career and technical education is rooted in training for jobs and family life directly after high school, it historically placed great value on teachers' occupational skills; educational background was considered less important than practical experience. Current federal career and technical education policy, however, emphasizes improving the academic achievement of CTE students. In this climate, the academic skills of career and technical education teachers may be of increasing importance, although it is not known how these skills translate into effective teaching practice and student achievement in a career and technical education setting.

Among new teachers, those who are in career and technical fields are more likely to come from industry. Career and technical teaching continues to draw men and women with other work experiences (Levesque, 2004).

Candidates for career and technical education teaching positions are less academically prepared than their counterparts who seek other teaching jobs (U.S. Department of Education, 2004). Given the way that federal policy has evolved, it appears increasingly important to attract new CTE teachers who can support students' academic learning. However, recent data on the PRAXIS—a series of tests administered by the Educational Testing Service and required for state teacher licensure in 31 states—indicate that candidates for career and technical education teaching jobs consistently score lower in reading, writing, and mathematics than candidates for other secondary subjects. In reading and writing, in fact, prospective secondary vocational teachers have lower scores than those planning to teach at the elementary school level. Compared to other secondary teachers, CTE teacher candidates also have lower undergraduate GPAs and lower pass rates on the basic skill PRAXIS assessments based on the score their states set (Cramer, 2004). Case studies suggest that these assessments probably do not include individuals entering the profession laterally from industry (Stasz and Bodilly, 2004).

A high and increasing share of career and technical education teachers qualify through alternative certification routes, but there is no evidence to suggest how this affects students. Past research has stressed the importance of teacher education training and a teaching certificate as indicators of quality, although that notion has been challenged (Goldhaber and Brewer, 2000). This debate is particularly relevant for career and technical education, where industry experience has long been presumed to be an equitable, if not better, trade-off for more traditional credentials such as a college degree and certification.

Perhaps due to teacher shortages or the expansion of alternative entry routes, an increasing share of high school teachers were working without regular or standard certification over the last decade. In particular, new teachers were far more likely to enter high schools without certification in 2000 than in 1991 (Table 8.3). The proportion of both new career and technical education and new non-career and technical education teachers who were not certified about doubled during that period. Some evidence suggests that a higher share of new career and technical education teachers were drawn directly from industry, perhaps entering through alternative certification routes (Levesque, 2004).

There is currently little research to evaluate the relative or unique contributions of teacher certification and industry experience to career and technical education teaching. No rigorous evaluations have examined the

Table 8.3   Percentage of New High School Teachers without Teacher Certification, by Teaching Assignment: 1991 and 2000

| | Percentage of New Teachers without Certification | | Change between |
Teaching Assignment and School Type	1991	2000	1991 and 2000
All CTE	11.7	22.1	10.4
All non-CTE	7.8	17.9	10.1*

* Differences were statistically significant at the 0.05 level.
Note: Calculations were performed on unrounded numbers.
Source: U.S. Department of Education. (2004). National assessment of vocational education: Final report to Congress, p. 79. Washington, DC: Office of the Under Secretary, Policy and Program Studies Service.

relationship between the credentials of CTE teachers and the occupational and technical competencies of their students. One recent survey indicates that, compared to those with a baccalaureate or post-baccalaureate degree, new career and technical education teachers who have alternative certifications are less likely to feel confident about pedagogy but more likely to feel well-prepared in their CTE subject area. There were no differences, however, between the two types of teachers in terms of their confidence in their classroom skills, ability to work with special populations, or plans to remain in teaching (Ruhland and Bremer, 2002). A review of research on the importance of industry experience in predicting CTE teacher quality reports that "there is no reliable correlation between years of occupational experience or scores on occupational competency tests and such variables as teacher qualifications, satisfaction, or effectiveness" (Lynch, 1998, p. 47).

Historically, vocational educators have argued that work experience is indispensable for teaching students how to perform certain kinds of jobs. Indeed, it is hard to see how teachers who have never been auto mechanics, welders, or electricians could teach auto mechanics, welding, or electrical wiring to students. According to the National Assessment of Vocational Education (NAVE) (1994), the findings across many studies conducted over a period of forty years suggest that extensive occupational experience confers no particular benefits on vocational teaching, although a few years' experience has a positive impact. Formal postsecondary education is positively associated with desirable teacher and student outcomes. In essence, trade and industry teachers would be better off with more formal education and less occupational experience.

Implications for Career and Technical Teacher Preparation

Career and technical education is changing as a result of reform activities at the federal, state, and local levels. States and localities are responding to the reforms called for in the Perkins Act. Several states are undertaking fundamental reforms of secondary education to better prepare non-baccalaureate students for the workforce. The reforms for which teachers will need to be prepared include:

- An orientation toward workforce preparation for a majority of the secondary student body,
- Emphasis on developing cognitive and technical skills in an integrated context,
- Preparing nonbaccalaureate students for postsecondary education in community colleges and technical institutes through arrangements such as Tech Prep programs, and
- Student participation in work experience programs.

If such reforms are to be effected, there will have to be substantial changes in the way teachers are prepared in colleges and universities. Academic teachers will need more familiarity with the world of work, possibly through courses in business and technology, or through work experience outside of teaching. They will also need to learn how to apply features of their academic disciplines to work-related subjects. Career and technical education teachers will need more and more vigorous courses in the liberal arts. For many prospective vocational teachers, a greater emphasis on computers will be required. Beyond these changes in teacher education programs, states will need to tailor the preparation of their teachers to particular elements of reform in their system.

Bruening et al. (2001) reported several challenges for career and technical education teacher educators:

- The critical need to build the capacity of teacher education programs to produce CTE teachers. This is necessary due to the decline in the number of CTE teacher preparation programs.

- Emphasis on quality and rigor in teacher education necessitates recruiting students who can meet higher academic standards.

- Conflicting data suggest a need to ensure that CTE teachers understand the integration of academic and technical skills.

- Better ways to expand program delivery with the use of innovative methods are needed (Maurer, 2001).

Gray and Walter's (2001) recommendations for CTE preparation reform focused on several ways to address these challenges:

- Teacher preparation programs should ensure that teachers possess a good background in pedagogical knowledge, subject-matter knowledge, and general knowledge.

- Programs should be organized around mission, not titles. Programs are often downsized or altered due to the specific area they cover. By focusing CTE programs on the mission of preparation and instruction, more fields can be encompassed into a larger program structure, providing unique instruction in multiple areas.

- Alternative licensure models should be developed. With the large shortage of teachers in CTE, programs need to attract more prospective teachers (Maurer, 2001).

"The CTE profession is in a transitional period and is still forming new models" (Bruening et al. 2001, p. 53). The Bruening findings show both positive directions and some concerns about CTE teacher preparation, and Gray and Walter's synthesis provides information to guide policy and practice (Maurer, 2001).

Selected Entities Influencing Growth in CTE Programs

This final section discusses the organizations having the greatest impact on the growth in career and technical education programs: the Association for Career and Technical Education Research (ACTER), the Southern

Regional Education Board (SREB), the National Center for Research in Vocational Education (NCRVE), and the National Research and Dissemination Centers for Career and Technical Education (NCCTE).

Association for Career and Technical Education Research

The Association for Career and Technical Education Research (ACTER) (formerly AVERA) was organized in 1966. The name was changed from AVERA to ACTER at the December 2004 business meeting. ACTER is a professional association for scholars and others with research interests in the relationship between education and work. ACTER information can be accessed via the Internet (www.agri.wsu.edu/acter). Through participation in the ACTER members have the opportunity to:

- Stay current in research areas of interest that are of vital importance to professional roles.
- Present research to national audiences through various forums.
- Meet and interact with others who address professional interests and concerns through research.
- Assume national roles by serving as an officer and on committees that influence career and technical education research.
- Receive recognition for outstanding research accomplishments, contributions, and achievements.

Following is a list of ACTER resolutions:

- To stimulate research and development activities related to career and technical education.
- To stimulate the development of training programs designed to prepare persons for responsibilities in research in CTE.
- To foster cooperative effort in research and development activities within the total program of CTE.
- To facilitate the dissemination of research findings and the diffusion of knowledge.

Regular members actively engage in research and development activities. Members are entitled to the rights and privileges of the association without restriction. Student members of ACTER actively pursue graduate degrees as full-time resident students (as defined by the student's institution). Student members are entitled to the rights and privileges of ACTER members except they may not vote or hold elective office in the association. Emeritus members are those who have officially retired.

Annual business meetings of the association are held in conjunction with the Association for Career and Technical Education Convention. Between conventions, business of the association is conducted by an executive committee composed of the president, vice president (president elect), recording secretary, treasurer, membership secretary, historian, and the past president.

ACTER organizes presentations of research reports, symposia, and other programs of interest to research scholars. ACTER members who are also members of the American Educational Research Association (AERA) form the Special Interest Group on Vocational Education within AERA. During AERA meetings, this special-interest group conducts sessions on research in career and technical education. Publications originated by ACTER include *Career and Technical Education Research (CTER),* a refereed scholarly and quarterly publication. In addition, ACTER produces a directory of members and occasional monographs.

A new organization, the Academy for Career and Technical Teacher Educators (ACTTE), was formed in 2004. The primary purpose of this organization is to act as a vehicle for strengthening and supporting excellence in higher education programs that prepare and support career and technical teacher educators nationally and internationally. The first president of the ACTTE was Dr. William G. Camp of Cornell University.

The Southern Regional Education Board

The Southern Regional Education Board (SREB) developed a program in 1985 to address concerns by employers that high school graduates were not prepared for successful employment in the real world. Students who were not planning to continue their education in a four-year baccalaureate program were not receiving the type of education to prepare them for entry into the American workplace (Bottoms, 1992; Winterburn, 1995). The program promoted by the SREB, High Schools That Work (HSTW), emphasized integration of higher-level academic courses with vocational courses.

HSTW is founded on the conviction that most students can master rigorous academic and career/technical studies if school leaders and teachers create an environment that motivates students to make the effort to succeed.

According to ACTE (2006), Among the HSTW key practices for improving student achievement in career/technical studies and work-based learning are:

- Provide more students access to intellectually challenging career/technical studies in high-demand fields that emphasize the higher-level mathematics, science, literacy and problem-solving skills needed in the workplace and in further education. School leaders need to develop standards, conditions and agreements for awarding postsecondary credit in high-demand career/technical fields to high school students.
- Require senior projects with academic, technical and performance standards.
- Provide students opportunities to work toward a recognized employer certification.
- Enable students and their parents to choose from programs that integrate challenging high school studies and work-based learning and are planned by educators, employers and students.

The SREB High Schools That Work program is the nation's first large-scale effort to combine challenging academic courses and vocational studies to raise the achievement of career-bound high school students. The SREB–State Vocational Education Consortium, a partnership of states, school systems, and school sites, instituted the HSTW program in 1987. Superintendents, principals, teachers, and counselors in the multistate network became actively involved in making dramatic changes in the way they prepared students for work and further education in the twenty-first century. The number of High Schools That Work states increased from 13 in 1987 to 32 in 2006. More than 1,2000 HSTW sites in these 32 states are using the framework of HSTW goals and key practices to raise student achievement (SREB, 1999–2006).They are Alabama, Arkansas, Delaware, Florida, Georgia, Hawaii, Idaho, Illinois, Indiana, Kansas, Kentucky, Louisiana, Maryland, Massachusetts, Mississippi, Missouri, Nebraska, New Jersey, New Mexico, New York, North Carolina, Ohio, Oklahoma, Pennsylvania, South Carolina, South Dakota, Tennessee, Texas, Vermont, Virginia, Washington, and West Virginia. (SREB, 1999–2006).

The High Schools That Work program has been cited as a promising school-wide program for raising student achievement. It has two major goals:

1. To increase the national average in mathematics, science, communication, problem solving, and technical achievement of those students not in college-prep studies.

2. To blend the essential academic content of traditional college prep coursework with quality vocational and technical studies.

The HSTW program is based on applied learning theory and the premise that schools should require students to think differently than how they think in real life (Flowers, 2000). According to the National Council on Vocational Education (1991), those differences in thinking focused on four major areas: (1) individual learning vs. cooperative learning, (2) abstract thinking vs. concrete thinking, (3) symbol manipulation vs. reasoning with symbols, and (4) generalizing from concepts vs. generalizing from concrete examples. Therefore, the response to low achievement by HSTW was not simply to add more academic content to the curriculum for CTE students, but to add the academic content in an applied format that provided for group learning and use of mathematics and science concepts in concrete settings (Bottoms, Presson, and Johnson, 1992). In addition, CTE teachers were provided with tools to reinforce reasoning with symbols by integrating more academic content into the CTE courses they taught (Flowers, 2000). Fogarty (1991) explained that an integrated curriculum model provides students with better opportunities to make the relationships between academic and vocational content.

The SREB curriculum specifies that students in CTE courses complete a more rigorous program of studies than had been traditionally completed by vocational students. Students must complete at least three credits each in math and science, with two credits in each subject from courses that are comparable to college preparatory courses. Furthermore, the program of study should include science in both the junior and senior year of high school and math in the senior year. In English, students complete four courses with content equal to that of a college prep course. Students must also complete a sequence of courses in the major and two credits of related vocational or technical courses (Bottoms, 1992).

The underlying theoretical basis for HSTW is *expectancy value theory* (Murray, 1943). According to this theory, students will be motivated to learn only if they feel the task is within the appropriate range of challenge—not too easy and not extremely difficult. A second, critical component of the theory is that learning activities must be perceived by students to have some practical value (Brophy, 1987). Teaching academic subjects in an applied context not only challenges students, but also provides them with a practical application of mathematics, science, and English in a real-world setting (Flowers, 2000).

A preliminary assessment of SREB pilot sites showed evidence that HSTW had potential to improve the achievement of CTE students (Bottoms, Presson, and Johnson, 1992). Students who completed career and technical education programs at SREB pilot sites in 1990 completed the HSTW Assessment, which was developed using items from the National Assessment of Educational Progress (NAEP). Students who reported that their CTE teachers often stressed reading, mathematics, and science skills had significantly higher scores in all three subject areas than students who reported their CTE teachers did not emphasize those academic areas. Another measure of success included reports of increased enrollment in community college programs by students graduating from HSTW sites (Lozada, 1996).

All schools involved in the High Schools That Work program are dedicated to 10 goals, called "key practices" (Rose, 1998). These goals are:

1. *High expectations.* Setting higher expectations and getting career-bound students to meet them.

2. *Career/technical studies.* Increasing access to challenging career and technical studies, with an emphasis on using high-level mathematics, science, language arts, and problem-solving skills in the context of modern workplace practices.

3. *Academic studies.* Increasing access to academic studies that teach the essential concepts from the college preparatory curriculum through functional and applied strategies that enable students to see the relationship between course content and future roles.

4. *Program of study.* Having students complete a challenging program of study with an upgraded academic core and a major.

5. *Work-based learning.* When collaboratively planned by educator, employers, and workers, the outcome is an industry-recognized credential and employment in a career pathway.

6. *Teachers working together.* Having an organizational structure and schedule enabling academic and vocational teachers to have the

time to plan and provide integrated instruction aimed at teaching high-status academic and technical content.

7. *Students actively engaged.* Having each student actively involved in the learning process.

8. *Guidance.* Involving each student and his or her parent(s) in a career guidance and advising system to ensure completion of an accelerated program of study with a career and academic major.

9. *Extra help.* Providing a structured system of extra help to enable career-bound students to successfully complete an accelerated program of study.

10. *Keep score.* Using student assessment and program evaluation data to continuously improve curriculum, instruction, school climate, organization, and management to advance student learning.

Skill requirements for many occupations are changing, and workers require greater academic as well as occupational and employability skills. Consequently, the United States must develop a comprehensive system for skills development that takes into account those changing requirements. SREB information can be accessed via the Internet (http://www.sreb.org).

National Center for Research in Vocational Education

Funded by the Office of Vocational and Adult Education of the U.S. Department of Education, NCRVE played a key role in developing a new concept of workforce development. The center's mission was to strengthen school-based and work-based learning to prepare all individuals for lasting and rewarding employment, further education, and lifelong learning. NCRVE closed its operations on December 31, 1999.

National Research and Dissemination Centers for Career and Technical Education

Furthering the effort of NCRVE into the twenty-first century is the National Research and Dissemination Centers for Career and Technical Education. Its mission is to:

• Use practitioner-driven approaches in planning, development, conduct, and evaluation of all research, dissemination, and professional development activities.

• Develop a program that is national in scope, reflecting the strengths and needs of diverse national, state, and local practitioners across a range of geographic, socioeconomic, and cultural settings.

• Present a balanced research dissemination and professional development program for secondary and postsecondary practitioners and institutions.

For more information, visit the Web site for the Research and Dissemination Centers at http://www.nccte.com.

Summary

- Career and technical education at the secondary level is a large and complex system. CTE courses are available at various grade levels and include both introductory and advanced offerings.
- Secondary career and technical education is provided in a variety of settings.
- There are three types of secondary career and technical education courses: specific labor market preparative, general labor market preparative, and family and consumer sciences education.
- Career and technical education teachers are more likely to have industry experience than other secondary teachers but continue to be less academically prepared.
- Among new teachers, those who are in CTE fields are more likely to come from industry.
- Career and technical education teachers remain less likely than other high school teachers to hold a baccalaureate degree.
- Candidates for career and technical teaching positions are less academically prepared than their counterparts who seek other teaching jobs.
- A high and increasing share of career and technical education teachers come through alternative certification routes, but there is no evidence to suggest this affects students.
- The key practices of the High Schools That Work program are: high expectations, vocational studies, academic studies, program of study, work-based learning, teachers working together, students actively engaged, guidance, extra help, and keeping score.
- Among the entities that had an impact on the growth of career and technical education both prior to the 1990s and beyond are the Association for Career and Technical Education Research (ACTER), the Southern Regional Education Board (SREB), the National Center for Research in Vocational Education (NCRVE), and the National Research and Dissemination Centers for Career and Technical Education (NCCTE).

Discussion Questions and Activities

1. Describe the major program areas of career and technical education.
2. What types of classes are available to postsecondary students and adults who desire to engage in the study of career and technical education?
3. Interview a technology education instructor and prepare a report for the class about the changes in the program resulting from federal funding.

4. Select a career and technical education field, preferably one other than your area of concentration, and prepare a report on its history and impact on your local community or state.

5. Describe the preparation of CTE teachers for the eight major areas of career and technical education.

6. How does today's career and technical education compare with CTE in the early 1960s? What changes have occurred during the past four decades?

7. How large is the career and technical education field at both secondary and postsecondary levels, and is it growing, shrinking, or holding constant over time?

8. What types and how much career and technical education do students take at each level, and is this changing?

9. Who participates in career and technical education, and is this changing?

10. Extrapolate the trends in career and technical education teacher qualifications and experience over time.

11. Compare and contrast the 10 goals (key practices) of the High Schools That Work program with Prosser's Theorems (see Appendix C).

For Exploration

12. What skills do employers value, and how have skill requirements and worker proficiency changed in recent years?

13. Is the academic preparation of students who participate in career and technical education improving over time? Justify your answer.

14. Explain the role of work experience and work-based learning in students' courses of study.

15. What is the impact of career and technical education reform efforts at the local level? Explain.

16. Summarize the postsecondary and labor market outcomes associated with participation in career and technical education.

17. Extrapolate the labor market outcomes associated with participation in career and technical education. How do these outcomes compare with other kinds of preparation?

Thinking Critically

18. What are the economic and social challenges of our nation that make career and technical education at the secondary and postsecondary levels a good public investment by local, state, and federal government?

19. Why should career and technical education exist?

20. In your experience, what are the major assets and challenges of career and technical education in high schools and in community and technical colleges today?

21. How would you contrast the learning expectations/results and learning process for secondary/postsecondary career and technical education?

Library Research

22. Describe the instructional delivery system for a typical postsecondary career and technical education area.

23. Develop a research paper on the demand and supply of secondary and postsecondary career and technical education teachers for the past ten years.

References and Additional Reading

American Home Economics Association (1994). *A conceptual framework for the 21st century*. Alexandria, VA: Author.

American Vocational Association (1990). *The AVA guide to the Carl D. Perkins Vocational and Applied Technology Education Act of 1990*. Alexandria, VA: Author.

———. (1993). The state of certification. *Vocational Education Journal, 68*(6), 30–35.

———. (1997). Quick facts. *Techniques, 72*(4), 7.

Association for Career and Technical Education (ACTE) ((2006). Reinventing the American High School for the 21st Century: Strengthening a New Vision for the American High School through Experiences and Resources of Career and Technical Education. ACTE position paper. Retrieved February 20, 2007, from http://iacte.bizland.com/sitebuildercontent/sitebuilderfiles/actehsreform_paper.pdf.

Boesel, D., Hudson, L., Deich, S., and Masten, C. (1994). *National assessment of vocational education, final report to Congress. Volume II: Participation in and quality of vocational education*. Washington, DC: Department Education, Office of Educational Research Improvement (Issue Brief NLE 98-2023).

Bottoms, G. (1992, November/December). Closing the gap: SREB program blends academic standard, vocational courses, *Vocational Education Journal, 67*(8), 25–27, 70.

Bottoms, G., Presson, A., and Johnson, M. (1992). *Making high schools work*. Atlanta: Southern Region Education Board.

Britton, R. K., and Fick, S. L. (1956). Fifty years of progress in trade and industrial education. *American Vocational Journal, 31*(9), 83–90, 104.

Brophy, J. (1987). Synthesis of research on strategies for motivating students to learn. *Educational Leadership, 45*(2), 40–48.

Brown, T. C., and Logan, W. B. (1956). Fifty years of progress in distributive education. *American Vocational Journal, 31*(9), 57–66, 111.

Bruening, T. H., Sconlon, D. C., Hodes, C., Dhital, P., Shao, X., and Liu, S. T. (2001). *The status of career and technical education teacher preparation programs*. University Park: National Research Center for Career and Technical Education, Pennsylvania State University.

Bureau of Labor Statistics (2002). *Occupational outlook handbook*. Washington, DC: U.S. Department of Labor.

Calhoun, C. C., and Finch, A. V. (1982). *Vocational education: Concepts and operations*. Belmont, CA: Wadsworth.

Cox, D. E., McCormick, F. G., and Miller, G. M. (1989). Agricultural education model. *Agricultural Education Magazine, 61*(11), 9–12.

Cramer, K. (2004). The *vocational teacher pipeline: How academically well prepared is the next generation of vocational teachers?* Washington, DC: U.S. Department of Education, Office of the Under Secretary.

DECA Inc. (1992). *Marketing education and DECA: Essential factors in creating a quality work force*. Reston, VA: Report prepared by the Corporate National Advisory Board of DECA, an Association of Marketing Students.

Family and Consumer Sciences Education (2000). Subject matters: Addressing the critical shortage of FACS educators. *Techniques, 75*(8), 37, 41, 45.

Flowers, J. (2000). High Schools That Work and tech prep: Improving student performance in basic skills. *Journal of Vocational Education Research, 25*(3), 333–345.

Fogarty, R. (1991). *How to integrate the curricula*. Arlington Heights, IL: IRI Skylight Training and Publishing.

Foles, R. G., Coover, S. L., and Mason, W. R. (1956). Fifty years of progress in industrial arts education. *American Vocational Journal, 31*(9), 75–82.

Goldhaber, D. D., and Brewer, D. J. (2000). Does teacher certification matter? High school teacher certification status and student achievement. *Educational Evaluation and Policy Analysis, 22*(2), 129–145.

Gordon, H. R. D. (1985). Analysis of the postsecondary educational attainment of agricultural education graduates of the high school class of 1972. *Journal of Vocational Education Research, 10*(2), 11–18.

Gray, K. C., and Walter, R. A. (2001). *Reforming career and technical education teacher preparation and licensure: A public policy synthesis*. Columbus: National Dissemination Center for Career and Technical Education, The Ohio State University.

Haas, R. B. (1972). The origin and early development of distributive education—parts I, II, and III. In S. S. Schrumpf (Ed.), *The origin and development of distributive education* (p. 9). Hightstown, NJ: McGraw-Hill.

Hamlin, H. M. (1956). Fifty years of progress in agricultural education. *American Vocational Journal, 31*(9), 39–46.

Hudson, L., and Shafer, L. (2002). *Vocational education offerings in rural high schools*. Washington, DC: U.S. Department of Education, Office of Educational Research and Improvement, National Center for Education Statistics (Issue Brief NCES 2002-120).

International Technology Education Association (1993). *Technology education: The new basics*. Reston, VA: Author.

Lawson, D. S., and Creighton, M. (1956). Fifty years of progress in home economics education. *American Vocational Journal, 31*(9), 67–74, 104.

Lee, J. S. (1994). *Program planning guide for agriscience and technology education*. Danville, IL: Interstate Publishers.

Leventhal, J. I. (2002). The influence of marketing education. *Techniques, 77*(3), 30–33.

Levesque, K. (2004). *Teacher quality in vocational education*. A report prepared by MPR Associates for the National Assessment of Vocational Education. Washington, DC: U.S. Department of Education, Office of the Under Secretary.

Levesque, K., Lauren, D., Teitelbaum, P., Alt, M., Librera, S., and Nelson, D. (2000). *Vocational education in the United States: Toward the year 2000*. Washington, DC: U.S. Department of Education, Office of Educational Research and Improvement.

Lozada, M. (1996, September). A light beckons. *Techniques, 71*(6), 27–31.

Lynch, R. L. (1993). *Vocational teacher education in U.S. colleges and universities and its responsiveness to the Carl D. Perkins Vocational and Applied Technology Education Act of 1990.* Draft report prepared for the National Assessment of Vocational Education. Athens: University of Georgia, School of Leadership & Lifelong Learning.

———. (2000). High school career and technical education for the first decade of the 21st century. *Journal of Vocational Education Research, 25*(2), 155–198.

Mason, R. E., and Husted, S. W. (2002). *Cooperative occupational education,* 6th ed. Danville, IL: Interstate Publishers.

Maurer, M. J. (2001). *Career and technical teacher education programs,* No. 8. Columbus: National Dissemination Center for Career and Technical Education, The Ohio State University.

McMahon, G. G. (1970). Technical education: A problem of definition. *American Vocational Journal, 45*(3), 23.

Murray, H. A. (1943). *Thematic apperception test manual.* Cambridge: Harvard University Press.

National Assessment of Vocational Education (NAVE) (1994). *Final report to Congress, volume II: Participation in and quality of vocational education.* Washington, DC: Office of Educational Research and Improvement, U.S. Department of Education.

National Association of Trade and Industrial Education (NATIE) (1994). *Workforce 2020: Action report school-to-work opportunities national voluntary skill standards.* Leesburg, VA: Author.

National Center for Educational Statistics (NCES) (1992). *Vocational education in the United States: 1969–1990.* Washington, DC: Office of Educational Research and Improvement, U.S. Department of Education.

———. (2000). *Vocational education in the United States: Toward the year 2000.* Washington, DC: U.S. Department of Education, Office of Educational Research and Improvement.

National Council on Vocational Education (1991). *How we think and learn.* Washington, DC: Author.

Phillips, J. (1994). All business is global. In A. McEntire (Ed.), *Expanding horizons in business education* (pp. 35–45). Reston, VA: National Business Association, National Business Education Yearbook, No. 32.

Maurer, M. J. (2001). *Career and technical teacher education programs,* No. 8. Columbus: National Dissemination Center for Career and Technical Education, The Ohio State University.

Reese, S. (2004). Family and consumer sciences education: The compassionate curriculum. *Techniques, 79*(3), 18–21.

Rose, M. (1998). High schools that work: Making the link between academic and vocational education. *American Teacher, 82*(8), 12–13, 19.

Ruhland, S. K. and Bremer, C. D. (2002). *Alternative teacher certification procedures and professional development opportunities for career and technical education teacher.* St. Paul: National Center for Research in career and technical education, University of Minnesota.

Sands, W. F. (1971). The healthcare crisis: Can vocational education deliver? *American Vocational Journal, 46*(9), 24.

Scott, J. L., and Sarkees-Wircenski, M. (1996). *Overview of vocational and applied technology education.* Homewood, IL: American Technical Publishers.

Southern Regional Education Board (SREB) (1999–2006). *High schools that work.* Retrieved February 20, 2007, from http://www.sreb.org/Programs/hstw.hstwindex.asp.

Stasz, C., and Bodilly, S. (2004). *Efforts to improve the quality of vocational education in secondary schools: Impact of federal and state policies.* Santa Monica, CA: RAND.

Stewart, D. (1994). Home economics division considers name change. *Vocational Education Journal, 69*(6), 53–54.

U.S. Department of Education (2004). *National assessment of vocational education: Final report to congress.* Washington, DC: Office of the Under Secretary, Policy and Program Studies Service.

U.S. Department of Labor (1993). The American work force: 1992–2005. *Occupational Outlook Quarterly, 37*(3), 2–44.

———. (2007). *Career Guide to Industries.* Bureau of Labor Statistics. Retrieved February 12, 2007, from http://www.bls.gov/oco/cg/cgs035.htm.

Venn, G. (1964). *Man, education, and work.* Washington, DC: American Council on Education.

Vo, C. D. (1997, April). This is agriculture? *Techniques, 72*(4), 30–33.

Walker, A. L., Huffman, H., and Beaumont, J. A. (1956). Fifty years of progress in business education. *American Vocational Journal, 31*(9), 47–54, 104.

Winterburn, P. (1995, April). Learning to trust. *Vocational Education Journal, 70*(4), 28–29, 44.

chapter 9

Development of Career and Technical Education Student Organizations

Career and technical education's commitment to student organizations stems from the belief that the total development of individuals is essential to the preparation of competent workers. Research and experience have shown us that student-organization activities are the most effective way to teach some of the critical skills that are necessary if students are to reach their fullest potential. The organizations are designed to allow students a vehicle for exploring their interest in an occupational field and to learn and refine leadership, social, and citizenship skills (Threeton, 2006; Reese, 2003; Zirkle and Connors, 2003; Harris and Sweet, 1981).

Career and technical student organizations (CTSOs) bring together students interested in careers in specific vocational fields, providing them with a range of individual, cooperative, and competitive activities designed to expand their leadership and job-related skills. Some CTSO activities are incorporated into the regular classroom curriculum, while others support curricular efforts outside the classroom. Student members take part in chapter meetings; serve on committees; run for elected positions; participate in local, state, or national workshops, conferences, and competitive events; help with chapter fund-raising activities and community service projects; and serve as mentors for other CTE students. This chapter provides an overview of the following areas: Public Law 81-740, organizational structure and role of the vocational student organizations, and federally recognized career and technical student organizations.

Public Law 81-740

Commonly referred to as Public Law 740, this act was passed in 1950 and was the only act to federally charter a vocational student organization. It clearly established the integral relationship of a vocational student organization to the instructional program and represented the first time that the U.S. Office of Education was recognized for being associated with vocational youth organizations. Public Law 740 allowed USOE officials to work with such organizations (Vaughn, 1998).

Although the law chartered only one vocational student organization (the one for vocational agriculture), it established the pattern of treating existing and future vocational student organizations as integral parts of vocational instruction. It is because of this act that all CTSOs are now recognized as essential components of the education provided for CTE students (Vaughn, 1998).

Organizational Structure and Role of the CTSOs

CTSOs are organized into local chapters that are typically formed by CTE students in a class or from several classes within a vocational program area. Each chapter is sponsored by an instructor who serves as the chapter faculty and advisor. State departments of education typically support CTSO activities by designating state advisors for each vocational program area, and by providing administrative or financial assistance for local, state, and national meetings and conferences. Each CTSO also has a national office focusing on policies, guidelines, and curricula to assist instructors in implementing CTSO programs.

Leadership skills are fostered by encouraging students to participate in chapter planning and decision making, as well as running for chapter offices. Fund-raising and community service are also common activities that help build team spirit and individual initiative. In addition, local, regional, state, and national contests serve as "vocational skill Olympics."

While CTSO contests can vary, the national contests follow a set format in which students complete industry-developed written and performance tests of job-related skills. The written tests focus on relevant academic knowledge, while the performance tests assess vocational skills. For example, construction students may be required to build a cabinet or the corner of a house; marketing students may develop an advertising campaign; business students may perform word processing or electronic bookkeeping assignments; and livestock or crops raised by agriculture students may be judged on a variety of dimensions. Other performance tests assess leadership abilities through such activities as speeches and mock job interviews. While only a small percentage of students may make it to the national competition, many more participate in state competitions, with even more in regional and local competitions.

Because of such opportunities for student skill development, recognition, and leadership, CTSO membership is widely regarded as a valuable adjunct to more formal education, particularly as a means to increase student motivation and professionalism (Threeton, 2006; Zirkle and Connors, 2003).

Membership Status of CTSOs

In the 1980s, membership growth that had continued in the 1960s and 1970s was stagnant or beginning to decrease for many CTSOs (Hannah, 1993). Only FFA and the newer CTSOs, such as Technology Student Association (TSA) and Health Occupations Students of America (HOSA), have had a continuing increase in membership size. This increase was probably attributed to the expanding opportunities in these fields. Table 9.1 shows membership distribution of selected years.

Hannah (1993) describes four reasons that may impact membership status of career and technical student organizations.

1. *Fewer students.* The population of school-age children was lower in the 1990s. Some call this the "baby bust" generation that began in 1965 and ended in 1976. According to census data from 1990, the number of 14- to 17-year-olds plunged 18 percent in the 1980s, and the number of 18- to 24-year olds dropped 11 percent.

2. *Fewer electives.* With more students directed toward the college track, fewer students have the time or desire to take career and technical programs. While most CTSOs have been able to maintain their membership as a percentage of the career and technical student population, overall membership dropped because of a decline in career and technical course enrollment.

3. *Reduced state role.* Because of state budget cuts and the reduction in federal funds for CTSO activities, many state supervisors have been told to limit their student organization time to 5 to 15 percent. Teachers say today they are held more accountable for students' success in meeting curriculum objectives, so they have less time for CTSOs.

4. *Fewer teachers.* There has been a reduction in programs to prepare teachers in career and technical education areas, which in turn affects CTSOs. Many chapter advisors became associated with student organizations through their college experience. However, many career and technical teachers today come from other disciplines or from industry and often don't recognize student organizations as a valuable learning opportunity.

Federally Recognized CTSOs

The term *federally recognized* CTSOs includes student organizations for each vocational program area at the middle school, secondary (high school), postsecondary, and (in one case) adult level. The following CTSOs are associated with the vocational program areas:

Agriculture

- National FFA Organization (formerly Future Farmers of America)
- National Postsecondary Agricultural Student Organization (PAS)
- National Young Farmers Educational Association (NYFEA)

Table 9.1   Nationally Recognized Career and Technical Student Organizations (CTSOs)

Organization	Year Founded	Education Levels Served	Membership Size[a] (1996–1997)	Membership Size[b] (2001–2002)	Membership Size[c] (2005–2006)
National FFA Organization (FFA)	1928	Secondary, Postsecondary	452,885	455,000	495,046
Future Business Leaders of America—Phi Beta Lambda FBLA-PBL)	1943	Middle, Secondary (FBLA), Postsecondary (PBL)	250,000	233,000	237,000
Distributive Education Clubs of America (DECA)	1945	Secondary, Postsecondary	136,511	170,000	187,000
Family, Career and Community Leaders of America (FCCLA)	1945	Middle, Secondary, Postsecondary	242,000	222,000	217,550
SkillsUSA	1965	Secondary, Postsecondary	245,000	250,000	284,527
Health Occupations Students of America (HOSA)	1976	Secondary, Postsecondary	61,000	60,000	80,000
Technology Student Association (TSA)	1977	Elementary, Middle, Secondary	150,000	121,000	130,000
National Postsecondary Agricultural Student Organization (PAS)	1979	Postsecondary	1,122	1,115	1,254
National Young Farmer Educational Association (NYFEA)	1982	Adult	14,403	15,000	N/A
Business Professionals of America (BPA)	1988	Secondary, Postsecondary	45,314	50,000	55,100

[a] Information pertaining to membership size for 1996–1997 was obtained through personal communications with the CTSOs, April 14–25, 1997.
[b] Information pertaining to membership size for 2002 was obtained through personal communications with the CTSOs, February 25, March 11, 2002.
[c] Information pertaining to membership size for 2005–2006 was obtained through personal communications with CTSOs, October 10–December 15, 2006.
N/A = not available
Source: National Assessment of Vocational Education. (1994). *Final Report to Congress volume IV: Access to programs and services for special populations*, p. 138. Washington, DC: Office of Educational Research and Improvement, U.S. Department of Education.

Business/Office
- Business Professionals of America (BPA)
- Future Business Leaders of America–Phi Beta Lambda (FBLA-PBL)

Family and Consumer Sciences Education
- Family, Career and Community Leaders of America

Marketing
- Distributive Education Clubs of America (DECA)

Health Occupations
- Health Occupations Students of America (HOSA)

Trades and Technical Fields
- SkillsUSA

Technology Education (formerly Industrial Arts)
- Technology Student Association (TSA)

More information on the structure of each CTSO is provided in Table 9.1. Although CTSO participation is obviously dependent on student interest and enrollment in each vocational field, it also seems to be related to the length of time the CTSO has been in existence.

Linked through 10 national associations, state and local CTSO affiliates have long been a popular component of many career and technical education programs. The organizations provide skill competitions, training, and other after-school activities, as well as classroom resources and strategies that CTSOs encourage participating teachers to integrate into their career and technical education courses. CTSO efforts are designed to emphasize both building technical skills and developing other competencies, such as teamwork, leadership, communication, critical thinking, and basic academic proficiency.

Stasz and Bodilly (cited in U.S. Department of Education, 2004) suggested that more than two-thirds of all career and technical education teachers report that their classes are linked to a CTSO at the national level. According to the U.S. Department of Education (2004), career and technical education teachers are more likely than other teachers to have their students listen to lectures, write essays, take tests or quizzes, and participate in discussion of exploration of careers (see Table 9.2). Stasz and Bodilly also reported that many career and technical education teachers are involved in CTSO efforts at the local level, with emphasis on some integration approaches.

Future Farmers of America (FFA)

The FFA is an intracurricular activity for CTE agriculture. For many years prior to the FFA movement, vocational agriculture clubs existed in many parts of the United States. The movement received its first definite recognition as a state organization in Virginia. Professor Henry C. Groseclose of Virginia Tech, while confined to a hospital in 1926, wrote the constitution and bylaws of the FFA, which soon attracted national attention.

Table 9.2   Percentage of CTE Teachers Reporting That Various Student Activities Occur Frequently, by Whether Class Is Linked to a CTSO: 2001

Student Activity	Percentage of Teachers Reporting Activity Occurs Frequently in Class[1]	
	No CTSO Link	CTSO Link
Listen to a lecture	45.8	62.7**
Write a paragraph or more	32.2	42.5**
Receive a homework assignment	33.5	32.8
Take a test or quiz	30.4	43.7**
Use computers	60.5	53.2
Use appropriate instruments, tools, or equipment	64.5	67.0
Work in groups during class	61.5	67.3
Work on extended projects (two or more days)	60.2	52.4
Use commercially available "applied academics" curriculum materials (e.g., CORD, AIT)	11.0	11.4
Discuss or explore careers	17.7	28.3**
Apply academic skills to tasks that might be found in a job or career	61.4	67.9

[1] "Frequently" = one to two times each week or almost daily.
**Statistically different from academic teachers at the 0.001 level.
Note: CORD = Center for Occupational Development; AIT = Agency for Instructional Technology.
Source: U.S. Department of Education (2004). National assessment of vocational education: Final report to Congress, p. 56. Washington, DC: Office of the Under Secretary, Policy and Program Studies Service.

Leaders of vocational education in agriculture in other states soon realized that such an organization was exceedingly worthwhile. Within two years after the FFA was founded, six states in the southern region had similar organizations. A national organization meeting was held in November of 1928 in Kansas City, Missouri. At this meeting national officers were elected and the national constitution and bylaws adopted (Phipps and Osborne, 2002).

Prior to 1965, states that had separate schools for White and Black students had two youth organizations for agriculture students—The Future Farmers of America and The New Farmers of America (NFA) (Roberts, 1971). The NFA was started as early as 1928, and the first convention was held at Tuskegee Institute in August of 1935. Thirteen states were represented in the organizational meeting (Hawkins, Prosser, and Wright, 1951). In 1965, the NFA merged with the FFA (Vaughn, 1998).

The FFA was expanded in 1963 to include students from off-farm agricultural programs, and girls were officially admitted into the organizations in 1969 (Vaughn, 1998). The organization changed its name in 1988 from Future Farmers of America to the National FFA Organization to reflect its evolution in response to expanded agricultural opportunities encompassing science, business, and technology in addition to production farming (Mason and Husted, 2002).

Today, FFA members are preparing for agricultural careers through secondary high schools, technical schools, and four-year colleges and universities.

Contact information:
Future Farmers of America
P.O. Box 68960, 6060 FFA Drive
Indianapolis, IN 46268-0960
Phone: (317) 802-6060
Fax: (317) 802-6061
Web site: http://www.ffa.org
E-mail: webmaster@ffa.org

Future Business Leaders of America (FBLA) and Phi Beta Lambda (PBL)

The purpose of FBLA-PBL is to provide as an integral part of the instructional program additional opportunities for students in business and office education to develop vocational and career supportive competencies and to promote civic and personal responsibilities.

The FBLA concept was developed in 1937 by Hamden L. Farkner of Teachers College, Columbia University, New York City (Vaughn, 1998). Early in the 1940s, leading teachers in the South saw an opportunity to help young people achieve success in their business careers through a national organization with state and local chapters. Sponsored by the National Council of Business Education, the Future Business Leaders of America established its first chapter in Johnson City, Tennessee, on February 3, 1942 (Santo, 1986). However, it did not become a national organization until 1946.

A separate postsecondary division of FBLA, Phi Beta Lambda (PBL) was established in 1958 and achieved independent status in 1969 (Binkley and Byers, 1982).

Contact information:
FBLA PBL Inc.
1912 Association Drive
Reston, VA 20191-1591
Phone: 1-800-FBLA-WIN
Fax: (703) 758-0749
Web site: http://www.fbla-pbl.org
E-mail: general@fbla.org

Distributive Education Clubs of America (DECA)

The mission of DECA is to enhance the education of students with interests in marketing, management, and entrepreneurship. Roberts (1971) points out that DECA had its ori-

gin in local clubs organized during the years 1938 to 1942. These local clubs, known under various names such as Future Retailers, Future Merchants, Future Distributors, and Distributive Education Clubs, were organized to meet the need for social and professional growth and the common interests of students in cooperative classes.

DECA began in 1947 as the Distributors Clubs of America. The first interstate conference was held that year in Memphis, Tennessee. In 1950, the name was changed to Distributive Education Clubs of America (Vaughn, 1998). A postsecondary division of DECA-Delta Epsilon Chi (DEC) was established in 1961 to meet the needs of students enrolled in marketing and distributive education programs in junior colleges, community colleges, technical institutes, and area vocational technical schools. The first Junior Collegiate (postsecondary) National Conference was held in 1965 in Chicago (DECA Handbook, 1995).

Contact information:
Distributive Education Clubs of America
1908 Association Drive
Reston, VA 20191
Phone: (703) 860-5000
Fax: (703) 860-4013
Web site: http://www.deca.org
E-mail: www.decainc@aol.com

Family, Career and Community Leaders of America (FCCLA)

The Future Homemakers of America voted to change its name to Family, Career and Community Leaders of America at its national leadership meeting in July of 1999. According to the American Association for Career and Technical Education (1999):

> "Since our name had become outdated, we found it much harder to communicate to teens what our organization is really about—building leadership skills and addressing important personal, family, work and societal issues," said Brandon Abbott, 18, of the FCCLA national presidents, in a press release. (p. 12)

Family, Career and Community Leaders of America is a nonprofit national vocational student organization for young men and women in family and consumer sciences education in public and private school through grade 12. Once exclusively geared toward future housewives, FCCLA now has men as members. FCCLA focuses on consumer home economics and on balancing work and family. FCCLA is the only in-school student organization with the family as the center focus.

As early as 1920, high school home economics students belonged to home economics clubs. The clubs had many different names (e.g., Junior Homemakers, Betty Lamp Clubs, and Future Homemakers) and structures. In Chicago on June 11, 1945, a group of national officer candidates and a group of advisers drew up a tempo-

rary constitution. They also selected the name for the proposed national youth organization for students of home economics education: Future Homemakers of America (FHA/HERO Chapter Handbook, 1991).

The New Homemakers of America (a national organization for Black students enrolled in homemaking) was founded on June 19, 1945 at Tennessee Agricultural and Industrial State College, Nashville (Hawkins, Prosser, and Wright, 1951). Prior to the New Homemakers of America, Blacks participated in developing homemaking clubs such as New Homemakers, Progressive Homemakers, and Young Homemakers. In 1965, New Homemakers of America merged with Future Homemakers of America (Vaughn, 1998). Future Homemakers of America, Inc. (1996) cites Dr. Hazel Frost as the first national adviser for both FHA and NHA.

FCCLA expanded its organization in 1971 to include a division of Home Economics Related Occupations (HERO) for students studying occupational home economics (FFA/HERO Chapter Handbook, 1991). HERO was created for students who intended to be gainfully employed in one of the many subfields of home economics (Adams, 1993).

Today's FCCLA is a dynamic and effective national student organization that helps young men and women become leaders and address important personal, family, work, and societal issues though family and consumer sciences education. Chapter projects focus on a variety of youth concerns, including teen pregnancy, parenting, family relationships, substance abuse, peer pressure, environment, nutrition and fitness, teen violence, and career exploration.

Involvement in FCCLA offers members the opportunity to expand their leadership potential and develop necessary life skills—planning, goal setting, problem solving, decision making and interpersonal communication—in the home and workplace.

Contact information:
Family, Career and Community Leaders of America
1910 Association Drive
Reston, VA 20191-1584
Phone: (703) 476-4900
Fax: (703) 860-2713
Web site: http://www.fcclainc.org
E-mail: kmuleta@fcclainc.org

SkillsUSA

The first national organization for students in trade and industrial (T&I) education, the Future Craftsmen of America, was formed by educators during the 1920s (SkillsUSA Leadership Handbook, 2004). The Future Craftsmen of America grew out of recognition of the needs of students for

industrial occupation. The organization failed in its second year of operation, but individual states kept the idea alive with organizations of their own (Binkley and Byers, 1982). Santo (1986) points out that the Future Craftsmen organization was destined for failure because its founders had not involved industry and labor.

In 1960, interest resurfaced for a national organization for T&I students among state supervisors and teacher trainers. At the American Vocational Association Convention, a committee was established to study the possibility of a national organization. By February of 1965, existing vocational education groups agreed to finance the start-up effort, including those from Alabama, Arkansas, Georgia, Indiana, Ohio, Oklahoma, North Carolina, Missouri, South Carolina, Tennessee, Texas, Virginia, and West Virginia. The Future Farmers of America made the first financial contribution (SkillsUSA Leadership Handbook, 2004).

VICA (Vocational Industrial Clubs of America) was officially started at a Trade and Industrial Youth Conference in Nashville, Tennessee, in May 1965. The Postsecondary Division was officially formed in 1969. On September 1, 2004, the organization's name officially changed to SkillsUSA. Today,

Heating, Ventilation and Air Conditioning (HVAC) is designed to provide students with skills to acquire employment and build a profitable career in the field. EPA Refrigeration Certification is desirable for HVAC students

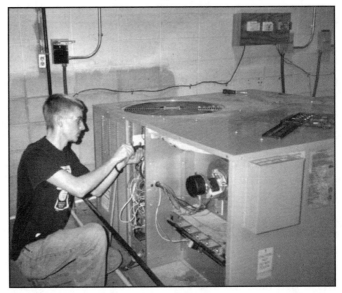

SkillsUSA works directly with business and industry to maintain American productivity, quality, and competitiveness.

Contact information:
SkillsUSA
P.O. Box 3000
Leesburg, VA 20177-0300
Phone: (703) 777-8810
Fax: (703) 777-8999
Web site: http://www.skillsusa.org
E-mail: anyinfo@skillsusa.org

Business Professionals of America (BPA)

Shortly after the passage of the Vocational Education Act of 1963, the need for a student organization to provide for students enrolled in vocational office programs was recognized. In 1964 at the AVA meeting, it was suggested that a study group be established to determine if state supervisors of office education wanted a youth group similar to those serving other curriculum areas of vocational education. Most did, and in July 1966, Iowa, Kansas, and Wisconsin formed the Vocational Office Education Clubs of America. The group was later incorporated as the Office Education Association (OEA). In 1988, the name of OEA was changed to Business Professionals of America with new logo, emblem, and colors (Business Professionals of America, 1988).

These BPA students are thoroughly engaged in a project involving office machines and quantitative applications.

Unlike the FBLA, the BPA is intended for only those secondary and postsecondary students enrolled in vocational business and office education. Its aims are to develop the leadership abilities of its members, to promote interest in the nation's business system, and to encourage competency in business office occupations (Mason and Husted, 1997).

Contact information:
Business Professionals of America (BPA)
5454 Cleveland Avenue
Columbus, OH 43231-4021
Phone: (614) 895-7277
Fax: (614) 895-1165
Web site: http://www.bpa.org
E-mail: bpa@ix.netcome.com

Health Occupations Students of America (HOSA)

The Health Occupations Students of America was formed in 1976 through the guidance of AVA's Health Occupations Division. The constitu-

tional convention that formally established HOSA was held in Arlington, Texas, November 10–13, 1976 (Santo, 1986). HOSA serves secondary and postsecondary students enrolled in health occupations. HOSA's twofold mission is to promote career development and opportunities in the health-care industry and to enhance the delivery of quality health services to all people. HOSA is the only student organization recognized

Health Occupations Students of America (HOSA) serves secondary and postsecondary students enrolled in health occupations such as nursing and medical technology.

by the Health Occupations Education (HOE) Division of the American Vocational Association.

Contact information:
HOSA
6021 Morris Rd., Suite 111
Flower Mound, TX 75028
Phone: 1-800-321-HOSA
Fax: (972) 874-0063
Web site: http:/www.hosa.org
E-mail: info@hosa.org

Technology Student Association (TSA)

Industrial arts student groups have been in existence since the first industrial arts teachers decided to do something extra with their students after school (Santo, 1986). Desire on the part of students and advisors of industrial arts clubs triggered the establishment of the American Industrial Arts Association (AIASA, pronounced I-A-Sa). In 1957, an article written by Dr. Rex Miller regarding his high school club in Iowa generated interest in a national organization for students in industrial arts. Under Dr. Miller's leadership, the American Industrial Arts Student Association was officially organized at the 27th American Industrial Arts Association Convention in Tulsa, Oklahoma, in March 1965 (Vaughn, 1998).

Technology Student Association

AIASA was organized as a sponsored program of the American Industrial Arts Association and in 1978 was officially incorporated (Binkley and Byers, 1982). At the

1988 national conference, delegates voted to change the name to the Technology Student Association to reflect a commitment to the dynamic field of technology and the future (Scott and Sarkees-Wircenski, 1996). TSA is different from the other nine student organizations in vocational education in that the students may be in elementary school, middle school, or high school.

According to Taylor (2006), TSA students report improvements in problem-solving, creativity, and communication skills, a better understanding of technology, and motivation to do their best work.

Contact information:
Technology Student Association
1914 Association Drive
Reston, VA 20191-1540
Phone: (703) 860-9000
Fax: (703) 758-4852
Web site: http://www.tsaweb.org
E-mail: general@tsaweb.org

National Postsecondary Agricultural Student Organization (NPASO or PAS)

The formation of PAS began in 1966 with a national seminar sponsored by the U.S. Office of Education at Cobleskill, New York, to identify curriculum

content, facilities, and requirements for postsecondary programs in agriculture (Vaughn, 1998). According to Santo (1986), PAS was founded in 1979 and had its first Board of Directors meeting in Washington, DC, the same year.

Today, PAS chapters are formed in postsecondary institutions that offer associate degrees or vocational diplomas and certificates in agricultural fields.

Contact information:
National Postsecondary Agricultural Student Organization (PAS)
6060 FFA Drive
P.O. Box 68960
Indianapolis, IN 46278-1370
Phone: (317) 802-4214
Fax: (317) 802-5214
Web site: http://www.nationalpas.org
E-mail: info@nationalpas.org

National Young Farmers Educational Association (NYFEA)

NYFEA is a student organization for adults enrolled in agricultural education beyond the high school level. There was a Young Farmers Organization in existence prior to the development of the NYFEA. However, Vaughn

NYFEA provides for the development and improvement of urban-rural network relationships for students enrolled in agricultural education beyond the high school level.

(1998) cites May 23, 1985 as the year when Assistant Secretary for Vocational and Adult Education Dr. Robert Worthington officially recognized the NYFEA as a vocational student organization. In April of 1988, the NYFEA was included in the U.S. Department of Education policy statement on vocational student organizations (Vaughn, 1998).

The Association for EDUCATING AGRICULTURAL LEADERS

This organization provides for the development and improvement of urban-rural network relationships and is especially appropriate for young farmer leaders when they leave the National FFA organization.

Contact information:
National Young Farmers Educational Association, Inc.
P.O. Box 20326
Montgomery, AL 36120
Phone: (334) 213-3276
Fax: (334) 213-0421
Web site: http://www.nyfea.org
E-mail: office@nyfea.org

Career and Technical Student Organizations and Work-Based Learning

Clearly, the CTSOs and their students have been tremendous ambassadors to the business/industry/labor environment for years. The local CTSO advisor and his or her students can play an active role in contacting and recruiting potential employers to become involved with developing local partnerships.

Employers today increasingly emphasize that academic and technical skills are not the only skills needed by students in order to enter the workplace. Today's high-performance workplace requires a diversity of general skills, such as teamwork, problem solving, positive work attitudes, employability, and participative skills, as well as critical thinking. These competencies make up the core of the educational programs on which CTSOs are founded.

CTSOs can play an integral role providing quality paid and nonpaid work experiences through school-based entrepreneurial and cooperative programs. Especially in rural areas, where even fewer opportunities exist for work-based learning, the CTSOs can provide guidance and development strategies for initiating or expanding operating school-based enterprises.

The national CTSO offices provide leadership at the national level in underscoring for Congress the important role that CTSOs have provided for years in the delivery of vocational-technical education. For years the various CTSOs have provided extended learning competencies related to a variety of vocational areas. Their contribution has been even more valuable because the instruction the CTSOs provide is comprehensive enough to ensure that the student understands and can competently navigate the area beyond the prerequisite academic and technical skills. This kind of well-rounded employee can integrate a variety of skills and competencies that will be demanded by the high-performance workplace of tomorrow.

The CTSOs' long-standing relationship with business/industry representatives is an ideal conduit for these students to access work-based learning opportunities. Member interaction through regional and state workshops, conferences, and contests should make the matching of students with appropriate employers an instinctive process. The reader is urged to consult Appendix D to learn more about the Fair Labor Standards Act.

Summary

- Public Law 740 is the only act to federally charter a vocational student organization. This act, passed in 1950, clearly established the integral relationship of a vocational student organization to the instructional program and represented the first time that the U.S. Office of Education was recognized for being associated with vocational youth organizations.

- The interest in and support for CTSOs derives from their role in working to foster the career, leadership, and personal development of CTE students. These basic goals are reflected in CTSO operations and activities. Leadership skills are fostered by encouraging students to participate in chapter planning and decision making, as well as running for chapter offices. Fund-raising and community service are also common activities that help build team spirit and individual initiative. In addition, local, regional, state, and national contests serve as "vocational skill olympics."

- The ten federally recognized CTSOs include student organizations for each vocational program area, at the middle school, secondary (high school), postsecondary, and (in one case) adult level.
- Career and Technical Student Organizations are regarded as an important integration strategy. Through CTSOs, young people are learning more than just skills for a future career. Guided by the career and technical educators who are their advisers, they are also learning to become good citizens who will contribute greatly to their communities and to their nation.

Discussion Questions and Activities

1. How do FFA organization activities provide educational experiences for student learners? How do they differ from other occupational areas?
2. Name the vocational student organizations associated with each vocational field. What contributions do these groups make toward realizing the goals of career and technical education?
3. Select at least two vocational student organizations with which you are unfamiliar. Interview a student member and find out his or her impressions of the contributions of the organization to its individual members, the department, and the school.
4. How do the activities provided by a health occupations student organization provide educational experiences for student learners?
5. How do the activities of the FHA-HERO student organization provide educational experiences for student learners?
6. How do DECA activities provide educational experiences for student learners?
7. Describe each vocational student organization.

For Exploration

8. Identify some of the barriers that students from special needs populations may experience in becoming involved in CTSOs.
9. What are some of the major values students can acquire from membership in a CTSO?
10. Describe the federal legislation that has guaranteed all students the right to participate in CTSO activities.
11. Describe how you would establish a local career and technical student organization.
12. Identify some of the benefits and advantages for students, teachers, schools, and communities that are provided by active CTSOs.

13. Assume you are the advisor of a local chapter. Write a lesson plan in which you introduce the topic of the student organization to the related class.

14. Volunteer your services as a judge for CTSO competitive events held statewide.

15. Research has shown that there is a decline in membership for CTSOs. Describe at least five solutions for increasing the membership rate for individual CTSOs.

Recommended Educational Media Resources

- *CTSOs' role in integrating academic, technical, and employability skills* (streaming video, 2/16/2006)
  View online at http://www.nccte.org/webcasts/descriptiondca2.html (downloadable transcript also available).

- *Contributions of CTSOs: Policy makers and CTSO student views*
  A 2005 Webcast of a panel discussion featuring leaders in the nation's career and technical education student organizations. (A downloadable transcript is also available.)
  National Dissemination Center for Career and Technical Information. Available from two sources:
  http://whitepapers.techrepublic.com/com/webcast.aspx?docid=133614
  or
  http://www.nccte.org/webcasts/description4c29.html

References and Additional Reading

ACTE Online (2006). Panel commemorates CTE week with look at value of CTSOs. Retrieved April 17, 2007, from http://www.acteonline.org/members/news/frontpage_news/frontpage22206.cfm.

Adams, D. A. (1993). The organization and operation of vocational education. In C. Anderson and L. C. Rampp (Eds.), *Vocational education in the 1990s, II: A sourcebook for strategies, methods, and materials* (pp. 35–59). Ann Arbor, MI: Prakken Publishing.

Association of Career and Technical Education (1999). A new future in store for FHA. *Techniques, 74*(6), 12.

Binkley, H. R., and Byers, C. W. (1982). *Handbook on student organizations in vocational education*. Danville, IL: Interstate Publishers.

Business Professionals of America (1988). History and organization: Office education association. *Chapter Management Reference*, 11–13. Columbus, OH: Author.

DECA, Inc. (1995). *DECA handbook*. Reston, VA: Distributive Education Clubs of America.

FHA/HERO (1991). *Chapter handbook*. Reston, VA: Future Homemakers of America.

Future Homemakers of America, Inc. (1996). *History*. Reston, VA: Author.

Hannah, G. (1993). Shift or drift. *Vocational Education, 68*(4), 21–25.

Harris, T., and Sweet, G. (1981). Why we believe in vocational student organizations. *Vocational Education, 56*(6), 33–35.

Hawkins, L. S., Prosser, C. A., and Wright, J. C. (1951). *Development of vocational education*. Chicago: Harper & Row.

Mason, R. E., and Husted, S. W. (2002). *Cooperative occupational education,* 6th ed. Danville, IL: Interstate Publishers.

Phipps, L. P., and Osborne, E. W. (2002). *Handbook on agricultural education in public schools,* 5th ed. Upper Saddle River, NJ: Pearson/Prentice Hall.

Reese, S. (2003). Career and technical student organizations: Building our future. *Techniques, 78*(2).

Roberts, R. W. (1971). *Vocational and practical arts education,* 3rd ed. New York: Harper & Row.

Santo, G. (1986). Through the decades: A family album. *Vocational Education Journal, 61*(8), 39–57.

Scott, J. L., and Sarkees-Wircenski, M. (1996). *Overview of vocational and applied technology education*. Homewood, IL: American Technical Publishers.

SkillsUSA. (2004). *Leadership Handbook*. Leesburg, VA: SkillsUSA Inc.

Stasz, C., and Bodilly, S. (2004). *Efforts to improve the quality of vocational education in secondary schools: Impact of federal and state policies*. Santa Monica, CA: RAND.

Taylor, J. S. (2006, Spring). Student perceptions of selected Technology Student Association Activities. *Journal of Technology Education, 17*(2).

Threeton, M. (2006, Fall). The importance of career and technical student organizations (CTSOs) in career development: A literature review. *Workforce Education Forum, 33*(2).

U.S. Department of Education (2004). *National assessment of vocational education: Final report to Congress*. Washington, DC: Office of the Under Secretary, Policy and Program Studies Service.

Vaughn, P. R. (1998). *Handbook for advisors of vocational student organizations,* 4th ed. Athens, GA: American Association for Vocational Instructional Materials.

Zirkle, C., and Connors, J. J. (2003, Fall). The contribution of career and technical student organizations (CTSOs) to the Development and Assessment of workplace Skills and Knowledge: A Literature Review. *Workforce Education Forum, 30*(2).

chapter 10

The Effectiveness of School-to-Work

When the School-to-Work Opportunities Act (STWOA) was passed in 1994, it was visualized as a comprehensive effort to help students better prepare for careers and college by providing work-based learning experiences. The legislation evolved out of studies revealing that, compared with our competitors, the United States lacked a coherent system to connect education with employment in the part of the labor market where four-year college degrees are not required. The contrasting experience of Germany is most often cited to highlight the absence of a U.S. system that fosters the transition from school to work.

According to most sources, School-to-Work has been a real success story. President Bill Clinton stated that "School-to-Work helps students see the relevance of their studies for their futures, motivating them to attend classes and study hard, and has created thousands of new partnerships between businesses and schools" (Cutshall, 2001, p. 18). As of 2001, there were about 1,000 local School-to-Work (STW) partnerships involving 26.3 million students in 50,000 schools. Approximately 3,450 postsecondary institutions were working with these partnerships (Cutshall, 2001).

Schools using work-related curricula increased from 66 percent in 1996 to 81 percent in 1999. Over the same four-year period, schools integrating vocational and academic curricula increased from 59 percent to 69 percent, and those connecting work-based learning to integrated curricula increased from 51 percent to 64 percent. More than 2.5 million secondary school students received classes with a career-related curriculum in 1998, up from 1 million in 1997. Between 1997 and 1999, there were increases of *job shadowing* from 55 percent to 71 percent, school-based enterprises from 40 percent to 51 percent, and student internships from 34 percent to 45 percent. The percentage of employers nationally who became involved in partnerships grew from 25 percent in 1996 to 37 percent in 1998 (Cutshall, 2001).

This chapter describes the effectiveness of School-to-Work based its impact on youth, teachers, and employers of School-to-Work components.

Historical Background of School-to-Work

In the 1980s, several trends led to an extensive national discussion of education reform and workforce development. The 1983 report, *A Nation at Risk* (National Commission on Excellence in Education, 1983), claimed that profound weaknesses in the education system were undermining U.S. productivity and competitiveness. Researchers were documenting and analyzing the changing nature of work and changing skill requirements (Bailey, 1989; 1991). Increasingly, young people without some postsecondary education could not expect to earn enough money to support a family. *America's Choice: High Skills or Low Wages* (Commission on the Skills of the American Workforce, 1990) pointed out that many young adults were spending their early years in the workforce moving form one low-wage, dead-end job to another.

At the same time, developments in research on learning and pedagogy emphasized the effectiveness of "learning in context" (Collins, Brown, and Newman, 1989; Lave and Wenger, 1991; Resnick, 1987). Cognitive psychologists argued that students learn most effectively if they are taught skills in the context in which they will use those skills. Advocates of constructivism argued for a pedagogic approach in which students are more active learners, guided by their teacher in such a way that they "construct" their own knowledge. These approaches were believed to be promising in helping to ameliorate the problem of students' disengagement from school (Hughes, Bailey, and Mechur, 2001).

The education reform and workforce development agenda that emerged contained several principles that were eventually included in a series of bills passed in the early 1990s (see Bailey and Morest, 1998, for a more detailed discussion of these principles and their origins). The School-to-Work Opportunities Act (STWOA) of 1994 was the most comprehensive attempt to implement the principles, including the following goals: improved academic skills; strengthened SCANS skills; a greater emphasis on standards; innovative pedagogy, including the integration of academic and vocational instruction and work-based learning; participation of many institutions, including employers, in education;

This School-to-Work student is learning valuable skills that will help her to reach her goal of opening her own business after she graduates high school.

making pathways into particular occupations more transparent; and facilitation of the transition of the "forgotten half" to postsecondary education.

The STWOA was not designed to establish a new secondary school program, but instead distributed seed money to support states in planning and establishing statewide School-to-Work transition systems. To many, it is this goal of system building that differentiates the STWOA from other education or workforce development initiatives. States were to use the short-term federal funding to amend or incorporate existing career preparation activities and create links between school reform and workforce development efforts. Once the federal appropriation was distributed, the new systems were to be supported by other long-standing education and workforce development funding streams.

By 1997, more than 90 percent of secondary students in federal grantee states attended schools in districts with partnerships, the local collaborations responsible for stimulating and implementing School-to-Work reforms (Hershey, Silverberg, and Haimson, 1999). One of the hallmarks of the legislation was the flexibility allowed to the states in determining their own forms of School-to-Work; thus, the structure and specific activities of these partnerships vary from state to state. Some states highlighted efforts already underway, such as partnership academies in California, while others began new efforts, such as teacher externships in New Hampshire. Wisconsin chose to invest the funding in youth apprenticeship programs, which the state had previously initiated (Hughes, Bailey, and Mechur, 2001).

"School-to-Work" is an umbrella term encompassing a variety of initiatives, some intensive and others much less so. While it seems clear that School-to-Work themes have spread across the country and impacted a broad cross-section of students, researchers have also found that brief work-site visits and job shadowing are the most prevalent activities engaged in by students. A survey of high school seniors in eight of the first states that received STWOA grants found that only three percent had participated in all three components called for by proponents: career related academics, comprehensive career development activities, and paid or unpaid work experience linked to school (Hershey, Silverberg, and Haimson, 1999).

The rapid phase-in of the less intensive activities is likely due to their being easiest to implement and least controversial. School-to-Work has faced criticism and a number of challenges (American Youth Policy Forum, 2000; Urquiola et al., 1997), despite vocal support by many policy makers, professional associations, and nonprofit organizations. Some of the opposition originally centered on the chosen name, "School-to-Work," which was taken to imply that the initiative would focus on preparing high school students to go directly to work, threatening the college-preparatory curriculum. As a result, in many localities, education officials changed the term to "school-to-careers," or devised a new name altogether (Hughes, Bailey, and Mechur, 2001). The final round of federal funding was administered on October 1, 2001.

Related Studies on School-to-Work

This section summarizes the results of various studies that document the impact of the School-to-Work legislation on career and technical education students.

Academic Achievement

School-to-Work students maintain good grades and take difficult courses.

Students in School-to-Work initiatives earn GPAs that are at least comparable to those of other students, if not higher.

- Student grades rose as they spent more time in career academies. This study compared student grades before and after enrollment in the academics (Foothill Associates, 1997).

- In state and national surveys, students who participated in School-to-Work had similar grades to nonparticipants, even though the School-to-Work students tended to take more difficult classes (Westchester Institute for Human Services Research. Inc., 1998; Bishop, Mane, and Ruiz-Quintilla, 2000).

- Participation in well-implemented (measured by program characteristics) career academies raised students' GPAs. This conclusion was based on a comparison to non-academy students in the same district (Maxwell and Rubin, 2000).

- Students who participated in an intensive work-based mentoring program showed increased grade point averages when compared to students who were eligible for but not enrolled in the program (Linnehan, 1998).

- Students in a California academy achieved similar GPAs to students in magnet programs in the same schools, even though the magnet programs were more selective than the academy (Hanser and Stasz, 1999).

Students with intensive participation in School-to-Work take more rigorous courses, including science and math courses, than their non-participating counterparts.

Students in School-to-Work take challenging classes.

- In New York State, students with intensive participation in School-to-Work (measured by the number and types of School-to-Work activities in which they participate) took more rigorous courses, including advanced math and science courses, than those who did not participate (Westchester Institute for Human Services Research, 1997).

- In Santa Ana Unified School District, enrollment in AP U.S. History, English, Physics, and Chemistry rose significantly after career pathways were instituted in the high school (Santa Ana Unified School District, 1999).

- A national survey found that students who participated in one or more School-to-Work activities took more lab courses than nonparticipating students (Bishop, Mane, and Ruiz-Quintilla, 2000).

- Analysis of NLSY97 data revealed that for Black and Hispanic youth, participation in at least one of a variety of School-to-Work programs was linked to increased future course-taking in science and math (Rivera-Batiz, 2000).

Students in School-to-Work stay in school and complete their diploma.

Almost every study shows that students in School-to-Work have better attendance than comparable students. None indicate that they come to school less often.

- Career academy students originally considered to be "high risk" were less likely to be chronically absent from school than randomly assigned control group students (Kemple and Snipes, 2000).

- In a New York State survey, students who actively participated in School-to-Work had better attendance and missed fewer classes than students who did not (Westchester Institute for Human Services Research, Inc. 1997).

- Wisconsin apprentices maintained good school attendance throughout their time in the program. Comparison students' attendance rates fell over the same time period (Orr, 1996).

- Students in a California academy achieved similar attendance rates to more rigorously screened magnet students in the same schools (Hanser and Stasz, 1999).

School-to-Work students are less likely to drop out of school. This is especially true for those who are considered at a high risk of not graduating.

- Participation in career academy reduced the dropout rate for high-risk students by 34 percent, compared to non-academy students in a randomly selected control group (Kemple and Snipes, 2000).

- Students in California Partnership Academies had lower dropout rates than the statewide average, even though the academies enrolled a higher percentage of "at-risk" students than the state average (Foothill Associates, 1997).

- Analysis of NLSY97 data shows that participation in at least one of a variety of School-to-Work programs significantly reduces the likelihood of dropping out of school (Stone and Alliaga, 2005; Rivera-Batiz, 2000).
- A study of urban career academies with a Junior Reserve Officers Training Corps (JROTC) component found that a significantly higher proportion of students who were in the program in the 9th grade graduated than would have been expected for those same students in the standard JROTC program or in no program (Elliott, Hanser, and Gilroy, 2000).

School-to-Work students are more likely than comparable students to complete the requirements for graduation and graduate on time.

- High-risk career academy students were more likely to complete the credits needed to graduate on time than non-academy comparison (randomly assigned) students (Kemple and Snipes, 2000).
- Students in a California academy were just as likely to graduate from high school and go to college as were students in the "academic" track (Maxwell and Rubin, 1997).

It is unclear how School-to-Work participation affects students' test scores.

- The MDRC random-assignment study found that academy participation had no effect, either positive or negative, on standardized test scores (Kemple and Snipes, 2000).
- ACT scores for Wisconsin apprentices were comparable to the scores for non-apprentices (Center on Education and Work, 1999).

School-to-Work students are prepared for college.

School-to-Work students are just as likely to attend college as other students. Some studies suggest that they are even more likely to do so.

- In a New York State survey, the college enrollment rate for intensive School-to-Work participants was statistically equivalent to that of the comparison group (Westchester Institute for Human Services Research, Inc., 1998).
- Graduates of a California career academy were 40 percent more likely to enroll in a four-year college than non-academy students in the same school district (Maxwell and Rubin, 2000).
- In both North Carolina and Colorado, statewide surveys of students and graduates found that School-to-Work participants were 10 percent more likely to enroll in college than other students (Metis Associates, Inc., 1999a).

School-to-Work students have the opportunity to earn college credit in high school.

- Wisconsin youth apprentices were able to earn between 3 and 12 credits of advanced standing at state technical colleges. Students reported that this was a major reason they wanted to enter an apprenticeship (Phelps, Scribner, Wakelyn, and Weis, 1996).

- Students graduating from the Wisconsin Youth Apprenticeship Program in printing earned at least one semester of college credit prior to entering postsecondary school. Many students stated that this encouraged them to plan for and pursue higher education after high school (Orr, 1996).

Graduates of School-to-Work are more likely than other students to choose a major early in their college career.

- Forty-three percent of Colorado students who had three or more School-to-Work experiences during high school had chosen a major upon entering college; only 28 percent of students without this many School-to-Work experiences did so (Colorado School-to-Career Partnership, 1999).

- A year after high school graduation, more of the students who had actively participated in School-to-Work activities had chosen a college major than comparison students (Westchester Institute for Human Services Research, Inc., 1998).

Research on the postsecondary experience of School-to-Work participants suggests positive effects, and more research is currently underway.

- Career academy graduates who enrolled in a nearby state university were less likely to need remedial coursework and more likely to receive their bachelor's degrees, compared to other graduates from the same district (Maxwell, 1999).

Career Preparation

School-to-Work students are able to define their career interests and goals for the future.

- The ability of Arizona tenth graders to define a career interest is directly related to the number of School-to-Work activities in which they participated (Larson and Vandegrift, 2000b).

- Both college-bound and noncollege-bound participants in School-to-Work feel that their career exploration experiences were valuable in helping them clarify their career goals (Hershey, Silverberg, and Haimson, 1999).

- The same study found that students who changed their career goals were just as likely to view School-to-Work activities as useful as those who did not change their goals. Thus the School-to-Work activities had value outside of the career area around which the student's School-to-Work schooling was organized (Hershey, Silverberg, and Haimson, 1999).

- Of the youth apprentices surveyed from a small Wisconsin printing program, 80 percent believed that their experience offered them valuable career information, focus, and direction (Orr, 1996).

- Apprentices in a New York State School-to-Work initiative reported that their experience allowed them to identify career paths and the appropriate "steps along them" (Hamilton and Hamilton, 1997).

School-to-Work helps young people become prepared for the world of work.
Students in School-to-Work are exposed to many different career development activities.

- Career academy students were significantly more likely than randomly selected comparison students to participate in both in-school career development activities, such as receiving instruction on how to act on the job, and out-of-school development activities, such as career-related field trips (Kemple, Poglinco, and Snipes, 1999).

- Almost two-thirds of seniors in School-to-Work partnerships surveyed reported participating in four or more of the following five career development activities: taking interest inventories, having employer talks at school, discussing careers with school personnel, taking a work-readiness class, or having a job-shadowing experience (Hershey, Silverberg, and Haimson, 1999).

School-to-Work teaches students job-readiness skills.

- Eighty-six percent of academy alumni surveyed said that the experience helped them gain job-interviewing skills. Of the academy seniors surveyed, 79 percent said that their internship was better at teaching them how to prepare for a job than other jobs they had (Academy for Educational Development, 1995).

- In a Colombia, MO, survey of students in schools with School-to-Work initiatives, approximately 60 percent indicated that these activities helped them learn skills like writing a resume or conducting a job search (Institute for Workforce Education, 1998).

Students who acquire their jobs through School-to-Work are likely to learn skills that employers value.

- Students in a variety of School-to-Work activities reported that their internships allowed them to make decisions, solve problems, and work in groups or as part of a team (Academy for Educational Development, 1995; Stasz, 1999).

- Seventy-two percent of Wisconsin youth apprentices believe that the skills they learned through their apprenticeship prepared them well for employment (Center on Education and Work, 1999).

Students involved in School-to-Work report that their internships prepare them well for employment.

- The majority of Boston employers who supervise students in work-based learning said that their students work with computers, are involved in customer-relations activities, and perform multi-step tasks (Almeida, Goldberger, and Lalbeharie, 1999).

During their work-based learning experiences, School-to-Work students learn how to behave in a professional environment and to work well with other people.

- Students in a variety of work-sites learned to understand the social expectations of work, and to behave in ways that were appropriate for their jobs (Stasz and Kaganoff, 1997).
- Apprentices in a New York State School-to-Work initiative learned the importance of teamwork and how individual jobs fit into the larger company. In interviews, they also frequently mentioned improved ability to relate to and communicate with coworkers (Hamilton and Hamilton, 1997).
- Wisconsin youth apprentices reported that their work helped them learn to act professionally, relate to adults, and understand what is expected of them once they began their postsecondary experiences. Parents concurred, noting that their children's self-confidence and self-esteem increased through their apprenticeship (Phelps, Scribner, Wakelyn, and Weis, 1996).

Employers believe that School-to-Work students perform well on the job.

- Ninety-nine percent of employers involved in New York State's School-to-Work initiative said that they were satisfied with the performance of the students, and 97 percent planned to continue their involvement with the program (Westchester Institute for Human Services Research, Inc., 1998).

- The majority of Wisconsin Youth Apprenticeship employers rated their apprentices as better than other entry-level employees in their computer skills, understanding of the company, technical skills, and ability to act responsibly and professionally (Orr, 1996).

The jobs that students obtain through School-to-Work tend to be different from and of higher quality than the jobs they would normally get.

- Academy students were significantly more likely than randomly assigned comparison students to say that their jobs gave them opportunities to learn new things (Kemple, Poglinco, and Snipes, 1999).

- Students in school-sponsored work-based learning have access to more diverse workplaces than youth who do not obtain their jobs through school (Hershey, Silverberg, and Haimson, 1999).

- School-to-Work internships were more likely to be in the service sector, which includes health, education, and business services, rather than in retail trade, where American youth typically work (Bailey, Hughes, and Barr, 2000).

- Wisconsin youth apprentices work in areas such as finance, health, manufacturing, machining, printing, and biotechnology (Phelps, Scribner, Wakelyn, and Weis, 1996).

- Students whose paid work is through School-to-Work spend more time in training, and were much more likely to receive quality feedback about their performance, than students who found paid positions on their own (Hershey, Silverberg, and Haimson, 1999).

Graduates of School-to-Work programs have better labor market outcomes than do other high school graduates.

Employers believe that young people who participated in School-to-Work are better prepared for work than are other high school graduates.

- North Carolina employers who hired former School-to-Work participants reported that the former students required less training, had a greater ability to work in teams, and had better work ethics than other new hires (Metis Associates, 1999b).

- Ninety percent of 1999 Wisconsin Youth Apprenticeship graduates received offers of part- or full-time employment from their Youth Apprenticeship employers following completion of the program (Scholl and Smyth, 2000).

School-to-Work participation is related to greater success in gaining employment after high school.

- Eighty-five percent of Wisconsin apprentices believed that their School-to-Work experiences had helped them get their current job (Center on Education and Work, 1999).

The jobs held by School-to-Work graduates are more likely to be within meaningful career paths and to offer high wages than the jobs of other high school graduates.

- New York State graduates who had participated intensively in School-to-Work, and who were attending college and working, were more likely than comparison students to report that their jobs allowed them to use their skills and abilities, helped them learn new skills, and fit in with their long-term career plans (Westchester Institute for Human Services Research, Inc., 1998).

- In the same study, former School-to-Work participants who opted to work full time rather than attend postsecondary school were more likely than other graduates to indicate that their jobs fit in with their long-term career plans and indicated a higher level of satisfaction with their jobs (Westchester Institute for Human Services Research, Inc., 1998).

- In Wisconsin, 70 percent of graduates from the Youth Apprenticeship program believed that they had obtained high-wage employment as a result of their apprenticeship participation (Center on Education and Work, 1999).

- One year after graduation, those who had participated in a Maryland Career and Technology Education program reported significantly higher hourly wages, more hours worked in a week, and greater relevancy of their high school studies to both their current jobs and current postsecondary school or training than did nonparticipants (Griffith, Wade, and Loeb, 1998).

School-to-Work participants are likely to view work as a way to learn new things and prepare for the future.

- In qualitative studies, students in School-to-Work commented that they discovered the value of "learning how to learn" through their experiences (Hamilton and Hamilton, 1997; Stasz, 1999).

Youth Development

School-to-Work helps students plan for the future and act in ways that will help them achieve their goals.

- In a survey given to Columbia, MO, junior high and high school students to evaluate the effectiveness of the career paths School-to-Work initiative, most of the students reported using the career paths for exploration and to help plan for the future. Most students anticipated linking their high school courses to one or more paths (Institute for Workforce Education, 1998).

- School-to-Work students in New York State indicated a higher degree of long-term career planning than did comparison students, and they stated that their experiences helped them make their career decisions (Westchester Institute for Human Services Research, Inc., 1997).

- Wisconsin youth apprentices stated that they gained an understanding of the education and skills needed for careers in their chosen fields. They used this information to make decisions about postsecondary education and employment (Phelps, Scribner, Wakelyn, and Weis, 1996).

School-to-Work students feel that their teachers and peers make up a supportive "second family."

- Students frequently commented on the "family-like atmosphere" of career academies and the fact that their teachers were supportive and approachable. Academy students were also more likely than a comparison group to believe that their peers were supportive of them (Kemple, 1997).
- In focus group interviews, academy students indicated that the sense of community and support that they received from the program gave them an incentive to attend school and apply themselves in school (Academy for Educational Development, 1995).

Students are more confident about themselves when they learn new skills in their School-to-Work activities.

- In a study of New York State youth apprentices, evidence from multiple sources indicated that the apprentices' pride and self-esteem rose as their knowledge and skill level increased (Hamilton and Hamilton, 1997).
- In observations of students in a variety of work-based experiences, researchers found that the students felt confident in their skills and were often encouraged to try new things (Stasz and Kaganoff, 1997).

Students report that School-to-Work activities make them more interested in school.

- When compared to students who did not intensely participate in School-to-Work, New York State School-to-Work students had a higher level of interest in school (Westchester Institute for Human Services Research, Inc., 1998).
- In Peoria, Illinois, half of all academy students reported that they had become more interested in school since entering the program (Peoria Public Schools, 1995).

Students state that School-to-Work helps them understand why school is important.

- In Wisconsin, 80 percent of youth apprentices indicated that their apprenticeship had influenced their educational plans, and many indicated that they planned to attend a four-year, rather than a two-year, college as a result of their experiences (Orr, 1996).
- Two-thirds of academy students said that the academy helped them understand why staying in school is important (Peoria Public Schools, 1995).
- In Columbia, Missouri, of the elementary students surveyed who participated in School-to-Work activities, nearly all indicated an under-

standing of the fact that school can help them prepare for the work they will do in the future (Institute for Workforce Education, 1998).

School-to-Work brings adults and youth together.

The adults involved in School-to-Work can positively influence students' educational achievement.

- Students who spent more time with adult mentors at the workplace had higher grade point averages and better attendance than students who spent less time with mentors (Linnehan, 1998).

- In interviews with employers involved in a New York State youth apprenticeship program, employers frequently described themselves as role models and "advice givers" who emphasize the importance of education to the students (Hamilton and Hamilton, 1997).

School-to-Work employers can help students make decisions about college and careers.

- Apprenticeship supervisors in New York State noted in interviews that they make an effort to help guide students through the process of choosing a career path (Hamilton and Hamilton, 1997).

- The majority of employers involved in Boston School-to-Work initiatives indicated that they discussed with students their futures, postsecondary plans, current classroom work, and personal interests (Almeida, Goldberger, and Lalbeharie, 1999).

School-to-Work can provide students with a network of supportive adults.

- As School-to-Work expanded in Arizona, the numbers of middle and high school students who indicated that they found the adults in their life helpful increased substantially (Larson and Vandegrift, 2000a).

- In a survey, Wisconsin apprentices noted that their relationships with adults at work gave them a network that supported their learning and career development (Orr, 1996).

- In a study of ten career academies, the quantitative and qualitative data showed that academy teachers were more likely to emphasize personal support for their students than were non-academy teachers (Kemple, 1997).

- Wisconsin youth apprentices indicated that they feel they have business contacts who will help them get jobs in the future (Phelps, Scribner, Wakelyn, and Weis, 1996).

Teachers' Perceptions of School-to-Work

Teachers believe that School-to-Work is good for students.

- Over 60 percent of Kentucky teachers surveyed said that they were involved in School-to-Work because they believed that it was effective (Blasczyk and Bialek, 1999).

- In Arizona, educators' support for the state's School-to-Work initiative grew significantly in the three years following its implementation, indicating that the more familiar educators are with School-to-Work, the more they believe in its value (Vandegrift and Wright, 1999).
- The same study found that 69 percent of the state's teachers and 70 percent of administrators believe that School-to-Work is so valuable that support for it should be incorporated into the state budget once federal funding ends (Vandegrift and Wright, 1999).
- The majority of teachers in Charleston County believe that School-to-Work is appropriate for students at all grade levels, regardless of whether they plan to attend college (Charleston County School District, 1999).

Teachers can benefit from participating in work-based professional development.

- Some teachers who spent time in businesses through School-to-Work externships reported that their teaching improved and that they became more proficient in offering their students work-based learning and hands-on activities (McPherson, Rainey, Roach, Rogers, and Wamba, 2000).
- In Charleston County, teachers who participated in work-based experiences were more likely to use cooperative learning strategies and integrated curricula than other teachers in the district (Charleston County School District, 1999).

Teachers report that participating in School-to-Work keeps them motivated to teach.

- In Peoria, Illinois, 73 percent of academy teachers indicated that teaching in the academy "rekindled their enthusiasm for teaching" (Peoria Public Schools, 1995).
- In a study of ten career academies, academy teachers were more likely than their non-academy peers to feel that they were part of a teacher community and were more satisfied with their work (Kemple, 1997).

Employers' Perceptions of School-to-Work

Surveys of employers find that vast majorities support the School-to-Work vision and initiative.

- Over 90 percent of employers surveyed in Maryland said that improving or expanding technical training in high schools is important in helping to improve the job skills of the workforce (Maryland Business Research Partnership, 1997).
- In New York State, 88 percent of participating employers surveyed said that School-to-Work was a good direction for education to take (Westchester Institute for Human Service Research, Inc., 1998).
- Participating New York State employers also indicated that School-to-Work supports academics (Westchester Institute for Human Service Research, Inc., 1998).

- Over 90 percent of employers participating in the Wisconsin Youth Apprenticeship program would recommend the program to other employers (Phelps and Jin, 1997).
- Almost all of the New York State participating employers surveyed said they would definitely or probably continue their participation (Westchester Institute for Human Service Research, Inc., 1998).

Employers' participation in School-to-Work partnerships and in work-based learning activities is widespread.

- In 1997, 26 percent of all establishments employing 20 or more people were participating in a School-to-Work partnership (Cappelli, Shapiro, and Shumanis, 1998).
- From 1996 to 1998, business membership in individual partnerships expanded from an average of 16 to 30 firms (Hulsey, Van Noy, and Silverberg, 1999).
- Even those employers not participating in formal partnerships have increased their participation in work-based learning (Shapiro, 1999).
- According to a 1997 national survey of employers, 39 percent were participating in some form of work-based learning (Cappelli, Shapiro, and Shumanis, 1998).
- In surveys of School-to-Work partnerships in the 1995–1996 and 1996–1997 school years, the percent of schools receiving employer support across a wide range of activities increased (Hershey, Silverberg, and Haimson, 1999).

Employers participating in School-to-Work serve as resources to students and schools.

- Work-based learning placements for students tend to be different from the typical after-school jobs youth have (Bailey, Hughes, and Barr, 2000; National Center for Postsecondary Improvement and the Consortium for Policy Research on Education, 1997).
- Participating employers in Boston tended to provide work-based learning placements that require and teach skills (Almeida, Goldberger, and Lalbeharie, 1999).
- Students who obtained paid or unpaid work-based learning positions through schools were more likely than students who obtained their positions outside of school to see substantive connections between their studies and work experience (Hershey, Silverberg, and Haimson, 1999).
- Employers reported that they discussed schoolwork, personal interests, and postsecondary and other future plans with their student interns (Almeida, Goldberger, and Lalbeharie, 1999).
- Students with paid work-based learning positions were significantly more likely to spend at least half of their time at the worksite in training, and more likely to discuss possible careers with their employers,

than students with paid positions not related to school (Hershey, Silverberg, and Haimson, 1999).

- Some employers provide work-based learning placements for teachers as well as other school staff development assistance (Hershey, Silverberg, and Haimson, 1999).

- Employers who participate tend to have more favorable perceptions of their local high schools and tend to use school information in their hiring decisions (Shapiro and Goertz, 1998).

Employers speak well of their student interns.

- In a survey of participating New York State employers, 99 percent of those providing work-based learning said that they were satisfied or very satisfied with the performance of the students (Westchester Institute for Human Service Research, Inc., 1998).

- More than 80 percent of intern supervisors surveyed in Boston rated their students as similar or superior to their typical hires on skills ranging from productivity to job-related math and communication skills (Almeida, Goldberger, and Lalbeharie, 1999).

- Participating employers surveyed tended to rate their interns' skills as being comparable to or better than those of their regular entry-level workers, particularly soft skills such as attitude and attendance (Bailey, Hughes, and Barr, 2000).

Employers see real benefits to their firms from participation.

- The benefits to employers, such as reduced recruitment and training costs, the value of student interns' work, and higher productivity and morale for existing workers, can be higher than the costs (National Employer Leadership Council, 1999; Bassi and Ludwig, 2000).

- Over 80 percent of participating Wisconsin employers said that the Youth Apprenticeship program benefited their company "somewhat" or "a lot" (Phelps and Jin, 1997).

- Data from the National Employer Survey indicate that employer involvement with local high schools is associated with better experiences in hiring local graduates as well as having lower turnover of their youth employees (Shapiro and Iannozzi, 1998).

- In the Boston employer survey, over 80 percent of intern supervisors said that students' contribution to productivity was a major or moderate benefit (Almeida, Goldberger, and Lalbeharie, 1999).

- Employers who hired their former interns said that, compared to other employees, the former interns performed more effectively: they required less training, had better work ethics, better respect for supervisors, and greater ability to work in teams (Metis Associates, 1999b).

- A study of career academy graduates found a direct positive impact of the academy program on later job performance, compared with non-academy graduates (Linnehan, 1996).

Research indicates that participation in School-to-Work can improve students' attendance, grades, and graduation rates. School-to-Work has (1) improved attendance, academic achievement, graduation rates, and academic rigor in classrooms; (2) prepared students for college entrance and decreased attrition rates; and (3) helped prepare young people for employment and helped them obtain higher-quality jobs with better wages than they might normally get (Brown, 2002). The early fears that School-to-Work would turn students' focus away from academic achievement were unfounded. Instead, School-to-Work students, regardless of their risk of school failure, have comparable or better attendance and graduation rates than students in comparison groups. School-to-Work advocates argue that participants can become more motivated academically because their experiences help them see the practical relevance of their class work.

However, research regarding School-to-Work students' achievement on standardized tests is inconclusive. The few existing studies indicated that there is little, if any, effect on test scores; for example, some School-to-Work students' scores improve in one area but remain stagnant in another. Some educators argue that the standardized tests typically used to evaluate learning do not measure many of the nonacademic and practical skills that students learn in School-to-Work initiatives, but assessments of these nonacademic skills are also lacking. Regardless, in comparison to similar students, School-to-Work students maintain good grades, which allows them to complete the coursework necessary for college admissions. Finally, studies indicate that School-to-Work students attend college in greater numbers than their peers, and that they are better able to choose a major (Hughes, Bailey, and Mechur, 2001). School-to-Work students displayed more positive attitudes about school experiences and the future, better academic performance, and higher postsecondary enrollment rates (MPR Associates, 2002).

Implications of School-to-Work Research

The evidence suggests that policy makers and practitioners should build on the best of School-to-Work, dedicate more energy to address the shortcomings, and integrate School-to-Work into the broader high school reform and youth development movements (Griffith, 2001; Stone, 2002; Hairston, 2002; Yan, Goubeaud, and Fry, 2005). A major factor in sustainability of STW will be the commitment of educators to the STW philosophy. Career and technical educators must play a major role in the implementation of School-to-Work programs. Getting teachers out of the classroom and into the workplace—for example, through teacher externships—has been successful in many states.

Summary

- According to most sources, School-to-Work has been a real success story.
- Research shows that School-to-Work students take more challenging classes, earn higher grades, and are more likely to graduate from high school and enroll in college.
- Participating employers and teachers have embraced School-to-Work as a good strategy for building a competitive workforce.
- School-to-Work contributes significantly to students' career preparations through exploration activities and work-based learning experiences.
- School-to-Work fosters broader youth development goals: increased access to caring adults, enhanced motivation, and better planning for the future.
- Overall, research studies support the value of School-to-Work; however, this should be regarded as promising, not conclusive.

Discussion Questions and Activities

Thinking Critically

1. Discuss ways that federal policies can help students prepare for careers in today's technological workplace.
2. Are School-to-Work programs sustainable? Discuss and give examples to support your opinions.
3. Extrapolate the factors that make a School-to-Work program sustainable.
4. Critically examine selected School-to-Work programs in your state.
   a. What are some of the best practices in STW?
   b. What are some of the weaknesses in STW?
   c. List some steps you would recommend to strengthen STW programs.
5. Devise an evaluation instrument for a School-to-Work program in your community.
6. What are the essential attributes of quality School-to-Work curriculum materials?

References and Additional Reading

Academy for Educational Development (1995). *Academy of travel and tourism: 1993–94 evaluation report*. New York: Author.

Almeida, C., Goldberger, S., and Lalbeharie, V. (1999). *Boston supervisor survey: Findings and recommendations*. Boston: Jobs for the Future.

American Youth Policy Forum and The Center for Workforce Development (2000). *Looking forward: School-to-work principles and strategies for sustainability*. Washington, DC: American Youth Policy Forum and Center for Workforce Development.

Bailey, T. R. (1989). *Changes in the nature and structure of work: Implications for skill requirements and skill formation*. New York: National Center on Education and Employment. Teachers College, Columbia University.

———. (1991). Jobs of the future and the education they will require: Evidence from occupational forecasts. *Educational Researcher, 20*(2), 11–20.

Bailey, T. R., Hughes, K. L., and Barr, T. (2000). Achieving scale and quality in school-to-work internships: Findings from two employer surveys. *Educational Evaluation and Policy Analysis, 22*, 41–64.

Bailey, T. R., and Morest, V. S. (1998). Preparing youth for the world of work. In S. Halperin (Ed.), *The forgotten half revisited: American youth and young families, 1988–2008* (pp. 115–136). Washington, DC: American Youth Policy Forum.

Bassi, L., and Ludwig, J. (2000). School-to-work programs in the United States: A multi-firm case study of training, benefits, and costs. *Industrial and Labor Relations Review, 53*, 219–239.

Bishop, J., Mane, F., and Ruiz-Quintilla, A. (2000). *Who participates in school-to-work programs? Initial tabulations*. Ithaca, NY: Bishop Associates.

Blasczyk, J., and Bialek, S. (1999). *Improving & sustaining Kentucky's system of school-to-work: Summary report and data supplement*. Madison, WI: Center on Education and Work.

Brown, B. L. (2002). *School-to-work after the School-to-work Opportunities Act*. Myths and Realities. (ERIC Document Reproduction Service No. ED 472365).

Cappelli, P., Shapiro, D., and Shumanis, N. (1998). *Employer participation in school-to-work programs*. Philadelphia: University of Pennsylvania, National Center on the Educational Quality of the Workforce.

Center on Education and Work (1999). *Wisconsin Youth apprenticeship: Another road to success . . . a synthesis of findings and outcomes form evaluation and research studies*. Madison, WI: Author.

Charleston County School District (1999). *Annual curriculum survey of teachers and counselors*. Charleston, SC: Author.

Collins, A., Brown, J. S., and Newman, S. (1989). Cognitive apprenticeship: Teaching students the craft of reading, writing, and mathematics. In L. B. Resnick (Ed.), *Knowing, learning and instruction: Essays in honor of Robert Glaser* (pp. 453–494). Hillsdale, NJ: Erlbaum.

Colorado School-to-Career Partnership (1999). *What works? Colorado high school senior survey, initial results*. Denver, CO: Author.

Commission on the Skills of the American Workforce (1990). *America's choice: High skills or low wages*. Rochester, NY: National Center on Education and the Economy.

Cutshall, S. (2001). School-to-work: Has it worked? *Techniques, 76*(1), 18–21.

Elliott, M. N., Hanser, L. M., and Gilroy, C. L. (2000). *Evidence of positive student outcomes in JROTC career academies*. Santa Monica, CA: RAND National Defense Research Institute.

Foothill Associates (1997, Summer). *California partnership academies: 1995–96 evaluation report*. Nevada City, CA: Author.

Griffith, J. (2001). An approach to evaluating school-to-work initiatives: Postsecondary activities of high school graduates of work-based learning. *Journal of Vocational Education and Training: The Vocational Aspect of Education, 53*(1), 37–60.

Griffith, J., Wade, J., and Loeb, C. (1998). *Postsecondary school activities of Montgomery County Public Schools graduates: High school students' profiles associated with postsecondary school activities*. Rockville, MD: Montgomery County Public Schools.

Hairston, J. E. (2002). Perceived knowledge level, utilization, and implementation of school-to-work by pre-service teacher educators in Ohio. *Journal of Vocational Education Research, 27*(2), 243–255.

Hamilton, M. A., and Hamilton, S. F. (1997). *Learning well at work: Choices for quality*. Washington, DC: National School-to-Work Office.

Hanser, L., and Stasz, C. (1999). *The effects of enrollment in the transportation career academy program on student outcomes*. Paper prepared for the meeting of the American Educational Research Association. Santa Monica, CA: RAND.

Harber, G. (2005). Career and technical education enrollment disparities and disability status. *Workforce Education Forum, 32*(1), 40–57.

Hershey, A. M., Silverberg, M. K., and Haimson, J. (1999, February). *Expanding options for students: Report to Congress on the national evaluation of school-to-work implementation*. Princeton, NJ: Mathematica Policy Research.

Hollenbeck, K. (1996). *In their own words: Student perspective on school-to-work opportunities*. New York: Academy for Educational Development.

Hollingsworth, Christine (2005). *CTSOs: Do they matter and how?* Retrieved April 17, 2007, from http://lists.more.net/archives/mofacts/2005-November/02239.html.

Hughes, K. L. (1998, June). *Employer recruitment is not the problem: A study of school-to-work transition programs*. (Working Paper No. 5). New York: Institute on Education and the Economy, Teachers College, Columbia University.

Hughes, K. L., Bailey, T. R., and Mechur, J. M. (2001). *School-to-work: Making a difference in education*. New York: Teachers College, Columbia University.

Hulsey, L., Van Noy, M., and Silverberg, M. K. (1999). *The 1998 national survey of local school-to-work partnership: Data summary*. Princeton, NJ: Mathematica Policy Research.

Institute for Workforce Education (1998). *The school-to-work system in Columbia, Missouri: A quantitative evaluation*. Columbia, MO: Author.

Kemple, J. J. (1997). *Communities of support for students and teachers: Emerging findings from a 10-site evaluation*. New York: Manpower Demonstration Research Corporation.

Kemple, J. J., Poglinco, S., and Snipes, J. C. (1999). *Career academies: Building career awareness and work-based learning activities through employer partnerships*. New York: Manpower Demonstration Research Corporation.

Kemple, J. J., and Snipes, J. C. (2000). *Career academies: Impacts on students' engagement and performance in high school*. New York: Manpower Demonstration Research Corporation.

Larson, E. H., and Vandegrift, J. A. (2000a). *Seventh grade students' perceptions of career awareness and exploration activities in Arizona schools: Three-year trends and 1999 results* (Arizona School-to-Work Briefing Paper #18). Tempe, AZ: Morrison Institute for Public Policy.

———. (2000b). *Tenth grade students' perceptions of career preparation and work experience in Arizona schools: Three-year trends and 1999 results* (Arizona School-to-Work Briefing paper #19). Tempe, AZ: Morrison Institute for Public Policy.

Lave, J., and Wenger, E. (1991). *Situated learning: Legitimate peripheral participation*. Cambridge, England: Cambridge University Press.

Linnehan, F. (1996). Measuring the effectiveness of a career academy program from an employer's perspective. *Educational Evaluation and Policy Analysis, 18*, 73–89.

———. (1998). *The effect of work-based mentoring on the academic performance of African American, urban high school students*. Unpublished manuscript. Philadelphia: Drexel University.

Littrell, Joseph J. (2006). *From School to Work.* Tinley Park, IL: Goodheart-Wilcox.

MacAllum, K., Yoder, K., Kim, S., and Bozick, R. (2002). *Moving forward: College and career transitions of LAMP graduates. Findings from the Lamp longitudinal study.* (ERIC Document Reproduction Service No. ED 475156).

Maryland Business Research Partnership (1997, October). *The Maryland employers' workforce skills development and workforce preparedness survey.* Baltimore, MD: Author.

Maxwell, N. L. (1999, November). *Step to college: Moving from the high school career academy through the four-year university.* MDS-1313. Berkeley, CA: National Center for Research in Vocational Education.

Maxwell, N. L., and Rubin, V. (1997). *The relative impact of a career academy on post-secondary work and education skills in urban, public high schools.* Hayward, CA: The Human Resource Investment Research and Education Center.

———. (2000). *Career academy programs in California: Implementation and student outcomes.* Hayward, CA: Human Investment Research & Education Center.

McPherson, B., Rainey, C., Roach, T. D., Rogers, H., and Wamba, N. G. (Delta Pi Epsilon Research Team) (2000). *Perceptions and attitudes of school personnel towards educator externships.* Unpublished manuscript.

Metis Associates, Inc. (1999a). *Evaluation of the North Carolina JobReady initiative: 1998 graduate follow-up survey.* New York: Author.

———. (1999b). *Evaluation of the North Carolina JobReady Initiative: Survey of employers.* New York: Author.

Miller, V. R. (2002). *The role of career and technical education in high school* (ERIC Document Reproduction Service No. ED 466941).

MPR Associates (2002). *California school-to-career: Helping students make better choices for their future.* Final evaluation report. (ERIC Document Reproduction Service No. ED 474218).

National Center for Postsecondary Improvement and the Consortium for Policy Research on Education (1997). *Bringing School-to-Work to scale: What employers report: First findings from the new administration of the national employers survey* (NES-II) (NCPI-2-04). Stanford, CA: Author.

National Commission on Excellence in Education (1983). *A nation at risk.* Washington, DC: U.S. Department of Education.

National Employer Leadership Council (1999). *Intuitions confirmed: The bottom-line return on school-to-work investment for students and employers.* Washington, DC: Author.

Neumark, David (2007). *Improving School-to-Work Transitions.* New York: Russell Sage Foundation Publications.

Neumark, D., and Allen, A. (2003). What do we know about the effects of school-to-work? A case study of Michigan. *Journal of Vocational Education Research,* 28(1), 59–84.

Orr, M. T. (1996). *Wisconsin youth apprenticeship program in printing: Evaluation. 1993– 1994.* Boston: Jobs for the future.

Peoria Public Schools (1995). *Career academies program evaluation, 1994–1995 school year.* Peoria, IL: Author.

Phelps, L. A., Scribner, J., Wakelyn, D., and Weis, C. (1996). *Youth apprenticeship in Wisconsin: A stakeholder assessment.* Madison, WI: Center on Education and Work.

Phelps, L., and Jin, M. (1997). *Wisconsin youth apprenticeship employer survey.* Madison, WI: Department of Workforce Development. Division of Connecting Education and Work.

Resnick, L. B. (1987, November). Learning in school and out. *Educational Researcher, 16*, 13–16.

Rivera-Batiz, F. L. (2000). *The impact of school-to-work programs on minority youth.* Paper presented for the national invitational conference: What do we know about school-to-work: Research and practice. Philadelphia: Temple University Center for Research in Human Development and Education, December 4–5, 2000.

Santa Ana Unified School District (1999). *First quarter report summary, third year: 1998–1999.* Santa Ana, CA: Author.

Scholl, L., and Smyth, C. (2000). *Exit survey of 1999 Wisconsin youth apprenticeship graduates.* Madison, WI: Center on Education and Work.

Shapiro, D. (1999, January). *School-to-work partnerships and employer participation: Evidence on persistence and attrition from the national employer survey.* Unpublished manuscript. Philadelphia: Institute for Research on Higher Education, University of Pennsylvania.

Shapiro, D., and Goertz, M. (1998, April). *Connecting work and school: Findings from the 1997 national employer survey.* Paper presented at the annual meetings of the American Educational Research Association, San Diego, CA.

Shapiro, D., and Iannozzi, M. (1998). Benefits to bridging work and school. *Annals of the American Academy of Political and Social Science, 559*, 157–166.

Stasz, C. (1999). *Students' perceptions of their work-based learning experiences: A comparison of four programs.* Paper prepared for the annual meeting of the American Educational Research Association, Montreal, Quebec.

Stasz, C., and Kaganoff, T. (1997). *Learning how to work: Lessons from three high school programs* (MDS-916). Berkeley, CA: National Center for Research in Vocational Education. (RP-667). Santa Monica: RAND.

Stone, J. R., III. (2002). The impact of school-to-work and career and technical education in the United States: Evidence from the national longitudinal survey of youth. *Journal of Vocational Education and Training, 54*(4), 533–582.

Stone, J. R., III, and Alliaga, O. A. (2005). Career and technical education and school-to-work at the end of the 20th century: Participation and outcomes. *Career and Technical Education Research, 30*(2), 125–144.

Stull, W., Sanders, N., and Stull, J. (2000). The effects of school size and leadership on participation in the school-to-work movement. *Journal of Vocational Education Research, 25*(4), 472–502.

Urquiola, M., Stern, D., Horn, I., Dornsife, C., Chi, B., Williams, L., Merritt, D., Hughes, K. L., and Bailey, T. R. (1997, November). *School to work, college and career: A review of policy, practice, and results 1993–1997.* Berkeley, CA: National Center for Research in Vocational Education.

Vandegrift, J. A., and Wright, J. (1999). *Arizona's school-to-work initiative: Four-year trends in public opinion* (Arizona School-to-Work Briefing Paper #17). Tempe, AZ: Morrison Institute for Public Policy.

Westchester Institute for Human Services Research, Inc. (1997). *New York State school-to-work opportunities system: Interim evaluation report, lessons learned.* White Plains, NY: Author.

———. (1998, April). New York employers show strong support for School-to-Work. *The School-to-Work Reporter, 1*(1).

———. (1998, July). New York State school-to-work initiative demonstrates promising student results. *The School to Work Reporter, 1*(2).

———. (1999). Presentation slides. New York University School-to-Work Conference.

Wonacott, M. E. (2001). *Students with disabilities in career and technical education,* No. 230. Columbus: ERIC Clearinghouse on Adult, Career, and Vocational Education, The Ohio State University.

Yan, W., Goubeaud, K., and Fry, C. (2005). Does school-to-work make a difference? Assessing students' perceptions and practices of career-related skills. *Journal of Vocational Education and Training, 57*(2), 219–235.

chapter 11

The Aging Workforce

From hula hoops to cell phones.
                —Howard Smead

The growth of our aging population presents America with some of the greatest challenges and opportunities. By the year 2030, 21.8 percent of our population will be 65 years and older. Because of advances in health care and the environmental sciences as well as changes in our lifestyles, older people will live longer, further increasing the ranks of the elderly. The number of people over age 85 will triple by the year 2030 (Yaukey et al., 2007; Harper, 1990).

According to the National Health Interview Survey (as cited in AARP, 2006, p. 26), 47 percent of the 50+ population reported their health as "excellent or very good" on a scale ranging from "poor, fair, or good" to "very good or excellent." This is a decline of one half of one percentage point over the past year. The results for the 50+ population mask fairly dramatic differences in reported levels of health status within the group, ranging from 54.3 percent of 50- to 64-year-olds to 31.9 percent of those age 75+ reporting excellent or very good health. You've heard the news stories about George H. W. Bush, parachute jumping out of airplanes at age 75; and John Glenn, at the age of 77, riding the shuttle into space. Older people not only are healthier but also are enjoying increased life spans. In 1999, there were about 57,000 people in the United States aged 100 or over; another 15 million are older than the current average life expectancy of almost 80 for women and 73 for men (NEUS, 1999).

As we look ahead to a more highly competitive world economy, we must use our resources more efficiently. We must offer older people affordable retraining opportunities and create flexible working environments to meet their special needs. We must prepare workers to care more effectively for the elderly who are no longer physically able to care for themselves. Above all, we must begin individually to prepare for the process of aging as simply another stage of our lives. This chapter describes selected population characteristics, population aging and its impact on the workforce.

Selected Population Characteristics

According to Hankin (2005), by 2025, workers age 55 and older will comprise more than 20 percent of the total workforce—more than one in five. Among the reasons why the size of this portion of the labor force is growing are:

- The sheer volume of baby boomers.
- Health improvements.
- Less physically taxing occupations.
- Financial considerations—people simply can't afford to retire.
- A growing interest in making a meaningful contribution through work (Walsh, 2001).

Population Size and Composition

Women outnumber men among older adults. In 2002, 26.6 million men and 33.0 million women in the civilian non-institutionalized population were aged 55 and over, yielding a sex ratio (men per 100 women) of 81. The sex ratio dropped steadily with age. In the 55-to-64 age group, the sex ratio was 92, and in the age group 85 years and over, the sex ratio was 46. As a corollary to the declining sex ratios with age, the age distribution of women was older than for men among the population aged 55 and over. For example, 41 percent of women and 47 percent of men were 55 to 64, whereas 7 percent of women and 4 percent of men were 85 and older (Yaukey et al., 2007; Smith, 2003).

Diversity is less evident among the older population than among the younger population. Non-Hispanic Whites accounted for 69 percent of the total population in 2002; however, the proportion varied greatly with age— 66 percent of the population under age 55, and 81 percent of those aged 55 and over. The percentage of non-Hispanic Whites increased with age: 79 percent for those 55 to 64, 80 percent for those 65 to 74, 86 percent for those 75 to 84, and 87 percent for those 85 and over. The age distribution of the older population varied considerably among racial and ethnic groups. Non-Hispanic Whites had the oldest age distribution in 2002, with 42 percent in the 55-to-64 age group and 6 percent who were aged 85 and over. American Indians and Alaska Natives, Asians and Pacific Islanders, and Hispanics had the youngest age distribution, with 51.7 percent, 51.1 percent, and 50.6 percent in the 55-to-64 age group and only 3.6 percent, 2.9 percent, and 4.1 percent in the group aged 85 and over (Yaukey et al., 2007; Smith, 2003).

Educational Attainment

Among the older population, men are more likely than women to have a bachelor's degree or more education. High school completion rates vary among the older population. In 2002, 84 percent of people aged 55 to 64 and 71 percent of those aged 65 to 84 had completed high school, compared with only 58 percent of those 85 and over. The percentage of people with less than a ninth grade education also varied. At the older ages, 27 percent of people 85 and over had less than a ninth grade education, compared with only 7 percent of people aged 55 to 64 and 15 percent of people aged 65 to 84. In most age categories, women and men aged 55 and over were equally likely to be high school graduates. The proportions were 84 percent for both men and women among those 55 to 64; 71 percent and 72 percent, respectively, for those 65 to 84; and 61 percent and 57 percent, respectively, for those aged 85 and over. Among the older population, however, men were more likely than women to have a bachelor's degree or more education. The populations were 31 percent and 22 percent, respectively, among those 55 to 64; 22 percent and 13 percent, respectively, for those 65 to 84; and 17 percent and 12 percent, respectively, for people 85 and over (Smith, 2003).

Labor-Force Participation

Older men are more likely than older women to be in the civilian labor force. Men aged 55 and over were more likely than women to be in the civilian labor force, and that proportion declined with age for both sexes. In March of 2002, 77 percent of men aged 55 to 59 were in the civilian labor force, compared with 63 percent of women. Among people aged 60 to 64, these proportions were 57 percent for men and 44 percent for women, whereas for people aged 65 and over they were 18 percent and 10 percent, respectively. Among the people aged 55 and over in the civilian labor force, 3.8 percent were unemployed (Smith, 2003).

Population Aging and Perceptions of an Older Workforce

Our nation's elderly population is growing at a rapid pace due to increased life expectancy, lower fertility rates, advancement in medicine, and improvements in working conditions (Yaukey et al., 2007; Davis, 2001). Organizations have raised concerns about the physiological decline of the aging workforce for some time (Ashcraft, 1992; Fox 1951; Robinson, 1983; Welford, 1976). Although Kupritz (1999) reported that laboratory studies indicate some decline in cognitive functions (e.g., cognition, cognitive speed, decision making, memory, sensory factors, and perceptual motion), negative effects of this decline appear to be absent from job performance (Salthouse, 1982). Salthouse (1982) theorizes that this may be because of the minimal demand level of most on-the-job activities when compared to laboratory tests, as well as work and life experiences gained from increasing age.

Our knowledge of older workers as a rich resource does not seem to match our attitudes and actual treatment of older workers (Palmore, 1993). Davis (2001) reports that the American Association of Retired Persons provided training and retraining opportunities to their older employees for three reasons:

1. To train new employees into their respective jobs;

2. To prevent skill antiquation; and

3. To avoid additional expense and time in training someone more skilled.

Despite proven success and evidence that age is not a handicap to continued learning, employers remain reluctant to hire, train, and retrain the aged. Employers' reservations—legitimate or not—about older workers and their capacity to deal with technology serve as a barrier to employment (Yaukey et al., 2007; Davis, 2001). High unemployment of the elderly has been linked to a number of causes, among them job discrimination, outdated skills, and dislocation and opposition (Kupritz, 2001; Czaja, 1990).

Regardless of legislation that favors older workers, negative stereotypes of performance abilities persist along with reduced opportunities for retraining and promotional discrimination (Davis, 2001). Rix (1996) reported that training resources are mostly reserved for workers between the ages of 25 and 44. The existence of stereotypes in the workforce may encourage older workers to opt for early retirement, while a more supportive environment might encourage older workers to remain employed.

Companies seem to lack information associated with cost-benefit of employing older workers and also lack information on what to include in training programs for older workers (Imel, 1991). In order to effectively manage an older workforce, employers will need to adjust their attitudes and increase their knowledge of older workers (Mor-Barak and Tynan, 1993). Career and technical education can serve as a change agent in educating employers about the value in hiring, training, and retraining older workers. Other suggestions for effectively managing an older workforce include:

- Encouraging employees to participate in gerontology workshops and conferences;
- Linkages between career and technical education institutions and labor organizations;
- Partnerships with local area agencies on aging;
- Keeping supervisors aware of the Age Discrimination and Employment Act; and
- Providing older workers with performance feedback and career counseling.

Participation Characteristics of the Aging Workforce

The older adult learner faces many problems when attempting to participate in career and technical education/workforce education and continuing education. One of the most important is a general slowing of the perceptual and motor skills inherent in the older adult learner. Also, the working memory capacity declines with age and becomes a difficult barrier when the complexity of the instruction is increased (Echt, 1997). While there is no doubt that there are decreases in certain functions such as hearing, eyesight, and response time, the vast majority of older adult learners compensate for these losses without drastic complications and without noticeable impact on achievement (Myers, 1992).

Machado and Smith (1996) investigated the impact of certain variables on productivity of work teams (i.e., service order completion) for service technicians at Bell South. Findings determined that the teams at the top ten percent in productivity were older, had much more time on the present job, and had much more service with the company than teams at the bottom ten percent in productivity. Research also indicates that productivity can decline with age where specific job tasks or occupations relate to the degree and type of physical effort, such as reaction time and speed of performance (Ashcraft, 1992; Robinson, Coberly, and Paul, 1985; Sheppard, 1976).

Robinson, Coberly, and Paul (1985) reviewed a number of studies on occupational performance and age, concluding that environmental conditions are important in mitigating the effects of decline in aging workers. Zeisel (1984) describes barriers as the physical elements in the workplace that keep people apart or join them together, physically and symbolically, through walls, screens, objects, and partitions. He describes field characteristics as the physical elements of the work environment that perceptually alter the physical context through shape, size, orientation, lighting, acoustics, and air quality. Health professionals caution that structural changes in workplace design may need to be made to support the physiological decline that occurs for older workers (Ashcraft, 1992).

However, Kupritz (1999) reported that older and younger workers perceive similar types of office features as impacting work, regardless of the physiological changes occurring in aging workers. Older workers do not seem to need different physical features or special design adaptations to facilitate job performance. Research also indicates that privacy is a primary concern of both older and younger workers that should not be overlooked when addressing the needs of an organization and its employees (Kupritz, 2001).

Over the longer term but on just as significant a scale, the aging of the population will profoundly alter the characteristics of the workforce. Declining birth rates and increasing life spans are showing their effects. Longman (1999) reported that older persons in some developed countries outnumbered youth. Within the first half of the twenty-first century, more than one out of every five people in the world will be over the age of 60 (Yaukey et al., 2007). Even if men and women remain in the workforce for more years than they do at present, an eventual decline in numbers of available workers will result in less productivity (Daines, Hartenstein, and Birch, 2000).

Given that older adults are participating in career/technical and adult education (National Center for Education Statistics, 2001), what motivates them to enroll and what are they interested in learning? Ventura and Worthy (1982, p. 28) conclude, "There is no question that the predominant motivation for older adults enrolling in educational programs is to learn." Dellman-Jenkins, Fruit, and Lambert (1984) would agree. Their analysis of eight studies on intergenerational programs indicated that older participants were motivated by an intrinsic need for intellectual growth. Courtenay (1989) reported that older adults take courses that provide a sense of control or ability to cope—courses in areas such as business education, health care, family and consumer sciences, and physical education.

Possible barriers to participation by older students include poor health, lack of time, prohibitive costs, fear of being out at night, lack of transportation, lack of information about the activity, inconvenient location of parking facilities, and inconvenient location of the activity itself. Other barriers are psychological, such as fear of competition with younger students, fear of exposure of what older students may perceive as their inadequate backgrounds, or fear of the unknown.

Influence of an Older Workforce on Career and Technical Education

The present increase in the older population will create and expand opportunities for careers providing high-quality care to older people and helping prepare them and their families for productive retirement and the aging process (Lockwood, 2003). The burgeoning older population also can be viewed as a valuable resource that can help offset the shortage of skilled workers. Career and technical education, it seems, is in the unique position of influencing the quality of education that older people, their caregivers, and the corporate sector will receive.

While there are more and more older people wanting to enhance the quality of their lives after retirement through education and embarking on new careers, many others will be unable to work and will require a substantial amount of care instead (Harper, 1990). Career and technical education will be responsible for preparing many of the workers who will provide health care and other types of services for the aging workforce.

The present increase in the older population will create and expand opportunities for careers providing high-quality care to the elderly.

Improving care for the aging workforce has not been a priority of many federal, state, and local agencies. In federal appropriations, adult vocational education is combined in a "set-aside" allocated to postsecondary education. However, there have been quite a number of different pieces of legislation that have provided for the advancement of career and technical vocational education throughout the years, many of which are still an integral part of career and technical education today. Harper (1990) stated that:

Despite the fact that many federal, state, local agencies, academic centers, and professional organizations have set goals to improve the quality of care, their budgets seldom include many funds for preservice, inservice, or career and technical education for family caregivers, nurse's aides, and practical nurses. (p. 14)

There is a general belief that older people want to leave work; however, many would prefer to delay retirement or return to the workforce after retirement due to such factors as:

- increased longevity
- better health
- uncertain economic conditions
- more interesting work opportunities
- use of alternative work patterns, such as flextime and part-time employment (Winkfield, 1985).

Although adults and the unemployed are specifically mentioned in the Vocational Education Amendments of 1976, the needs of older persons to upgrade their job skills are not addressed. Winkfield (1985) reported that such upgrading and retraining of the elderly can result in reduced federal transfer payments, a greater supply of trained older workers as the pool of younger workers diminishes, and increased opportunity for continued growth and change for the elderly throughout their life spans.

Related Career Opportunities

Career and technical educators can help address some of the issues of the aging workforce by beginning to develop and expand comprehensive programs for all types of caregivers. Harper (1990) suggested that preretirement training for older people and referrals for families are two areas that career and technical educators must consider. In today's aging workforce, many career opportunities require specific career and technical education preparation, which educators can provide at the postsecondary level. Some of the extremely fast-growing occupations include (U.S. Department of Labor, 2007):

Home health and personal care aides	Emergency medical technicians
Occupational therapists	and paramedics
Nurses	Chiropractors
1. Registered nurses (RNs)	Physical therapist assistants and aides
2. Licensed practical nurses (LPNs)	Medical assistants
3. Licensed vocational nurses (LVNs)	Dental hygienists
Respiratory therapists	Surgical technologists
Physician assistants	Dental assistants

The need for preparation in these selected career areas—and many others— shows an integral part that career and technical education can play in the future delivery of health and social services to the aging workforce. Accord-

Area student nurses provide health-care seminars to the elderly at this underserved medical center.

ing to Harper (1990), "When today's medical students, nurses, dentists, pharmacists, and administrators reach the prime of their careers, they may find themselves spending as much as 75 percent of their practice time with older people" (p. 16). Career and technical educators need to plan to meet the needs of our older population. The workforce of tomorrow will need to prepare for changing demographics. The call for creative recruitment, retention, training, and retraining solutions will amplify as our older population decides to remain in or reenter the workforce.

Generations and the Workforce

Hankin (2005, p. 48) provides a vertical timeline of four distinct and different generations that are now in the workforce.

The Silent Generation

- Born 1922 to 1945
- Key Influences: The Great Depression and the New Deal; World War II; the Holocaust; Hiroshima; radio and movies
- Other Names: The Veterans; Seniors; The Greatest Generation

The Baby Boomers

- Born 1946 to 1964
- Key Influences: the Vietnam War; assassinations of JFK, Martin Luther King, Jr., and Robert Kennedy; putting a man on the moon;

Watergate; the Cold War and bomb shelters; television; women's liberation, sexual revolution; environmental concerns

- Other Names: Boomers; "Me" Generation

Generation X

- Born 1965 to 1976
- Key Influences: Demolition of the Berlin Wall; the *Challenger* disaster; the skyrocketing growth of the stock market and the abundant economy in the 1980s and 1990s; 24-hour live, remote news coverage; the dot-com economy; hi-tech start-ups
- Other Names: Baby Burst; Xers

Baby-Boom Echo

- Born 1977 to 2000
- Key Influences: the Oklahoma City bombing; the Columbine High School and Virginia Tech massacres; Y2K; the Internet; September 11, 2001, terrorist attacks; corporate scandals (e.g., Enron); video games; instant messaging.
- Other Names: Generation Y, Nexters, Internet Generation, Millennials (for those born in the 1980s and 1990s)

Characteristics of the Silent Generation

The Silent Generation is considered the most traditional: working fathers, nuclear families, and traditional work ethics. They are more likely to be highly disciplined, hardworking, and loyal employees. Although they may not hold managerial positions, many of these senior employees are natural workplace leaders. They can assist younger workers in finding information they need or in determining who is the right person to go to in a given situation. Much of this type of knowledge is not written down in employee handbooks and job descriptions—it is simply woven into the fabric of a workplace. Still, it is vital in maintaining a thriving team atmosphere (Hankin, 2005).

According to Hankin (2005):

> A natural affinity is developing between this generation and the Baby Boom Echo Generation. The indication for employers is that a mentor relationship between a Senior and an Echo would be a match. While the Silent Generation has felt undervalued for quite a while, it seems that the tide is turning and that they are becoming open to remaining at work (or coming back to the workplace after they reach retirement age) if given adequate flexibility. (p. 51)

Demographic Characteristics of the Baby-Boom Generation

The U.S. baby-boom generation is categorized by demographers into two distinct groups: the first half of the generation, born between 1946 and 1955, and the second half, born between 1956 and 1964. The early segment of the cohort—those born between 1946 and 1955—averaged 3.5 million births per year, while annual births for the latter group—those born between 1956 and 1964—averaged 4.2 million per year (Poulos and Nightingale, 1997).

The baby boomers, who increased the *size* of the labor force when they reached working age, are now raising the average *age* of the workforce. When they entered the workforce, the median age of the labor force decreased; as they aged, the median age of the labor force aged. The highest median age of the labor force before the baby-boom generation was 40.5 years in 1962. The median declined until 1980 and then begin rising again as the baby boomers aged (Fullerton, 1995).

The baby-boom generation has, for the most part, had higher labor-force participation levels than previous generations. For example, in 1985, when the baby boomers were between 21 and 39 years of age, their participation rate was 82 percent, compared to a participation of 74 percent for 21- to 39-year-olds in 1975 and a participation rate of 69 percent in 1965 (Fullerton, 1995). This increase is generally attributed to an overall increase in labor-force participation for persons under fifty years of age (not just baby boomers) and to an especially sharp increase in women's labor-force activity since 1970 (Yaukey et al., 2007; Poulos and Nightingale, 1997).

Labor-force participation has been declining since the mid-1970s for all age groups of men. Baby boomers are particularly affected because they comprise such a large portion of the population. Several explanations have been put forth for the declining labor-force participation rates among prime-age men, including increased job-market competition for the baby boomers because of the large workforce. Some of the participation decline is also probably related to inadequate education and skills that are in demand. The decreases have been greatest, for example, for men with less than a high school education (Blank, 1995).

Education accounts for most of the differences in income among subgroups of baby boomers and the differences between the baby boomers and their parents' generation. According to the Congressional Budget Office Study, in 1960 only three-fifths of the population of 25- to 29-year-olds had a high school degree, and just one out of ten had completed four years of college. By 1990, four-fifths of the 25- to 29-year-old population had completed high school, and 25 percent had completed four years of college.

The baby-boom generation, because of its vast size, has the ability to force societal change and cause economic unrest. What started out as a society in which baby boomers shaped economic patterns at every stage of their lives by crowding schools in the 1950s and 1960s, and overwhelming labor and housing markets in the 1970s and 1980s, is turning into a society ill-prepared to deal with the challenges of mass population aging (Cork, 1998; Davis, 2001).

Impact of the Aging Baby-Boom Generation on the Workforce

From Woodstock to woodstoves, to the World Wide Web.

—Howard Smead

When President Clinton turned 50, his birthday was met with great celebration and fanfare. To many Americans it was about more than the president of the United States reaching a personal milestone, it symbolized a milestone for a whole generation—the baby-boom generation.

The post–World War II generation referred to as the Baby Boomers has had a profound effect on public policy and on society in general. Between 1946 and 1964, about 75 million children were born in the United States—an average of about 4 million births each year, compared to an annual average of less than 3 million in the preceding 20 years. Births peaked at over 4.2 million a year in the early 1960s. In 1996, the baby-boom generation in the United States (that is, persons between the ages of 32 and 50) totaled over 80 million, including those born in other countries but not residing here (Yaukey et al., 2007; Poulos and Nightingale, 1997).

At each stage in the life cycle, this generation has changed the demand for public services and the market for a range of products. In the 1950s and 1960s, the public-policy challenge centered on the need to expand public elementary and secondary schools to educate the baby boomers. By the mid-1960s when the baby boomers began entering adulthood, the labor market and institutions of higher education were challenged to absorb larger numbers of individuals than in previous years. Beginning in the 1970s and continuing into the twenty-first century, the presence of a large cohort of child-bearing adults also contributed to redefinition of a number of social and economic institutions such as family and work, and presented major new business opportunities created by the expanded market for goods and services preferred by young adults and families.

The social and policy phenomena associated with the baby boom resulted from a complex interaction of (a) the sheer numbers of people in this generation, and (b) the coincident occurrence of important events and developments in society and the economy as a whole. Major changes have occurred in the nation since World War II that have influenced this generation of workers. The workplace, for example, has changed dramatically as the structure of work, the role of computers and communication technology, and the globalization of labor markets replaced the earlier industrial-based market. Baby boomers have faced and continue to face a very different work world than that of earlier generations (Poulos and Nightingale, 1997).

Demographic shifts, especially increased life expectancy and reduced fertility, have also changed the way individuals and families think about their work years and their "old age." The baby-boom generation is now passing through the phase of the life cycle in which individuals are, or should be, at their peak in terms of earnings potential, wealth accumulation, and career success. In 1996, the first of the baby boomers reached the age of 50. Just as the baby boomers redefined the popular notion of what other life-cycle phases mean, there is evidence that they are now contributing to a redefinition of aging, what it means to be a mature adult or an older worker, and what it means to retire (Sheehy, 1995; Friedan, 1993).

The baby-boom generation is now contributing to a redefinition of aging.

Some 76 million baby boomers are expected to live 30 or more years longer than their predecessors did in 1900 (Dychtwald and Flower, 1990). This aging population is changing the demographic profile of the American workforce (AARP, 1996; Brill, 1993; Hopkins, Nestleroth and Bolick, 1991). The median age of the workforce was approximately 35 years in 1980 and 37 years in 1990. The American Association of Retired Persons (2006) projects that the majority of the baby-boom generation will reach age 65 between the years 2010 and 2030.

Numerous reports emphasize the enormous spending power of the boomer generation (as cited in Gist, 2006) compared with today's 60- to -70-year-olds. More than one such report suggested that boomers will spend twice as much—one trillion dollars a year—as their elders did. According to Gist and Wu (2006), based on the 2004 Federal Reserve Survey of Consumer Finances, the medial total net worth of the entire boomer generation was about $146,000 in 2004, but only about $50,000 is left after housing equity. Medians—the value at which half the population falls above and half below—are generally used rather than means to characterize wealth distributions because wealth is so skewed toward the top (Gist, 2006).

For over twenty years policy makers, analysts, and social scientists have been concerned with the effect the baby boomers' retirement will have on the nation (Inskeep, 2004; Pifer and Bronte, 1986). As the baby boomers approach retirement age, economists warn of an impeding economic crisis during the twenty-first century. The flood of retirees, coupled with an anticipated decline in the American workforce, is expected to place unprecedented strain on the social security program (Yaukey et al., 2007).

Retirement often means that a new workforce will depend on training programs. With such a gap in the need for employees, career and technical education and training will be in great demand.

A broad array of policies and programs have been developed or modified over the past several years to address the needs of the aging population in general and in anticipation of the baby boomers approaching retirement age:

- Changes to the social security system have increased the official age of retirement, encouraging individuals to work longer.
- Changes to pension and benefit regulations have removed many disincentives to continue working beyond age 65.
- Older worker employment and training programs receive continued political support.
- Laws prohibiting age discrimination in the workplace have been enacted (Poulos and Nightingale, 1997).

Characteristics of Generation X

Hankin (2005) describes Generation Xers as fascinating, lack political awareness, and a generation raised with more of a "silver spoon" and a sense of entitlement. However, some Xers are considered as hard-core traditionalist-optimistic and hard working. Hankin (2005) argues that some "Xers are like a second wave of hippies and narrow-minded believers in gender roles and stereotypes" (p. 55). However, some of these labels ascribed to the Xers are too general, and can be viewed merely as misleading.

The divorce rates of Generation Xers have often been cited as the greatest influence on them. Hankin (2005) reported that the high rate of divorce and increased number of working mothers led to Xers being the first generation of latchkey children. Thus, resilience and adaptability are often among their attributes. Other worthwhile traits of Xers include working well in a multicultural environment, their pragmatic ways of accomplishing tasks, and giving ongoing feedback.

Characteristics of Baby-Boom Echo

According to Zemke et al. (2000), seven attributes characterize the Baby-Boom Echo:

1. Their supervisory style is flexible. How closely they monitor and manage is a product of each individual's track record and personal preferences. Control and autonomy are a continuum, not solitary options.
2. Their leadership style is situationally varied. Some decisions are consensually made; others are made by the manager, but with input and consultation.
3. They depend more on personal power than on positional power.
4. They know when and how to make personal policy exceptions, without causing a team riot.

5. They are thoughtful when matching individuals to a team, or matching a team or individual to an assignment.

6. They balance concern for tasks and concern for people. They are neither slave drivers nor country club managers.

7. They understand the elements of trust and work to gain it from their employees. They are perceived as fair, inclusive, good communicators, and competent in their own right.

Strauss and Howe (1991) reported that the Baby-Boom Echoes are expected to become politically active and will require even more dramatic employment adjustments, such as pay equity among workers and fewer job definitions.

Implications for Education

According to a workplace study by Padgett, Maldonado, and Saddler (2006):

> As the workforce becomes more diverse in age, companies will face a challenging environment. The "one size fits all" approach to employee incentives will no longer prove to be effective, and employers will need to take a hard look at who their employees are and what motivates them. As the labor pool tightens and turnover rates continue to rise, there will be fierce competition for top performers in Corporate America. Companies will need to take a proactive approach to employee retention if they are to remain competitive in today's labor market. (p. 56)

Society was comfortable telling young Gen-Xers to go it alone, keep their distance from the system, and learn from individual failures. Society does not see Millennials going down the same path. Parents have high expectations and don't want these children to fail. The children themselves don't expect to settle for second best. These expectations have given rise to great pressure for a new system to be put in place—one that won't fail, won't leave anyone behind, and will guide individuals in the right direction.

One of the biggest challenges facing career and technical education is the pressure to reshape programs to help children become college ready or to be their best, whatever they choose. An example comes from a policy paper issue by the Bill and Melinda Gates Foundation (2003) entitled "Closing the Graduation Gap: Toward High Schools That Prepare All Students for College, Work and Citizenship." There is pressure today for teacher education programs to incorporate academic rigor that not only colleges but also employers expect. The answer, however, lies in getting away from at-risk and damage control in education, and moving to a new model based on confidence and teamwork and mastery of the future. That's what young Millennials want, and that's where we should aspire to go.

Implications for Career and Technical Education Programs

Policy makers should consider expanding older worker programs and refocusing general employment and training programs to better meet the needs of the impending increase in disadvantaged older workers (Nichols, 2000). Alternatively, there are ways that the number of older workers in need of employment and training services might be reduced. Policies that encourage workers to continue working beyond retirement age and those that allow older workers to pursue occupational retraining or skill upgrading, for example, could reduce the number of unemployed and disadvantaged older workers. In addition, the aging of the baby-boom generation presents an expanding pool of potential volunteers to perform productive community service, since the rate of voluntarism is highest among older persons, particularly retirees.

To ease the earnings and income distribution problem that is evident among baby boomers, it is important to emphasize the feasibility of continued retooling and education for mature workers. Most baby boomers, especially the earlier group, are and will continue to be well prepared for the modern workplace. Highly educated workers with technical and other skills in demand will continue to be valued, especially if the current shortage of highly skilled workers continues. When necessary or desirable, such workers generally make fairly smooth transitions to new jobs. On average, they are earning wages that should allow them to retire with adequate income.

However, the less educated and less skilled among them will face greater problems as maturing workers than did previous generations. It is no longer assumed that individuals will be employed long term, with one employer or in one industry. Workers increasingly must plan for the job and career changes and for continuous retooling. Technological change requires that workers at all levels be able to adapt quickly to new technology and acquire new skills as necessary. To keep pace with new skills in demand, there may be a need for more ongoing training and retraining of workers, by individuals themselves as well as by employers, community colleges, and government programs.

There is an immediate need, therefore, to invest more funds and give a higher priority to encouraging continuous training, retooling, and learning for the current working-age baby-boom generation, especially for those who have less than a college education. The return on the investment in career and technical education will benefit individuals and society.

Challenges for Career and Technical Educators

Career and technical educators need to spend more time on issues related to aging. We must play a role in maximizing the contribution that older Americans can make to their country's future. This challenge means

addressing two critical issues: preparing workers to care for the elderly, and helping older people remain active.

As educators, we need to help people understand that the choices they make today will have a lot to do with the quality of their elderly years. Another challenge will be capturing the extensive expertise of retirees by using them as teachers' aides in our career and technical education laboratories and technology shops. This experience will benefit not only the students but also instructors who have not had the opportunity to spend many years in business or industry developing their skills.

An additional educational challenge will be to involve older persons as students. When mature adults share life experiences, they can learn from each other. Young people from single-parent homes may benefit from the opportunity to interact with a second adult. If career and technical educators are to play a role in transforming the challenges that face America into opportunities for cultural enrichment, then all education must evaluate the issues and put forth solutions to prepare for this changing workforce.

Summary

The aging population is a megatrend creating a diversified workforce in age and physiological makeup as well as work and life experiences. Older adults represent a significant clientele for career and technical educators over the next several decades. Current participation data, though limited to institutionalized learning, reflect the variety of interests among individual older learners and serve to rebut the myth that older adults cannot learn or are not interested in learning. The changes in the composition of the labor force and the changing personal needs of older people are creating powerful incentives for them to remain in or reenter the workforce. For many, this will mean job training or retraining. Although employers rate older workers highly in terms of dependability, loyalty, and commitment, they are less positive about their ability to learn new skills. They also question whether older individuals will stay on the job long enough to make training pay off. However, both research and practice show that deterioration of cognitive processes is by no means universal. Some studies have shown that older workers can adjust to new technology, can perform nearly as well as younger counterparts, and stay on the job longer.

The aging of the baby-boom generation presents real challenges to policy makers, since the huge cohort of older workers includes a proportionately large number of disadvantaged persons. At the same time, the generation offers enormous opportunities, especially because of the high levels of educational achievement of its members. A number of factors can guide policy considerations:

- On average, the post–World War II baby-boom generation has done better in terms of education, income, and wealth than any prior generation in history. However, the success has not been shared consistently by the generation as a whole. Those in the earlier segment of the gen-

eration have done somewhat better than those in the younger (and larger) cohort.

- About 25 to 30 percent of baby boomers have four or more years of college (more than double the rate of their parents' generation); but still 11 to 13 percent lack a high school diploma. Those without high school or without a college education, particularly men, have seen their earnings decline during their peak employment years. The baby-boom generation has been affected particularly by the changing structure of the U.S. labor market, since the structural shift from manufacturing to services coincided with their peak employment years (mid-1970s to mid-1990s).

- Traditionally, there has been strong public and policy support in the United States for allowing maximum individual choice in decisions related to retirement and working. While many older persons have always worked well into their older years, the clear preference currently is for earlier retirement. Provisions in social security and pension policies influence the age at which individuals retire.

- Life expectancy is increasing, as is "healthy" life expectancy. This means that individuals are not only living longer after they retire but also are healthy enough to continue working or performing other productive activities longer than previously has been the case.

- The structure of work has changed and continues to change dramatically in the postindustrial era. The predominance of computer and communication technology and the value placed on "soft skills" rather than physical strength in the workplace provide broad new opportunities for continuing work later in life for those who have up-to-date skills. In contrast, those without the skills that are in demand will have fever options in their older years, just as they did during their younger years.

- Finding and keeping the best and the brightest from all the generations will be the challenge of the future. Management, compensation, scheduling, and training will be impacted by the multigenerational workforce. These will be ongoing challenges for career and technical educators.

Discussion Questions and Activities

Thinking Critically

1. Within the next few decades more than one out of every five people in the world will be over age 60. From your point of view, how will workforce/career and technical education needs and societal obligations to people be met?

2. What characteristics of our older population will influence career paths in the future?

3. Should the ultimate purpose of career and technical education for older adults be directed toward advocacy—enabling older persons to improve their situations? Or should the ultimate purpose of educational opportunities for the elderly be to enable them to be influential and contributing members of society?

4. Should career and technical education experiences for older persons address the need to learn for the sake of learning or to learn for the experience of transcending the mundane activities of reality?

5. To what extent is funding a barrier to participation of older persons?

6. Will the working-age population be able to support the large number of retirees, or will the baby boomers have saved enough for retirement?

7. Will there be an adequate supply of labor to replace the retiring baby boomers?

8. Are baby boomers unique in any way that might suggest a need for new public programs related to maturing workers?

9. Are there any subgroups of the baby-boom population that might need special targeting as they mature (e.g., those with low incomes, low skill or education levels, or limited work experience)?

10. How can career and technical educators be more responsive to the educational planning and employment needs of older persons?

11. What is the Millennial Generation? What sets them apart from earlier generations?

12. What impact have the changing generations had on career and technical education?

Instructor-Related Activity

13. Have students conduct a role-play activity to address selected characteristics of the following generations:

    a. The Greatest Generation

    b. The "Me" Generation

    c. The Baby Bust

    d. The Internet Generation

Recommended Educational Media Resources

- *FRONTLINE: Can you afford to retire?*
- *Living old*
- *Generation next: Speak up, be heard*
- *Boomer Century: 1946–2046*
  PBS Home Video
  P.O. Box 609
  Melbourne, FL 32902-0609
  Web site: http://www.shoppbs.org

The National Center for Career and Technical Education offers a 2004 Webcast by the National Research Center for Career and Technical Education at the University of Minnesota (2004): *Labor force projections from the Bureau of Labor Statistics*. A downloadable transcript is also available in PDF and Word formats, as well as a PowerPoint presentation (http://www.nccte.com/webcasts/description78d5.html).

References and Additional Reading

American Association of Retired Persons (AARP) (2006). *The state of 50+ America 2006*. Washington, DC: Author.

Ashcraft, D. M. (1992). Health in the workplace. In K. Kelley (Ed.), *Issues, theory, and research in industrial/organizational psychology* (pp. 259–283). New York: Elsevier Science Publishing.

Blank, R. (1995). Outlook for the U.S. labor market and prospects for low-wage entry jobs. In D. S. Nightingale and R. A. Howen (Eds.), *The work alternative: Welfare reform and the realities of the job market* (pp. 33–69). Washington, DC: Urban Institute Press.

Brill, M. (1993). *Now offices, no offices, new offices . . . wild times in the world of office work*. Marlton, NJ: Jecknion.

Congressional Budget Office (1993). *Baby boomers in retirement: An early perspective*. Washington, DC: U.S. Government Printing Office.

Cork, D. (1998). *The pig and the python*. Rocklin, CA: Prima Publishing.

Courtenay, B. C. (1989). Education for older adults. In. S. B. Merriam and P. M. Cuningham (Eds.), *Handbook of adult and continuing education* (pp. 525–536). San Francisco: Jossey-Bass.

Czaja, S. J. (1990). *Human factors: Research needs for an aging population*. Washington, DC: National Academy Press.

Daines, J. (1993). *Preparing the workforce for the 21st century: Postsecondary education in the midst of paradigm shift* (The Leadership Academy Monograph Series). St. Paul: University of Minnesota, College of Education.

Daines, J., Hartenstein, A., and Birch, M. (2000). Women, education, and training: Old challenges in a new age. In D. R. Herschbach and C. P. Campbell (Eds.), *Workforce preparation: An international perspective* (pp. 22–33). Ann Arbor, MI: Prakken Publications.

Davis, S. K. L. (2001). Meeting the needs of an older workforce. *Workforce Education Forum, 28*(1), 12–26.

Dellman-Jenkins, M., Fruit, D., and Lambert, D. (1984). Exploring age integration in the university classroom: Middle age and younger students' educational motives and instructional preferences. *Educational Gerontology, 10*, 429–440.

Dychtwald, K., and Flower, J. (1990). *Age wave*. New York: Bantam Books.

Echt, K. V. (1997). *Effects of age and training formats on basic computer skills acquisition in older adults*. Unpublished master's thesis, University of Georgia, Athens.

Federal Reserve Board (2007, February). Testimony of Donald L. Kohn before the Special Committee on Aging, U.S. Senate. Retrieved April 18, 2007, from http://www.federalreserve.gov/boarddocs/testimony/2007/200702282/default.htm.

Fox, H. (1951). Utilization of older manpower. *Harvard Business Review, 29*, 40–54.

Friedan, B. (1993). *The fountain of age*. New York: Simon and Shuster.

Fullerton, H. N. (1995, November). The 2005 labor force: Growing, but slowly. *Monthly Labor Review, 118*(2), 29–44.

Gates, B., and Gates, M. (2003). *Closing the graduation gap: Toward high schools that prepare all students for college, work, and citizenship*. Seattle, WA: The Bill and Melinda Gates Foundation.

Gist, J. (2006). Boomer wealth: Beware of the median. *Data Digest,* 143. Washington, DC: AARP Public Policy Institute.

Gist, J., and Wu, K. (2006). The distribution of wealth among baby boomers. Washington, DC: AARP Public Policy Institute.

Goodman, John C. (2005). Baby boomer retirement: The nightmare in Our Future. Testimony before the House Ways & Means Committee. National Center for Policy Analysis. Retrieved May 14, 2007, from http://www.ncpa.org/sub/dpd/index.php?Article_ID=1709.

Hankin, H. (2005). *The new workforce: Five sweeping trends that will shape your company's future.* New York: AMACOM.

Harper, M. (1990). The greying of America. *Vocational Education Journal,* 65(1), 14–16.

Hopkins, K. P., Nestleroth, S. L., and Bolick, C. (1991). *Help wanted—how companies can survive and thrive in the coming worker shortage*. New York: McGraw-Hill.

Imel, S. (1991). *Older worker training: An overview* (Report No. EDO-CE-91-114). Washington, DC: Office of Educational Research and Improvement (ERIC Document Reproduction Service No. ED 334-470).

Inskeep, Steve (2004, September 6). The impact of an aging workforce. *Morning Edition,* National Public Radio. Retrieved April 18, 2007, from http://www.npr.org/templates/story/story.php?storyId=3892041.

Kupritz, V. W. (1999). The impact of office design on performance for older and younger workers. *Workforce Education Forum,* 26(2), 1–15.

———. (2001, Spring). Aging worker perceptions about design and privacy needs for work. *Journal of Architectural and Planning Research, 18*(1), 13.

Lockwood, Nancy R. (2003, December). The aging workforce: The reality of the impact of older workers and eldercare in the workplace. *HR Magazine Online*. Retrieved April 16, 2007, from http://findarticles.com/p/articles/mi_m3495/is_12_48/ai_n5989579.

Longman, P. (1999, March 1). The world turns gray: How global aging will challenge the world's economic well-being. *U.S. News & World Report, 126*, 30–39.

Machado, A. D., and Smith, D. H. (1996). *The relationship of training and team diversity on the productivity of service technicians at Bell South*. Proceedings of the Academy of Human Resource Development, USA, 106–113.

Meredith, G., and Schewe, C. (1994). The power of cohorts. *American Demographics, 16*(12), 22–29.

Mills, Q. (1987). *Not like our parents*. New York: William Morrow and Company.

Mor-Barak, M. E., and Tynan, M. (1993). Older workers and the workplace: A challenge for occupational social work. *Social Work, 38*(1), 45–55.

Myers, D. E. (1992). Searching learners of all ages. *Music Educators' Journal, 79*, 23–26.

National Center for Education Statistics (2001). *Digest of education statistics*. Washington, DC: Office of Educational Research Improvement, U.S. Department of Education.

Neus, E. (1999). Special, but not alone. Huntington, WV: *The Herald Dispatch*, pp. 1D, 5D.

Nichols, Kenneth L. (2001). Optimizing the silver collar worker: In the shoes of the older employee. *Journal of Organization Theory and Behavior, 4*(3–4), 225–246.

Padgett, V. L., Maldonado, C., and Saddler, S. (2006). Retention in the workplace today: Are we ready for generation Y? *Workforce Education Forum, 33*(1), 55–69.

Palmore, E. B. (1993). United States. In E. B. Palmore (Ed.), *Developments and research on aging* (pp. 355–374). Westport, CT: Greenword Publishing Group.

Pifer, A., and Bronte, L. (1986). *Our aging society: Paradox and promise.* New York: W.W. Norton.

Poulos, S., and Nightingale, D. S. (1997). *The aging baby boom: Implications for employment and training programs.* Washington, DC: Urban Institute.

Rix, S. E. (1996). The challenge of an aging workforce: Keeping older workers employed and employable. *Journal of Aging & Social Policy, 8,* 2–3, 79–96.

Robinson, P. K. (1983). *Organizational strategies for older workers.* New York: Pergamon Press.

Robinson, P. K., Coberly, S., and Paul, C. E. (1985). Work and retirement. In R. Binstock and E. Shanas (Eds.), *Handbook of aging and the social sciences* (pp. 503–527). New York: Van Nostrand Reinhold.

Salthouse, T. (1982). *Adult cognition: An experimental psychology of adult cognition.* New York: Springer-Verlag.

Schweitzer, Tamara (2007). *Report: Retiring baby boomers expected to hurt U.S. companies.* Breaking Entrepreneurial News. New York: Mansueto Ventures LLC. Retrieved April 16, 2007, from http://www.inc.com/criticalnews/articles/200703/boomers.html.

Sheehy, G. (1995). *New passages: Mapping lives across time.* New York: Random House.

Sheppard, H. L. (1976). Work and retirement. In R. Binstock and E. Shanas (Eds.), *Handbook of aging and the social sciences.* New York: Van Nostrand Reinhold.

Smith, D. (2003). *The older population in the United States: March 2002.* Current Population Reports (P20-546). Washington DC: U.S. Census Bureau.

Strauss, W., and Howe, N. (1991). *Generations: The history of America's future, 1584 to 2069.* New York: William Morrow and Company.

The Commonwealth Fund (2006, January). *Health coverage for aging baby boomers: Findings from the Commonwealth Fund survey of older adults.* New York: Author. Retrieved April 16, 2007, from http://www.cmwf.org/publications_show.htm?doc_id=340370.

U.S. Department of Labor (2007). *Career Guide to Industries.* Retrieved February 13, 2007, from http://www.bls.gov/oco/cg/cgs035.htm.

Ventura, C., and Worthy, E., Jr. (1982). *Education for older adults: A synthesis of significant data.* Washington, DC: National Council on the Aging.

Walsh, M. W. (2001). Reversing decades-long trend: Americans retiring later in life. *New York Times,* February 26, p. A1.

Welford, A. T. (1976). Thirty years of psychological research on age and work. *Journal of Occupational Psychology, 49,* 129–138.

Winkfield, P. W. (1985). *Retirement policy: Overview.* ERIC Digest No. 38.

Yaukey, D., Anderton, D. L., and Lundquist, J. H. (2007). *Demography: The study of human population,* 3rd ed. Long Grove, IL: Waveland Press.

Zeisel, J. (1984). *Inquiry by design.* Cambridge: Cambridge University Press.

Zemke, R., Raines, C., and Filipczak, B. (2000). *Generations at work: Managing the clash of veterans, boomers, xers, and nexters in your workplace.* New York: AMACOM.

chapter 12

Globalization of Career and Technical Education

The smallness of the world, the interdependence of all human beings, and the need for a global outlook are concepts that remind us of the similarities of human beings (McBreen and Perry, 1985). Career and technical education generally has focused on helping people to understand the relationship between education and work and to acquire employment skills. Today, the "new economic order" is a global one. Policy makers, educators, business, and industry are all concerned with strengthening the ability of the United States to compete in this area. Career and technical educators throughout the nation are affected by what goes on internationally. Each day, new developments—improved communication, faster travel, and increased commerce—make the world we live in smaller. In the national interest, we must prepare our students to compete in a global market.

This chapter focuses on the global role of career and technical education. The chapter also discusses the influence of Western thinking in the shaping of career and technical education in third-world countries.

Global Awareness and Interdependence

The evolving global economy is based on a number of factors: decreasing transportation and communication costs, new political structures and economic alliances (such as the European Community, G8, and the North American Free Trade Agreement [NAFTA]), and homogenization of tastes influenced by media and travel (Herr, 1990). With the growth of multinational corporations and increased trade among nations, workers need to understand global conditions, development, and trends. Such issues as population growth, wealth distribution, environmental concerns, diseases, and political and social problems, as well as cultural issues such as religious beliefs, customs, and family structure, have implications for a country's business activity and practices (Tan, 2004). The study of such issues will enhance students' abilities to engage in job-related problem solving and decision making in ways that reflect knowledge and respect for other cultures (McLaughlin, 1996).

The most important influence is the emergence of flexible, information-based technologies (Carnevale, 1991). Profound economic and social changes are creating new market standards (productivity, quality, variety, customization, convenience, timeliness) and integrating producers and consumers into networks for delivering goods and services globally or locally. Meeting these standards requires changes in organizational structures, skill needs, and jobs (Kerka, 1993).

We are in a world in which global interdependence is growing daily. Many U.S. colleges and universities are promoting international education. Internationally, there are many agencies and associations promoting globalization of career and technical education, for example:

- Food and Agriculture Organization (FAO);
- Inter American Development Bank (IADB);
- International Labour Organization (ILO);
- New International Economic Order (NIEO);
- Newly Industrializing Countries (NICs);
- North Atlantic Treaty Organization (NATO);
- The Peace Corps;
- United Nations Development Program (UNDP);
- United Nations, Scientific and Cultural Organization (UNESCO);
- United States Agencies for International Development (USAID);
- World Bank; and
- World Health Organization (WHO).

International students face many challenges in adjusting to their new environment.

Marcelo Suárez-Orozco, who hosted the 2004 HSGE–Nieman Foundation/Ross Institute Conference on Globalization and Education, says that the definition of the term *globalization* differs, depending on which academic discipline is doing the defining (quoted in Choy, 2004):

> The term "globalization" conjures up multiple meanings, particularly in regards to education. Two weeks ago, I visited a high school outside of Stockholm, in Kista, more or less the Silicon Valley of Europe, and what I saw there defines globalization today, as I see it. The students in the biology class I observed were from Somalia, Ethiopia, the former Yugoslavia, Iraq, Iran, Chile, and even a few students from Sweden. More than 80 percent of the students in the school were of immigrant and refugee origin; approximately 40 percent of all students in Stockholm schools are foreign-born or children of foreign-born parents. The kids at this school all spoke English, in addition to their own home languages, and, of course, Swedish. Of particular interest to me was that they all had wireless PCs and were quite involved in an Internet-based research project, visiting sites in multiple languages, and e-mailing each other across the aisles, as well as companions around the world.
>
> This is a scene that is increasingly common in schools all over the world, which encapsulates the main vectors that define globalization today: the movement of people, ideas, goods, services, and capital across the world—from Santiago to Stockholm and back to Santiago. This back-and-forth movement is fueled by the high octane of new information, communication, and media technologies as well as ever more affordable and efficient mass transportation systems.

According to Suárez-Orozco (quoted in Choy, 2004), there are four factors at the heart of the current wave of globalization:

- Growing worldwide immigration,
- The power and ubiquity of new global technologies,
- The post-nationalization of production and distribution of goods and services, and
- The area of back-and-forth cultural flows.

Richard Lynch (cited in Richardson, 2004), an occupational studies professor, represented the United States at a United Nations Educational, Scientific and Cultural Organization (UNESCO) international conference on the qualifications of vocational and technical teachers. Lynch remarked:

> The leadership at UNESCO and its collaborators are trying to address the need to train teachers who can teach (through education programs), technicians, health workers, repair persons, engineers, and such. . . . There is a critical shortage worldwide of teachers for technical, vocational education, and training—especially in developing countries.

Benefits of Global Interdependence

- Career and technical education provides learning experiences for both the host country and the visiting international students.

- New ideas and concepts are exchanged and lasting friendships formed.
- Degree programs at most U.S. universities/colleges and in some other developed countries help to provide the seed for growth in developing nations.
- International programs are tailored to focus on the needs of developing countries. Agencies and universities are partners in planning, conducting, and evaluating foreign projects. Many of these projects have supported the establishment and strengthening of cooperative extension services in developing countries (Remigius, 1989).
- Career and technical education provides linkages within developed and developing nations. Various agencies, organizations, and self-sponsored students can increase their efforts in international development. Career and technical educators are in the best position to contribute to the improvement of this trend. Resources within the host countries, foreign experts, students, and visitors should be utilized to enrich curriculum and curriculum offerings in both countries.

Internationalizing the Curriculum

Classroom study, even when it includes international content, cannot provide the extent of global awareness that one can achieve through international experiences. In a study of chief executive officers, 53.8 percent of the respondents stressed the importance of foreign exchange and internship programs in preparing workers for international business positions. Experience, travel, and overseas assignments also emerged as important considerations (Hart, 1994).

The new competitive framework requires a broader set of skills. Both "hard" (technical) and "soft" (interpersonal and communication) skills are equally important (Carnevale, 1991). Global workers need flexibility, problem-solving and decision-making ability, creative thinking, self-motivation, adaptability, and the capacity for reflection.

The literature describes a number of examples on which career and technical educators can rely as guides to internationalizing the curriculum. Many of them involve comparing U.S. systems (e.g., agriculture, transportation, and family living) with those of other countries. Ibezim and McCracken (1994) stress the importance of internationalizing the curriculum with specific reference to agricultural education:

> It has become clear that for a student to be considered educated in agriculture, he or she must be cognizant of the interrelationships of various agricultural systems and the governments, cultures, and societies in which they function. It is no longer sufficient to know how to produce food and fiber. (p.10)

In a study of the internationalization of a secondary-level agricultural program—a study involving agricultural teachers in 12 states of the North

Language competence is a major factor in teaching and learning for international students.

Central Region—"the most integrated dimensions were the origin of crops, agriculture technology, agricultural trade, geographical factors, economic factors, and political factors" (Ibezim and McCracken, 1994, p. 46).

Smith and Steward (1995) offer the following suggestions for upgrading communication curricula to take students beyond awareness of other cultures to competent intercultural communication:

1. Provide a cognitive instructional framework from which students can develop communication strategies related to elements of (a) oral and written intercultural communication, including negotiations; (b) techniques to overcome language barriers, both oral and written; and (c) advantages and disadvantages of using interpreters.

2. Lead students to examine the emotional (or affective) aspects of intercultural communication, e.g., sensitivity to intercultural differences and different value systems; the impact of culture on personal attitudes, behaviors, and communication; and the distinction between true and false perceptions in reaching a true understanding of a foreign culture's communication process.

3. Provide experiences through which students can engage in real-life application of the skills they learn. For example, students should be given opportunities to write letters, memoranda, and reports for intercultural audiences; make presentations using interpreters and telecommunications technology; engage in simulated intercultural experiences; and so forth.

Wismer (1994) recommends that colleges (1) establish a cross-functional task force to develop a comprehensive plan for international education and training; (2) form alliances with government, business, and industry to develop competencies for students and business employees that also strengthen local economic development; and (3) establish advisory boards from local business and industry to provide valuable input into training programs. Tech Prep programs offer another strategy for infusing international content into vocational programs. Sutliff (1996), who visited London to share Tech Prep tips, suggests broadening the scope of Tech Prep to focus on preparing a world-class workforce for global competition.

Faculty development is crucial to the implementation of programs that have an international component. Ibezim and McCracken (1994) suggest that "agricultural teachers who exhibit higher degrees of cultural awareness would be more likely to internationalize their agricultural instruction" (p. 48). Since many teachers have had no international education, opportunities such as staff development workshops and seminars, externships in other countries, study tours, continuing education courses in international business, and participation in business associations and organizations that promote international education would add valuable insight into issues they should be addressing in their instruction and classroom curriculum (Brown, 1997).

International Comparisons

To meet the challenge of building a world-class workforce, we need to know how career and technical education in the United States compares with that of other nations. A report by Warnat (1991) revealed several training strategies used to prepare work-bound youth for employment in the United States and four competitor nations—England, Germany, Japan, and Sweden. The findings are as follows:

- The four competitor nations expect all students to do well in school, especially in the early years. U.S. schools accept that many will lag behind.
- The competitor nations have established competency-based national training standards that are used to certify skill competency. U.S. practice is to certify program completion.
- All four foreign nations invest heavily in the education and training of work-bound youth. The United States invests less than half as much for each work-bound youth as it does for each college-bound youth.
- To a much greater extent than in the United States, the schools and employment communities in competitor countries guide students' transition from school to work, helping students learn about job requirements and assisting them in finding employment.
- Young adults in the four competitor nations have higher literacy rates than the comparable population segment in the United States.

Enrollment rate comparisons for the United States and four competitor nations—England, Germany, Japan, and Sweden—revealed the following findings (Warnat, 1991):

Country	% Youth in Vocational Curriculum	% At Postsecondary Level	% At University Level
U.S.	30	57	36
England	18	21	8
Japan	28	30	24
Sweden	50	37	25
Germany	70	30	26

Career and Technical Education Delivery Systems

The *quality* of career and technical education in Germany and Korea is regarded to be uniformly good; in Japan, fair to good; in the United States, greatly variable from poor to excellent. In terms of *availability*, career and technical education is universally available in Germany and Korea and of limited availability in Japan. In the United States, availability tends to be concentrated in more populous areas. *School-to-work transition* in Germany focuses on apprenticeship; in Korea employers recruit directly from the schools; in Japan it depends on a close relationship between employers and individual local schools; in the United States some employers have transition ties with local schools (Warnat, 1991).

Western Influence on Career and Technical Education in Developing Countries

Keating and others (as quoted in Brown, 2003) reported that:

> Across the international spectrum, CTE reflects a country's economic social investment in education and the strategies used to enhance the skill development of workers and foster their employability. The purpose of these efforts is to raise the country's level of productivity and competitiveness in a global market.

For most third-world countries, the history of having been colonized by Europeans is central to their national identity, foreign policy, and place in the world. Colonialism had certain negative economic implications. The most easily accessible minerals were dug up and shipped out of the country. The best farmland was planted in export crops rather than subsistence crops and was sometimes overworked and eroded. The education and skills needed to run the economy were largely limited to Whites. As a result, when colonies attained independence and many of the Whites departed, what remained was an undereducated population with a distorted economic structure and many of the valuable natural resources gone (Goldstein, 2001).

The economic effects were not all negative, however. Colonialism often fostered local economic accumulation. Much of the infrastructure that exists today in many third-world countries was created by colonizers. In some cases colonization brought disparate communities together into a cohesive political unit with a common religion, language, and culture, thus creating more opportunities for economic prosperity. In other cases, the local political cultures replaced by colonialism were themselves oppressive to the majority of the people (Goldstein, 2001).

The early settlers brought apprenticeship programs from Europe to colonial America. The schools of Pestalozzi and Fellenberg in Switzerland were used as patterns for the work-study schools of the United States in the early nineteenth century. Industrial education was influenced by the Russian system of manual training and the Scandinavian sloyd. France and Italy influenced instruction in the arts and crafts, and Germany contributed the idea of continuation schools to vocational education programs in the United States.

Pressures from the West on developing countries largely have come from bilateral and multilateral agencies. A UNESCO conference on technical education held in 1976, for example, urged developing countries to diversify their secondary-school curriculum, that is, to introduce practical and technical subjects along with academic subjects and to develop technical education both at basic levels and in higher education (NEIDA, 1982). Corvalan commented on Latin America in the late 1980s,

> the main issues are not necessarily diversification and vocationalism but how to provide for a better integration of science, technology and the socio-technical reality of working life, and how to combine education with productive work. (1988, p. 95)

Kenya's vocationalism of both the primary and secondary school curricula was influenced by the International Labour Organization in 1972 (Sifuna, 1992) and the Swedish International Development Agency in 1976 (Foster, 1987), while both World Bank and UNESCO thinking influenced the meeting of African Ministers of Education in Lagos in 1976, which adopted a major policy shift in African education:

> African states should provide a new form of education so as to establish close ties between the school and work: such an education based on work and with work in mind should break the barriers of prejudice which exist between manual and intellectual labour, between theory and practice, between town and country . . . and therefore productive practical work should generally be introduced in school, offering technical and vocational courses whether at primary, secondary or higher level. (Watson, 1994, p. 90)

Arguments against Career and Technical Education

It would appear that the crises facing many developing countries fit into two categories: (1) socioeconomic issues, and (2) problems relating to career and technical education (Watson, 1994).

1. At the socioeconomic level there is a growing financial crisis, brought on partly because of the world economic recession but also because of the debt problem. In a number of African countries, the problem is

compounded by rising population growth, rapid urbanization, rising unemployment, and falling output. CTE has been unable to address these problems. In many instances, it has actually exacerbated them because much of the training has been towards high-tech industrial employment, which requires only a few highly skilled personnel, rather than intermediate or low-tech jobs (Watson, 1994). According to Toffler (1971, 1981, 1990), the speed of change is so great that unless developing countries try to catch up or at least to be involved, they will fall much further behind in the technology race than they are currently.

2. The problems and criticisms leveled against CTE are numerous. Of all the educational fields, it is one that has been studied the least. In the eyes of many academics and governments, it is of less importance than, say, the school system, teacher training, and higher education (Watson, 1994).

Much of the criticism leveled against vocational education is based on economic rather than pedagogical arguments (Watson, 1994). Foster's (1965) *Vocational School Fallacy* argued that while governments might advocate vocational education, most pupils and parents rejected it in favor of academic schooling because the latter paved the way to greater career opportunities and higher financial rewards. Foster (1987) noted that:

> The relatively high costs of vocational education programs are not justified in terms of major cognitive or affective curricular effects, nor is there any compelling evidence with respect to positive labor market outcomes. (p. 138)

External bodies, such as ILO and the World Bank, have all been influential in shaping Kenya's policies. Yet the evidence from Kenya, Colombia, and Tanzania (Psacharopoulos and Loxley, 1985) would indicate that CTE students neither earn more nor get better jobs nor prove more likely to go into technical areas of the labor market than do those from general education courses.

Sifuna (1992) shares these views and argues that, because of an absence of basic resources, poor teaching, underqualified teachers, lack of parental support, and underresourcing—regardless of the pressures from international agencies—the diversified curricula program was doomed to failure. According to Sifuna:

A continuing decline in international student enrollment has lessened CTE's ability to attract the best and brightest.

> Although schools are expected to impart some useful occupational skills through the teaching of prevocational subjects, they are certainly not the right institutions for such training in depth. The main task of schools is to prepare pupils for post-school occupational training although they may expose pupils to prevocational skills. (p. 144)

In the context of Latin America, Corvalan (1988) argues that the real failure of secondary career and technical education is that it is generally unrelated to other sectors of the education system, let alone the labor market; it is too inflexible; teachers are inadequately trained; and both parents and pupils regard it as second best.

In the Caribbean, governments often view vocational education as a solution to the problem of school learner unemployment; it is ill directed, underresourced, and fails to take local variations into consideration (Lewis and Lewis, 1985).

Psacharopoulos (1991) cites seven reasons for the failure of CTE programs in third-world countries.

1. Most families and children regard it as inferior to the academic discipline.
2. The speed of global technological change has made it difficult to prepare students for unpredictable labor markets.
3. Forward planning has proved notoriously difficult, not only because of (2) above, but also because inadequate databases have made accurate forecasting impossible. In addition, many of the skills and jobs required have been based on Western concepts of employment and have failed to take into account the local cultural dynamic.
4. There is a lack of retraining programs built into the curricula to deal with changes in technology.
5. Governments rather than parents usually have made the decision to expand career and technical education.
6. Teachers invariably are inadequately trained or simply untrained.
7. CTE costs are at least twice the amount of general education costs because of the need to equip vocational classrooms, and because technical teacher education is much more expensive than comparable academic training.

Watson (1994) conducted an extensive review of literature and observations to determine the main reasons for the failure of so many CTE programs in developing countries. The reasons are as follows:

1. Too many governments have been swayed by the arguments put forward by multinational agencies, with the result that there has frequently been a disturbing disregard for indigenous cultures, local employment opportunities, and the reality of the local environment.
2. The dependency culture, seen in terms of overseas training, course evaluations and assessment, as well as the use of expatriate staff and

Western equipment, has prevented the development of indigenous programs, except where intermediate technology/self-help programs have prevailed.

3. Whatever the claims made for vocational education, the costs cannot justify the programs and have distorted investments in other areas of the education sector.

Arguments for Career and Technical Education

Foster (1987) has argued that there are many arguments in favor of CTE that have sound pedagogical roots. Writers as diverse as Marx, Dewey, Plato, Nyerere, and Gandhi have all advocated a balanced curriculum incorporating both practical and academic subjects. Some of the justifications put forward for CTE are that it would:

- transmit certain values and attitudes necessary to perform certain skills in the modern sector of the economy;
- provide specific skills for employment in a wide range of job categories;
- help to alleviate mass unemployment and the resulting public disaffection;
- alleviate obsolete work practices and improve job performance by upgrading or reorienting existing work skills;
- promote a work ethic and sensitize learners to the importance of practical work and practical skills application;
- help to prevent mass movements of dropouts from rural to urban areas;
- enable young persons to acquire skills for self-employment;
- prepare citizens for technical and technological change; and
- provide a necessary antidote to "overacademic education."

The Global Role of Career and Technical Education

The shift to a global context changes the content and focus of career and technical education. Employment security is becoming "employability security" (Kanter 1991, p. 9), the knowledge that one has the competencies demanded in the new economy and the ability to expand and adjust those competencies as requirements change.

According to Heraty, Morley, and McCarthy (2000, as cited in Brown, 2003), because lifelong learning is a critical component of today's competitiveness, international career and technical education and training requires a learning environment in which thinking is combined with doing, all of which requires a strong commitment from both the state and individual employers to facilitate the development of a knowledge-based and knowledge-driven economy.

Zwerling (1992) advocates a curriculum that focuses on the generic skills needed at different career stages. He outlines a comprehensive program that identifies the tasks, events, preferred learning styles, and formats of each life stage and suggests programming related to the life and career planning needs of each stage.

Occupational information, a vital component of career and technical education, can be bewildering as the quantity, distribution, and quality of jobs change continuously in the new economy. In an information age, the ability to locate information is necessary both to find a job and to do a job. People must be equipped with mental maps of how the new labor market works (Wegmann et al., 1989). Skills in processing the information acquired, including critical reasoning skills to select and evaluate the most relevant information, are also essential (Jarvis, 1990).

In the global economy, jobs increasingly may be shaped by the qualities of those performing them, and status and compensation may be attached to people, not positions (Tan, 2004; Kerka, 1993). Therefore, career and technical educators need to help people become individual career negotiators and to rethink work and career to identify how they can contribute to an organization according to their abilities.

Herr (1990) recognized a number of psychological issues for which workers must be prepared in the event of potential mergers, downsizing, relocation, and constant change. Adjustment is the key word: helping people assess the meaning of work, prepare for retraining, cope with uncertainty, and possibly deal with a move to "a less satisfying and less well-paying job for which life satisfactions and rewards will need to be found in roles and opportunities outside the work force" (p. 157). Those who relocate will need help in adjusting to living and working in a different culture, as well as in helping their families make the transition, a new dimension of work-family issue.

Skills needed for work in the global economy are reflected in current curricular emphases such as development of critical thinking skills, Tech Prep, the integration of CTE and academic education, and the competencies of the Secretary's Commission on Achieving Necessary Skills (SCANS). The challenges of the global economy are an opportunity not only for organizations to redesign themselves across national borders, but also for career and technical education to transcend its national boundaries and re-envision ways to prepare people for life and work.

The global workplace is a reality. Global competition as well as the General Agreement on Tariffs and Trade (GATT) and the North American Free Trade Agreement (NAFTA) have stimulated growth of multinational corporations as well as increased trade among nations (McLaughlin, 1996). The U.S. population will continue to reflect cultural diversity, which requires awareness, understanding, and networking of people from diverse backgrounds who can work together to accomplish family, community, and economic goals (Tan, 2004). Career and technical education can make a contribution by adding international perspectives to its programs.

In today's changing international marketplace and workforce, workers must be prepared to upgrade their education and skills. Career and technical education prepares both youth and adults for a wide range of careers in the twenty-first century economy.

Efficacy of Career and Technical Education on Global Competitiveness

Although higher productivity and new management and hiring practices have had some influence on the loss of jobs, a growing number of companies are moving their operations to other countries where the cost of wages is cheaper than in the United States (Benjamin and Perry, 2003). Many of these job losses have been in the manufacturing industry, involving mostly blue-collar workers. Also, many white-collar jobs are exported to India (for financial services) and China (for manufacturing) (Benjamin and Perry, 2003; Edgardio et al. 2003; Kelly et al. 2003; Lee, 2003; Rossheim, 2003). Several researchers (Benjamin and Perry, 2003; Lee, 2003) reported that U.S. financial institutions plan to ship more than 500,000 jobs abroad as a way to reduce their operating cost. "John C. McCarthy of Forrester Research Inc., predicts that at least 3.3 million white collar jobs and $136 million wage will shift from the U.S. to low-cost countries by 2015" (Edgardio et al. 2003, p. 51).

Haglund (2003) argues that it is the increased productivity of American workers rather than globalization that is costing jobs in the long run. However, Reich (2002) asserts that as the mix of job changes, workers must be prepared to upgrade their education and skills. He states that:

> Even if a country were to erect a wall around itself and secede from the global economy, many jobs would still disappear and the people who once performed them would be likely to find themselves in new jobs paying less than old, especially if they lack the skills for the new. (p.120)

Newbury (2001) reported that employees who work in more interdependent offices where they are exposed to shared clients from other countries are more likely to see the career benefits from global integration than do those in more locally embedded offices. Based on a report of the Census Bureau, it is estimated that labor demand will exceed supply by the year 2013, and by 2031, "the American workforce may be 27.9 million short of the 57.1 million new workers the country will need" (Osterman et al., 2002). These shortages will be more likely to occur in fields that require higher degrees in education and increased skill levels realized through postsecondary training (Reich, 2002). Rossheim (2003) suggests that although globalization may result in the loss of lower-end jobs to other countries, jobs in fields where the level of expertise is high will remain in the United States.

Workers with a high school education or less are more likely to experience the downside of globalization. "From November 2000 to November 2001, the unemployment rate for persons with less than a high school diploma increased from 8.2% to 10.0% (Osterman et al., 2002, p. 740). Many of the job losses were in assembly and machine operating, production crafts, services, and transportation occupations. During the same time period, jobs in managerial, technical specialties, professional groups, and protective services grew by one million (Osterman et al., 2002).

Career and technical education affects not only the skill and earning power of U.S. workers, but those in other countries as well. There has been an explosion of college-educated men and women in New Delhi, Manila, Shanghai, Budapest, Bulgaria, Romania, and South Africa who are being tapped by the global market for their services (Edgardio, et al., 2003). Low-end jobs are more likely to be exported to countries where labor is cheap and jobs that are mentally challenging and require high levels of expertise are exported to countries where workers are educated (Cohen and Zaidi, 2002; Rossheim, 2003). According to Nadesan (2001), the highest skills and jobs are more likely to concentrate among the most privileged groups in all nations. There is significant global movement toward hiring of temporary skilled workers, particularly in countries where skill shortages require that temporary workers be imported until the country can develop its own pool of skilled workers (Iredale, 2001). According to Harvard economist David Bloom (quoted in Choy, 2004),

> . . . the returns for each additional year of schooling in the developing world today grow exponentially—each year of schooling in developing countries is thought to raise individuals' earning power, which is closely linked to productivity, by about 10 percent. Children and youth with the skills, competencies, and sensibilities to proactively and critically engage globalization's new grammar will have huge advantages over those without them.

Career and technical education has generally focused on helping people understand the relationship between education and work and acquire employability skills. However, people need assistance in realizing the opportunities and meeting the challenges of the international workplace. "America's economic competitiveness is at the forefront of a national policy debate with federal, state, and local leaders examining ways to keep the country at the top of international innovation as other countries make technological and economic gains" (ACTE, 2006, p.1). During the reauthorization of the 2006 Carl D. Perkins Career and Technical Education Improvement Act, Members of Congress recognized that one area missing from almost all of these policy proposals was a focus on career and technical education. They added a new clause to the Act: "Providing individuals with opportunities throughout their lifetimes to develop, in conjunction with other education and training programs, the knowledge and skills needed to keep the United States competitive" (U.S. Congress, 2006).

President Bush has stated, "The bedrock of America's competitiveness is a well-educated and skilled workforce" (ACTE, 2006, p. 1). Viable career and technical education programs are critical to preparing this well-educated and skilled workforce. Expanded investments in career and technical education are vital to meeting the administration's goals of:

- A system of education through secondary level that equips each new generation foundation for future study and inquiry in technical subjects and that inspires and sustains their interest;

- Institutions of higher education that provide American students access to world-class education and research opportunities in science, technology, engineering and mathematics fields; and

- Workforce training systems that provide more workers the opportunity to pursue the training and other services necessary to improve their skills and better compete in the twenty-first century (Domestic Policy Council, Office of Science and Technology Policy, 2006).

High-quality career and technical education can ensure America's future competitiveness through increased student engagement, the innovative integration of math, science and literacy skills, and by meeting the needs of both employers and the economy as a whole (ACTE, 2006). Career and technical education prepares both youth and adults for a wide range of careers in the twenty-first-century economy. These careers may require varying levels of education—from high school and postsecondary certificates to two- and four-year college degrees. According to the U.S. Department of Education's Office of Vocational and Adult Education (OVAE), 97 percent of all high school students take at least one career and technical education course, and one in four students take three or more courses in a single program area. One-third of college students are involved in career and technical education, and as many as 40 million adults engage in short-term postsecondary occupational training. (U.S. Department of Education, 2004).

Career and technical education programs help students achieve academic success, experience increases in earnings and improved employment outcomes, reduce dropout and absentee rates, and achieve postsecondary success. Nations enrolling a large proportion of upper-secondary student in career and technical education programs that include heavy doses of work-based learning have significantly higher school attendance rates, upper-secondary completion rates and college attendance. (Bishop and Mane, 2004). Career and technical education supports strong economic competitiveness by assisting secondary and postsecondary education programs meet the following goals (ACTE, 2006):

- Increase student engagement,
- Improve math, science, and literacy,
- Meet employer needs for highly skilled workers, and
- Meet America's workforce needs.

Table 12.1 Distribution of Occupations Expected to Grow the Fastest and their Corresponding Career Clusters (2005–2014)

Occupation	Cluster
Home health aides	Health Science
Network systems and data communications analysts	Information Technology
Medical assistants	Health Science
Physician assistants	Health Science
Computer software engineers, applications	Information Technology
Physical therapist assistants	Health Science
Dental hygienists	Health Science
Computer software engineers, systems software	Information Technology
Dental assistants	Health Science
Personal and home care aides	Health Science
Network and computer systems administrators	Information Technology
Database administrators	Information Technology
Physical therapists	Health Science
Forensic science technicians	Law, Public Safety & Security
Veterinary technologists and technicians	Agriculture, Food & Natural Resources/ Health Science
Diagnostic medial sonographers	Health Science
Physical therapist aides	Health Science
Occupational therapist assistants	Health Science
Medical Scientists, except epidemiologists	Health Science
Occupational therapists	Health Science

Source: U.S. Department of Labor (2006). *Occupational Outlook Handbook:* 2006–2007 edition. Washington, DC: Bureau of Labor Statistics.

Over the past decades, career and technical education has evolved with the economy to focus on high-skill careers in high-demand and high-growth industries. Career and technical education programs help prepare students for all 20 (see Table 12.1) of the fastest growing occupations identified in the U.S. Department of Labor's 2006–2007 *Occupational Outlook Handbook* (U.S. Department of Labor, 2006), and in all 14 job sectors identified by the Department of Labor's high-growth job training initiative (ACTE, 2006).

If the United States is to remain a player in the global economy, it needs to budget more money for education—or at the very least to spend existing funds more wisely. Money will only get tighter in the years ahead as Social Security, Medicaid, and Medicare spending reaches critical mass. Corporations and other institutions nationwide are reevaluating their payment structures for employee pension plans. Many of these companies look overseas and see the opportunity to move their business to places where employee benefits are nonexistent or minimal in comparison to domestic requirements (Daggett and Pedinotti, 2005). Most jobs in the twenty-first century will probably require increasing levels of technical knowledge. Career and technical education programs can provide this exposure of technical skills to most students, regardless of their future goals. From the standpoint of globalization, work need not rely on taking assignments in other countries. However, employment in the global economy will require understanding and appreciation of a wide variety of cultures and the ability to work cooperatively and collaboratively in teams and across cultures (Nordgren, 2002).

Summary

- Career and technical education can help people realize the opportunities and meet the challenges of the international workplace.
- Future workers will need to develop global awareness, and an understanding of competitive cultural and economic factors that influence ways of doing business, to work in the international arena.
- Career and technical education, the educational program area specifically designed to prepare students for work, must infuse international concepts into programs so the youth of today are prepared for the global workplace.
- With the growth of multinational corporations and increased trade among nations, workers need to be aware of global conditions, developments, and trends.
- Career and technical educators must internationalize the curriculum.
- Career and technical educators need to adopt instructional practices that incorporate international dimensions. For example, communication curricula could be upgraded to take students beyond awareness of other cultures to competence in intercultural communication.

- Increased corporate input is necessary for international business program development. The firsthand knowledge and experiences of corporate representatives working in firms that conduct international business offer a current and practical basis for upgrading curricula.
- Faculty development is crucial to the implementation of programs that have an international component.
- Western paradigms have been influential in shaping less developed countries in terms of economic development, technological development, and vocational education/career and technical education.
- Students must be exposed to future career opportunities during their formal education, and it is critical to get students interested in science, technology, engineering and mathematics-related occupations early in their educational careers.

Discussion Questions and Activities

Thinking Critically

1. What is a global economy?
2. What skills do people need to participate in a global economy?
3. How can career and technical education infuse international concepts into CTE programs so that the youth of today are prepared for the global workplace?
4. Compare and contrast career and technical education in *developed* and *developing* counties.
5. Debate the pros and cons of career and technical education in developing countries.
6. Design a career and technical education project with emphasis on the integration of international concepts for three of the following program areas:
   - Agriculture
   - Business Education
   - Family and Consumer Sciences Education
   - Health Occupations Education
   - Marketing Education
   - Technical Education
   - Technology Education
   - Trade and Industrial Education
7. In North and South America, independence from colonialism was won by descendants of the colonists themselves. In Asia and Africa, it was obtained mainly by local populations with a long history of their

own. How do you think this has affected postcolonial history of CTE in one or more specific countries from each group?

8. Describe and give examples of your global perspectives for career and technical education.

Recommended Educational Media Resources

- *Learn from the past, plan for the future*
- *The intercultural classroom: A different place* (DVD)
  Insight Media
  2162 Broadway
  New York, NY 10024-0621
  1-800-233-9910 or (212) 721-6316
  Web site: http://www.insight-media.com

References and Additional Reading

Association for Career and Technical Education (2006). *ACTE issue brief: American competitiveness*. Alexandra, VA: Author.

Bates, Richard (2005). Can we live together? Towards a global curriculum. *Arts and Humanities in Higher Education, 4*(1), 95–109.

Benjamin, M., and Perry, J. (2003, August 11). The new job reality. *U.S. News and World Report, 135*(4), 24.

Bishop, J., and Mane, F. (2004). The impacts of career-technical education on high school labor market success. *Economies of Education Review, 23*(3), 381–402.

Brown, B. L. (1997). *Adding international perspectives*. Washington, DC: Office of Educational Research Improvement (ERIC Document Reproduction Service No. ED 407 575).

Brown, Bettina (2003). International models of career-technical education. *Trends and Issues Alert*, no. 42. Retrieved March 21, 2007, from http://www.calpro-online.org/eric/docgen.asp?tbl=tia&ID=165.

Burbules, N., and Torres, C. (Eds.) (2000). Globalization and Education: Critical Perspectives. Oxford, UK: Routledge.

Carnevale, A. P. (1991). *America and the new economy*. Alexandria, VA: American Society for Training and Development (ERIC Document Reproduction Service No. ED 333 246).

Choy, Carol P. (2004). Education and globalization (interview with Marcelo Suárez-Orozco). *HSGE News*, April 1. Harvard Graduate School of Education. Retrieved April 18, 2007, from http://www.gse.harvard.edu/news/features/mso04012004.html.

Cohen, M. S., and Zaidi, M. A. (2002). *Global skill shortages*. Cheltenham, UK; Northhampton, MA: Edward Elgar Publishing.

Corvalan, V. (1988). Trends in technical-vocational and secondary education in Latin America. *International Journal of Educational Development, 8*, 73–78.

Daggett, W. R., and Pedinotti, J. (2005). Globalization: *Tipping the scale of economic supremacy*. Rexford, NY: International Center for Leadership in Education.

Domestic Policy Council, Office of Science and Technology Policy (2006). *American competitiveness initiative*. Retrieved November 8, 2006, from www.whitehouse.gov/stateoftheunion/2006/aci/aci06-booklet.pdf.

Edgardio, P., Bernstein, A., Kripalani, M., Balfour, F., Grow, B., and Green, J. (2003, February 3). Is your job next? *Business Week*, 3818, 50–60.

Foster, P. J. (1965). The vocational school fallacy in development planning. In C. A. Anderson and M. J. Bowman (Eds.), *Education and economic development* (pp. 142–166). Chicago: Aldine Publishing.

———. (1987). Technical vocational education in the less developed countries. *International Journal of Educational Development*, 7, 137–139.

Goldstein, J. S. (2001). *International relations,* 4th ed. Boston, MA: Addison Wesley Longman.

Haglund, R. (2002, June 1). American workers' proficiency costs jobs in the long run. *The Plain Dealer* (Cleveland), pp. G1, G3.

Herr, E. L. (1990). Employment counseling in a global economy. *Journal of Employment Counseling*, 27, 147–159.

Hart, S. (1994). A survey of corporate executives' perceptions of collegiate international business preparation. *Delta Pi Epsilon Journal*, 36(2), 96–109.

Ibezim, D. O., and McCracken, J. D. (1994). Factors associated with internationalization of secondary agricultural education programs. *Journal of Agricultural Education*, 35(3), 44–49.

Iredale, R.(2001). The migration of professionals: Theories and typologies. *International Migration*, 39(5), 7–26.

Jarvis, P. S. (1990). A nation at risk: The economic consequences of neglecting career development. *Journal of Career Development*, 16(3), 157–171.

Kanter, R. (1991). Globalism/localism. *Harvard Business Review*, 69(2), 9–10.

Kelly, A., Brannick, T., Hulpke, J., Levine, J., and To, M. (2003). Linking organizational training and development practices with new forms of career structure: A cross-national exploration. *Journal of European Industrial Training*, 27(2–4), 160–168.

Kerka, S. (1993). *Career education for a global economy*. Washington, DC: Office of Educational Research Improvement (ERIC Document Reproduction Service No. ED 255 457).

Lee, K. (2003). Financial services companies to export 500,000 jobs. *Employee Benefit News*, 17(8), 1, 34.

Lewis, T. and Lewis, N. V. (1985). Vocational education in the Commonwealth Caribbean and the United States. *Comparative Education*, 21, 157–172.

McLaughlin, C. H. (1996). Implications of global change: Technology education's role. *Technology Teacher*, 55(5), 14–18.

McBreen, E. L., and Perry, C. S. (1985). Catalyst for African development. *Agricultural Education Magazine*, 57(7), 16–18.

Nadesan, M. H. (2001, February). "Fortune" on globalization and the new economy: Manifest destiny in a technological age. *Management Communication Quarterly,* 14 (3), 498–506.

Network in Education Innovation for Development in Africa (NEIDA) (1982). *Education and productive work in Africa: A regional survey* (Dakar: UNESCO, Regional Office for Education in Africa).

Newbury, W. (2001). MNC interdependence and local embeddedness influences on perceptions of career benefits form global integration. *Journal of International Business Studies*, 32(3), 497–507.

Nordgren, R. D. (2002). Globalization and education: What students will need to know and be able to do in the global village. *Phi Delta Kappan*, 84(4), 318–321.

Osterman, P., Kochman, T. A., Locke, R., and Piore, M. J. (2002). Working in America: A blueprint for the new labor market (Review Symposium). *Industrial and Labor Relations Review, 54*(4), 715–745.

Psacharopoulos, G. (1991). Vocational education theory, voced 101: Including hints for vocational planners. *International Journal of Educational Development, 11,* 193–199.

Psacharopoulos, G., and Loxley, W. (1985). *Diversified secondary education and development evidence form Colombia and Tanzania.* Baltimore: Johns Hopkins University Press.

Reich, R. B. (2002). The challenge of decent work. *International Labour Review, 141*(1-2), 1, 5–122.

Remigius, F. O. (1989). International development: An agricultural education. *The Agricultural Education Magazine, 61*(10), 20–21.

Richardson, Nicole (2004). Lynch Speaks at UNESCO Conference on Vocational-Technical Teachers. Retrieved February 14, 2007, from http://www.uga.edu.coenews/fac_staff.0606Lynch.html.

Rossheim, J. (2003). The great labor shortage: Job creation, job destruction and globalization. *Monster Featured Reports.* Retrieved November 8, 2006, from http://featuredreports.monster.com/laborshortage/globalization/

Sifuna, D. N. (1992). Prevocational subjects in primary schools in the 8-4-4 education systems in Kenya. *International Journal of Educational Development, 12,* 133–145.

Smith, M. O., and Steward, J. F. (1995). Communication for a global economy. *Business Education Forum, 49*(4), 25–28.

Suárez-Orozco, Marcelo M., and Baolian Qin-Hilliard, Desirée (2004). *Globalization: Culture and education in the new millennium.* Berkeley: University of California Press.

Sutliff, L. (1996). The English translation. *Vocational Education Journal, 71*(4), 38–39, 57.

Tan, J-S. (2004, December). Cultural intelligence and the global economy. *Leadership in Action, 24*(5), 19–21.

Toffler, A. (1971). *Future shock.* New York: Bantam Books.

———. (1981). *The third wave.* New York: Bantam Books.

———. (1990). *Power shift.* New York: Bantam Books.

U.S. Congress (2006). *The Carl D. Perkins career and technical education act.* Retrieved November 8, 2006, from http://www.actonline.org/policy/legislative_issues/upload/Perkins_Changes_Summary.doc.

U.S. Department of Education (2004). *National assessment of vocational education.* Final report to Congress. Washington, DC: Office of the Under Secretary, Policy and Program Studies Service.

U.S. Department of Labor (2006). *Occupational Outlook Handbook: 2006–07 edition.* Bureau of Labor Statistics. Retrieved November 7, 2006, from http://www.bls.gov/oco/oco2003.htm.

Warnat, W. I. (1991). Preparing a world class work force. *Vocational Education Journal, 66*(5), 22–25.

Watson, K. (1994). Technical and vocational education in developing countries: Western paradigms and comparative methodology. *Comparative Education, 30*(2), 85–97.

Wegmann, R., Chapman, R., and Johnson, M. (1989). *Work in the new economy.* Alexandria VA: American Association for Counseling and Development (ERIC Document Reproduction Service No. ED 308 322).

Wismer, J. N. (1994, April). *Training for trade: Role of American community colleges*. Paper presented at the meeting of the American Council on International and Intercultural Education, Colorado Springs, CO (ERIC Document Reproduction Service No. ED 371 789).

World Bank (2002). *Higher education in developing countries: Peril and promise*. Washington, DC: Report of the Task Force on Education and Society.

Zwerling, L. S. (1992, Spring). Liberal learning and the world of work. *New Directions for Adult and Continuing Education, 53*, 99–113.

chapter 13

Issues and Trends Impacting the Growth and Future of Career and Technical Education

Traditionally, individuals of the agrarian society had access to only a rudimentary level of education. Generally, children completed their formal schooling by age 14, so as to begin working on a full time basis. The change to an economy based on manufacturing required more people to be educated to assume leadership positions in business, industry, government and various communities. However, since the publication in 1983 of *A Nation at Risk*, the American schools have experienced pressure from political and business leaders to raise the academic standards for all students.

At the beginning of the twenty-first century, states were required to implement new standards and state assessments in compliance with the No Child Left Behind (NCLB) legislation. NCLB required each district, school, superintendent, principal, and teacher to look at new and different ways of educating their students if they are to be successful in raising academic standards and student performance as defined by NCLB. This chapter provides information on factors (issues and trends) that the author perceives as impacting career and technical education in general and our students in particular: the changing image of career and technical education, the CTE teacher shortage, diversity and multicultural education, closing the achievement gap, selected learning models, career clusters, and the impact of twenty-first century globalization.

The Changing Image of Career and Technical Education

Today's world of career and technical education is an informative, exciting, and innovative arena where students are learning more than just career skills. Career and technical education in the twenty-first century is more challenging, more academic, and more relevant. However, there are still many negative perceptions of career and technical education. Hull (2003) stated that

> while some career and technical education programs do an excellent job
> of preparing students for future, career and technical education is still

widely viewed as a "dumping ground" for academically struggling students, and therefore a way for our education system to hide its failure. (p. 30)

According to Blank (1999), the terminology used to describe our field has evolved through many changes. Some of the terms used included vocational education, technical education, and occupational education. Another dimension of Blank's perspectives on vocational education was the less-than-positive perceptions by policy makers, potential students, parents, and academic educators.

> The label vocational education has triggered less-than-flattering images in the minds of many people. These images sometimes include the notions of a dumping ground, a place of last resort for troubled youth, lack of rigor, or nation training and preparation for low-wage/obsolete jobs. While these negative images are most often ill deserved and in no way characterize the many high quality, progressive vocational education programs in existence, such negative stereotypes are unfortunately, all too prevalent. (Blank, 1999, p. 282)

> Why the rejection of CTE in particular? In part, it stems from stereotypes about CTE—it prepared students only for work after high school, and its students are mostly male, too often minorities, academically backward, and destined for dead-end jobs. While this characterization may or may not have been correct in the past, it is not accurate today. (Gray, 2004)

The underlying theme that emerged from a study (*Major needs of career and technical education in the year 2000: Views from the field*) conducted by Lewis (2001) was "the need to improve the image of career and technical education." Participants reported that career and technical education was perceived as offering an inferior curriculum, appropriate only for students who cannot meet the demands of a college preparatory program. There are many secondary and postsecondary career and technical education programs in the United States that provide much more than job training; however, they still have to fight for respect. How do you change the perception of career and technical education? As CTE educators, we have to create a positive image of career and technical education so that it is viewed as a kaleidoscope of opportunities for pursuing a plethora of career choices. The following strategies/challenges can be useful for career and technical education educators to present a positive image of career and technical education as a viable strategy for education and work:

1. *Infuse career and technical education into the curriculum of public schools.* Motivation to learn is high when classes and activities relate to the real world, to real career choices and real job opportunities.

2. *Highlight the marketability of career and technical education program completers.* Invite members of the media to serve on task forces.

3. *Collaborate with business and industry to ensure a highly trained workforce.* Through collaboration we can elevate the image of career and technical education through the perceptions of students, parents and the public.

4. *Establish constant communication with parents.* Address misconceptions concerning the need that all students seek college degrees. Describe viable career and technical education options that might meet the needs of their children.

5. *Reeducate guidance counselors.* The adage "you are not college material" is a myth and also reduces one's self-esteem. Career and technical education advocates must work to ensure that school counselors understand the benefits of career and technical education and how it fits into the school's curriculum.

All school-to-career education programs hinge on the integration of academic and career and technical education. Through a collaborative effort, students can obtain a multitude of experiences and knowledge. Improving its image will not happen by chance, but rather by the concerted effort of those who have a paramount interest in ensuring that career and technical education students are well prepared for the global village of the workforce.

This teacher educator shows dedication to the well-being of students in her CTE program.

The Shortage of Career and Technical Education Teachers

Research suggests that the number of colleges and universities offering career and technical education teacher training programs declined by about 10 percent between 1991 and 2001 (Bruening et al., 2001), but the increase in teachers entering the profession through alternative certification routes suggests that pre-service programs are not necessarily a constraint. Some states and local communities report teacher shortages, often blaming the lack of career and technical education teacher training programs in state universities (Stasz and Bodilly, 2004). Increased primary and secondary student enrollment, recent expansion of secondary technology education programs, teacher attrition, and the decreasing number of universities offering technology education degrees have led to a nationwide shortage of technology teachers (Gray and Daugherty, 2004). National data suggest a gap between supply and demand for career and technical education teachers (Levesque, 2004):

- The number of students in high school grew by 17.9 percent between 1991 and 2000; however, the average number of career and technical education courses taken remained constant at approximately 4.0 credits per student. These trends suggest that the total number of career and technical education courses taken by students increased during the decade.

- During the last decade, the proportion of career and technical education teachers at retirement age remained steady while the proportion of new hires increased. These trends resulted in a substantial net gain of teachers into career and technical education classrooms: between 1991 and 2000, an estimated 55,000 new career and technical education teachers were added to the workforce. These new hires were concentrated in areas of increased student enrollment—computer science and health care, for example—while the number of new teachers in business, trade and industry, and technology education declined, which was also consistent with student enrollment (U.S. Department of Education, 2004). According to Levesque (2004), career and technical education class sizes, which declined in the late 1980s, began to increase in 1991 following a pattern similar to that of academic high school classes (Table 13.1).

The data from Table 13.1 reveals that during the 1990s, the average size of career and technical education class increased by more than two students (18.1 to 20.5) but, in 2000, career and technical education classes still contained fewer students than academic classes by about four students (20.5 compared to 23.6).

The proportion of high schools seeking career and technical education teachers remained the same between 1991 and 2000 (at about one-third),

Table 13.1   Average Class Size for High School Teachers, by Teaching Assignment and School Type: Selected Years 1991–2000

Teaching Assignment and School Type	Average Class Size			Change between 1991 and 2000
	1991	**1994**	**2000**	
All career and technical education	18.1	18.9	20.5	2.4*
At comprehensive high school	18.2	19.1	20.6	2.4*
At career and technical education school[1]	15.7	15.9	18.8	3.1*
At other type of school[2]	16.9	17.8	19.3	2.4
All non-career and technical education	22.6	23.3	23.6	1.0*

[1] CTE schools include full-day CTE high schools and area or regional CTE centers that may serve students part-day or part-time.
[2] "Other" school include alternative schools or special schools serving students with disabilities.
* Differences were statistically significant at the 0.05 level.
Note: Calculations were performed on unrounded numbers.
Source: U.S. Department of Education (2004). National assessment of vocational education: Final report to Congress, p. 81. Washington, DC: Office of the Under Secretary, Policy and Program Studies Service.

while the share of schools with vacancies for academic teachers and special education teachers increased substantially. Schools reported growing difficulty filling vacancies in all subjects, but the proportion that found it very difficult or impossible to fill career and technical teacher vacancies more than doubled (see Table 13.2).

Table 13.2   Percentage of High Schools Reporting It Was Very Difficult or Impossible to Fill Teacher Vacancies, by Teaching Field: 1991 and 2000

Teaching Field	Percentage of Schools		Change between 1991 and 2000
	1991	**2000**	
Career and technical education	18.1	40.3	22.2*
Computer science	n/a	34.6	n/a
English/language arts	5.0	9.2	4.1*
Math	12.9	43.3	30.4*
Biology or life sciences	15.2	29.9	14.6*
Special education	26.9	40.9	14.0*

n/a = not available or missing data
* Differences were statistically significant at the 0.05 level.
Note: Calculations were performed on unrounded numbers.
Source: U.S. Department of Education (2004). National assessment of vocational education: Final report to Congress, p. 82. Office of the Under Secretary, Policy and Program Studies Service, Washington, DC.

Today's CTE teacher educators are training teachers of tomorrow to carry on their legacy.

In 1990, over 50 percent of all technology teachers were over the age of 50 (Dugger et al., 1991; cited in Gray and Daugherty, 2004). This aging workforce has led to an increased number of retirees. With as many as 76 million baby boomers approaching retirement age, this trend is likely to continue and will impact the classroom (Dohm, 2000; cited in Gray and Daugherty, 2004).

By 2000, one out of 15 schools did not fill their career and technical education teacher vacancies, one possible signal of teacher shortages. Another indicator of excess demand was that average salaries increased more for career and technical education teachers than for academic teachers (Levesque, 2004). Stasz and Bodilly (2004) reported that twelve sites in five states reported anticipated career and technical education shortages. Five of these reported that shortages had affected programs. Sites in California, Michigan, and Florida reported that lack of teacher training programs in the state contributed to these shortages. As some teachers retire and others enter outside professions, the shortage of teachers may become critical. If career and technical education is to remain alive and well, there must be sufficient teachers, not only for career and technical education programs but also for the academic courses that make up the core curriculum.

Diversity, Multicultural Education, and CTE

We could learn a lot from a box of crayons. . . . Some are *sharp*. . . . Some are *pretty*. . . . Some are *dull*. . . . Some have *weird* names. . . . And all are different *colors*. . . . But they all live in the same box.

—Anonymous

Workforce Diversity of Career and Technical Education Teachers

The demographic composition of society and the workforce has changed considerably and is expected to continue undergoing dramatic changes in the near future. Researchers agree that modern society is undergoing an historic transition from a predominantly white society rooted in Western culture to a global society composed of diverse racial and ethnic minorities (Thomas, 1996; Triandis, Kurowski, and Gelfand, 1994).

Diversity is included as one of the standards used by the National Council for Accreditation of Teacher Education (NCATE). It is mandatory that teacher education candidates have experiences "working with diverse higher education and school faculty, diverse candidates, and diverse students in P–12 schools" (NCATE, 2002, p. 10). Banks and others (2005) noted that although there was an increase in diversity among public school students, diversity among teachers was not increasing. America's teaching force is not representative of our student population.

Minority role models are essential to the survival of CTE programs.

The changing workforce is one of the most significant challenges facing career and technical education teacher educators. A study conducted by Bruening and others (2001) revealed that career and technical teacher educators were 90 percent white, 4 percent African American, and 3 percent Hispanic. A previous study reported by the National Center on Educational Statistics (NCES) in 1992 (as cited in Bruening et al., 2001) indicated that the higher education faculty were 89 percent white, 4.9 percent African American, and 2.5 percent Hispanic. Goodlad (1990) argued that teacher preparation programs seem to have problems with both minority recruitment and teacher preparation for the multicultural classrooms. The bottom line is that this statistic was unchanged over a 10-year period. Shure (2001) stated that "an overwhelming majority of American's teachers are white females. African-American, Hispanic, Asian, and American Indian—and even male—teachers are dangerously underrepresented in our schools" (p. 32).

Shure further noted that:

> A lack of minority role models inside our school building is just one consequence of this shortage. With fewer minority teachers at the head of

the class, fewer minorities are looking to teaching as a potential career. Certainly, some of the lack of interest in teaching comes from wealth of job opportunities available today, for everyone across the board. But, many minorities simply do not see themselves joining, or having never considered, a profession that is dominated by white females. (p. 32)

Alternative certification holds the promise of diversifying the teacher workforce.

An excellent exploratory study was conducted by Wakefield and colleagues (2006) to examine the perceptions of selected agricultural education teachers' perceptions toward diversity. Although the sample size was small, this study provided a rich source of baseline data concerning student teachers' perceptions regarding diversity. The researchers concluded that student teachers were leaving their teacher preparation programs without experiencing interactions with others from diverse groups. The study further revealed that participants were demographically, predominantly White, male, and from rural communities. Surprisingly, participants reported that they had no experiences with minorities prior to college, but did have moderate interactions with minorities outside of college classes. Amazingly, of the 12 student teachers, only one taught more than five students from a minority group.

According to Ruhland and Bremer (2002):

> The racial and ethnic diversity of teachers is also part of the alternative teacher certification debate. Many believe that minority students benefit by seeing teachers in their school who look like them and who can serve as role models. Feistritzer (1993) reported that just 9% of teachers, but 26% of students, are minorities. They estimated that by the year 2000, 5% of teachers and 33% of students would be minorities. Houston, Marshall, and McDavid (1993) argue that alternative certification holds the promise of diversifying the teacher workforce. They studied the characteristics of participants in alternative and traditional certification programs in the Houston school district and found that alternatively certified teachers represented much greater diversity than traditionally certified teachers. Specifically, alternatively certified teachers were more likely than traditionally certified teachers to be male (24% vs. 6%); more

likely to be African American (29% vs. 13%); less likely to be Anglo (48% vs. 67%); and more likely to be 30 to 40 years of age (42% vs. 14%). (p. 10)

Given the apparent intractability of the problem of teacher shortages, pragmatic approaches aimed at helping alternatively certified teachers are increasingly evident. In reviewing the research comparing traditional and alternative certification, Miller, McKenna, and McKenna (1998) stated, "alternative certification is here to stay; researchers should investigate not whether such programs work, but which ones work best" (p. 166). In other words, it is more important to focus on strategies for developing teaching competence rather than the teacher certification route. (p. 12)

Multicultural Education

There are several theoretical approaches to multicultural education. Sleeter and Grant (2007) described five noteworthy approaches:

- *Assimilation approach.* Proposes that we should all be culturally similar as "Americans" and strive to make all students capable of being productive citizens and fitting into the dominant culture. These teachers ignore differences or actively work to eliminate them.
- *Human relations approach.* Values each student as an individual, works to eliminate stereotypes, and promotes tolerance. Teachers and schools following this approach actively promote the cultural enrichment of all students and the enhancement of all students' self-esteem.
- *Ethnic studies approach.* Focuses on an ethnic group such as Jewish Studies or African American studies. Pre-service students may take courses in these areas, but ethnic studies are typically not seen at the high school level.
- *Integrated multicultural education approach.* Seeks to promote the equality of all through pluralism.
- *Social reconstructionist approach.* Extends the previous approach and aims to teach students how to change society. Alleviating oppression and equalizing power are key outcomes of this approach.

Multicultural Suggestions and Challenges for CTE Educators

The increasingly diverse demographics of the U.S. population should be an indication that CTE should explore ways to reach and educate the changing student population's needs. Sabo (2000) reported that racial and ethnic minorities will soon comprise one-half of all Americans. According to Brotherton (2000), the changing diversity of the population includes not only racial and ethnic minorities, but also people with disabilities. These demographic shifts are likely to affect not only CTE classrooms, but also the changing workforce. The integrated multicultural approach is accepted as the best model for the school and is applied through a democratic and equitable process (Birkel, 2000). CTE has a responsibility to create challenging and equal environments for all students and teachers.

The following suggestions and challenges are useful for CTE educators to develop a model or framework based on societal goals, school goals, curriculum, instruction, and other aspects of classroom and school-wide concerns (Birkel, 2000).

- Focus on intercultural sensitivity of CTE teachers (acceptance of cultural differences).
- Respect and encourage differences of opinion and perspective.
- CTE students should be taught to respect those who are different from themselves.
- Emphasize the importance of communication.
- Assign team-based projects.
- Encourage workplace experiences.
- CTE educators should teach students about the ways in which various cultures have influenced various vocations.
- CTE activities should be representative of a wide variety of cultures.
- Students should have an equal opportunity to learn and succeed in CTE.
- Specific objectives should target program content related to cultural diversity.
- Infuse cultural factors in selected courses.
- Conduct professional development on selected theoretical approaches to multicultural education.
- Design urban-based field experiences/projects.
- CTE educators should be more inclusive of all students by making changes in content and teaching methods/styles.
- Invite role models to serve as resource personnel.

Implications for Career and Technical Education Practitioners

- Recruit minority teachers from business and industry. Though career and technical education teacher education programs offer the best option for increasing the numbers of minority teachers and minority students, that effort can be supplemented by luring minority professionals from the world of work and into career and technical education teaching. Barriers to formal certification can be waived, and alternative certification can be allowed. Schools should consider providing relocation assistance and other incentives especially for teachers who choose to move into the local community.
- Introduce alternative teaching strategies in pre-service and in-service teacher training programs. A body of knowledge can be developed specific to instructional and learning styles most beneficial to minority students in career and technical education (Gordon and Yocke, 2005).

These styles can be included in pre-service teacher training programs and explored during in-service professional growth opportunities. Federal funds and grants designated for the research of alternative teaching styles can be developed. Professional organizations such as the *Association for Career and Technical Education Research* and *Academy for Career and Technical Teacher Education* should work closely with higher education and governmental bodies in directing this research.

- Career and technical education programs must also make efforts to recruit both diverse students and diverse faculty. A diverse faculty will help students better deal with diversity in the workplace. A diverse faculty and student body provide a way of practicing diversity as a reality.

- The primary reason attributed to the failure of diversity initiatives is a lack of accountability. Therefore, it is essential to promote diversity objectives among administrators and other school personnel assessments.

- Career and technical education practitioners should develop faculty/ student training and developmental programs to increase awareness, sensitivity, understanding, and appreciation of cultural and other differences through workshops, training programs, and seminars.

- By engaging in strategies to attract and retain minority teachers in career and technical education, the field can fulfill its mission to provide capable graduates for the world of work. Today's workplace is multicultural and diverse, and this should be reflected in career and technical education programs. The inclusion of minority teachers in CTE instruction is important to the integrity and vitality of the profession.

Closing the Achievement Gap

Much has been written regarding ideal ways of teaching to attain higher student achievement. Green and Winters (2005), reported that too many young people leave school before earning diplomas. Their analysis revealed that in 1991–2002 the graduation rate for students earning a high school diploma (excluding the GED) was 71 percent. This probably suggests that academic programs often fail to help students engage in the high school experience. Only 34 percent of 2002 high school graduates were prepared for postsecondary education (Green and Winters, 2005). A large part of this problem may be attributed to a so-called *achievement gap* in education.

In a position paper on "Reinventing the American High School," the Association for Career and Technical Education (2006, p. 5) reported three achievement gaps in the United States:

1. The *domestic achievement gap*—the disparity in learning among American students correlated to racial and economic status.

2. The *international achievement gap*—the gap between U.S. students and young people from other nations who are more highly educated and,

in many cases, able to carry out skilled work for relatively low wages, compared to what skilled U.S. workers command in the marketplace.

3. The *ambition gap*—aspects of American culture that devalue hard work, personal achievement, exerting effort toward reaching future goals, and other aspects of strong character, resulting in an overall lack of focus and purpose among American youth.

Regarding the domestic achievement gap, Henson (2006) believes that closing the gap between white and Asian students and their black and Hispanic counterparts should be a major thrust of the work ahead. Although minority students have made considerable gains, a gap still remains. Socioeconomic factors, such as racial-ethnic differences in family income and parents' educational levels, play a role in this gap. The National Center for Education Statistics (2002) states that poverty has a negative correlation with school achievement, and black and Hispanic children are more than twice as likely to live in poverty as white children. Yet teachers in schools with high minority enrollments or high poverty rates are somewhat less likely to have a master's degree or a college major or minor in their main field of assignment than teachers in schools with few minority children or low poverty rates.

To close achievement gaps, states and school districts should make special efforts to:

- Recruit and hire teachers for high-poverty and high-minority schools who have academic backgrounds and full certification in the fields they are teaching;
- Encourage all middle-school students to take rigorous coursework; and
- Make low-income students aware of programs to help finance the costs of AP exams, as well as the costs of postsecondary education (Center on Education Policy, 2000).

The ACTE has made recommendations for closing achievement gaps in education. Among them are several suggestions that are particularly pertinent to career and technical education (Association for Career and Technical Education, 2006):

- *Recommendation 1—Establish a clear system goal of career and college readiness for all students.*
  - Enroll students in career and college readiness coursework upon entering high school, utilizing structures already in place such as career clusters or career academies.
  - Design the master schedule in a way that students can take advanced academic and CTE courses, including through dual enrollment and Tech Prep options.

- *Recommendation 2—Create a new school culture that stresses personalization in planning and decision making.*
  - Begin structured career development and postsecondary planning activities in eighth grade (or earlier) and continue in each year of high school.
  - Provide electronic tools for career development.
  - Provide local support for career development facilitation skills among teachers, counselors, and other educational staff who engage in career development activities with students.
  - Offer summer externships in business and industry to build teacher career awareness.
- *Recommendation 3—Create a positive school culture that stresses personalization in relationships.*
  - Provide structures and activities to promote personalization—advisory periods, smaller learning communities, CTSOs or other organizations, and individual career development and postsecondary planning meetings with students and their parents/guardians.
  - Increase the percentage of students involved in extra curricular and co-curricular activities.

Selected Learning Models for Career and Technical Education Students

This section reviews three teaching and learning models and explains the application of these theories to career and technical education.

Behaviorism has served as the basic teaching and learning model for Career and Technical Education (Doolittle and Camp, 1999). It continues to be seen in performance objectives, criterion-referenced measures, task lists as a source of curriculum, and specific, predetermined skills demonstrated by industry standards. Another theory developed at about the same time (1910–1920) was constructivism.

Constructivism

Constructivism is a set of assumptions about the nature of human learning that guide constructivist learning theories and teaching methods of education. Constructivism values developmentally appropriate teacher-supported learning that is initiated and directed by the student. The theory of constructivism rests on the notion that there is an innate human drive to make sense of the world. Instead of absorbing or passively receiving objective knowledge, learners actively construct knowledge by integrating new information and experiences into what they have previously come to understand, revising and reinterpreting old knowledge in order to reconcile it with the new (Billett,

1996). During the 1970s and 1980s, Piaget's works also inspired the transformation of European and American education, including both theory and practice, leading to a more "child-centered" approach. In *Conversations with Jean Piaget*, he says: "Education, for most people, means trying to lead the child to resemble the typical adult of his society . . . but for me and no one else, education means making creators. . . . You have to make inventors, innovators—not conformists" (Bringuier, 1980, p. 132).

Today, constructivist theories are influential throughout much of the so-called informal learning sector.

According to Parnell (1996), the philosophical position of academic education has been "learning to know is most important; application can come later"; of career and technical education he says: "learning to do is most important; knowledge will somehow seep into the process" (p. 19). In addition, the behaviorist position (Prosser) has predominated over the pragmatic/constructivist position (Dewey) in career and technical education for most of the twentieth century (Lynch, 1997). Elements of constructivist situated learning may be seen in developments such as Tech Prep, School-to-Work, and integration of career and technical education and academic education. Barriers such as time constraints, administrative procedures, and lack of consensus on the goals and purposes of education limit teachers' ability to implement constructivist approaches.

The career and technical education teacher's role is not to set tasks, but rather to organize experiences that allow learners to develop their own knowledge and understanding. The learning environment should reproduce the key aspects of communities of practice: authentic activities sequenced in complexity, multiple experiences and examples of knowledge application, access to experts, and a social context in which learners collaborate on knowledge construction.

Brooks and Brooks (as cited in Wardlow and Scott, 2000, p. 628) listed the following traits of constructivist teachers:

- Encourage and accept autonomy and initiative.
- Use raw data and primary source, along with manipulative, interactive and physical models.
- When framing tasks, constructivist teachers use cognitive terminology such as "classify," "analyze," "predict," and "create."
- Allow student responses to drive lessons, shift instructional strategies, and alter content.
- Inquire about students' understandings of concepts before sharing their own understandings of those concepts.
- Encourage student inquiry by asking thoughtful, open-ended questions and encouraging students to ask questions of each other.
- Seek elaboration of students' initial responses.
- Engage students in experiences that might engender contradictions to their initial hypotheses and then encourage discussion.

- Allow wait time after posing questions.
- Provide time for students to construct relationships and create metaphors.
- Nurture students' natural curiosity through frequent use of the learning cycle model.

Contextual Learning

Contextual learning is a conception of teaching and learning that helps instructors relate subject-matter content to real-world situations. Contextual instruction has been demonstrated by hands-on experience in a land laboratory or "shop setting." The following are examples of contextual teaching and learning strategies:

- Emphasize problem solving;
- Recognize the need for teaching and learning to occur in a variety of contexts such as home, community, and work sites;
- Teach students to monitor and direct their own learning so they become self-regulated learners; and
- Encourage students to learn together and from each other.

Research shows that not all students learn best through an abstract modality. In fact, most people learn best through informal, contextual experiences (Gardner, 2006; Kolb, 1984). Therefore, accommodating the learning styles of all learners requires the use of a variety of learning strategies, multiple ways of organizing curriculum content, and diverse contexts for learning opportunities.

Bond (2004) reported that contextual learning systems are defined by the following characteristics:

- *Centralization of pragmatic life/work issues.* The major concern in contextual/concrete learning systems is to fill the gap between what students know to compete in a global economy.

- *Integration of academics with real-life experiences.* Contextual learning systems integrate academic subjects,

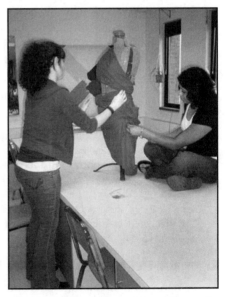

Visual Merchandising includes the use of elements and principles of design to manipulate materials—props, background, lighting, mannequins, and much more.

such as science, mathematics and English, with applications in the workplace.

- *Personalization of instruction.* Contextual learning personalizes academic content for the student. Declarative or factual knowledge is transferred to a personal experience for the student so the knowledge is internalized.

- *Visualization of abstract ideas.* Although visualization of abstract ideas and concepts in the mind's eye may be beneficial for many students, it may not work for all.

- *Demonstration of utility.* Contextual teaching methods demonstrate the utility of the material being taught. A student should not need to ask, "Why do I have to take this course?" (p. 4)

Decisions about what instructional system to use to impart knowledge depend on three major factors (Bond, 2004):

1. Teachers, principals, curriculum planners and guidance personnel must realize that all students do not perceive and organize information in the same way. Teachers must understand these differences and apply strategies that enable all their students to use their natural, dominant abilities to the maximum.

2. Teachers must realize that all students do not necessarily perceive and organize information the way they themselves do.

3. Any contextual teaching system must use strategic planning and implementation of lessons. Lessons that match a student's learning style with the teaching methods greatly help the student obtain and use factual knowledge. (p. 5)

Traditionally, career and technical educators developed and used a task-based curriculum. Students were trained to perform the specific duties required for a job. Berns and Erickson (2001) stated that:

> Although learning skills to perform such tasks may be important in some career and technical education programs, contextual teaching and learning requires that portion of the curriculum to be placed in a broader framework that integrates other subject content into the learning process for the students. Learning goals are elevated to higher-order thinking skills in the process of learning how to find information, adapt to change, and communicate effectively unlike relating appropriately to others. (p. 4)

Rigor and Relevance Curriculum Framework

A rigorous and relevant education is a product of effective learning, which takes place when standards, curriculum, instruction, and assessment reinforce each other. The 1983 government publication *A Nation at Risk* concluded that our schools were in danger of not preparing students to compete in the twenty-first century. The focus of this report was to strengthen academic requirements for graduation, more tests, and emphasis on standards and accountability. Daggett (2004) stated that:

> In 1983, as now, the impetus for change came primarily from the business community, not higher education. And business continues to feel firsthand the skills gap between what students are learning in school and what they actually need to be competitive in the high-tech, global economy. (p. 1)

Research has shown that students understand and retain knowledge best when they have applied it in a practical and relevant setting. An instructor who relies on lecturing does not provide students with maximum learning opportunities. According to the International Center for Leadership in Education (n.d.), relevance is critical if we want to get students to rigor. Relevance can create the conditions and motivation needed for students to make a personal investment in rigorous work for optimal learning. Students are more likely to invest more of themselves, work harder, and learn better when the topic is connected to something that they already know and in which they have an interest.

The Rigor/Relevance Framework is a tool developed by personnel of the International Center for Leadership in Education to examine curriculum, instruction, and assessment. The Rigor/Relevance Framework is based on two dimensions of higher standards and student achievement. First is the

Figure 13.1   Rigor/Relevance Framework®

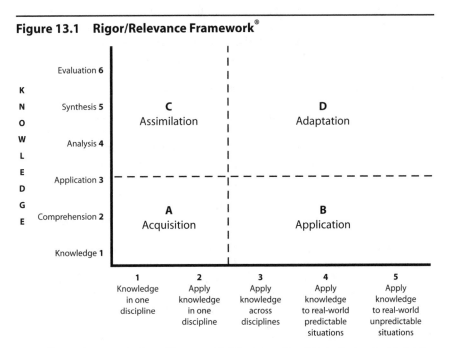

Personal communication with personnel of the International Center for Leadership in Education, October 5, 2006. Reprinted with permission.

Knowledge Taxonomy, a continuum based on the six levels of Bloom's Taxonomy, which describes the increasingly complex ways in which we think. The low end involves acquiring knowledge and being able to recall or locate that knowledge. The high end labels the more complex ways in which individuals use knowledge, such as taking several pieces of knowledge and combining them in both logical and creative ways.

The second continuum, the Application Model, is one of action. Its five levels describe putting knowledge to use. While the low end is knowledge acquired for its own sake, the high end signifies use of that knowledge to solve complex real-world problems and to create unique projects, design, and other works for use in real-world situations. The Rigor/Relevance Framework has four quadrants. Each is labeled with a term that characterizes the learning or student performance at that level.

Daggett (2005, p. 3) suggests the following various ways to incorporate the Rigor/Relevance Framework in instruction. When instruction and expected learning is in Quadrant A, the focus is on *teacher work*. Teachers expend energy to create and assess learning activities—providing lesson content, creating worksheets, grading students' work. When instruction and expected learning move to Quadrant B, the emphasis is on the student doing *real-world work*. This work involves more real-work tasks than Quadrant A and generally takes more time for students to complete. When instruction and expected learning falls in Quadrant C, the *student* is required to *think* in complex ways—to analyze, compare, create, and evaluate. Traditionally, this has been the level of learning at which students graduated from high school. Quadrant D learning requires the student *to think and work*. Roles have

Figure 13.2   Rigor/Relevance Framework Quadrants

Quadrant C—Assimilation	Quadrant D—Adaptation
Students extend and refine their acquired knowledge to be able to use that knowledge automatically and routinely to analyze and solve problems and create solutions.	Students have the competence to think in complex ways and to apply their knowledge and skills. Even when confronted with perplexing unknowns, students are able to use extensive knowledge and skills to create solutions and take action that further develops their skills and knowledge.
Quadrant A—Acquisition	Quadrant B—Application
Students gather and store bits of knowledge and information. Students are primarily expected to remember or understand this knowledge.	Students use acquired knowledge to solve problems, design solutions, and complete work. The highest level of application is to apply knowledge to new and unpredictable solutions.

: Personal communication with personnel of the International Center for Leadership in Education, October 5, 2006. Reprinted with permission.

shifted from teacher-centered instruction in Quadrant A to student-centered learning. Quadrant D requires that students thoroughly understand the standard or benchmark being taught, but equally important, they must also understand and conceptualize relevant applications to the content being covered.

At the secondary level, career and technical education programs provide the most effective learning opportunities. Not only are students applying skills and knowledge to real-world situations in their CTE programs, but they are also drawing on knowledge learned in their core subjects. Students who participate in career and technical education programs should be well prepared for state exams because the academics they learn are used in Quadrants B and D. The goal is to link academics to core content areas. In this respect, career and technical education teachers can be a great asset to language arts, math, and science teachers by reinforcing the skills and concepts that students learn in those subjects (Daggett, 2005).

Rigor and relevance must be the cornerstones of career and technical education. CTE must not only be challenged with a rigorous curriculum, but that curriculum should also be presented in a relevant manner, engaging students in real-life situations. Career and technical education students must learn to apply knowledge if they are going to be successful in their future. Since change is the constant for our students' future, learning to apply knowledge in that changing world is the most important quality that schools can teach students. Although schools must continue to teach a rigorous curriculum, career and technical education must also teach students the relevance of education and make application of that rigorous curriculum a top priority. Thus, the responsibility of teachers is to provide students with active learning opportunities in exploring patterns, raising their own questions, and building their own models.

Career Clusters: A Plan of Education for a Global Economy

The Career Clusters Initiative began in 1996 in the United States as the Building Linkages Initiative, a collaborative effort between the U.S. Department of education, the Office of Vocational and Adult Education (OVAE), the National School-to-Work Office (NSTWO), and the National Skill Standards Board (NSSB). The purpose of the initiative was to establish linkages among state educational agencies, secondary and postsecondary educational institutions, employers, industry groups, other stakeholders, and federal agencies. The goal was to create curriculum frameworks in broad curriculum clusters, designed to prepare students to transition successfully from high school to postsecondary education and employment in a career area (*Federal Register*, 2000).

U.S. Department of Education Structure
of Career Clusters, Pathways, and Specialties

Career clusters are broad groupings of related careers representative of types of occupations in the world of work. There are 16 career clusters in the U.S. Department of Education model (Vocational Technical Education Consortium of States, 2000):

1. Agriculture, food, and natural resources
2. Architecture and construction
3. Arts, audio/video technology, and communications
4. Business, management, and administration
5. Education and training
6. Finance
7. Government and public administration
8. Health science
9. Hospitality and tourism
10. Human services
11. Information technology
12. Law, public safety, and security
13. Manufacturing
14. Marketing, sales, and service
15. Science, technology, engineering, and mathematics
16. Transportation, distribution, and logistics

In the U.S. Department of Education model, the 16 career clusters are linked to 74 more specific career pathways. (Examples include natural resources systems, construction, telecommunications, human resources, teaching/training, financial and investment planning, foreign service, travel and tourism, family and community services, network systems, legal services, production, and e-marketing.) A pathway level represents the more specific skill and knowledge, both academic and technical, necessary to pursue a full range of career opportunities within a pathway—ranging from entry level to management and including professional career specialties. Within the 74 career pathways, 1800 career specialists are defined. (Examples include bookkeeper, epidemiologist, marketing manager, and geoscientist.) The U.S. Department of Education career clusters framework is useful for connecting students with courses of study and careers via career assessment. It allows students to learn general, more transferable skills at the cluster level, with more specific skills and knowledge acquired at the career pathways and specialty levels (*Federal Register*, 2000).

Impact of Career Clusters on CTE

ACTE (2007) reported that career clusters are more likely to:

1. Provide a quality education system that integrates both academic and technical preparation.
2. Support the development of a new framework for CTE by promoting academic achievement.
3. Foster successful transitions from secondary to postsecondary education.
4. Assess students' skills and meet new accountability requirements in a more uniform and systematic manner.
5. Provide flexibility for states to implement the clusters based on their local labor market data.
6. Assist guidance counselors in developing individualized education plans for students.
7. Expose parents and students to various career options.

During a forum held at the National Dissemination Center for Career and Technical Education, Kim Green, executive director of the National Association of State Directors of Career Technical Consortium (cited in ACTE, 2007) remarked, "We now have a tool that anybody can use . . . to be able to look at their curriculum and decide whether or not they are meeting current needs of the economy, or whether or not they need to do some updating."

Career Clusters and the Global Economy

The National Association of Manufacturers (NAM) (2005) reported that manufacturers are taking business overseas because America is not producing the human capital to meet their projected needs. NAM (2005) further noted that the "skills gap" may be the most critical business issue facing the United States in the twenty-first century. Friedman (2006) attributes the "ambition gap" as a major indicator of the widening skills gap. Friedman's thesis is supported by a report published by the U.S. Department of Education, National Center of Education Statistics (2005), which suggests that American students do not demonstrate the same drive academically to achieve as do international students.

In a report titled "Toward a New Framework of Industry Programs for Vocational Education (as cited in Wonacott, 2001), Hoachlander suggests that CTE needs to prepare students to keep pace with changing technology and global economic trends. A new framework of CTE would feature (1) broad, long-term conception of work; (2) strengthened academic foundation; (3) strong secondary-postsecondary connections; and (4) emphasis on long-term careers beyond entry-level jobs.

In a career cluster, instruction initially begins at the foundation level so that learners are exposed to an entire industry and understand how different careers interact and rely on one another. Without knowledge of what careers really exist, students rely on their own perceptions as well as those of family and friends to help them choose a career (EPIC-MRA, 2002). According to Meeder (2006), there are several reasons why we need career clusters and pathways:

- In a global context, America's preparation system must be highly effective and efficient, accessible to students.
- As the pace of change quickens, CTE must emphasize flexible career preparation.
- Embedded college preparation options are more likely to appeal to a broad array of students.
- Opportunities are provided for students to master academic content by applying it to real-world contexts.
- Stronger personal motivation is created for students to complete high school and work toward academic achievement.

Impact of Globalization on Career and Technical Education in the Twenty-First Century

Since the early 1990s, the pace of change in the global economy has rapidly accelerated, giving rise to "flattening forces" that impact the economy (Friedman, 2006). T. L. Friedman's examples of the flattening of the world range from the widespread outsourcing of customer service of U.S. companies to the rising power and prevalence of bloggers and blog sites in the media. While at times a bit overstated, Friedman nonetheless argues convincingly that companies, businesses, and nations that fail to build bridges are more likely to be left behind in the growing global community. Friedman (2006, pp. 150–159) suggests that globalization has evolved through three distinctive stages:

- *Globalization 1.0* (1492–1800). This phase was about national power—how much a country had and how well that country deployed it. For example, Columbus was sent out to explore other regions and discovered not only that the world was round, but also that a whole "new world" existed. In this stage of globalization the "size" of the world changed from large to medium.
- *Globalization 2.0* (1800–2000). This phase was about multinational corporations "going global" for materials, markets and labor. Falling transportation and communications costs contributed to the ability of corporations to move into a worldwide arena.
- *Globalization 3.0* (2000–present). This phase marked the death of distance as a primary economic factor and the birth of the empowered individual.

According to Friedman (2006) and Yost (2006), there are ten flattening forces that made the world smaller and launched America and the world into a globalized economy:

1. *The fall of the Berlin Wall* in 1989 marked the beginning of a period when the free-market economy was the only mind-set left. Microsoft released Windows 3.0, the first version of Windows to make computing really attractive to the average user. This resulted in an explosion of computer purchasing.

2. *Netscape went public* in 1995. The personal computer became even more useful, in turn causing an explosion in demand for all things digital and sparking the Internet boom. This resulted in communication between more people than ever before in human history.

3. *Workflow software* (free), a communication program, became available to provide communication with other software. This allowed knowledge to be broken down, disseminated, and then reassembled by the most efficient producer in each step. Most important of all, workflow software created a platform for a global workforce of people and computers.

4. *Open sourcing* via The Internet browser, Fire Fox, enabled thousands of people worldwide to come together to create what they wanted in a browser versus depending on a corporation(s) to provide the service. The best result of open sourcing is a free product for worldwide use.

5. *The Y2K problem* loomed large and required a great deal of inexpensive brainpower to fix. This is where India came into play and marked the beginning of mass-scale outsourcing. Y2K was followed by the downfall of the Dot Coms. As a result, we have become interdependent with India in an effort to save operating costs.

6. *Offshoring* refers to the process where by entire companies began relocating outside of America. This meant that the developed world would move away from making anything labor intensive and toward more highly skilled occupations. However, it stimulated American production, and companies ended up exporting to themselves.

7. *Supply chaining* forced the adoption of common standards between companies, thereby encouraging global collaboration. Wal-Mart set the standard for supply chaining.

8. *Insourcing* is a partnership between companies, in which the partner company comes into another company, learns their processes, improves them, and then executes on their behalf. This allows small companies to act big and the big to act small. United Parcel Service, the premier pioneer of insourcing, worked with Toshiba to reduce the time required to turn service work around to the customer. This concept set the stage for other companies to develop the same services. Insourcing worked so well that more than 60 major U.S. companies now have moved their operations closer to the Louisville UPS hub.

9. *In-forming* is the individual's personal analog to open-sourcing, insourcing, supply chaining, and offshoring—the ability to build and deploy one's own personal supply chain of information, knowledge, and entertainment. In-forming enabled people to become their own self-directed and self-empowered researchers, editors, and selectors of entertainment, without having to go to the library or the movie theater. In-forming is searching for knowledge, seeking like-minded people and communities. Google's phenomenal global popularity shows how hungry people are for this form of self-collaboration. As a result of in-forming (using search engines), today's consumers are much more efficient and can find information, products, and services faster than through traditional means. People are better informed about issues related to work, health, and leisure.

10. *The steroids* are what Friedman refers to as items embraced globally (such as iPod, Burger King, cell phones, laptop computers, and all things digital, mobile, personal, and virtual) that amplify and turbo charge all the other flatteners.

Friedman (2006) argues that in 2000 a triple convergence was responsible for the final flattening of the world:

1. All ten flatteners came together.
2. China joined the World Trade Organization.
3. Corporations became addicted to India's less expensive workforce and began outsourcing to them at a rapidly increasing rate.

Globalization, as described by Friedman, provides firm evidence that America must look to career and technical education to prepare its workforce for the twenty-first century. Both students and workers must be aware of global conditions, developments and trends.

Summary

- The image of career and technical education is greatly enhanced when state-of-the art equipment is available for students to use when engaging in hands-on learning. Working with equipment that meets workplace standards and is used by industry workers not only improves the quality of learning, but is also perceived by students as being "cool" (Ries, 1998).

- Lack of accurate labor market information may cause students to overlook career and technical education because they believe that only a college degree will ensure employment success.

- Three groups that could have a positive role on image building are guidance counselors, student organizations, and local business representatives.

- The decline in standard forms of teacher certification and other factors may be signals of a career and technical education teacher shortage.

- Growth in high school enrollments, coupled with little change in overall percentage of CTE course taking among students, has resulted in an increased demand for career and technical education.

- The proportion of high schools seeking career and technical education teachers remained the same between 1991 and 2000. However, there are twenty-first-century indications that career and technical education vacancies are becoming difficult to fill.

- Using a constructivist approach, teachers facilitate learning by encouraging active inquiry, guiding learners to question their tacit assumptions, and coaching them in the knowledge construction process. This contrasts with the behavioralist approach that has dominated education, in which the teacher disseminates selected knowledge, measures learners' passive reception of facts, and focuses on behavior control and task completion. A constructivist teacher is more interested in uncovering meanings than covering prescribed material.

- For contextual teaching and learning approaches to be most effective in student learning, teachers must plan, implement, reflect upon, and revise lessons. To implement contextual teaching and learning, a variety of teaching approaches (problem-based learning, cooperative learning, project-based learning, service learning, and work-based learning) may be used.

- The Rigor/Relevance Framework requires a rigorous academic discipline for all students, but it is equally important that students understand and conceptualize relevant applications for each academic standard and benchmark being taught. Studies have shown that students understand and retain knowledge best when they have applied it in a practical, relevant setting. A teacher who relies solely on lecturing does not provide students with optimal learning opportunities.

- When implementing the Rigor/Relevance Framework in a classroom, it is important to develop assessments that measure "D quadrant" (adaptation) skills (Daggett, 2005). This enables students not only to gain knowledge but also to develop skills such as inquiry, investigation, and experimentation as well as learning how to use trial and error.

- Career clusters provide a way for schools to organize instruction and student experiences around 16 broad categories that encompass virtually all occupations from entry through professional levels. Clusters are designed to include the foundation, pathway, and specialty levels of knowledge and skills.

- Demographic developments will continue to make society, the marketplace, and the workforce more diverse in the future. If students are going to function efficiently in a world that is increasingly multicultural and globally linked, their education should help prepare them for this challenge.

Discussion Questions and Activities

1. Discuss some of the reasons why it can be very difficult to fill career and technical education teacher vacancies.
2. Debate the pros and cons of the following teaching and learning models of career and technical education:

    a. Behaviorism versus Constructivism

    b. Constructivism versus Contextual teaching and learning

3. For a number of years, marketing professionals have urged career and technical educators to get serious about image building. List at least 10 steps for marketing career and technical education.
4. How will an increasingly diverse student clientele and declining minority teacher population impact career/technical education, and what appropriate actions will need to be taken?
5. What recruitment and retention measures should be considered to attract and retain quality career/technical education teachers?

Research Activities

6. With the guidance of a professor/graduate teaching assistant, conduct small-scale research to determine the demand and supply of career and technical education teachers in your school district or state.
7. List and discuss at least five trends and issues impacting career and technical education in your school district or state.
8. Research the impact of selected pieces of legislation in the 1980s and 1990s on the development of career clusters.

Recommended Educational Media Resources

- *A teacher's culture*
- *Studies in constructivist teaching*
- *Creating the constructivist classroom*
- *Different kinds of smarts: Multiple intelligences*
- *Teaching to multiple intelligences*
- *The theory of multiple intelligences on the hands-on, test-free school* (DVD)
- *Learning styles*
- *Learning styles and the learning process* (DVD)

     Insight Media
     2162 Broadway
     New York, NY 10024-0621
     1-800-233-9910 or (212) 721-6316
     Web site: http://www.insight-media.com

References and Additional Reading

Association for Career and Technical Education (2006). *Reinventing the American high school for the 21st century*: A position paper. Alexandria, VA: Author.

———. (2007). Officials: *Career clusters foster link between CTE and academics*. Alexandria, WV: Author. Retrieved March 25, 2007, from http://www.acteonline.org.

Banks, J. A., Cookson, P., Gay, G., Hawley, W. D., Irvine, J. J., Neeto, S., Schofield, W. J., and Stephan, W. G. (2005). Education and diversity. *Social Education, 69*(1), 36–40.

Berns, R., and Erickson, P. (2001). An *interactive web-based system for the professional development of teachers in contextual teaching and learning*. Bowling Green, OH: Bowling Green State University.

Billet, S. (1996). Towards a model of workplace learning: The learning curriculum. *Studies in Continuing Education, 18*(1), 43–58.

Birkel, L. F. (2000). Multicultural education: It is education first of all. *The Teacher Educator, 36*(1), 22–28.

Bond, L. P. (2004). Using contextual instruction to make abstract learning concrete. *Techniques, 79*(1), 1–9. Retrieved October 9, 2006, from http://www.acteonline.org/members/techniques/Jan04_featured4.cjm.

Blank, W. (1999). Future perspectives in vocational education. In A. J. Pautler, Jr. (Ed.), *Workforce education: Issues for the new century* (pp. 281–289). Ann Arbor, MI: Prakken Publications.

Bringuier, J.-C. (1980). *Conversations with Piaget.* Chicago: Chicago University Press.

Brotherton, P. (2000). Diverse solutions. *Techniques, 75*(2), 18–21.

Bruening, T. H., Scanlon, D. C., Hodes, C., Dhital, P., Shao, X., and Liu, S. T. (2001). *The status of the career and technical education teacher preparation program*. University Park: National Research Center for Career and Technical Education, Pennsylvania State University.

Center on Education Policy/American Youth Policy Forum (2000). *Do you know the good news about American education?* Retrieved February 25, 2005, from http://www.ctredpol.org.

Daggett, W. R. (2005). *Achieving academic excellence through rigor and relevance*. Rexford, NY: International Center for Leadership in Education.

———. (n.d.). *Reforming American high school: Why, what, and how*. Rexford, NY: International Center for Leadership in Education.

Doolittle, P. E., and Camp, W. G. (1999). Constructivism: The career and technical education perspective. *Journal of Vocational and Technical Education, 16*(1), 23–46.

EPIC-MRA (2002). *Decisions without direction: Career guidance and decision-making among American youth*. Comprehensive report and data summary. Conducted for Ferris State University's Career Institute for Education and Workforce Development. Retrieved March 24, 2007, from http://www.ferris.edu/careerinstitute/report.pdf.

Federal Register (2000). Career clusters: Cooperative agreements. Vol. 65, No. 235 (December 6), 76523–76543.

Friedman, T. L. (2006). *The world is flat: A brief history of the twenty-first century.* New York: Farrar, Straus and Giroux.

Gardner, H. (2006). *Multiple intelligences: New horizons.* New York: Basic Books.

Goodlad, J. (1990). *Teachers for our nation's schools.* San Francisco, CA: Jossey-Bass.

Gordon, H. R. D., and Yocke, R. J. (2005). Analysis of productivity and learning style preferences of beginning and experienced career and technical teachers in West Virginia. *Workforce Education Forum, 32*(1), 1–19.

Gray, Kenneth (2004, October). Is high school career and technical education obsolete? *Phi Delta Kappan, 86*(2), 128–134.

Gray, Michael, and Daugherty, Michael (2004, Spring). Factors that influence students to enroll in technology education programs. *Journal of Technology Education, 15*(2), 5–19.

Green, J., and Winters, M. (2005). *Public high school graduation and college-readiness rates, 1991–2002*: Education working paper. New York: Center for Civic Innovation at the Manhattan Institute.

Henson, Kenneth T. (2006). *Curriculum planning: Integrating multiculturalism, constructivism, and education reform*, 3rd ed. Long Grove, IL: Waveland Press.

Hull, D. (2003). Redefining career and technical education: Seizing a unique opportunity to help the "neglected majority" become world-class students, workers and citizens. *Techniques, 78*(5), 30–36.

Hyslop-Margison, E. J. (2001, Spring). An assessment of the historical arguments in vocational education reform. *Journal of Career and Technical Education, 17*(1), 23–30.

International Center for Leadership in Education (n.d.). *Rigor and relevance for all students: Rigor/relevance framework*. Retrieved October 5, 2006, from http://www.leadered.com/rigor.html.

Kolb, D. (1984). *Experiential learning: Experience as the source of learning and development*. Upper Saddle River, NJ: Prentice Hall.

Levesque, K. (2004). *Teacher quality in vocational education*. A report prepared by MPR Associates for the National Assessment of Vocational Education. Washington, DC: U.S. Department of Education, Office of the Under Secretary.

Lewis, M. V. (2001). *Major needs of career and technical education in the year 2000: Views from the field*. Columbus: National Dissemination Center for Career and Technical Education, The Ohio State University.

Lynch, R. L. (1997). *Designing vocational and technical education for the 21st century*. Columbus, OH: ERIC Clearinghouse on Adult, Career, and Vocational Education.

Meeder, H. (2006). *Globalization 3.0: Why career clusters matter more than ever!* Adel, IA: Visions Unlimited.

National Association of Manufacturers (2005). *2005 skills gap report: A survey of American manufacturing workforce*. Washington, DC: Author.

National Center for Education Statistics (2002). *The condition of education*. Washington, DC: Author.

National Commission on Excellence in Education (1983). *A nation at risk: The imperative for school reform*. Washington, DC: U.S. Government Printing Office.

National Council for Accreditation of Teacher Education (2002). *Professional standards for the accreditation of schools, colleges, and departments of education*. Washington, DC: Author.

Parnell, D. (1996). Cerebral context. *Vocational Education Journal, 71*(5), 33–35, 60.

Piaget, J. (1950). *The psychology of intelligence*. New York: Routledge.

Ries, E. (1998). At the table and in the mix: Making education and career connections. *Techniques, 73*(7), 14–17.

Ruhland, S. K., and Bremer, C. D. (2002). *Alternative teacher certification procedures and professional development opportunities for career and technical education teachers*. St. Paul: National Research Center for Career and Technical Education, University of Minnesota.

Sabo, S. R. (2000). Diversity at work. *Techniques, 75*(2), 26–28.

Shure, J. L. (2001). Minority teachers are few and far between. *Techniques, 76*(5), 32.

Sleeter, C. E., and Grant, C. A. (2007). *Making choices for multicultural education*: *Five approaches to race, class, and gender*, 4th ed. New York: Maxwell Macmillan.

Stasz, C., and Bodilly, S. (2004). *Efforts to improve the quality of vocational education in secondary schools*: Impact of federal and state policies. Santa Monica, CA: RAND.

Thomas, R. R., Jr. (1996). *Redefining diversity*. New York: AMACOM.

Triandis, H. C., Kurowski, L. L., and Gelband, M. J. (1994). Workplace diversity. In H.C. Triandis and M. Dunnett (Eds.), *Handbook of industrial organizational psychology* (pp.770–827). Palo Alto, CA: Consulting Psychologists Press.

U.S. Department of Education (2004). *National assessment of vocational education: Final report to Congress*. Washington, DC: Office of the Under Secretary, Policy and Program Studies Service.

———. (2005). *Trends in international mathematics science study 2003*. Washington, DC: USDOE, National Center for Education Statistics.

Vocational Technical Education Consortium of States (2000). *V-TECS career cluster frameworks*. ERIC Document Reproduction Service, No. ED 454–384.

Wakefield, D., Talbert, B. A., and Pense, S. (2006). A descriptive study on the preparation of student teachers to work with diverse populations. *Online Journal for Workforce Education and Development* (5), 1–12. Retrieved October 20, 2006, from http://wed.siu.edu/Journal/volInum5/diverse_populations.htm.

Wardlow, G. E., and Scott, F. (2000). Beliefs about a constructivist model for teaching compared with traditional teaching methods among teacher education students. Proceedings of the 27th National Agricultural Education Research Conference, San Diego, CA, pp. 626–637.

Wonacott, M. E. (2001). Career clusters. *The Highlight Zone: Research @ Work,* no. 6. Columbus: National Dissemination Center for Career and Technical Education, The Ohio State University.

Yost, D. M. (2006, Fall). *Career and technical education in the twenty-first century*. (Available from the Department of Adult and Technical Education, Marshall University, Huntington, WV 25755).

Appendix A
European-American Evolution of Vocational Education

1802	Factory Act (England) required instruction for apprentices and limited children's hours of labor
1806	Lancastrian Schools, New York City
1820–1876	Mechanics Institutes (America)
1820	Common Schools (elementary)
1820	Boston Apprentices' Library
1821	First high school (Boston)
1827	Christian Brothers combine general and technical instruction
1827	Lyceum movement begins in United States
1832	School Workshops, France (Cesar Fichet)
1836	Lowell Institute (Massachusetts)
1846	Associations formed to extend instruction in Sloyd, Sweden
1847	Sheffield Scientific School at Yale
1857	N.E.A. is organized
1860	First U.S. Kindergarten (Froebel)
1862–1890	Land-Grant College Act (Morrill Act)
1865	Imperial Technical School, Russia (Della Vos). Large-group instruction to speed up training of apprentices
1868–1906	Rise of Trade Schools in France, England, Germany, America
1871	Opening of "The Whittling School" in Boston
1873	First free manual training school—Salicis Manual Training School, France (Gustave Salicis)
1876	Manual training introduced to high schools, Philadelphia
1876	Introduction of Manual Arts and Arts and Crafts
1876	Boston School of Mechanical Arts (Runkle)
1880	First manual training school in St. Louis (Woodward—"put the whole boy in school")
1881	New York Trade School
1882	Sloyd School in Naas, Sweden, entirely for teacher training
1884	First public high school for manual training in Baltimore
1884	Industrial Education Association formed in New York City

1887	Hatch Act, providing federal funds for support of agricultural experiment stations
1888	Sloyd Association of Great Britain and Ireland formed. A system of manual training developed from a Swedish system included use of tools.
1893	Manual training school, Boston—first public-supported manual training school
1898	Technical high school established at Springfield, Massachusetts
1902	First Junior College in United States—Joliet, Illinois
1903	Term "Manual Arts" introduced at N.E.A. convention
1906	Massachusetts Commission on Industrial Education reports, state aid given for industrial education courses
1906	National Society for the Promotion of Industrial Education formed in New York City (Beginning of Industrial Education)
1907	Wisconsin adopts vocational education.
1908	New York adopts vocational education.
1908	Beginning of cooperative education with formation of cooperative schools
1908	Beginning of formalized vocational guidance (Frank Parsons and Jim Brewer), Vocational Bureau and Breadwinners Institute opened in Boston
1909	First Junior High School, Berkeley, California
1912	N.S.P.I.E. promotes state and national legislation for vocational education (Prosser)
1913	Bonser proposes that industrial arts is both a subject and a method (*School Arts Magazine*)
1914	Smith-Lever Bill passed aid to agricultural education
1914	European involvement in World War I
1917	First Federal Publication of Policies for Vocational Education
1917	Russian Revolution
1917	U.S. involvement in World War I

Appendix B
Quotations of Booker T. Washington

Any movement for elevation of the Southern Negro in order to be successful must have to a certain extent the cooperation of the Southern white.

We shall prosper in proportion as we learn to glorify and dignify labor and put brains and skill into the common occupations of life. It is at the bottom of life that we must begin and not at the top; nor should we permit our grievances to overshadow our opportunities.

An educated man on the street with his hands in his pockets is not one whit [sic] more benefit to society than an ignorant man on the streets with his hands in his pockets.

I have learned that it is important to carry education outside of the school building and take it into the fields, into homes, and into the daily life of the people surrounding the school.

The Negro should be taught book learning, yes, but along with it he should be taught that book education and industrial development must go hand in hand. No race which fails to do this can ever hope to succeed.

There is as much dignity in tilling a field as in writing a poem.

Learn all you can, but learn to do something, or your learning will be useless.

It seems to me that the temptation in education and missionary effort is to do for people that which was done a thousand years ago, or is being done for people a thousand miles away, without always making a careful study of the needs and conditions of the people we are trying to help. The temptation is to run all people through a certain educational mold, regardless of the condition of the subject or the end to be accomplished.

One of the weakest points in connection with the present development of the race is that so many get the idea that the mere filling of the head with a knowledge of mathematics, the sciences, and literature means success in life.

Is there not as much mental discipline in having a student think out and put on paper a plan for a modern dairy building as having him merely commit to memory poetry that somebody else thought out years ago?

The great thing for us as a race is to conduct ourselves so as to become worthy of the privileges of an American citizen, and these privileges will come. More important than receiving privileges is the matter of being worthy of them. Nobody likes to come in contact with a whining individual and nobody likes to be connected with a whining, despairing race.

When people, regardless of race or geographical location, have not been trained to habits of industry, have not been given skill of hand in youth and taught to love labor, a direct result is the breeding of a worthless, idle class, which spends a great deal of its time trying to live by its wits.

So long as the Negro is permitted to get education, acquire property, and secure employment, and is treated with respect in the business or commercial world, I shall have the greatest faith in his working out his own destiny in our Southern states.

The foundation of every race must be laid in the common everyday occupations that are right about our door.

A man's position in life is not measured by the heights which he has attained, but by the depths from which he has come.

We shall succeed not by abstract discussions, not by depending upon making empty demands, not by abuse of some other individual or race, but we will succeed by actually demonstrating to the world that we can perform the service which the world needs, as well or better than anyone else.

There are definite rewards coming to the individual or the race that overcomes obstacles and succeeds in spite of seemingly insurmountable difficulties. The palms of victory are not for the race that merely complains and frets and rails.

The colored boy has been taken from the farm and taught astronomy— how to locate Jupiter and Mars—learned to measure Venus, taught about everything except that which he depends upon for daily bread.

One of the saddest sights I ever saw in the South was a colored girl, recently returned from college, sitting in a rented one-room log cabin attempting day by day to extract some music from a second-hand piano, when all about her indicated want of thrift and cleanliness.

Source: Moore, G. E. (1993). *An informal conversation with Booker T. Washington and W.E.B. DuBois*. Raleigh: North Carolina State University, University Council for Vocational Education.

Appendix C
Charles Prosser's Sixteen Theorems

1. Vocational education should occur in the most realistic setting that replicates the work environment.
2. Vocational education should only be given where the training jobs are carried on in the same way, with the same tools, and with the same machines as in the occupation itself.
3. Vocational education should provide students with thinking habits—technical knowledge and scientific problem-solving skills—and the manipulative skills required in the occupation itself.
4. Vocational education should be planned and delivered in a manner that capitalizes on the student's interest, aptitudes, and intrinsic intelligence to the highest degree.
5. Vocational education is not for everyone, but for those individuals who need it, want it, and are able to profit from it.
6. Vocational education should provide opportunities for students to repeat operations of thinking and manipulative skills until habits are formed characteristic of those required for gainful employment.
7. Vocational education should be taught by instructors who have successful experience in the application of skills and knowledge required of competent workers.
8. For every occupation there is a minimum of productive ability which an individual must possess in order to secure or retain employment in that occupation.
9. Vocational education should prepare individuals for the occupations as they currently exist in the workforce and for future labor markets as a secondary concern.
10. Vocational education should provide opportunities for students to perform operations on actual jobs and not only simulated work tasks.
11. The only reliable source of content for specific training in an occupation is in the experiences of masters of the occupation.

12. For every occupation there is a body of content which is peculiar to that occupation and which practically has no functioning value in any other occupation.

13. Vocational education should meet the needs of individuals when it is needed and in such a way that they can benefit from it.

14. Vocational education is more effective when its methods of instruction are best suited to the particular characteristics of any particular group which it serves.

15. The administration of vocational education should be as efficient in proportion as it is elastic, and fluid rather than rigid and standardized.

16. While every reasonable effort should be made to reduce per capita cost, there is a minimum level at which effective vocational education cannot be given, and if the course does not permit this minimum of per capita cost, vocational education should not be attempted.

Source: Prosser, C. A., and Allen, C. R. (1925). *Vocational education in a democracy*. New York: Century Company.

Appendix D
School-to-Work Opportunities and the Fair Labor Standards Act

Exhibit 1. Standards for 16- and 17-Year-Olds

The following standards apply to 16- and 17-year-old youths employed in nonfarm jobs.

Hours Limitations

- None under FLSA: Federal law does not limit either the number of hours nor the time of day that the youth 16 years of age and older may work.
- Some state laws do restrict the hours that 16- and 17-year-olds may work.

Occupation Limitations

Minors may perform all work except in 17 occupations considered too hazardous for all youth under the age of 18. The Hazardous Occupations Orders (HOs) are:

HO1   Manufacturing and storing explosives;

HO2   Motor-vehicle driving and outside helper, including driving motor vehicles or working as outside helpers on motor vehicles or driving as part of any occupation;

HO3   Coal mining;

HO4   Logging and sawmilling;

HO5*   Work using power-driven woodworking machines, including the use of saws on construction sites;

HO6   Work where exposed to radioactive substances;

HO7   Work involving the operation of power-driven hoisting devices, including the use of fork lifts, cranes and nonautomatic elevators;

HO8*   Work using power-driven metal forming, punching, and shearing machines (but HO8 permits the use of a large group of machine tools used on metal, including lathes, turning machines, milling machines, grinding, boring machines and planing machines);

HO9   All mining other than coal mining, including work at gravel pits;

HO10*   Work involving slaughtering or meatpacking, processing, or rendering, including the operation of power-driven meat slicers in retail stores;

HO11   Work involving the operation of power-driven bakery machines;

HO12*   Work using power-driven paper-products machines, including the operation and loading of paper balers in grocery stores;

HO13   Work in manufacturing of brick, tile and kindred products;

HO14*   Work involving the use of circular saws, band saws, and guillotine shears;

HO15   All work in involving wrecking, demolition and ship-breaking;

HO16*   All work in roofing operations; and

HO17*   All work in excavating, including work in a trench as a plumber.

Exceptions to Occupation Limitations

Special Provisions for Student-Learners and Apprentices—The seven HOs identified with an asterisk permit the employment of apprentices and student-learners in vocational education programs under certain conditions. Student-learners in STW programs will meet the student-learner exemption if the student is employed under a written agreement which provides that:

1. All hazardous work will be performed under the direct and close supervision of a qualified and experienced person;

2. Safety instructions will be given by the school and reinforced by the employer with on-the-job training;

3. The job training follows a schedule which reflects organized and progressive skill developments; and

4. The work in the hazardous occupation is intermittent and for short periods of time and is under the direct and close supervision of a journeyman as a necessary part of such apprenticeship training.

The written agreement must be signed by the employer and placement coordinator (or school principal). Copies of the agreement must be kept on file by both the school and the employer.

Note: To qualify as an apprentice, one must obtain the appropriate certificate from the local U.S. Department of Labor Bureau of Apprenticeship and Training (BAT) office, or a state office approved by BAT.

Exhibit 2. Standards for 14- and 15-Year-Olds

The following standards apply to 14- and 15-year-old youths employed in nonfarm jobs.

Hours Limitations

The hours 14- and 15-year-olds may work are limited to:

- outside school hours,
- no more than 3 hours on a school day,
- no more than 18 hours in a school week,
- no more that 8 hours on a nonschool day,
- no more than 40 hours in nonschool weeks,
- between 7 AM and 7 PM (between June 1 and Labor Day they may work as late as 9 PM).

Occupation Limitations

In addition to the Hazardous Occupations listed in Exhibit 1 that are prohibited for minors under the age of 18, 14- and 15-year-olds may not work in the following occupations:

- cooking, other than at lunch counters and snack bars, and within the view of the customer;
- manufacturing, mining, processing;
- most transportation jobs;
- most jobs in warehouses and workrooms;
- construction jobs, except in the office;
- any job involving hoists, conveyor belts, power-driven lawn mowers, and other power-driven machinery.

No Exceptions to Occupation Limitations

Occupation limitations are strictly enforced for 14- and 15-year-old youths, with no exceptions. The student-learner provisions applicable to some Hazardous Occupations for youths 16 and 17 years of age (as listed in Exhibit l) do not apply to minors under the age of 16.

Exhibit 3. Special Provisions for 14- and 15-Year-Olds under WECEP

The Work Experience and Career Exploration Program (WECEP) includes special provisions that permit 14- and 15-year-old STW enrollees to be employed during school hours and in occupations otherwise prohibited by regulation.

WECEP is designed to provide a carefully planned work experience and career exploration program for 14- and 15-year-old youths, including youths in STW programs, who can benefit from a career-oriented educational program. WECEP is designed to meet the participants' needs, interests, and abilities. Among other things, the program helps dropout-prone youths to become reoriented and motivated toward education and helps to prepare them for the world of work.

A state education agency with a school-to-work program may obtain approval from the Department of Labor for STW enrollees participating in WECEP to be employed:

- up to 3 hours on a school day,
- up to 23 hours during a school week,
- any time during school hours,
- under variances granted by the Wage and Hour Administrator that permit employment of WECEP participants in otherwise prohibited activities and occupations.*

Any representative of the Governor who is interested in establishing a WECEP may forward a letter of application to the Administrator of the Wage and Hour Division, U.S. Department of Labor, Room 53502, 200 Constitution Avenue, N.W., Washington, DC 20210. The provisions for WECEP are set by Regulations 29 CFR Part 570.35a. Approval to operate a WECEP is granted by the Administrator of the Wage and Hour Division for a two-year period.

Note: The Regulations do not permit issuance of WECEP variances in manufacturing, mining, or in any of the 17 hazardous occupations orders listed in Exhibit 1.

Exhibit 4. Standards for Farm Jobs

The following standards apply to minors employed in farm jobs.

Hours Limitations

- Minors 16 years old may be employed in any farm job at any time.
- Fourteen- and fifteen-year-old farm workers may be employed outside school hours in any occupation not declared hazardous. Children who move from a school district where schools have closed for summer vacation and live in another district where the schools are still in session may work during the hours that the school is in session in the new district. After May 15, it is assumed that school is closed for the summer.
- With written parental consent, 12- and 13-year-olds may be employed outside school hours in any nonhazardous job on the same farm where their parents are employed.
- Minors under 12 years of age may be employed outside school hours in any nonhazardous job with written parental consent but only on farms not subject to the minimum wage provisions of FLSA.
- Minors of any age may perform work at any time on a farm owned or operated by the minor's parents or persons standing in place of the parents.

Occupation Limitations

- Once teenagers reach age 14, they may perform the same agricultural work as an adult except occupations that involve the agricultural hazardous occupations orders.
- Agricultural hazardous occupations orders apply to minors under age 16. These orders are listed in Child Labor Bulletin 102—The Child Labor Requirements in Agriculture under the Fair Labor Standards Act.

Exemptions

Exemptions from the agricultural hazardous occupations orders applicable to tractors and certain other farm machinery apply to 14- and 15-year-old student-learners enrolled in vocational education programs and holders of certificates of completion of training under 4-H programs.

Source: Adapted from U.S. Departments of Education and Labor. (1995). *School-to-work opportunities: Work-based learning and the fair labor standards act.* 1st ed. Washington, DC: Authors.

Recommended Educational Video

- *Lost futures: The problem of child labor*
  American Federation of Teachers
  555 New Jersey Avenue, NW
  Washington, DC 20001-2079
  (202) 879-4400
  Web site: http://www.aft.org

Appendix E
Time Line of Federal Vocational/CTE Legislation

1917   The **Smith-Hughes Act** (P.L. 64-347) was the first vocational education act for high schools. Federal money for training in agriculture, home economics, trades, industry, and teacher training.

1918   The **Smith-Sears Act** (P.L. 65-178) provided federal funds for establishing retraining programs for World War I veterans.

Commission on Reorganization of Secondary Education issues its famous "**Cardinal Principles of Secondary Education**": health, command of fundamental processes, worthy home membership, development of a vocation, civic education, worthy use of leisure time, and ethical character.

1920   The **Vocational Rehabilitation Act.** (P.L. 66-236) Training for handicapped persons.

The **Smith-Bankhead Act** (P.L. 66-236) authorized grants for vocational rehabilitation programs.

1923   **Gordon Bonser** advocated the inclusion of industrial arts into the elementary school with a study of manufacturing industries as the curriculum base, with the goal of developing an understanding of the functioning of our industrial society. Industrial arts was to be a general education subject desirable for all to take.

1925   Federal vocational education programs extended to territory of Hawaii (P.L. 68-35).

1926   The **American Vocational Association** was formed out of the merger of the National Society for Vocational Education (formerly NSPIE) and the Vocational Association of the Middle West.

Vocational enrollment exceeded 850,000; states received $7.2 million for programs.

1929   The **George-Reed Act** (P.L. 70-702) expanded vocational education in agriculture and home economics.

1934   The **George-Ellzey Act** (P.L. 73-245) increased supplemental funding for agriculture, home economics, and trade and industrial education programs authorized by the Smith-Hughes Act of 1917.

1935   The **Bankhead Jones Act** (P.L. 74-182) authorized grants to states for agriculture experiment stations.

The **Social Security Act** (P.L. 74-271) provided vocational training for handicapped persons.

The **National Youth Administration** provided vocational training and employment.

The **Works Project Administration and Public Works Administration** provided vocational training, employment, and work relief.

1936   The **George-Deen Act** (P.L. 74-673) authorized an annual allotment of $12 million for agriculture, home economics, and trade and industrial education. Marketing occupations were recognized for the first time, and $1.2 million was authorized for them annually.

1938   The Civil Aeronautics Authority sponsored vocational training for pilots.

1940–   A series of ten **Vocational Education for National Defense Acts**
1946   (P.L. 78-156, P.L. 78-248, P.L. 78-338) were passed as war emergency measures to provide for vocational education programs to prepare war industry workers.

1944   The **Serviceman's Readjustment Act** ("GI Bill") (P.L. 78-346) provided vocational education opportunities for veterans.

1946   The **George-Barden Act** (P.L. 79-586) authorized an appropriation of $28.5 million annually for the further development of vocational education. It is also known as the Vocational Education Act of 1946. It replaced the George-Deen Act of 1936.

1950   Federal vocational education program extended to the Virgin Islands (P.L. 81-462).

1956   The **Health Amendments Act** (P.L. 84-911) added practical nursing and health occupation programs to the list of vocational programs eligible to receive federal funds.

Federal vocational education programs extended to Guam (P.L. 84-896).

The **George-Barden Act Fishing Amendment** (P.L. 84-911) provided vocational education training in fishing trades, industry, and distributive occupations.

1958   The **National Defense Education Act** (NDEA) (P.L. 85-864) provided funds to support technical programs.

1961   The **Area Redevelopment Act** (P.L. 82-27) was an emergency measure born out of a recession, which authorized $4.5 million annually to be used for vocational education until 1965. It recognized the critical need for training due to unemployment and underemployment in economically distressed areas.

1962   The **Manpower Development and Training Act** (MDTA) (P.L. 87-415) authorized funds for training and retraining of unemployed and underemployed adults.

1963   The **Health Professions Educational Assistance Act** (P.L. 88-129) provided federal funds to expand teaching facilities for health programs and for loans to students preparing for the health professions.

The **Vocational Education Act** (P.L. 88-210) for the first time mandated that vocational education meet the needs of individual students, not just the employment needs of industry. Its major purposes were to maintain, extend, and improve existing programs of vocational education and to provide part-time employment for young people who needed the earnings from such employment to continue their schooling on a full-time basis.

The **Higher Education Facilities Act** (P.L. 88-204) authorized a five-year program of federal grants and loans to colleges and universities for the expansion and development of physical facilities.

1964   The **Civil Rights Act** (P.L. 88-352) established basic human rights and responsibilities in the workplace and prohibited discrimination on the basis of race, gender, national origin, or handicap. Other issues addressed equal employment opportunities, voting rights, equal education, fair housing, and public accommodation.

The **Economic Opportunity Act** (P.L. 88-452) authorized grants for college work-study programs for students of low-income families; established a Job Corps program and authorized support for work-training programs to provide education and vocational training and work experience for unemployed youth; provided training and work experience opportunities in welfare programs; authorized support of education and training activities and of community action programs including Head Start, Follow Through, Upward Bound; authorized the establishment of the Volunteers in Service to America (VISTA).

1965   **Appalachian Regional Development Act** (P.L. 89-4). The purpose of this act was to provide public works, economic development programs, and the planning and coordination needed to assist in the development of the Appalachian region.

Higher Education Act of 1965 (P.L. 89-329) provided grants for university community service programs, college library assistance, library training and research; for strengthening developing institutions and teacher training programs; and for undergraduate instructional equipment. Authorized insured student loans, established a National Teacher Corps, and provided for graduate teacher training fellowships.

1967   The **Educational Professions Development Act** (P.L. 90-35) provided federal funds to address the training of teachers in critical shortage areas and provided fellowships for teachers and other educational professionals. This act was instrumental in providing a vital source of college and university vocational teacher educators.

1968   The **Vocational Amendments** (P.L. 90-576) broadened the definition of vocational education to bring it closer to general education and provided vast sums of money to address the nation's social and economic problems. The act established a National Advisory Committee, expanded vocational education services to meet the needs of disadvantaged students, and established methods of collecting and disseminating information about vocational education. This act placed more emphasis on vocational programs at the postsecondary level. It also added cooperative education as one of the vocational education programs eligible to receive federal funds.

1971   The **Nurse Training Act** (P.L. 92-158) increased and expanded provisions for nurse training facilities.

1972   The **Education Amendments** (P.L. 92-318) established a National Institute of Education; general aid for institutions of high education; federal matching grants for state student incentive grants; a National Commission on Financing Postsecondary Education; state advisory councils on community colleges; a Bureau of Occupational and Adult Education; state grants for the design, establishment, and conduct of postsecondary occupational education; and a bureau-level Office of Indian Education.

1973   The **Comprehensive Employment and Training Act** (CETA) (P.L. 93-203) intended to continue the goals of the previous MDTA legislation plus expand the previous services MDTA made available. It recognized the high unemployment level at that time, the increasing number of welfare recipients, the increasing number of economically disadvantaged rural and urban communities with hardcore unemployed, the significantly large number of youth unable to find part-time or full-time employment, and the increasing number of people in minority groups who were unskilled and unemployed.

1974   The **Education Amendments** (P.L. 93-380) encouraged the development of individualized education plans (IEPs) for children with special needs participating in Title I of the 1965 Elementary and Secondary Education Act (ESEA). These amendments also included the Women's Educational Equality Act of 1974, which was designed to assist states in bringing about educational equity for women. Other important provisions of these amendments included support for career education, establishment of the National Center for Educational Statistics, and research into the problems of providing bilingual education.

1975   The **Education of All Handicapped Children Act of 1975** (P.L. 94-142) launched an organized effort to provide a free and appropriate education for all handicapped children ages 3–21. This act spelled out the assurances for handicapped youngsters including due process, written individualized education plans, bias-free testing and assessment, and measures to protect the confidentiality of records. In addition, a number of terms related to handicapped individuals were clearly defined. This act provided a number of grants to states and local school systems to improve vocational education and related services for handicapped individuals.

1976   The **Educational Amendments** (P.L. 94-482) continued the trend of omnibus legislation to extend and revise previous legislation and to redirect American education in an attempt to correct some of the nation's problems, including changing the public's attitude toward the roles of men and women in society. This act required the development of programs to eliminate sex discrimination and sex stereotyping. It also required the development of a national vocational education data-reporting and accounting system and required states to develop an evaluation system.

1978   The **Career Education Act** (P.L. 95-207) established the comprehensive career development concept, which viewed the individual as progressing through various planned experiences, a series of dimensions that total a complete cycle. These dimensions begin with career awareness at an early age, add employability skills, and end with educational awareness.

The **Comprehensive Employment and Training Amendments of 1978** (P.L. 95-524) provided for continuation of the Comprehensive Employment and Training Act of 1973 and the Manpower Development and Training Act of 1962. Ensured coordination and cooperation among all federal, state, and local private and public agencies involved in the vocational education and training of workers.

1982   The **Job Training Partnership Act** (JTPA) (P.L. 97-300) replaced CETA and enlarged the role of state governments and private industry in federal job training programs, imposed performance standards, limited support services, and created a new program of retraining for displaced workers.

1984   The **Carl D. Perkins Vocational Education Act** (P.L. 98-524) amended the Vocational Education Act of 1963 and replaced the amendments of 1968 and 1976. It changed the emphasis of federal funding in vocational education from primarily expansion to program improvement and at-risk populations.

1990   The **Carl D. Perkins Vocational and Applied Technology Education Act** (P.L. 101-392) amended and extended the previous 1984 Perkins Act. The intent of this act was to assist states and local school systems in teaching the skills and competencies necessary to work in a technologically advanced society for all students. A major goal of this legislation was to provide greater vocational opportunities to disadvantaged individuals. The act provided funds for the integration of academic and vocational education and the tech prep programs, and articulated programs between high schools and postsecondary institutions. The act eliminated set-asides for support services for special populations, giving states and local agencies greater flexibility in how funds are best used to serve special populations.

1992   The **Job Training Reform Amendments** (P.L. 101-367) revised the JTPA of 1982 to change the focus of manpower programs toward improving services to those facing serious barriers to employment, enhancing the quality of services provided, improving accountability of funds and the programs they serve, linking services provided to real labor-market needs, and facilitating the development of a comprehensive and coherent system of human resource services. One of the new provisions of special interest to vocational educators was the requirement for on-the-job training contracts and the development of individual service strategies (ISSs), an individualized employability development plan for each JPTA participant. This act is devoted to serving special populations who face the greatest employment barriers.

1993   Family and Consumer Science became the new name for home economics education.

1994   The **Goals 2000: Educate America Act** (P.L. 103-227) was a blueprint for improving America's schools through the establishment of eight national goals and the development of voluntary academic and skill standards to assist state and local agencies in helping every child meet criteria to ensure that youngsters are learning what they need to learn in order to function as a family member, involved community member, and competent worker. The act identified ten elements that constitute a suggested framework for developing a local Goals 2000 Plan.

The **Improving America's School Act** (P.L. 103-382) was a reauthorization of the Elementary and Secondary Education Act (ESEA) of 1965, which placed primary emphasis on serving disadvantaged students. The major goal of Title I has been revised to improve the teaching and learning of children in high-poverty schools to enable them to meet the challenging academic and performance standards being established by the Goals 2000 Act. This act increased opportunities for vocational and applied technology education to provide input into state and local educational plans and strengthened vocational and applied technology education in fourteen different areas.

The **School-to-Work Opportunities Act** (STWOA) (P.L. 101-239) provided a framework to build a high-quality, skilled workforce for our nation's economy through partnerships between educators and employers. This act emphasized preparing students with the knowledge, skills, abilities, and information about occupations and the labor market that facilitated the transition from school to continuing education and work. Key elements of this act included collaborative partnerships, integrated curriculum, technological advances, adaptable workers, comprehensive career guidance, work-based learning, and a step-by-step approach.

1997   **The Individuals with Disabilities Education Act Amendments** (P.L. 105-17) were designed to ensure that all children with disabilities have access to free appropriate public education that emphasized special education and services to meet their unique needs. There were three major changes that distinguished IDEA '97 from the previous version:

1. General education teachers could participate in the Individualized Education Program (IEP).
2. Schools had greater flexibility in disciplining special needs students.
3. There was greater emphasis on integrating special needs students into the general education curriculum.

1998   The **Workforce Investment Act** (P.L. 105-220) provided the framework for a unique national workforce preparation system designed to meet the needs of both the nation's businesses and job seekers, and those who wanted to further their careers.

1998   The **Carl D. Perkins Vocational and Technical Education Act of 1998** (P.L. 105-332) consisted of two major focus areas. The first area was to increase accountability and provide states with more flexibility to use funds. The second area emphasized the use of technology in vocational-technical education and made a commitment to professional development. A separate authorization and funding stream for Tech Prep was provided in the law, in a manner similar to the previous Perkins Act.

2001   The **No Child Left Behind Act/ESEA** (P.L. 105-110). The Elementary and Secondary Education Act (ESEA), renamed the No Child Left Behind (NCLB) Act of 2001, established laudable goals—high standards and accountability for learning of all children, regardless of their background and ability.

2004   The **Individuals with Disabilities Education Act (IDEA)** (P.L. 108-446) was authorized on December 3, 2004. IDEA is a critical federal investment in the future of our nation by ensuring that all students with disabilities have access to a free appropriate public education in the least restrictive environment. This law provides a framework for school systems across the nation to use in delivering individualized education programs. The Association for Career and Technical Education identified four key areas in IDEA that are of particular importance to career and technical educators: a greater focus on the importance of comprehensive transition planning, authorization of more funding, cutting the paperwork burden for teachers, and a compromise on discipline provisions.

2006   The **Carl D. Perkins Career and Technical Education Improvement Act** (Also known as Perkins IV). (P.L. 109-270) The law includes three top priorities: using the term *career and technical education* instead of *vocational education*, maintaining the Tech Prep program as a separate federal funding stream within the legislation, and maintaining state administrative funding at 5 percent of a state's allocation. The law also includes specific requirements for "programs of study" that link academic and technical content across secondary and postsecondary education, and strengthened local accountability provisions that will ensure continuous program improvement. The Perkins Act provides almost $1.3 billion in federal support for CTE programs in all 50 states. The law will extend through 2012.

Appendix F
Fastest-Growing Occupations and Occupations Projected to Have the Largest Numerical Increases in Employment between 2004 and 2014*

Education of training level	Fastest-Growing Occupations	Occupations Having the Largest Numerical Job Growth
First professional degree	Pharmacists Physicians and surgeons Chiropractors Optometrists Veterinarians	Physicians and surgeons Lawyers Pharmacists Veterinarians Chiropractors
Doctoral degree	Medical scientists, except epidemiologists Postsecondary teachers Computer and information scientists, research Biochemists and biophysicists Clinical, counseling, and school psychologists	Postsecondary teachers Clinical, counseling, and school psychologists Medical scientists, except epidemiologists Computer and information scientists, research Biochemists and biophysicists
Master's degree	Physical therapists Occupational therapists Hydrologists Substance-abuse and behavioral-disorders counselors Instructional coordinators	Physical therapists Clergy Education, vocational, and school counselors Instructional coordinator Rehabilitation counselors

356

Education of training level	Fastest-Growing Occupations	Occupations Having the Largest Numerical Job Growth
Bachelor's or higher degree, plus work experience	Education administrators, preschool and child care center/program Computer and information systems managers Training and development managers Actuaries Medical and health-services managers	General and operations managers Management analysts Financial managers Computer and information systems managers Sales managers
Bachelor's degree	Network systems and data-communications analysts Physician assistants Computer software engineers, applications Computer software engineers, systems software Network and computer systems administrators	Elementary school teachers, except special education Accountants and auditors Computer software engineers, applications Computer systems analysts Secondary school teachers, except special and vocational education
Associate degree	Physical therapist assistants Dental hygienists Forensic science technicians Veterinary technologists and technicians Diagnostic medical monographers	Registered nurses Computer support specialists Dental hygienists Paralegals and legal assistants Medical records and health information technicians
Postsecondary vocational award	Preschool teachers, except special education Surgical technologists Gaming dealers Emergency medical technicians and paramedics Fitness trainers and aerobics instructors	Nursing aides, orderlies, and attendants Preschool teachers, except special education Automotive service technicians and mechanics Licensed practical and licensed vocational nurses Hairdressers, hairstylists, and cosmetologists

Education of training level	Fastest-Growing Occupations	Occupations Having the Largest Numerical Job Growth
Work experience in a related occupation	Self-enrichment education teachers Emergency management specialists Gaming managers Construction and building inspectors First-line supervisors/managers of fire fighting and prevention workers	First-line supervisors/managers of food preparation and serving workers First-line supervisors/managers of office and administrative support workers First-line supervisors/managers of construction trades and extraction workers Self-enrichment education teachers First-line supervisors/managers of retail sales workers
Long-term on-the-job training	Fire fighters Tile and marble setters Athletes and sports competitors Coaches and scouts Interpreters and translators	Carpenters Cooks, restaurant Police and sheriff's patrol officers Plumbers, pipe fitters, and steamfitters Electricians
Moderate-term on-the-job training	Medical assistants Dental assistants Hazardous materials removal workers Social and human service assistants Residential advisors	Customer service representatives Truck drivers, heavy and tractor-trailer Maintenance and repair workers, general Medical assistants Executive secretaries and administrative assistants
Short-term on-the-job training	Home health aides Personal and home-care aides Physical therapist aides Amusement and recreation attendants Occupational therapist aides	Retail salespersons Janitors and cleaners, except maids and housekeeping cleaners Waiters and waitresses Combined food preparation and serving workers, including fast food Home health aides

* By level of postsecondary education or training
Source: U.S. Department of Labor (2006). Bureau of Labor Statistics, Bulletin 2600. *Occupational Outlook Handbook 2006–2007*. Indianapolis: JIST Works.

Appendix G
Excerpts from the
Atlanta Compromise Address

The following excerpts reflect Booker T. Washington's belief that the future of his race lay in pursuing manual occupations in the South and in receiving an education that would inculcate the values of hard work.

Ignorant and inexperienced, it is not strange that in the first years of our new life we began at the top instead of at the bottom; that a seat in Congress or the state legislature was more sought than real estate or industrial skill; that the political convention of stump speaking had more attractions than starting a dairy farm or truck garden.

"Cast down your bucket where you are"—cast it down in making friends in every manly way of the people of all races by whom we are surrounded. Cast it down in agriculture, mechanics, in commerce, in domestic science, and in the professions.

Gentlemen of the Exposition, as we present to you our humble effort at an exhibition of our progress, [you] must not expect overmuch. Starting thirty years ago with ownership here and there in a few quilts and pumpkins and chickens, remember the path that has led from these inventions and production of agricultural implements, buggies, steam engines, newspapers, books, statuary, carvings, paintings, the management of drug-stores and banks, has not been trodden without contact with thorns and thistles.

The wisest among my race understand that the agitation of questions of social equality is the extremist folly, and that progress in the employment of all the privileges that will come to us must be the result of severe and constant struggle rather than of artificial forcing. In all things that are purely social we can be as separate as the fingers, yet one as the hand in all things essential to mutual progress.

In conclusion, may I repeat that nothing in thirty years has given us more hope and encouragement, and drawn us so near to you of the white race, as this opportunity offered by the Exposition.

Source: Washington, B. (1901). *Up from slavery*. Garden City, NY: Doubleday & Company.

Glossary

Academic integration—Including academic content and skills, such as math and writing skills, as part of the career and technical education program of study.

Academic rigor—Challenging each student toward individual excellence. Rigor is a careful, continual, self-motivated process toward excellence in thinking, feeling, analyzing, evaluating, relating to others, learning to learn, and becoming one's own best teacher.

Academics—Includes mathematics and science; letters, humanities, and communications; social sciences; art and design; and education, among other fields.

Achievement gaps—Academic disparities among racial and socioeconomic groups.

Adult education—College, vocational, or occupational programs, continuing education or noncredit courses, correspondence courses and tutoring, as well as courses and other educational activities provided by employers, community groups, and other providers.

Advisory committee—A group serving strictly in an advisory capacity, with the educational policy remaining under the control of the superintendent of schools. It usually consists of seven to twelve persons—teachers, businesspersons, labor leaders, parents, and students. If a steering committee is used, some members may be asked to serve on it.

Agricultural education—Instruction in crop production, livestock management, soil and water conservation, and various other aspects of agriculture—including instruction in food education, such as nutrition—to improve the quality of life for all people by helping farmers increase production, conserve resources, and provide nutritious foods.

Alternative certification—Any post-baccalaureate teacher education program, including emergency certification, intensive university-based programs, distance learning programs, and even programs created by school districts to recruit members of the community to become teachers. The main purpose is to entice mid-career professionals and subject-matter experts to bring a plethora of life experiences and professional endeavors into the classroom. Since teaching certificates are granted by state education departments, there are many variations in programs across the nation.

Alternative pathways—Use of non-traditional pathways to bring students into a teacher certification program. Articulation agreements with community colleges or recruitment from institutions that do not have a teacher certification program are examples.

Apprentice—A person who learns a trade by working under the guidance of a skilled master.

Apprentice training—Programs registered with the Department of Labor or a state apprenticeship agency in accordance with the act of August 16, 1937 (commonly known as the National Apprenticeship Act) that are conducted or sponsored by an employer, a group of employers, or a joint apprenticeship committee representing both employers and a union, and that contain all terms and conditions for the qualification, recruitment, selection, employment, and training of apprentices.

Apprenticeship—Programs registered with the Department of Labor or a state apprenticeship agency in accordance with the Act of August 16, 1937, commonly known as the National Apprenticeship Act, which is conducted or sponsored by an employer and a union, and which contains all terms and conditions for the qualification, recruitment, selection, employment, and training of apprentices.

Appropriations (federal funds)—Budget authority provided through a congressional appropriation process that permits federal agencies to incur obligations and to make payments.

Area CTE school/center—A high school, a department of a high school, a technical institute or technical school, a department or a division of a junior-community college, or a university used exclusively or principally to provide career and technical education to students who are entering the labor market.

Articulation—Uniting curricula or programs of study through a formal agreement between or among institutions.

Assessment—Evaluation measures used to provide information for monitoring and improving educational programs.

Association for Career and Technical Education (ACTE)—The largest national association dedicated to the advancement of education to prepare youth and adults for careers.

At-risk populations—Certain segments of society whose members have disabilities and/or disadvantages, such as minority groups, women, persons who are economically and/or academically disadvantaged, and those who are physically and/or mentally disabled.

Baby-boom generation—Persons born between 1946 and 1964.

Business Professionals of America (BPA)—The CTE organization for those secondary and postsecondary students enrolled in vocational business education programs.

Calling—Any vocation in which individuals are employed who regard their vocation as an end in itself and one from which they receive a high degree of personal satisfaction.

Career academy—A high school program that is usually a school-within-a-school—a smaller administrative unit operating within a larger school—that is occupationally focused. Usually brings together groups of students and teachers who get to know and value each other over a two- to three-year period of time. The career academy concept started with a single school in Philadelphia in 1969.

Career clusters—A grouping of occupations and broad industries based on commonalities to provide an organizing tool for schools, small communities, academies and magnet schools.

Career guidance and counseling—Programs that (a) pertain to the body of subject matter and related techniques and methods organized for the development in individuals of career awareness; career planning; career decision making; placement skills; and knowledge and understanding of local, state, and national occupational, educational, and labor market needs, trends, and opportunities; (b) assist individuals in making and implementing informed educational and occupational choices; and (c) aid students to develop career options with attention to surmounting gender, race, ethnicity, disability, language, or socioeconomic impediments to career options and encouraging careers in nontraditional employment.

Career major—A group of CTE courses and academic courses that focus on a career cluster (e.g., business, health, construction), or a particular occupation (e.g., data processing, carpentry).

Career objective—A particular occupation within a career cluster that has special interest for the student.

Career pathway—A coherent sequence of rigorous academic and technical courses that prepare students for successful completion of state academic standards and support transition to more advanced postsecondary coursework related to a career area of interest.

Career and technical education—Organized educational programs offering a sequence of courses directly related to the preparation of individuals in paid or unpaid employment and in current or emerging occupations requiring other than a baccalaureate or advanced degree. Such programs should include competency-based applied learning that contributes to an individual's academic knowledge, higher-order reasoning, problem-solving skills, work attitudes, general employability skills, and the occupational specific skills necessary for economic independence as a productive and contributing member of society. This term also includes applied technology education.

Career and technical high school—Includes full-time vocational high schools and area or regional vocational schools. The latter type of school may serve postsecondary and adult students in addition to high school students.

Career and technical student organizations (CTSOs)—Organizations for individuals enrolled in CTE programs that engage in activities as an integral part of the instructional program. Such organizations may have state and national units that aggregate the work and purposes of instruction in vocational education at the local level.

Carl D. Perkins Reauthorization Act (2006)—Also known as Perkins IV, the act authorizes the legislation through FY 2012, for a total of six years instead of five. Other major changes include a section on local accountability that did not exist in the 1998 law, the separation of performance indicators for secondary and postsecondary programs, and requirements for "Career and Technical Programs of Study."

Certification—The process by which professional recognition is granted to an individual who has met certain predetermined qualifications.

Certification area—A specific content area in which professional licenses are issued.

Commission on National Aid to Vocational Education (1914)—A commission formed to determine (1) the need for vocational education, (2) the need for federal grants, (3) the kinds of vocational education for which grants should be made, (4) the extent and conditions under which aid should be granted, and (5) proposed legislation.

Community college—A public institution that awards associate's degrees or less-than-four-year, sub-baccalaureate certificates as its highest award type.

Competency—Something a student will be able to do after completing a course. To master a competency, a student must be able to apply it to real-world situations and be able to explain basic concepts surrounding its application.

Comprehensive high school—The typical U.S. high school offering, at minimum, academic studies and usually some CT education.

Constructivism—A set of assumptions about the nature of human learning that guide constructivist learning theories and teaching methods.

Contextual learning—Learning designed so that students can carry out activities and solve problems in a way that reflects the nature of such tasks in the real world.

Contextual teaching and learning—Relates subject matter to real-world situations and motivates students to make connections between knowledge and its applications.

Cooperative education—Programs that allow students to earn course credit for paid or unpaid employment that is related to a specific occupational program of study. These programs usually involve employers in developing a training plan and evaluating students. (In contrast, general work experience is not connected to a specific occupational program.)

Cooperative extension system—A partnership of the federal, state, and county governments to distribute information gathered by land-grant universities and the U.S. Department of Agriculture to farmers, families, and young people.

Core content—Content all students in a major are expected to master.

Course—A subdivision of a subject matter area program which presents a meaningful subset of the content of that matter area (e.g., algebra within mathematics, physics within science, and introduction to microcomputers within career and technical education).

Curriculum—Courses, experiences, and assessments necessary to prepare candidates to teach or work with students of a particular age or in a specific subject level.

Developing countries—Countries in the global South, the poorest regions of the world—also called third-world countries, less-developed countries, and undeveloped countries.

Disabled—Referring to those students, ages 3 to 21, who are disabled mentally, educationally, and/or physically. They may be in public elementary and secondary schools or they may have been placed in private schools by public agencies.

Disadvantaged—Characterizing individuals who are economically and/or academically disadvantaged to the extent that they cannot actively participate in CTE programs.

Distributive Education Clubs of America (DECA)—The national CTE organization for secondary and postsecondary students enrolled in marketing education programs. (DECA chapters are local student organizations consisting of marketing education students.)

Douglas Commission (1905)—A commission responsible for investigating the status of vocational education and making recommendations for any required modifications. The growing interest in vocational education during the first decade of the twentieth century led to the appointment of this commission by Governor William Douglas of Massachusetts.

E-mail—Electronic mail, which is a basic Internet service that allows users to exchange messages electronically.

English Poor Law (enacted in 1601)—Its basic intent was to equip the children of poor families in England with a salable skill. This approach was considered very successful and greatly influenced vocational education in America.

Enrichment/other—A high school curriculum including courses designed for students' personal enrichment, such as courses in general skills; health, physical, and recreation education; religion and theology; and military science.

Ethnic groups—Large groups of people who share ancestral, language, cultural, or religious ties and a common identity.

Family, Career, and Community Leaders of America, Inc. (FCCLA)—The national CTE organization for junior and senior high school students enrolled in family and consumer sciences occupations education. The organization's goal is to help youth assume active roles in society as wage earners, community leaders, and family members.

Family and consumer sciences—A discipline of study that synthesizes knowledge from (1) the physical sciences, (2) the social sciences, and (3) the humanities and applies this knowledge to an interdisciplinary study of various aspects of individual family life.

Federal Board for Vocational Education—In operation from July 1917 to October 10, 1933, this board's functions fell within three classifications: (1) efficient administration of federal funds; (2) research and studies to promote and improve vocational education; and (3) assistance to the states in their promotion and development activities.

Future Business Leaders of America (FBLA)—A national CTE organization for students enrolled in secondary business courses. Students do not have to be in a vocational program to belong.

Future Farmers of America (FFA)—The national CTE organization of secondary students in vocational agriculture programs.

General Agreement on Tariffs and Trade (GATT)—A world organization established in 1947 to work for freer trade on a multilateral basis; the GATT has been more of a negotiating framework than an administrative institution. It became the *World Trade Organization* (WTO) in 1995.

General work experience—Programs that allow students to earn course credit for paid or unpaid employment. Unlike cooperative education, general work experience is not connected to a specific occupational program of study.

Generation X—The generation following the post–World War II baby boom cohort, especially those born in the United States and Canada between 1965 and 1976.

Generation Y—Persons born between 1977 and 2000.

Globalization—The increasing integration of the world in terms of communications, culture, and economics; may also refer to changing subjective experiences of space and time accompanying this process.

Health Occupations Students of America (HOSA)—The national CTE organization for secondary and postsecondary students who are enrolled in health occupations education.

High Schools That Work (HSTW)—A program based on applied learning theory and the premise that schools require students to think differently than how they think in real life.

High technology—State-of-the-art computer, digital, microelectronic, hydraulic, pneumatic, laser, nuclear, chemical, telecommunication, and other technologies used to enhance productivity in manufacturing, communication, transportation, agriculture, mining, energy, commercial, and similar economic activity, and to improve the provision of health care.

Higher education—Study beyond secondary school at an institution that offers programs terminating in an associate's, baccalaureate, or higher degree.

Industrial Revolution—A rapid major change in an economy (as in England in the late eighteenth century) marked by the general introduction of power-driven machinery or by an important change in the prevailing types and methods of use of such machines.

In-service—Education that is delivered to teachers/administrators who work in schools as educators.

Integration—A curriculum development approach that makes academic coursework relevant to work. This may involve teachers across disciplines teaching related concepts concurrently using occupational themes.

Interdependence—A political and economic situation in which countries are simultaneously dependent on each other for their well-being.

Internet—A network of tens of thousands of computer networks that consist of over a million computer systems. These computers and networks communicate with each other by exchanging data according to the same rules, even though the individual networks and computer systems use different technologies.

Job shadowing—An opportunity to give students firsthand knowledge and experience in exploring the world-of-work. A student with a career interest is matched with, observes, and interacts with an adult in that career in the workplace. Students have an opportunity to learn about the education, skill requirements, and characteristics of the job.

Labor force—Persons employed as civilians, unemployed, or in the armed services during a given period of time. The "civilian labor force" comprises all civilians classified as employed or unemployed.

Land-grant college or university—An institution that has been designated by its state legislature or Congress to receive benefits of the Morrill Acts of 1862 and 1890.

Lyceum Movement—A movement that served as a means of building up useful knowledge in natural sciences among people of the smaller towns of America. It lasted until the middle of the nineteenth century.

Maintenance Act—Also known as the Second Morrill Act, it authorized additional funds from the sale or lease of public lands to more fully support and maintain the agricultural and mechanical arts programs established in the original Morrill Act.

Manual training—A course of training to develop skill in using the hands to teach practical arts (such as woodworking and metalworking).

Marketing education—The process of understanding and using various combinations of subject matter and learning experience related to the performance of activities that direct the flow of goods and services, including their appropriate utilization, from the producer to the consumer or user.

Morrill Act of 1862—Federal legislation that appropriated public lands for the establishment of a college of vocational education in each state (also known as the Land-Grant College Act).

Multicultural education—A philosophical concept built on the ideals of freedom, justice, equality, equity, and human dignity as acknowledged in various documents, such as the U.S. Declaration of Independence, the constitutions of South Africa and the United States, and the Universal Declaration of Human Rights adopted from the United Nations. It recognizes the role schools can play in developing the attitudes and values necessary for a democratic society. It values cultural differences and affirms the pluralism that students, their communities, and teachers reflect. It challenges all forms of discrimination in schools and society through the promotion of democratic principles of social justice.

Nation at Risk—An influential 1983 report of the National Commission on Excellence in Education reporting that the United States was losing ground in international economic competition and attributed the decline in large part to the relatively low standards and poor performance of the U.S. educational system.

National Association of Manufacturers (NAM)—Organized in 1895 in response to a period of economic depression, NAM was interested in securing an adequate supply of trained workers and in reducing the power of the growing labor movement.

National Association of State Universities and Land Grant Colleges (NASULGC)—A voluntary, nonprofit association of public universities, the nation's land-grant institutions, and many state university systems. NASULGC (pronounced *na SUL jick*) is the nation's oldest higher education association.

National Education Association (NEA)—A professional organization for teachers, supervisors, administrators, and others interested in education.

National Postsecondary Agricultural Student Association (NPASO or PAS)—The vocational organization for those students enrolled in agriculture/agribusiness and national resources programs in postsecondary institutions.

National Society for the Promotion of Industrial Education (NSPIE)—A society whose purpose was to bring to public attention the importance of industrial education (the term used then for vocational education) and to promote the establishment of institutions for vocational training.

National Young Farmers Educational Association (NYFEA)—The CTE student organization for adults enrolled in agriculture classes, usually through the local vocational program.

New basic standards—In the 1983 publication *A Nation at Risk*, the National Commission on Excellence in Education recommended that high school graduation requirements be strengthened and that, at a minimum, all students take 4 years of English; 3 years each of mathematics, science, social studies; and one-half year of computer science. The "core academic standards" referred to in this report include the recommendations for English, mathematics, science, and social studies.

No Child Left Behind Act—The centerpiece of President George W. Bush's domestic agenda, the act constitutes a blend of standards-based accountability, educational choice, and old-fashioned bureaucratic mandates, not all of which work together harmoniously. Teachers and lawmakers nationwide have criticized the measure, saying that it costs too much and its requirements are too strict.

Nontraditional students—Program enrollees, both male and female, who enroll in areas of study traditionally considered appropriate only for the opposite sex.

North American Free Trade Agreement (NAFTA)—A free-trade zone encompassing the United States, Canada, and Mexico since 1994.

One-stop delivery system—A cornerstone of the Workforce Investment Act that brings together under one roof a choice of training, education, and employment programs.

Postsecondary education—The provision of a formal instructional program whose curriculum is designed primarily for students who have completed the requirements for a high school diploma or its equivalent. This includes academic, CTE, and continuing professional education programs and excludes avocational and adult basic education programs.

Pre-service—Education that is pre-baccalaureate, generally to teachers not yet certified.

Professional development—Opportunities to develop new knowledge and skills through pre-service or in-service education, conference attendance, sabbatical leave, summer leave, intra- or inter- institutional visitations, and fellowships.

Program—A planned sequence of courses and experiences leading to a degree or recommendation for a state license.

Program of Studies—The entire array of courses that a student takes in high school, including academic and CTE courses. Courses should reinforce one another and reflect the student's career objective.

Prosser's theorems—Widely acknowledged as the father of U.S. career and technical education, Charles A. Prosser served as the first federal commissioner for career and technical education, a position created by the Smith-Hughes Act. His 16 theories provided a comprehensive foundation for career and technical education.

Rigor and Relevance Curriculum Framework—A tool developed by the staff of the International Center in Education to examine curriculum, instruction, and assessment.

Rural school—A school located in a community with a population of less than 2,500.

Russian system—Essentially a laboratory method of teaching, consisting of a set of exercises that were arranged in what was considered to be a logical order for teaching purposes.

School-based enterprise—A class-related activity that engages students in producing goods or services for sale or use to people other than the participating students themselves.

School-to-Work, early leaders in—Florida, Oregon, Tennessee, and Wisconsin were among the first states to enact statutory provisions for school-to-work initiatives. Washington state was recognized nationally as the first to pass legislation specifically to invest state funds in the development of school-to-work transition programs.

School-to-Work Opportunities Act (STWOA)—Legislation designed to address the nation's serious skills shortage through partnerships between educators and employers, signed into law by President Clinton on May 4, 1994, as Public Law 103-239. This act was a giant step toward the development of an educational system that matches students' educational attainment and corresponding skills more closely to job opportunities. It also reinforced the need to prepare students with high levels of technical skills and related academic competencies.

School-to-Work transition programs—See Apprentice training, Cooperative education; School-based enterprise, Tech prep, Work experience.

Secondary school—A nonprofit day or residential school that provides secondary education, as determined under state law, except that it does not include any education beyond grade 12.

Secretary's Commission on Achieving Necessary Skills (SCANS)—This 1991 report emphasized the importance of developing a range of work-related skills that spanned both academic and vocational programs. This report focused little, if any, emphasis on specific "difficult" skills, such as knowing how to operate a drill press or build a brick wall, and considerable emphasis on the development of thinking skills and interpersonal skills of the workplace.

Sex bias—Behavior, attitude, or prejudice resulting from the assumption that one sex is superior to another.

Sex discrimination—The denial of opportunity, privilege, role, or reward on the basis of sex.

Sex equity—The elimination of sex bias and sex stereotyping.

Sex stereotyping—Attributing behaviors, abilities, interest, values, and roles to an individual or group on the basis of sex.

Silent Generation—Persons born between 1922 and 1945.

SkillsUSA—A nonprofit national CTE organization for secondary and postsecondary students enrolled in trade and industrial occupations programs.

Sloyd System (Sweden)—A system advocating that manual labor in a prevocational sense should be taught as part of general education.

Smith-Hughes Act of 1917—Federal legislation that provided an annual grant of approximately $7.2 million in perpetuity to the states for the promotion of vocational education in agricultural, trade and industrial, and home economics education.

Socioeconomic status—Constructed from data on father's occupation, father's education, mother's education, family income, and material possessions in the household.

Southern Regional Education Board (SREB)—A consortium responsible for getting career-bound high school students to complete a challenging program of study and to reach or exceed the HSTW performance goals in reading, mathematics, and science. The intent is to prepare students for productive careers and future learning.

Special education—Curriculum provided to secondary students who have a disability and have developed an Individualized Education Plan (IEP).

Special populations—The federal regulations pertaining to the Carl D. Perkins Vocational and Applied Technology Education Act of 1990 define special populations as individuals with disabilities, educationally and economically disadvantaged individuals, individuals of limited-English proficiency, individuals who participate in programs designed to eliminate sex bias, and individuals in correctional institutions.

Specific labor market preparation—Courses organized into occupationally specific program areas that teach skills and provide information required in a particular vocation or occupation.

State plan—A written plan submitted to the U.S. secretary of education for a two-year period that shows how that state proposes to use funds provided through a particular vocational education act.

Statute of Artificers (passed in 1562)—Transformed apprenticeship from a local to a national system in England.

Sub-baccalaureate student—A postsecondary student who reported that he or she was currently seeking an associate's degree or postsecondary certificate, or was not seeking a postsecondary credential of any kind.

Suburban school—A school located either (1) within a standard metropolitan statistical area (SMSA) but outside the central city; or (2) outside a SMSA but in a town with a population of 2,500 or more.

Tech Prep—Programs consisting of the two or four years of secondary school preceding graduation and two years of higher education, or an apprenticeship program of at least two years following secondary instruction, with a common core of required proficiency in mathematics, science, communications, and technologies, designed to lead to an associate's degree or certificate in a specific career field (also referred to as 2 + 2 programs).

Technical/professional fields—A group of occupationally oriented fields of study, other than engineering and computer science, that includes agriculture and agricultural sciences, architecture, business and management, communications, education, health sciences, home economics, law, library and archival sciences, military sciences, parks and recreation, protective services, and public affairs.

Technology education—An applied discipline designed to promote technological literacy that provides knowledge and understanding of the impacts of technology including its organizations, techniques, tools, and skills to solve practical problems and extend human capabilities in areas such as construction, manufacturing, communication, transportation, power, and energy.

Technology Student Association (TSA)—The national organization for elementary, middle, and senior high school students who are enrolled in or have completed technology education courses.

Title IX—A comprehensive federal law that prohibits discrimination on the basis of sex in any federally funded education program or activity.

Trade and industrial education—A specific service area of career and technical education that trains public school students for careers in trades such as printing, drafting, building trades, and machining.

Tribal colleges/universities—Institutions cited in section 532 of the Equity in Educational Land-Grant Status Act of 1994, and any other institution qualifying for funding under the Tribally Controlled Community College Assistance Act of 1998, the Navajo Community College Assistance Act of 1978, or Public Law 95-471. Most of these institutions are tribally controlled and located on reservations. They are members of the American Indian Higher Education Consortium.

Urban school—A school located in the central city of a standard metropolitan statistical area (SMSA).

Urbanization—A shift of population from the countryside to the cities that typically accompanies economic development and is augmented by displacement of peasants from subsistence farming.

Vocationalism—The method used by schools, particularly high schools, to organize their curriculums so the students may develop skills, both vocational and academic, that will give them the strategic labor market advantages needed to compete for good jobs.

Work experience—Allows students to earn school credit in conjunction with paid or unpaid employment. In contrast with cooperative education programs, these programs may involve employment in the student's vocational field of study or may involve employers in developing a training plan and evaluating students.

Workforce Investment Act—A federal act that provides workforce investment activities through statewide and local workforce investment systems that increase the employment, retention, earnings, and occupational skills of participants.

World Wide Web—The collection of different services and resources available on the Internet and accessible through a Web browser.

Index